Professional Development in Home Economics

PROFESSIONAL DEVELOPMENT IN HOME ECONOMICS

Careers Serving Families and Consumers

Elizabeth Kendall Sproles
George B. Sproles
The University of Arizona

Macmillan Publishing Company
New York

Maxwell Macmillan Canada
Toronto

Maxwell Macmillan International
New York   Oxford   Singapore   Sydney

Editors: David Chodoff and Patrick Shriner
Production Supervisor: Patricia French
Production Manager: Nick Sklitsis
Text and Cover Designer: Jane Edelstein

This book was set in Century Schoolbook by V & M Graphics, Inc. and was printed and bound by Quinn-Woodbine.
The cover was printed by New England Book Components, Inc.

Macmillan Publishing Company
866 Third Avenue, New York, New York 10022

Macmillan Publishing Company is part of
the Maxwell Communication Group of Companies.

Maxwell Macmillan Canada, Inc.
1200 Eglinton Avenue East, Suite 200
Don Mills, Ontario M3C 3N1

Library of Congress Cataloging-in-Publication Data

Sproles, Elizabeth Kendall.
    Professional development in home economics : careers serving families and consumers / Elizabeth Kendall Sproles, George B. Sproles. — 2nd ed.
        p.   cm.
    Includes index.
    ISBN 0-02-363160-0 (paper)
    1. Home economics — Vocational guidance.   I. Sproles, George B.
    II. Title.
TX164.S67   1992
640'.23 — dc20   90–27448
                    CIP
Printing: 1 2 3 4 5 6 7   Year: 2 3 4 5 6 7 8

Preface

This is a book about professions serving families and consumers. Family- and consumer-oriented careers are found in all sectors of employment, including business, education, government, and the human services. In addition, many new, innovative, and nontraditional careers for men and women emerge almost daily. In short, careers centering on families and consumers are among the most abundant in our society.

The academic background that prepares men and women for family- or consumer-oriented careers is varied. Home economics has a long tradition of interest in families and consumers and has long provided graduates for professional fields such as foods, dietetics, textiles, clothing, consumer affairs, child development, family relations, housing, interior design, extension education, and home economics education. Newer programs in human development, human resources, human ecology, and family and consumer sciences have produced many successful professionals. The social sciences, business, and education offer valuable skills. Science, engineering, art, and design offer knowledge relevant to the aesthetic and technical development of products for consumers. Thus the range of skills and academic disciplines touching family- and consumer-oriented professions covers the full spectrum of knowledge created by our society.

We have written this book to increase students' awareness of the opportunities for those with degrees in family- and consumer-oriented fields. The book should be especially useful to students taking introductory courses in professional home economics or similar professional development courses. Much of the book is also directed at the graduating senior, with its practical information about identifying alternative career paths, job-seeking ideas, steps in résumé writing, and job descriptions of specific careers. We have included the broadest possible range of topics that are important to all college students planning careers.

The book is divided into four parts. Part I, "Foundations for Career Planning," is a four-chapter introduction to the family- and consumer-oriented professions. Part II, "Exploring Career Choices," has six chapters containing career profiles and introductions to specific family- and consumer-oriented careers in the arts, sciences, business, education, extension, human services, government, and innovative or nontraditional positions. Part III, "Professional Development for Careers," explains how to prepare professionally for a career. Included are detailed discussions of topics such as obtaining professional education, establishing career goals, preparing résumés and portfolios, and securing professional employment. Part IV, "Career Development Following Graduation," focuses on managing a career successfully, participating in professional organizations, and preparing for changes in the future.

This second edition of *Professional Development in Home Economics* differs from the first edition in a number of important respects. Most significantly, the introductory Chapters 1 and 2 have undergone major changes, giving these lead chapters a new focus. Chapter 1, "Professions Serving Families and Consumers," combines former Chapters 1 and 4 and gives a broad overview of the careers our profession offers. It is vital for students to see outright our many and varied careers in advance of making choices, and this is a significant change. Chapter 2, "The Growth and Status of Our Profession," is a new chapter that introduces the historical evolution and current issues of our profession. Many colleagues and reviewers suggested the value of an early introduction to this historical and contemporary perspective, and we concur. We have included many valuable exercises and references on this subject for further reading and class activities as well. The remaining chapters will be familiar to previous users of the book, although some specific changes should be noted: Chapters 2 and 3 of the first edition are now Chapters 3 and 4 of the second, and Chapter 20 now focuses entirely on trends that are changing family- and consumer-oriented careers. You will notice other changes in each chapter as well—updating of the text, addition of more Self-Assessment Exercises, additions to Career Profiles, and the addition of many new references to each chapter's bibliography.

Our writing has been influenced by literally hundreds of colleagues and professionals in family- and consumer-oriented fields. Many professors who teach courses such as Professional Development, Introduction to Home Economics, and Careers in Professional

Home Economics shared with us their course outlines and, especially, their needs. Numerous practicing professionals in every profession have assisted our classes or shared their views. Colleagues at The University of Arizona, including Amy Jean Knorr, Maureen Kelly, Naomi Reich, Ellen Goldsberry, Roger Kramer, Carl Ridley, Brenda Brandt, and Soyeon Shim have provided encouragement, ideas, and feedback. Our colleague, Robert Rice, was highly supportive, and our school's director, Jerelyn Schultz, provided encouragement for the importance of professional development as a key subject in our programs. Various colleagues from The University of Arizona Placement Center have also provided advice and materials, including Susan Young and Lois Meerdink. Instructors and teaching assistants have commented on the manuscript or helped in research, most notably Patricia Aaron, Kathleen Busch, Barbara Hemmerick, Lisa Kay, Mary Lopez, Michelle Sciame, Lisa Snyder, Kathy Sweedler, and Donna Swibold.

Photographs have been generously provided by the American Vocational Association; the American Institute for Property and Liability Underwriters and the Insurance Institute of America; the National Housewares Manufacturers Association; the Agricultural Sciences Communications and School of Family and Consumer Resources, The University of Arizona; the American Society of Interior Designers (Greg Komar, photographer); the American Apparel Manufacturers Association; and the National Restaurant Association.

Too many students to mention have shaped our thoughts or done key research for us, and we especially thank Laura Wilson and Jan Klobnak. Various secretaries and administrative assistants have contributed, especially Donna Snyder, Joyce O'Neill, Mary Miller, Verna Woolsey, and Earleen McGrew. Finally, we offer a special thanks to our colleagues at Macmillan, who have given us continued editorial support and helpful assistance in shaping both editions of this book.

Elizabeth Kendall Sproles
George B. Sproles

Contents

PART II EXPLORING CAREER CHOICES 75

Foundations for Career Planning

Part I establishes the foundations for family- and consumer-oriented professions. The four chapters are as follows:

- **Professions Serving Families and Consumers (Chapter 1)**
- **The Growth and Current Status of Our Professions (Chapter 2)**
- **Professional Career Planning — The First Steps (Chapter 3)**
- **The Career Market of Today — What to Expect (Chapter 4)**

These chapters present (1) an introduction to the varied careers serving families and consumers, (2) a view of what it means to be a family- and consumer-oriented professional, (3) a short historical perspective on the evolution and current status of our professions, (4) how to choose a professional career, and (5) the qualities that employers seek when hiring professionals.

CHAPTER 1

Professions Serving Families and Consumers

What does an education mean to me? What is the value of my college education? Where do I go from here? These are just some of the questions most college students ask some time during their college years.

The goals of a college education are numerous. Your professors view education as the development of broadened and reasoned thinking. Parents think of education as the final maturing step to adulthood. Society thinks of education as a passport to personal advance-

3

ment and success in life. And many people think of education as preparation for work, learning professional skills and earning entry into the occupational world.

Certainly you expect many returns from your education. Some will be personal, and others will be social and economic. For instance, consider the following:

1. *Personal returns:* You'll learn to think and reason. You'll acquire knowledge of many subjects, thereby enriching your life.
2. *Social returns:* You'll take the final steps toward maturation, the final growth stage for entry into adult life. You'll broaden your view of society and social life and perhaps learn ways to improve life for individuals and society.
3. *Professional returns:* You'll learn marketable skills, and you'll improve your future prospects by aiming toward a carefully planned career.

Perhaps you as a college student had thought of all these reasons, and more, for attending college. You have probably wondered what kind of education would be best to achieve your goals. Should you choose a liberal education with broad and general subjects or a specialized professional major? This is a difficult choice that college students must make. Particularly if you are considering a specific career, you may want to ask the following questions:

- What knowledge and skills do I need?
- Will I like the work?
- Can I help improve society?
- Will I be able to advance?
- What salary can I expect?
- Will a job be available for me?
- What kind of working conditions do I want?
- What are the job's advantages and disadvantages?
- What is the nature of this work?

This book answers many of these questions. Its focus is on one general category of professional careers, careers focused on families and consumers. Today we live in a family- and consumer-centered society, and so there are many opportunities in education, business, government, science, humanities, and public service.

Professions serving families and consumers offer the most career opportunities in our society. Examples of well-known and well-established careers are the following:

- Retail store manager
- Fashion buyer
- Fashion designer
- Residential interior designer
- Commercial interior designer
- Hotel manager
- Restaurant manager
- Dietitian
- Foods technologist
- Consumer affairs professional
- Consumer advocate
- Financial planner
- Financial counselor
- Marriage and family counselor
- Vocational and career counselor
- Child development specialist
- Day-care manager
- Social welfare worker
- Human services executive
- Family life educator
- Home economics educator
- Vocational educator
- Extension educator
- Journalist
- Research scientist
- Business owner

These are among our most widely available and popular professional careers, and in later chapters many more are discussed. In addition, the modern job market is continually creating new opportunities and new job titles. (For example, have you heard about such newer careers as biotechnologist, gerontological nutritionist, retirement counselor, or designer of products for the handicapped or others with special needs?) Professionals in family- and consumer-oriented specialties are finding innovative careers consulting, free-lancing, and starting a business, and in public service, nonprofit human service organizations, public relations, market research, and many others. Trained professionals in family and consumer fields are found in almost all parts of our occupational market.

Obviously, the family- and consumer-oriented professions are diverse, given their widespread availability in business, education, government, and human services. But they also have much in common as one professional field. First, they have a strong orientation toward service to families and consumers. And they offer excellent,

6

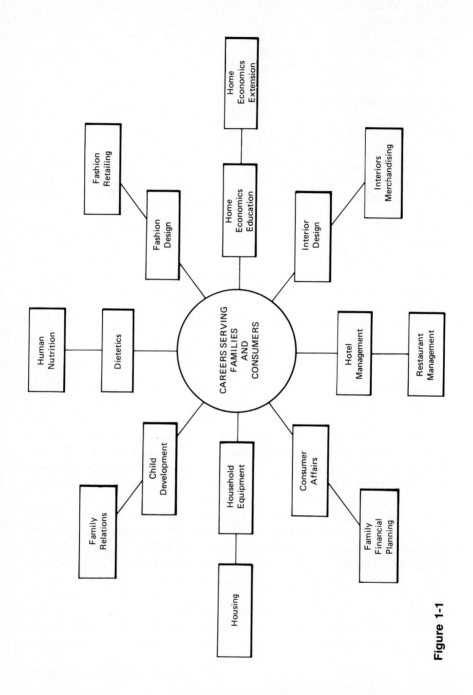

Figure 1-1

lifelong opportunities for men and women to grow professionally and serve. Finally, there are professional camaraderie and mutual respect among these professionals, a spirit fostering growth and excellence in the profession.

Philosophical Foundations for Family and Consumer Careers

Home life and family life are the foundations of our society. Family life-styles and forms of the American family are constantly evolving and changing. However, the institution of the family remains central to our well-being.

The consumption of products and services is also an important feature of our society. Consumption includes two activities, purchasing products and services from businesses or making products and services at home. We once produced everything we needed in our homes; today most products come from a complex business system that then sells them to us through retailers. This has created a need for professional careerists to manage and operate many consumer-oriented businesses efficiently and profitably.

Many academic disciplines serve the needs of families and consumers, but none has a more central interest than does home economics. Since its foundation early in the twentieth century, home economics has established a tradition of service to families and consumers. The main goal of home economics as a profession is to improve the quality of life for families and consumers. We are a people-oriented profession, and our fundamental values are humanitarian, altruistic, and service-oriented. The overall goal is to be a constructive force for the family and its individual members. To accomplish this, professional home economists work in a wide range of careers in business, education, government, and human services.

As a student interested in a career serving families and consumers, you are probably interested in learning about this broad field. Professionals from a broad range of academic disciplines and specialties are included under the umbrella of home economics. These include clothing and textiles, interior design, foods and nutrition, child development, family relations, housing and household equipment, family and consumer economics, home economics education, home economics extension education, home management, home economics in business, and journalism and communications home economics. The specialized knowledge of such professionals ranges from basic sciences like chemistry, psychology, and economics to applied sci-

STEPS IN CAREER PLANNING

Establishing Foundations
- Self-assessment
- Knowing What Employers Seek in Graduates
- Previewing Careers

Exploring Specific Careers
- Reading About Careers
- Talking with Professionals

Professional Development for Your Career
- Getting Your Education
- Gaining Work Experience

Placement in Your Career
- Presenting Your Credentials to Potential Employers
- Beginning Your First Job

Planning for Future Career Development and Changes

Figure 1-2

ences like product design, family life, and business management. These specialties are united as a single field with the purpose of serving the needs of families and consumers. Many home economists have long recognized that united they have a positive impact on society.

Professionals in family and consumer fields run businesses that serve consumers' needs; they design, develop, and test products; and they teach people to help themselves through programs of consumer education, parent education, and extension. They are journalists who write articles in magazines and newspapers. They are professionals who solve people's problems with inflation, budgets, marital lives, family roles, and family situations. They promote nutritional adequacy, product safety, product quality, and other issues of importance to the well-being of consumers. In short, family and consumer careerists serve a broad spectrum of socially beneficial

SELF-ASSESSMENT EXERCISE 1-1

Careers That May Interest You

Now that you have thought about various careers, which ones look potentially interesting to you? Be open-minded and list as many careers for yourself as possible.

1. _____

2. _____

3. _____

4. _____

5. _____

6. _____

7. _____

8. _____

9. _____

10. _____

Now look at your list again. Circle two or three "best preferences." Are there several others you need to learn more about? Indicate these with a check mark.

purposes. They are an important component of our society's professional work force.

Let us now take a broader look at the scope of careers in which you can serve families and consumers. This introduction will get you to think, and it will help to open your mind to the numerous possibilities discussed in the next chapters. We have organized careers into six focal points that we briefly introduce now and that we will examine in greater depth in Chapters 5 through 10. The six focal points are the following:

- Careers based on arts and sciences
- Careers in business
- Careers in education and the Cooperative Extension Service
- Careers in human services
- Careers in government and public policy
- Special and innovative careers

Careers in Arts and Sciences _____

Careers in arts and sciences are those that are founded on artistic and scientific skills. Careers emphasizing the arts and sciences are found in (1) product design and development, (2) product testing and quality control, and (3) scientific research and analysis. These careers pertain to fundamental consumer needs: foods, human nutrition, clothing, textiles, and housing and household furnishings (see Chapter 5 for details).

Product Design and Development. Product design and development includes many artistic careers in popular and exciting fields like fashion design, textile design, food science, interior design, and furniture design. There also are opportunities in product engineering and manufacturing. Positions are available with apparel and textile producers, food-processing companies, food stores, home builders, household equipment manufacturers, appliance manufacturers, home furnishing manufacturers, and interior design firms.

Product Testing and Quality Control. Manufacturers of all consumer products, including clothing, textiles, foods, and household equipment, are interested in ensuring the quality of their products. Retail stores are equally concerned with product quality. Therefore, there are important positions in testing products and ensuring that consumer products meet quality standards. In addition, the federal government and independent testing organizations also employ professionals trained to analyze the quality of consumer products.

Scientific Research and Analysis. Opportunities are available for professional scientists interested in investigating consumers' needs. Careers can be found in human nutrition, textile science, and special fields such as energy conservation for households. Some scientists also find opportunities in product engineering—for example, food processing engineering and the development of appliances. Positions are also available in manufacturing firms, universities, research institutes, testing companies, and government.

Are you suited for a career in the arts or sciences? To help you answer this question, you must know some characteristics of such a career. First, artistic careers such as those in fashion design or interior design require considerable artistic knowledge and skill and an appreciation of current tastes among consumers. Artists must be skilled in such areas as line drawing, illustration, color, and three-dimensional perspective. Increasingly, they must attain skills in computer-assisted design, which is now valued for careers in interior design, fashion design, and textile design. They must also have a thorough knowledge of the materials used in their artistic crafts. For example, textile designers must be familiar with many different fabrics, dyes, and finishes. Similarly, interior designers must have an extensive knowledge of drapery fabrics, upholstery materials, woods, paints, and floor coverings. And all designers must know how to use all these elements of design to make aesthetically pleasing products.

Careers in the sciences have different requirements. First, it is necessary to have a firm foundation in one or more of the physical sciences. For example, persons working in human nutrition must understand biochemistry and organic chemistry. Textile scientists find that physics and chemistry are fundamental to their fields. In addition, scientists must understand laboratory research methods and must enjoy working in a laboratory. This is highly intellectual and meticulous work, but it is also extremely interesting to study consumer products from a scientific viewpoint. Scientists also gain great satisfaction from knowing that they contribute to the most fundamental aspects of human health and welfare.

Careers in Business _____

Careers in business can be found in five main areas: (1) service businesses; (2) marketing, merchandising, and sales; (3) management and administration; (4) media and communications; and (5) business support services (see Chapter 6 for details).

Service Businesses. Service businesses include restaurants, hotels, resorts, travel agencies, entertainment facilities, recreation facilities, and other parts of the hospitality industry and the leisure industry.

Marketing, Merchandising, and Sales. There are marketing, merchandising, and sales positions with product manufacturers, service establishments, department stores, specialty stores, mass merchandisers, discount stores, mail-order retailers, supermarkets, public utilities, real estate firms, insurance companies, advertising agencies, public relations agencies, retail banks, savings and loans, credit unions, loan companies, and financial planning firms.

Management and Administration. There are positions for managers and administrators of service businesses, manufacturers, and all retail stores.

Media and Communications. Media and communications careers can be found in television and radio stations, magazines, newspapers, and all types of consumer-oriented businesses.

Business Support Services. There are jobs in business support services in personnel recruitment firms, advertising agencies, market researchers, public relations firms, management consultants, consumer services, complaint-handling bureaus, consumer credit services, and other business services.

What is a career in business like? Businesses want people with a broad range of skills in business subjects like marketing, merchandising, and accounting, plus skills in human relations and communication. You must be familiar with the products or services your business offers. To succeed, you must be committed to the business and its goals. Finally, you must be willing to be a leader and take responsibility.

There are business careers in every major field of study related to the family and consumers. Obviously, those graduates with merchandising skills and a knowledge of consumer products can find careers in retail marketing. But did you know that students with skills in education and family studies can find jobs in areas such as consumer relations, consumer education, merchandising, and sales?

Careers in Education and the Cooperative Extension Service

Careers in education and the Cooperative Extension Service have traditionally been among the most favored by family- and consumer-oriented careerists, particularly those with a home economics or family life education major. There is a broad range of occupations in education, perhaps broader than you thought (see Chapter 7 for details).

Primary and Secondary Education. Opportunities for teachers are found in preschool programs, primary teaching, secondary education, occupational home economics, consulting with schools, Future Homemakers of America, Home Economics Related Occupations programs, and vocational and technical schools.

Adult Education. Adult-oriented teaching opportunities can be found in formal degree-oriented programs, in-service programs, short courses, and workshops offered by local schools, community colleges, and city or county government. Family life education is an important area of growth for adult education.

Postsecondary Education. There are postsecondary education careers in community colleges, four-year colleges and universities, and vocational and technical institutes.

Cooperative Extension Service. Leaders in 4-H youth development, county extension agents, state extension specialists, and federal extension program directors have careers in the Cooperative Extension service.

Business. There are business opportunities in day-care and children's schools, consumer media, public relations, merchandising, consumer education, and vocational or educational programs run by employers. Today many teachers choose additional courses and experiences that will qualify them for these business opportunities as well as for traditional teaching careers.

Special Opportunities. Educators have unique opportunities available in state education agencies, federal government (e.g., the Department of Education, the Department of Labor, the Cooperative Extension Service), the armed forces, youth programs, (e.g., programs for incarcerated youths, delinquency programs, alcohol and other drug abuse programs), programs for young and/or unwed mothers and displaced homemakers, YMCA and YWCA programs, community services (e.g., United Way, Red Cross), orphan homes, halfway houses, and skill centers.

Careers in education have a number of characteristics in common. An educator can be a facilitator of learning, a guidance counselor, a mentor, and a "cheerleader" (an educator is an enthusiastic and positive role model). Education requires the use of many educational techniques and strategies, ranging from traditional lectures, labs, and classroom discussions to more innovative visual techniques, simulations, and computer-assisted instruction.

To be a successful educator, you first must have an area of expertise. Educators in general home economics need a broad range of knowledge. The subjects included are clothing, interior design, household equipment, housing, home management, child development, parent education, family life education, nutrition, food preparation, consumer education, and financial investments for families.

There is a trend for the home economics curriculum to focus on life management, including such topics as personal relationships, well-being, health, finances, and career development. You may be a specialist in one or more areas, but you also need knowledge with a global perspective in all areas. You also need versatile teaching strategies, especially because many students learn best when a variety of teaching approaches is used. Finally, you need classroom management skills and interpersonal sensitivity to succeed in the classroom.

Careers in Human Services

Among society's most important career opportunities are those in which one can help people. Many of the so-called human services careers are in community service agencies, nonprofit organizations, institutions (e.g., hospitals, clinics, universities), private businesses (e.g., family counseling services, day-care centers), and governmental agencies (see Chapter 8 for details).

Counseling and Guidance. There are counseling and guidance careers in marriage counseling, family counseling, financial planning, financial counseling, child guidance programs, career counseling, and educational counseling.

Social Welfare. Social welfare opportunities can be found in general welfare programs, employment programs, self-help programs, programs for the culturally disadvantaged, programs for the physically handicapped, programs for the mentally handicapped, programs for the homeless, support for AIDS patients, and special programs that provide food stamps and aid to families with dependent children. Important and growing opportunities are also available for family life educators.

Human Development. Many human development opportunities exist in such areas as child-care centers, youth programs, teenage programs, dependency control programs (e.g., child abuse, alcohol and other drug abuse programs), halfway houses, programs for teenage parents, diet therapy programs, and weight control programs. Some of these are operated by government and community service groups, and others are privately operated.

International Development. There is an increasing range of international careers. Some people have careers with the Peace Corps, foreign aid programs, missionary programs, and programs that aid Third World countries. As more businesses become international, new development careers may be created.

Institutional Human Services. Many types of institutions provide human services. Examples are hospitals, cafeterias, food services, universities, and established groups such as the Salvation Army and Goodwill Industries. Careers related to food service and nutrition are by far the best established in this category.

What is a career in human services like? Probably it is one of the most satisfying careers you can undertake because you help others, often on a personal, face-to-face basis and you witness the results of that help. You will solve family problems, serve individuals' needs, and increase the overall well-being of individuals and families. Certainly few activities could be more important, beneficial to society, and self-satisfying.

Human service careers are also challenging because you deal with stressful problems confronting individuals and whole families. The success or failure of the individual or family may depend on what you can do. You deal with the health, safety, and emotional stability of people and may confront major crises. To some people, all of this can be emotionally difficult. And so these are careers for the emotionally mature and for those who benefit from knowing they can help others lead better lives.

Careers in Government and Public Policy _____

Professionals in family and consumer fields find a wide range of opportunities on all levels of federal, state, and local government (city, county, and regional governmental bodies). Note that virtually every career that we have talked about in this chapter is available in some area of government (see Chapter 9 for details).

Federal Government. There are careers in the major departments of the federal government, including the Department of Agriculture, Department of Education, Department of Labor, Department of Health and Human Services, and Department of Housing and Urban Development. Opportunities can also be found in the special agencies of the federal government, such as the Federal Trade Commission, Consumer Product Safety Commission, Food and Drug Administration, National Bureau of Standards, and National Institutes of Health.

State Government. The fifty state governments contain a variety of agencies or departments offering family and consumer services. In general, all state governments provide career opportunities, particularly in education and human services.

City, County, and Regional Government. Perhaps you think of local government simply as providing human services such as public health programs, nutrition programs, consumer protection, garbage pickup, fire protection, and police protection. Certainly those are the major activities; however, local governments serve many other family and consumer needs. Local governments are the largest government employers, employing over half of all government employees. Nearly all the skills of family and consumer professionals are required.

Careers in government have many characteristics similar to those described for business, education, and human services. In addition, as a government employee, you are a manager and spender of public funds—money raised from taxes on businesses and individuals. Thus, you have a public responsibility for the expenditures you make. This requires you to consider the public interest in all your activities and expenditures. Your activities are also politically influenced by the political party currently in power and by grass-roots political groups. As a government employee, you serve those political constituencies.

Special and Innovative Careers

Would you like to develop your own special career tailored to your own skills, interests, and goals? Special careers can be created in areas such as consulting, writing, free-lancing, working for nonprofit organizations, starting a business, setting up a cottage industry (working out of your home), and working with political action groups (influencing public policy). Chapter 10 describes some important, innovative positions that are appropriate for family and consumer professionals.

What do you need for a special or innovative career? First, you must have a unique or unusual idea that can serve some special need of consumers or families. For instance, if you start your own business, your chances of success will be based on the uniqueness of the product or service you offer, as well as on whether consumers really need—or can be persuaded to buy—that product or service. Another determinant of success is your personal initiative and energy. A career in areas like consulting or free-lancing requires extensive effort to reach your goals. Finally, success depends largely on your courage, energy, determination, assertiveness, and enthusiasm in promoting your innovative career.

Professionalism in Family and Consumer Careers _____

Family- and consumer-oriented careers are professional careers. What does it mean to be a professional? First, a professional has a specialized knowledge of a particular subject. For example, a professional in child development has expertise in developmental psychology, the psychology of children, and the physical and biological development of children. A professional in fashion retailing understands economics, marketing, consumer products, and consumer demand.

Second, a professional is committed to serving the needs of his or her clients. The child development specialist focuses on the needs of the child, who is the client. Similarly, a fashion retailer focuses on the consumer who buys products from his or her store. What products does that particular consumer want? We cannot overemphasize how important this service orientation is—to succeed, you must make the client the center of all your activities.

There are other important criteria for professional behavior. The professional applies skills and knowledge directly to the solution of clients' problems, needs, and concerns. The professional also is committed to improving the standards of professional practice by continually increasing his or her knowledge of the subject matter and updating his or her skills. Finally, a professional follows a code of ethics or standards of good practice to ensure serving the client's best interests.

Professionalism is also a state of mind. It is a mental commitment to a specific goal and set of activities. To be a professional, you must be dependable, for others will count on you to complete each job in a timely manner. You must take a personal initiative and seek professional advice and assistance from others when necessary to accomplish your tasks. You are accountable for everything you do, including your mistakes. Finally, a professional does not work by the hour or expect to be paid by the hour; you must do your job no matter how long it takes.

To be a professional requires a lifelong commitment to learning and achievement. You are preparing yourself for a lifelong career, not just a job. College education only begins your career of continuous learning and development throughout your life. Your field will

continually change. As a functioning professional, you must keep
up to date on new discoveries. Realize also that a true professional
contributes to the field by developing new ideas, plans, and materials through publications, speaking engagements, and work in professional organizations and other activities to which you will professionally contribute.

In summary, being a professional in consumer and family careers
requires your commitment to excellence and service to others. Begin
that commitment now as you start working toward your career
goals.

The Goals and Use of This Book _____

This book is a complete guide to selecting and obtaining a professional career that is focused on serving the family and consumer
sectors of our world. In this chapter we have laid the foundations by
describing the overall picture of many and varied professional opportunities you can pursue. We hope this chapter has broadened your
perspective on the careers that may interest you. But what lies
ahead, and how can you use this book?

In the next chapters we briefly review the growth and status of
our professions (Chapter 2) and follow by giving some guidelines on
choosing your career (Chapters 3 and 4). We suggest a variety of
ways to clarify your career preferences and to identify your special
interests and values regarding careers. We also examine the career
market of tomorrow, including the qualities employers will be looking for and the types of jobs that are expected to be in plentiful
supply. This will complete your foundations for career planning.

Then we turn to the central part of the book, Chapters 5 through
10, which describe in detail the specific career opportunities we have
only briefly outlined in this chapter. The highlights of these chapters are the thirty-eight major Career Profiles, which give you perspectives on what is involved in key careers and what qualifications
and education are important. The Career Profiles focus your attention
on the best-established and most widely available areas for careers. At
the same time, remember that there are many more special and innovative opportunities as well (more on this in Chapter 10).

Chapters 11 through 16 suggest how to plan the appropriate education for your career and how to seek professional employment.
Some of the especially important topics are seeking internships or
other preprofessional employment (Chapter 12), how to plan a strategy for job seeking (Chapter 13), how to prepare your résumé and

portfolio of major accomplishments (Chapter 14), how to identify and learn about desirable employers (Chapter 15), and last—but certainly a major key to success—how to obtain professional interviews and job offers (Chapter 16). In total, Chapters 11 through 16 are a complete guide to your professional development and your search for professional opportunities.

The process of developing professionalism requires some perspectives on what you can expect in the early part of your career following graduation. Because that first job and the first several years on the job are so important, we have provided in Chapters 17 through 20 our views on what you might expect. First we look at such crucial topics as adjusting to your new job and integrating your career with your total life (Chapter 17). Then we offer suggestions for managing your successful career, including how to handle daily challenges and how to manage your time (Chapter 18). Next we reiterate the importance of your involvement in professional organizations and associations as well as in civic and service groups of your community (Chapter 19; also see the appendix, which lists many professional associations you can join). Finally, we look into the future and forecast some trends that are likely to affect the family- and consumer-oriented professions (Chapter 20). There is nothing so inevitable as change. Chapter 20 illuminates many of the changes taking place right now and some that are expected to take place in the future. These changes are making family and consumer professions some of the most interesting, exciting, personally rewarding, and socially beneficial endeavors available to any graduate with any major.

Questions and Exercises _____

1. What are the general characteristics of a professional?
2. What characteristics do you possess now that make you a professional?
3. What made you decide to get a college education? What benefits do you expect from it?
4. Write a general job description for a professional in the broad field of family and consumer careers. Include the following: (1) nature of the work, (2) responsibilities, and (3) qualifications.
5. Define home economics as a profession. Discuss how your specific career choice relates to it.
6. Organize into groups of three to six persons according to similar career interests (from those sectors outlined in Chapter 1). Each group member should research a specific career and create a career profile to share

with the other group members. This profile should contain the following information in outline form:
- Nature of the work
- Working conditions
- Qualifications
- Advantages and disadvantages
- Advancement potential

7. Compare and contrast the types of knowledge and skills needed for an artistic career as opposed to a scientific career.
8. What personal characteristics and skills will aid graduates entering profit-oriented and competitive business careers?
9. What can graduates with an interest in education and extension do to make themselves employable as teachers?
10. What type of personality is best for a career in human services? Consider the following aspects of personality:
    - Self-concept
    - Personal values
    - Attitudes toward others
    - Social skills
11. Discuss the characteristics of careers in government that differentiate these careers from careers in business, education, and human services.

Bibliography _____

Career Opportunity Index. Fountain Valley, CA: Career Research Systems, 1983.

Coulter, Kyle Jane, and Marge Stanton. *Graduates of Higher Education in the Food and Agricultural Sciences: An Analysis of Supply/Demand Relationships,* vol. II: *Home Economics.* U.S. Department of Agriculture, Science and Education Administration, Publication Number 1407, 1981.

Coulter, Kyle Jane, Marge Stanton, and Norma Bobbitt. *Employment Opportunities for College Graduates in the Food and Agricultural Sciences— Home Economics.* Washington, DC: U.S. Department of Agriculture, November, 1987.

Dictionary of Occupational Titles. Washington, D.C.: U.S. Government Printing Office, updated annually.

Dun's Marketing Services. *The Career Guide 1990: Dun's Employment Opportunities Directory.* New York: Dun & Bradstreet Corporation, 1990.

Evans, Rupert N., and Edwin L. Herr. *Foundations of Vocational Education,* 2nd ed. Columbus, OH: Merrill, 1978.

Goodman, Leonard H. *Current Career and Occupational Literature.* New York: Wilson, 1984.

Hoeflin, Ruth, Karen Pence, Mary G. Miller, and Joe Weber. *Careers for Professionals: New Perspectives in Home Economics.* Dubuque, IA: Kendall/Hunt, 1987.

Miller, Lawrence. *American Spirit: Visions of a New Corporate Culture.* New York: Morrow, 1985.

Parker, Frances J. *Home Economics: An Introduction to a Dynamic Profession,* 3rd ed. New York: Macmillan, 1987.

Powell, James. *The Prentice-Hall Global Employment Guide.* Englewood Cliffs, NJ: Prentice-Hall, 1983.

Reynolds, Caroline. *Dimensions in Professional Development,* 3rd ed. Cincinnati: South-Western, 1987.

U.S. Government Manual. Washington, DC: U.S. Government Printing Office, 1988.

CHAPTER 2

The Growth and Status of Our Profession

W e begin with an introduction to the historical growth and current status of our profession. Our focus is on professional home economics, which centers on improving the quality of life for families and consumers. Since its inception more than a century ago, professional home economics has become a general foundation for the family- and consumer-oriented careers. In addition, many specialized professions have evolved as central careers in which to serve the needs of families and consumers.

We shall survey the profession's development and offer a perspective on the profession today. Much has been written on the subject, and our treatment is necessarily brief. For those interested in further reading, the bibliography at the end of this chapter offers many excellent references, including *The Life of Ellen H. Richards* by

Caroline Hunt, *Caroline Hunt* by Marjorie East, *AHEA — A History of Excellence* by Helen Pundt, *Definitive Themes in Home Economics and Their Impact on Families 1909–1984* by the American Home Economics Association, and *Home Economics: Past, Present, and Future* by Marjorie East. The *Journal of Home Economics* devoted five issues to the seventy-fifth anniversary of the American Home Economics Association (Fall 1983 through Winter 1984) and always has excellent articles. Because family life and consumer life are the focal points of our society and our professions, it is also valuable to understand the forces shaping their evolution and change. For example, Steven Mintz and Susan Kellogg's *Domestic Revolutions: A Social History of American Family Life* has documented the historical shifts in family life from the traditional family to today's diverse family structures. In the consumer arena, Robert Mayer's *The Consumer Movement* surveys the rise of consumerism and the many consumer issues brought on by our mass-production and mass-consumption society. Much is to be learned from studying these and many other historical accounts of family and consumer environments.

Birth of the Profession

Let us start with a look at the early history of home economics. Did you know that

- A chemist is the recognized founder of home economics?
- The desire to adapt new scientific and technological developments to improve the health and efficiency of households was the main reason for establishing the home economics profession?
- The profession has been evolving for a century and a half, with the first home economics textbook being published in 1840?

The first woman to attend and graduate from the Massachusetts Institute of Technology, as well as its first woman faculty member, was a central figure in the profession's birth. She was Ellen Swallow Richards, one of the founders of home economics. It was her courage and determination in 1871 that allowed her to break down MIT's barriers against admitting women. And it was her interest in applying the sciences to home life that provided the profession's intellectual foundations.

Another woman, Catharine Beecher, shares some credit as one of the founders of home economics. In 1840 she wrote *Treatise of Domestic Economy,* which became the first home economics text accepted by a state department of education. She wrote on many subjects, including the following:

- Clothing, textiles, and related topics
- Equipment, housing, and home furnishing
- Family economics and home management
- Child development and family relations
- Nutrition and foods
- Health

Today these subjects remain as the core subjects and professions in home economics.

Ellen Swallow Richards is most often cited as the person who moved the profession forward during its early days. But when she began her college education at Vassar College in September 1868, she was concerned only about studying. As she wrote in her diary, "The only trouble here is they won't let us study enough . . . for the question is, can girls get a college degree without injuring their health?"[1] From Vassar, Richards moved to the Massachusetts Institute of Technology (MIT) and in 1873 received a bachelor of science degree in Chemistry. In addition, she received a master's degree from Vassar in the same year. It was at MIT that Richards became involved in public health programs. Over the next few years she pursued numerous projects related to increasing educational opportunities for women and improving living conditions.

In 1886 Richards became involved with the Society to Encourage Studies at Home, a correspondence school for women offering a variety of subjects such as history, language, and literature. Richards wanted to add a new area of correspondence lessons that concentrated on "sanitary science." Such education was thought appropriate because it was during this time that modern technology was beginning to enter the home. However, few women in the late 1800s knew how to use this technology safely and efficiently. Richards firmly believed that homemakers needed to understand the new household conveniences and to organize their households according to scientific principles. Her purpose was to educate people on the close relationship between science and everyday life.

In the early twentieth century, people became increasingly concerned about the rapid social and technological changes that were occurring and wondered whether society was progressing in the right direction. It was these issues that motivated the Lake Placid

---

[1] Caroline L. Hunt, *The Life of Ellen H. Richards* (Washington, DC: American Home Economics Association, 1980), pp. 22–23.

Conferences on Home Economics. These conferences led to a formal foundation for the profession and gave Ellen Richards another opportunity to influence the growth of this new profession. The conferences were attended by specialists in bacteriology, biology, chemistry, domestic sciences, economics, hygiene, physics, psychology, sanitary science, and sociology. Some of the issues raised at the first conference were the following:

> "What are the essentials which must be retained in a house if it is to be the home?"
> "What work may be done outside?"
> "What standards must be maintained within?"
> "What forces in the community can be roused to action to secure for the coming race the benefits of material progress?"[2]

Thus the first Lake Placid Conference brought further attention to the problems of home and family life and helped home economics to become a discipline of inquiry. More of the foundation for a family- and consumer-oriented profession was laid.

Ellen Richards is given credit for being the leading force that organized and directed the Lake Placid Conferences. One of the chief results was to bring focus, unity, and identity to the newly emerging field. After much deliberation, these people chose *home economics* as the name for this field. The *home* meant a place of shelter, nurturance of children, development of self-sacrificing qualities, and strength to meet the world. *Economics* reflected the management of the home in regard to time, energy and money.[3]

At the 1908 Lake Placid Conference, the question of organizing into a national body arose. The participants determined that the time had come, and so the annual Lake Placid Conference evolved into the American Home Economics Association. Its first meeting began on December 31, 1908, in Washington, DC. In its constitution, the American Home Economics Association stated its purpose as "the improvement of living conditions in the home, the institutional household and the community."[4] Richards was chosen as the association's first president. With her leadership and hard work, the organization grew. The first issue of the association's *Journal of Home Economics* was published in February 1909. Many other significant events followed. Ellen Swallow Richards continued her work until her death on March 30, 1911. Today her influence is still felt by

[2]Ibid., p. 119.
[3]Ibid., p. 123
[4]Helen Pundt, *AHEA—A History of Excellence* (Washington, DC: American Home Economics Association, 1980), p. 2.

many people. Her life and the events leading to the founding of home economics are documented in *The Life of Ellen H. Richards* by Caroline L. Hunt and *Ellen Swallow: The Woman Who Founded Ecology* by Robert Clarke.

Early History of the Profession _____

Many other forces helped shape the family- and consumer-oriented professions. The growth of public education for men and women has continually reshaped the home and family roles of both sexes, particularly the increase in women's educational opportunities outside the home, beginning in the late nineteenth and early twentieth century. The rise of mass production and the factory system in the Industrial Revolution took common household tasks like sewing out of the home and into factories. As these trends grew, women's time was freed to pursue education and to seek jobs. Family and consumer careers were reshaped by these social and economic forces, and that reshaping continues today.

Another important force in the early history of home economics was the 1862 Morrill–Land Grant Act, which established land-grant colleges in every state. These colleges fostered educational programs and scientific research related to home problems, and as a result, home economics prospered. Other important legislative measures were the 1914 Smith-Lever Act and the 1917 Smith-Hughes Act. The Smith-Lever Act appropriated funds for research, extension, and training in high school teaching. It also created agricultural experiment stations in each state, including funds for home economics research. The Smith-Hughes Act established home economics as a field of vocational education, and funds were provided to train professionals to work in cooperative extension. This helped home economics extension programs to grow.

Home economics was also affected by the stock market crash in 1929 and the Great Depression that followed. It was these events that encouraged research on the management of financial resources and on the family's efficient use of time, money, and energy.

World War II led to further development of home economics. The war necessitated interest in food services, journalism, sanitation, health, and environment. It also necessitated women's entering the labor market. This affected child care, the household management of tasks, family relationships, family welfare, and family economics. All this brought more attention to the home economics aspects of family life.

Thus home economics has evolved from its early focus on the needs and interests of women to its broad concern with all social and economic conditions. Home economists have helped improve consumer products, human nutrition, and legislation affecting families, health, and sanitation. Thus the original goals of the profession, to apply scientific principles to improving home and family life, are being met. From many historical rootings and evolutions has emerged this family- and consumer-oriented profession as we know it today.

The Profession Today _____

With this background in mind, let us look at where the profession serving families and consumers stands today

Focus on Family and Consumer Resources

Although there has been much change in the history of the profession, its focus has remained unchanged: to promote family life and the home as the center for family success and well-being. No other profession centers itself on the family.

Today the profession has two aims: (1) improving the lives of families and their members and (2) promoting the best selection and use of consumer products and services. The increasing complexity of contemporary life has led to the growth of many specializations serving families and consumers, as this book has indicated, but their overall purpose remains the same.

The Growth of Specializations

In many ways we are all generalists who know much about the diversity of families, cultural groups, and the many styles of family life. Understanding and appreciating the broad picture of family life is important, indeed crucial, to performing in our service-oriented professions. At the same time, the explosion of knowledge in our many fields has made specialization a virtual necessity to succeed. There is too much information to allow one to know everything. Furthermore, many of us have specialized interests that bring dedicated focus to our careers ("I love to design new things . . . ," "Teaching is one of the great joys of my life. . . ."). Thus where once we were professional home economists with the generalist's orientation, today we are more often interior designers, fashion buyers, child psychologists, family therapists, financial planners, restaurant managers, and so on. Each such person is a specialist, each with his or her own extensive array of professional skills and knowledge. Although there may be debates on the "generalist" versus "specialist" nature of our profession, there is no doubt that today's job market for our professions demands the deepened skills of the specialist.

With the growth of specializations has come the growth of many specialized professional organizations. Such umbrella associations as the American Home Economics Association (AHEA) have served as unifying forces for our professions for nearly a century and have promoted our common mission to improve the quality of family life. Today the AHEA has evolved much like a confederation of specializations, given its many professional sections and subject-matter specialties in all major family and consumer areas. Simultaneously, today there is a growing number of major professional organizations of specializations. Consider the following brief list of focused, highly specialized areas and their associated specialized organizations:

Specializations:	*Professional Organizations:*
Early childhood education	National Association for the Education of Young Children, Society for Research in Child Development
Family life	National Council on Family Relations, American Association of Marriage and Family Therapists
Home economics education	American Vocational Association, Home Economics Education Association
Home economics communications	National Association of Extension Home Economists, Home Economists in Business (AHEA)
Consumer interests	American Council on Consumer Interests, Society of Consumer Affairs Professionals in Business
Family finances	International Association for Financial Planning, Association for Financial Counseling and Planning Education
Nutrition and food sciences	American Dietetic Association, Society for Nutrition Education

Hotels and restaurants	National Restaurant Association, American Hotel and Motel Association
Retailing and store management	National Retail Federation, American Marketing Association
Textiles and clothing	The Fashion Group, American Association of Textile Chemists and Colorists
Interior design and housing	American Society of Interior Designers, National Home Fashions League

These are only a few examples of some leading specialized organizations for our professions; see the Appendix for many more examples.

The demand for specialization is a modern fact of life, but the knowledge of the generalist will always be relevant. The most successful professionals serving families and consumers integrate their generalized knowledge of the relation between humans and their environment with the particular knowledge of their specialties. Most constructive, for example, are the interior designer who understands how people live and interact in their homes, the financial planner who really knows a family's goals and life-style, the dietitian who appreciates how cultural preferences shape nutritional status. Each specializes, and each uses the perspective of the generalist to see clients in the context of their lives.

Professional Certifications and Licenses

Many professions now offer professional certifications or licenses to their practitioners. Some of these programs, such as teacher certification, have existed for a long time, whereas others, such as the program for certified financial planners, are relatively new. In general, to obtain certification you must complete a prescribed program of education, training and experience that is usually determined by a professional organization or governmental agency. For example, you may already be familiar with the requirements for certification of teachers that are mandated by each state. Teachers at the primary and secondary levels can obtain specialized certifications to teach in many areas, such as general home economics and vocational home economics. Specialized professional certifications can also be obtained through certain organizations, for example the following:

- Certified home economist (American Home Economics Association)
- Registered dietitian (American Dietetic Association)
- Certified financial planner (College for Financial Planning)
- Certified family life educator (National Council on Family Relations)

These are some examples of the professional credentials you can earn. You will learn more about each as you enter the courses for your major field of study. We recommend that you pursue the appropriate certifications standard for your field. Many of these have come into being only recently and will become more important in the future. In fact some certifications are even mandatory for practicing your profession (e.g., teacher certifications). Your professors will provide current information on the required or recommended certifications for your specialty.

A Contemporary Agenda

To accomplish its goals in serving families and consumers, our profession must take many actions. The following are some of those on its current agenda.

Promoting Education. Historically, family and consumer professionals have been active educators, and this role continues. Education comes from many arenas: schools, government, businesses, and human services organizations. The profession has achieved some of its greatest accomplishments in such areas as consumer education, family life education, nutrition education, home economics education, parent education, and early childhood education. This has taken place in both formal settings (e.g., schools) and informal settings (e.g., education through the media, continuing education programs).

Identifying Research Needs and Priorities. Home economics has become a research-oriented profession. The current priorities for research include nutritional adequacy of diets, healthfulness of products, safety of products, information for consumers, management of resources in families, child development, and management of family stressors (divorce, family violence, aging, and others).

Formulating Public Policy. The profession advocates legislation supporting families and consumers. Current legislative agendas include concerns for child welfare, family violence, displaced homemakers, labeling of consumer products, antipoverty programs, and family services programs. The profession is involved in such public service issues as formulating priorities for legislation, writing legislation, and lobbying for the passage of legislation.

Developing Professionalism. This book testifies to the importance of professional development in the family- and consumer-oriented professions. Developing professionalism means promoting high standards of work, involving oneself in professional organizations, and setting high standards and goals for professional productivity. When appropriate, professionalism also means developing programs for accreditation, certification, and licensing. These requirements have already become standard in professions such as medicine and law and are widely discussed in consumer and family professions as well.

Communicating a New Professional Image. Professionals want to be thought of as achievers, problem solvers, and leaders, and they must show that the profession has benefited society. Our profession was once thought of as mainly household arts, in particular cooking and sewing. Serving families and consumers means so much more today, yet this restricted image persists and must be defeated. The domestic arts are important, even crucial subjects to some audiences, especially in lower income and underdeveloped populations. But our society and our profession now place much greater priority on dealing with more pressing family and consumer issues—family violence, divorce, teenage pregnancy, malnutrition, personal finances, product safety, health, jobs, and consumer protection, to name a few.

Some programs in home economics are achieving a new image by a change of name hand in hand with a broadening of content or professional emphasis. For example, some programs of high school home economics have adopted such names for their curriculum as life management, essential living skills, family living, and others that escape old stereotypes. For similar reasons of image improvement and professional recognition, some colleges have adopted such names as human ecology or family and consumer sciences. Name changes are controversial, and some home economists fear that changes signal the demise of our profession. Others emphasize that our identity must change in step with inexorable changes in the society around us. The fact is that many renamed programs thrive today, as do the many that retain the term *home economics*. Regardless of name, the success of any program is determined exclusively by gaining and maintaining stature with the people we serve. As Armstrong says:

What is important is that, in spite of name change and diversity, we still retain the same primary objectives of almost a century ago: improving the life conditions of individuals and families and stimulating the optimal use of human and family resources. We are fortunate that, early in our profession's history, we realize the necessity for replacing the mask still worn by some professionals—that of friendly superficiality—with real interest in and involvement with the individuals and families with whom we work.[5]

Some experts recommend that we go beyond basic image improvement to actively and aggressively *marketing our profession.* This means (1) doing things that are important, that really serve a significant group of consumers, families, or the public at large, (2) communicating what we do that is important in an active and convincing way, and (3) being politically knowledgeable by knowing who has power to support our work and influencing their support. All of us are involved in this persuasive function: retailers selling products to consumers (the obvious case), consumer affairs professionals who promote the interests of consumers within their corporations, teachers who promote the value of their courses to students or administrators, service agency administrators who solicit funding from their communities, or interior designers who propose plans for a house to their clients. It is not enough to work well; people must be informed and believe in you. Marketing does count.

The most important thing a profession must do is show that its agenda reflects widely recognized national needs and priorities, some of which are the following:

1. Human health
2. Product safety
3. Conservation of resources
4. Concern for the disadvantaged, handicapped, or those with special needs
5. Economic cooperation and development
6. Building positive human and family relations
7. Promoting family financial security
8. Assuring the quality of products and services

Important Areas for Growth

The most important question a profession ever asks is: Where should we go next? Or asked in a slightly different manner: What areas and programs should receive new or renewed emphasis? The

---

[5]Barbara Armstrong, "A Cure for Future Shock," *Journal of Home Economics,* September 1976. p. 25.

following are some of the areas often suggested as requiring the greatest attention by the profession:

1. Solving problems created by family stresses, such as economic problems, divorce, and family violence
2. Helping remarried, reconstituted, and blended families adjust to new ways of life
3. Dealing with teenage pregnancy
4. Helping the single-parent family and the displaced homemaker
5. Helping families integrate work and family life
6. Coping with the problems created by an aging population (e.g., financial planning, retirement planning, nutritional planning, and other consumer issues)

SELF-ASSESSMENT EXERCISE 2-1

Important Issues Today

There are many more important issues today than those mentioned in this chapter. See how many current issues facing families and consumers you can *add* to the list.

1. _____
2. _____
3. _____
4. _____
5. _____

Now consider these issues and those listed in the chapter. Identify and rank what *you* consider the *five most important issues today*.

1. _____
2. _____
3. _____
4. _____
5. _____

These selections will help you to consider alternative careers in the coming chapters.

SELF-ASSESSMENT EXERCISE 2-2

What Will You Be Doing in a Few Years?

Describe what you think you will be doing five years from now.

_____

_____

_____

What special knowledge or skills must you acquire to do this job in the future?

_____

_____

_____

7. Taking a greater responsibility for all aspects of public policy, including advocacy, formation, enforcement, and analysis
8. Providing information for family financial analysis, resource management, and decision making
9. Providing information and education to assist consumers in understanding new complexities of markets and new issues associated with the regulation of consumer markets
10. Developing new technologies for producing foods, clothing, textiles, and appliances
11. Using computers in the home
12. Applying artificial intelligence, expert systems, or other informational aids to consumer decision making
13. Finding out more about human nutrition and health
14. Finding ways to cope with the internationalization of consumer markets
15. Renewing public concern for consumer health, safety, and protection
16. Studying the potential impacts of new energy problems and shortages
17. Promoting resource conservation

Within the listed global areas for growth there are numerous specific issues that command our attention and need solution. Consider the following headlines from the late 1980s and early 1990s:

Changing roles of women
Changing roles of men
New roles and life-styles for children
Day care for children
Latchkey children
Family communications
Divorce
Younger teenage pregnancy (age 13–14)
Work and the family
Cultural diversity
Family diversity
Child abuse
Family violence
Drugs
Designer drugs
Alcohol abuse
Malnutrition
Rising costs of health care
Product quality
Consumer protection
Fast foods
Biotechnology for foods and other products
Pesticides in the food supply
Cholesterol
Conservation of resources
Materialism
Voluntary simplicity
Family financial planning
Mass merchandising
Smart shopping
Information overload
The homeless
AIDS
Baby boomers
Aging baby boomers
Seniors — the mature market
YUPPIES
DINKS (Dual Income No Kids)
Leveraged buyouts
Economic globalization
Black Monday
The savings and loans crisis
Mergers
The environment

Oil supplies
Reunification of Germany
Rapid change ("future shock")

Many of the issues embodied in these headlines are old and seemingly perpetual, having lasted decades, but some are new creations of modern life. What are the new issues in today's headlines? One way to learn about the new issues leading to new agendas for our professions is to read the literature of the profession. Some helpful references are contained in the bibliography of this chapter, and the final chapter of the book offers perspectives on future directions for our family- and consumer-oriented careers. The daily news also offers banners that emphasize our new agendas. In concluding this chapter, we ask you what professions could be more exciting, more closely tied to contemporary life, and more beneficial to society than those that serve families and consumers? Our professions are mainstream and relevant, perhaps even more than any others in today's job markets. Let us continue to explore what to expect in the career market of tomorrow.

Questions and Exercises _____

1. What professional directions would you like to see our professions, and the field of home economics in general, take in the next ten years (toward the year 2000)?
2. Study the history of home economics by reading references such as those in the bibliography of this chapter. Why is understanding history important to your career?
3. Study the history of any professional area of our field (e.g., child development, family relations, nutrition, clothing, consumer affairs, interior design, housing, and family economics).
4. Learn more about a professional organization in your area of interest (see Chapter 19 and the Appendix for more information). What publications and services does it offer? How can it contribute to your career?
5. Learn about the certification or licencing of professionals in a specific area.
6. What are the advantages and disadvantages of being a generalist? A specialist?
7. How would you go about marketing your profession (i.e., persuasively promoting your profession to others)?
8. Scan a newspaper from a big city (e.g., *The New York Times*, *The Los Angeles Times*, *The Washington Post*) to identify major stories or issues facing families and consumers. How do these compare to issues raised in your local media? What are the implications for careers?

Bibliography

Armstrong, Barbara N. "A Cure for Future Shock," *Journal of Home Economics* 68 (September 1976), 23–25.

Bonde, Machelle. "Marketing Home Economics: Let's Stop Assuming and Start Selling," *Illinois Teacher* 33 (November/December 1989), 65–67.

Border, Barbara, ed. *Nontraditional Home Economics: Meeting Uncommon Needs with Innovative Plans.* Bloomington, IL: McKnight, 1983.

Burgess, Sharon L. "Home Economics and the Third Wave," *Journal of Home Economics* 75 (Fall 1983), 10–13, 59–60.

Butler, Sara, Linda Ade-Ridder, Susan Rudge, and Carol Sensbach. "Issues in Home Economics: Opinions of Specialists and Generalists," *Journal of Home Economics* 79 (Fall 1987), 13–18.

Byrd, Flossie M. "Home Economics: Reflections on the Past, Visions for the Future," *Journal of Home Economics* 82 (Summer 1990), 43–46.

Clarke, Robert. *Ellen Swallow: The Woman Who Founded Ecology.* Chicago: Follett, 1973.

Coulter, Kyle Jane, and Marge Stanton. *Graduates of Higher Education in the Food and Agricultural Sciences: An Analysis of Supply/Demand Relationships,* vol. II: *Home Economics.* U.S. Department of Agriculture, Science and Education Administration, Publication Number 1407, February 1981.

Coulter, Kyle Jane, Marge Stanton, and Norma Bobbitt. *Employment Opportunities for College Graduates in the Food and Agricultural Sciences— Home Economics.* Washington, DC: U.S. Department of Agriculture, November, 1987.

Crouse, Joyce, Kitty Coffey, Connie Ley, and Carol Townsend. "Certification: Making the Most of It," *Journal of Home Economics* 79 (Winter 1987), 52–54.

Deacon, Ruth E. "Visions for the 21st Century (1987 AHEA Commemorative Lecture)," *Journal of Home Economics* 79 (Fall 1987), 62–70.

Definitive Themes in Home Economics and Their Impact on Families 1909– 1984. Washington, DC: American Home Economics Association, 1984.

East, Marjorie. *Caroline Hunt: Philosopher for Home Economics.* University Park, PA: Division of Occupational and Vocational Studies, Pennsylvania State University, 1982.

_____. *Home Economics: Past, Present, and Future.* Boston: Allyn & Bacon, 1980.

"Ellen H. Richards (1842–1911), a Tribute," *Journal of Home Economics* 75 (Fall 1983), 3.

Feingold, S. Norman. "Tracking New Career Categories Will Become a Preoccupation for Job Seekers and Managers," *Personnel Administrator* 28 (December 1983), 86–91.

Gentzler, Yvonne S. "A Conceptualization of Competence: Constructs for Professional Development," *Journal of Home Economics* 79 (Winter 1987), 39–42.

_____."Certification: The Credentialed Professional," *Journal of Home Economics* 81 (Summer 1989), 56.

Horn, Marilyn J. "Undergraduate Majors in Home Economics: Integrate or Eliminate?" *Journal of Home Economics* 80 (Winter 1988), 28–32.

Hunt, Caroline L. *The Life of Ellen H. Richards.* Washington, D.C.: American Home Economics Association, 1980.

Jolly, Laura D., Renée A. Daugherty, and Peggy S. Meszaros. "C.H.E.C.K.ing into Home Economics Careers: A Computerized Approach," *Journal of Home Economics* 81 (Summer 1989), 15–19, 59.

Mayer, Robert N. *The Consumer Movement.* Boston: Twayne Publishers, 1989.

McFadden, Joan R. "Decades Ahead: Opportunities and Challenges for Home Economics," *Journal of Home Economics* 76 (Fall 1984), 14–16.

Meszaros, Peggy S., and Bonnie Braun. "Early Pioneers," *Journal of Home Economics* 75 (Fall 1983), 4–8.

Mintz, Steven, and Susan Kellogg. *Domestic Revolutions: A Social History of American Family Life.* New York: Free Press, 1988.

Morgan, George A., and Soyeon Shim. "University Student Satisfaction: Implications for Departmental Planning," *Home Economics Research Journal* 19 (September 1990), 47–66.

Naisbitt, John. *Megatrends: Ten New Directions Tranforming Our Lives.* Chicago: Nightingale Conant Corp., 1984.

Nickols, Sharon Y. "Families: Diverse but Enduring (1988 AHEA Commemorative Lecture)," *Journal of Home Economics* 80 (Fall 1988), 49–58.

Pundt, Helen. *AHEA — A History of Excellence.* Washington, DC: American Home Economics Association, 1980.

Rader, Bonnie, ed. *Significant Writings in Home Economics: 1911–1979.* Peoria, IL: Glencoe, 1987.

Selmat, Nevaleen Joy Schmitz. "Changing Role of Women," *Illinois Teacher* 25 (November/December 1981), 82–84.

Spitze, Hazel Taylor. "Home Economics in the Future," *Illinois Teacher* 68 (September 1976), 19–22.

Thompson, Patricia, ed. *Knowledge, Technology, and Family Change.* Bloomington, IL: McKnight, 1983.

Toffler, Alvin. *The Third Wave.* New York: Bantam, 1984.

Vaughn, Gladys Gary. "Home Economics: An Agenda for the '90s," *Journal of Home Economics* 82 (Summer 1990), 50–54.

Work, Clyde E., June H. Wheeler, and Jeanette V. Williams. "Guidance for Nontraditional Careers," *Personnel and Guidance Journal* 60 (May 1982), 553–556.

CHAPTER 3

Professional Career Planning—The First Steps

Now we begin planning your career. This chapter examines two topics:

1. General criteria for choosing your career: what you must consider as you plan your professional future.
2. Clarifying your career preferences: what you can do to find the specific careers in family and consumer professions that may be of interest to you.

Remember that there are no magic formulas or easy solutions for choosing the single best career for your life. We offer only guidelines, but your careful and thoughtful application of them should help you to find a career that is right for you.

General Criteria for Choosing Your Career _____

Choosing your career entails some risks and uncertainty. To help reduce those risks and to help you choose your career, you should consider the following criteria as you plan for your future.

Educational Requirements

What type of education does your profession require? Nearly every profession has special requirements for entry and advancement. In some careers, you may obtain an entry-level position with a two-year associate degree. But increasingly, professional careers require four-year college degrees or more, sometimes even a Ph.D. degree. For example, with a two-year associate degree, you can obtain technically skilled, entry-level positions in parts of the hotel and restaurant industry and in some areas of apparel technology. In other fields, such as fashion retailing and interiors merchandising, employers often look for a bachelor's degree. Teachers, on the other hand, may need to obtain a master's degree for long-term and continued employment in teaching programs. Many areas of child development, family relations, nutritional science, and textile science require advanced degrees, sometimes a Ph.D. It is important to be aware of such requirements as early as possible in order to choose the right major and plan for study. We give you more details on those requirements in later chapters.

Required Professional Skills

Every profession requires certain skills and knowledge. Academic and intellectual skills are foremost. Do you have the interest and aptitude to master the knowledge and skills you need? Professionals in foods and nutrition need a substantial knowledge of biochemistry, general chemistry, and other nutritionally oriented sciences. An interior designer requires a broad knowledge of art, design principles, and functional designs. A retailer must be familar with business subjects such as accounting, marketing, fashion prediction, consumer choice, personnel management, and public relations. An educator re-

Criteria for Choosing Careers

- Educational requirements
- Experience required
- Job prospects
- Your capabilities
- Personal interests
- Personal priorities
- Preferred life-style
- Geographic preferences
- Financial expectations
- Working conditions
- Advice from "significant others"

quires knowledge of many modern techniques for instructional development, ranging from traditional lecture and laboratory methods to new techniques of computer-assisted instruction and other student-centered techniques. Early in your college career you should learn more about the specific requirements of your career. Then try to acquire as many of the needed skills as possible.

New technological and quantitative skills are also becoming important in almost all careers. Nearly every career is affected by computers, and a growing array of computer-based skills is needed in all professions. All of us have become users of word processors for our written communications through letters, memos, and reports, and electronic mail through computer-to-computer communications has become commonplace. An array of spreadsheet mathematical programs and database managers has entered the business world. Computer-assisted design is a trend in most design professions. "Distance education" using television, microwave technologies, computers, and cable systems is used in an increasing range of instructional programs. Computerized financial planning, dietary analysis, and vocational and even personal counseling are being implemented. Although these and other skills of high technology are new (a growth phenomenon of the 1980s) and form only one facet of our careers, it is expected that technology will continue to grow in applications and become an indispensable tool for professionals.

Many occupations also require social skills. This is true for many of the family and human service professions, in which the professional must interact actively and frequently with family members.

Education is another profession requiring interaction with families and students. A fashion retailer interacts daily with consumers in stores, suppliers of goods, and other business associates. There are many instances in which you must learn social skills and human relations in order to interact successfully with clients.

Many other skills are important to specific professions. For example, physical skills and manual dexterity are important to an artist, an interior designer, or a laboratory scientist who must use complex scientific equipment. Leadership skills may be useful to many careers—for example, to a department store manager who must motivate sales employees or to a child development specialist who must lead the activities of a group of students. Look for these and other specialized requirements of your chosen career.

Some general skills are important to all careers. Communication skills—the ability to write and speak effectively—are necessary in business, government, and education. The ability to think analytically, or to solve problems and to make decisions, is often helpful. Personal qualities such as drive, initiative, innovativeness, self-motivation, and enthusiasm for your work are also highly regarded by employers.

Experience

For entry into some careers, work experience is desirable and, in some cases, mandatory. The range and type of experiences expected vary depending on the career you are entering. For example, students entering teacher education programs are expected to complete student teaching as a part of their certification requirements as teachers. Fashion retailing students are advised to obtain work expe-

---

SELF-ASSESSMENT EXERCISE 3-1

Key to Success

List three employers from whom you might gain work experience in a family- or consumer-oriented career:

1. _____

2. _____

3. _____

rience in sales and other levels of retail stores. Students in interior design or fashion design need to prepare elaborate portfolios displaying their creative talents and artistic skills. Child development specialists benefit from work in a day-care center. These are just some of the many examples of work experience that can be valuable as you enter your career.

How do you get these work experiences? You can take a part-time job during your school years or during the summers. There are also a number of ways in which you can gain experience and receive college credit for it. For example, some programs offer internships in specific subjects such as fashion merchandising or interior design. Some colleges have cooperative programs in which you may study for a semester and then work for a semester in your area of interest. These programs are carefully planned around the experiences you will receive and the types of employers with whom you will work. Organized programs, such as formal internships with employers, are especially recommended for professional career development, because these give you a more complete experience and credentials for future employment.

Your university may also have work-study programs and other job assistance programs available to you. Check with your financial aid office and the placement office for details on these opportunities.

Job Prospects

What are the current employment opportunities in your chosen career? How can you learn about current job prospects in your area of interest? There are resources that offer helpful forecasts of future jobs in your college placement office and in the library of your school or university. The *Occupational Outlook Handbook* published by the U.S. government is one general source of information that projects selected job demand into the near future. And from time to time, various government agencies study employment conditions and trends in various fields. For instance, the U.S. Department of Agriculture completed a study of career prospects for people in family- and consumer-oriented careers and projected a substantial demand for family and consumer professionals through 1990 (see Table 3.1).

The job expectations given in Table 3.1 have been borne out, and there continue to be extensive opportunities in the major career fields, according to updated studies. The most recent Department of Agriculture study forecasts a major demand for professionals in the family and consumer professions through 1995 and likely much longer. For example, the study identifies the following major areas of demand and the expected annual job openings:

TABLE 3.1 Average Annual Supply of and Demand for College Graduates Qualified for Employment in Home Economics and Related Fields, United States, 1977–1990

Occupational Cluster	Demand	Supply by Degree Level				
		Associate	Baccalaureate	Master's	Doctoral	Total
Administrators and managers	7,115	152	3,097	711	86	4,046
Design, manufacturing, and processing specialists	7,444	1,807	2,849	1,126	12	5,794
Marketing, merchandising, and sales personnel	17,069	918	9,901	1,739	23	12,581
Media specialists	1,626	14	1,453	440	29	1,936
Scientific and professional specialists	4,819	—[a]	3,915	574	89	4,578
Service specialists	7,253	1,321	5,678	795	100	7,894
Educators	8,904	—[a]	7,858	2,159	349	10,366
Total	54,230	4,212	34,751	7,544	688	47,195

Source: Coulter, Kyle Jane and Marge Stanton, *Graduates of Higher Education in the Food and Agricultural Sciences,* vol. II: *Home Economics.* U.S. Department of Agriculture, Publication 1407, 1981.
[a]This cluster requires a degree level higher than associate.

- Administrative and Managerial Professionals (e.g., directors of day-care centers, consumer affairs directors, customer service managers, hotel managers, restaurant managers, retail managers, managers of interior design firms, directors of fund development, food service managers)—6,500 openings annually for graduates with administrative and supervisory competencies
- Marketing, Merchandising, and Financial Professionals (e.g., account executives, buyers, financial planners, loan officers, marketing specialists, product analysts, sales managers, real estate agents—11,000 openings annually in the major areas of family and consumer products (foods, clothing, housing, furnishings, financial services)
- Scientific, Design, and Technical Professionals (e.g., apparel designers, biochemists, dietitians, energy conservation specialists, family science researchers, interior designers, nutritional scientists, quality control analysts, textile chemists, textile designers)—7,200 openings annually for graduates with degrees in science or design
- Information, Communication, and Education Professionals (e.g., counselors, curriculum specialists, teachers, media specialists, parenting educators, nutrition educators, consumer educators, public relations specialists, university professors, writers, journalists)—7,200 openings annually with new and innovative opportunities in business, adding to traditional choices in teaching and the media
- Family and Community Services Professionals (e.g., career counselors, child abuse case workers, family financial counselors, geriatric service counselors, home health care providers, marriage and family therapists, retirement counselors, youth counselors, community development specialists)—5,200 openings annually in the numerous family services at local, state, and national levels.

These expected opportunities are reinforced in the "Outlook 2000" analyses of growing occupations in the *Occupational Outlook Quarterly,* which forecasts excellent growth in such areas as social welfare, home health care, financial services, leisure services, correctional services, retailing, sales, management, and teaching. In a similar manner "hot" careers are regularly promoted in the popular media, including the widely read *Money Magazine, Working Woman,* and *National Business Employment Weekly.* Substantial demand for qualified professionals exists in all fields, and often there is keen competition for the best jobs. The employment experts therefore remind us that the need for appropriate education has never been greater and that gaining the education and experience is the best route to success.

Remember, however, that career opportunities are continually changing. A field that requires many new graduates right now may be saturated by the time you graduate. Therefore, interpret with caution the current demand for graduates in any particular career. However, do not choose your career solely on the basis of projected future opportunities for obtaining a job but, rather, on your own interests and its relevance to your future life. It would be unfortunate to enter a career with many opportunities only to find you are not happy and satisfied with it.

Your Capabilities

We all are good at something, but few of us are good at everything. What are your particular capabilities, skills, or aptitudes? Are you particularly good at math, chemistry, biochemistry, or other sciences? Do you have a natural ability to work well with others? Do you like working with others and understand the psychological, sociological, and behavioral aspects of interacting with others? Do you function best when analyzing and solving problems? How well do you communicate? Do you learn quickly and understand complex subjects?

You probably have many of these skills now and can learn many more. Furthermore, although you may feel uncomfortable with some of these skills, you can learn most of them. For example, some students speak of their difficulties with math, science, and problem-solving skills. Others tell us of their difficulty in interacting with others or with social relations and human interaction. But you can improve on any skill if you have self-confidence and make strong positive efforts.

What are your individual skills and aptitudes? There is no better time than now to sit down and do a careful self-analysis. Are you especially good in certain courses or subjects—writing, drawing, math, chemistry, psychology? Are your term projects and papers consistently high in quality, or do you make some of the best oral presentations in class? Are you particularly effective as an organizer or group leader? Or do you simply excel at working hard and putting in whatever efforts are needed to complete a job? Take just a moment to list these things you do best, for they are the leading clues to your best future. Many sources can help with this task. Parents, friends, teachers, and professors may help you in identifying your skills. In addition, you may wish to visit the guidance and counseling office of your school or your university placement office to find out about the available aptitude and interest tests. Some examples are the Strong-Campbell Interest Inventory and the Kuder Preference Record (Vocational). These types of tests can guide you in understanding more fully your personal skills, aptitudes, and interests.

Your Own Interests and Priorities

Your own interests and priorities are as important to your career decision as are your capabilities and will determine much of your satisfaction and enjoyment in life. It is not self-centered and selfish for a family- or consumer-oriented professional to consider personal satisfaction in choosing a career. If you are not interested in or satisfied with your career, you will do very little to serve either your clients or yourself. Thus a healthy self-interest is a legitimate criterion for a career choice.

It can be very hard to analyze your interests and priorities objectively, but try to answer such questions as: Do you seek status and prestige in your career, or would you rather be inconspicuous or less prominent? Do you enjoy working with people, or would you prefer to work by yourself? Would you enjoy a job that requires a lot of travel, or are you attracted to that job just because of its glamour? Would you really enjoy moving from one part of the country to another every two or three years, or would you like to return to your home town and live there for the rest of your life? Do you want material possessions, or would a simple life-style satisfy you? Do you need a large salary, or would a modest income be satisfactory for your long-term family and personal interests? Will your working life be the center of your life or merely a means for providing for your life after work? It is critical to your career planning to evaluate yourself honestly.

Should you need help, the counseling and guidance office and your college placement center can help. For self-help, you might wish to consult several books on career planning and job hunting. Some examples are Richard Nelson Bolles's *What Color Is Your Parachute?* and Howard Figler's *The Complete Job-Search Handbook.* Your college placement center or the academic advising office will provide these or similar references, and most colleges offer scheduled classes that include these job-search activities. A new approach gaining in popularity involves using computer programs for career guidance and planning, and some of these may be available in your placement center. For example, the *Discover* program provides a variety of self-paced exercises and helps you to identify personal interests in such general areas as arts, science and business. Other programs are designed for our specific careers, such as "C.H.E.C.K.ing into Home

Economics Careers." These and other books suggest specific exercises for identifying and analyzing your personal characteristics, skills, accomplishments, values, and interests. This book has the primary exercises serving this purpose—to help you understand your values, capabilities, and special preferences for careers.

Life-Styles

What are your daily activities and roles? Do you like to play tennis or golf? Do you go to the movies, or do you read a lot? Do you have a spouse, children, and a family life? What do you do with your time?

Your life-style has an important bearing on the career you pursue. Consider a family-centered life-style, for example. Family life tends to revolve around school hours, evenings, and weekends, and so obviously a career requiring you to work during these times could disrupt your family life. However, be prepared to make some compromises between career and life-style. Few people have the luxury of a perfect fit between their preferred way of living and the responsibilities of the professional world.

Geographical Preferences

To get the best job, you may need to be flexible in where you will live. The more flexible you are, the better your chances will be of finding the job you want and opportunities for advancement. Nevertheless, after graduating, many people wish to return to their home towns or states to begin their careers. Some even refuse to move from one part of the country to another or to a neighboring state. There is nothing wrong in having geographic preferences; in fact, it is easy to understand why people want to live near family and friends. But recognize the trade-off and sacrifices that can result. By insisting on a particular geographic preference, you limit the opportunities for finding a career and future advancement.

Some careers are located in specific geographic regions of the country. For instance, if you are interested in fashion design, you will find the best opportunities in New York and Los Angeles. However, there are opportunities in such fields as fashion merchandising, interior design, dietetics, and human services in nearly every city in the country, especially the larger cities. You will find, however, that most family- and consumer-oriented careers have opportunities in every geographic region of the country.

From time to time, certain geographic areas offer special opportunities. Currently, many careers in the family and consumer sectors are opening in large cities and the Sun Belt states, from

Florida through Texas to California. Nevertheless, there always are excellent opportunities in most northeastern, midwestern, and western states. You can look into opportunities in various states and regions of the country by contacting state employment offices, local employment offices, or chambers of commerce, which can give you current information on opportunities in various localities. You may also wish to consult the local newspapers and trade publications for information on current opportunities.

The Role of Influential Others

There is no question that the viewpoints of our parents, close friends, and other people who are significant to us influence our career choices. Perhaps they may even exert undue influence, as when a parent or friend pressures us toward a particular choice.

Who knows you better than your parents and friends? The great benefit of advice from them is they know your skills, interests, and capabilities in ways even you don't recognize. You can expect candor and honesty from them. You may not always like what they say, but they will have your best interests at heart, so listen carefully to them.

Other influential individuals include teachers, college professors, and guidance counselors. From time to time, you will have an opportunity to talk with people who are actually working in the field of your chosen career. Take advantage of every opportunity to talk with and question these experienced individuals. By talking with them, you can get up-to-the-minute advice for planning your career, choosing a major, choosing courses to take, and gaining entry into the field. These people will also serve as contacts as your career progresses. Start now to build a network of professionals in your career. Their expertise, experience, and advice can be your most valuable asset.

Financial Expectations

What salary do you expect to earn, and what is the probability of financial advancement in your career? The question of finances usually is central to many college graduates. Indeed, sometimes it is given more importance than it actually deserves.

There is a great deal of difference in the starting salaries from one field to another. Scientists, such as those going into textiles, nutrition, and product development, can expect higher-than-average starting salaries. But one can expect an average salary in many areas of business, such as retailing, interior design, fashion, communications, and personnel. Those graduates entering smaller businesses and proprietorships or some areas of volunteer work and human services will receive somewhat lower-than-average salaries.

Your starting salary should not be the principal reason for choosing a career. Of course, you must earn enough to maintain a satisfactory standard of living, but plan to live with a modest income for several years while launching your career. Most careers will provide you with salary advancements and financial rewards as your performance improves. Your starting salary is not as important to your decision as is what you expect to do in this career and the probability that your salary will advance as your career advances.

Working Conditions

Working conditions differ among careers. The hours you work, the office or environmental setting, the amount of paperwork involved, the level of supervision and interaction with other employees are just a few of the things that vary. One condition common to all professional careers is that you can expect to work long and odd hours sometimes. Few, if any, professional careers are paid by the hour, and very few are simply 8:00 A.M. to 5:00 P.M., Monday through Friday.

For example, a professional in fashion retailing or hotel and restaurant management may begin the day in midmorning and find it going on well into the evening. The activities of stores, restaurants, and hotels typically span a large range of daily hours and require professional attention for those periods. A day-care worker, on the other hand, may begin at 7:00 A.M. when the first clients arrive and complete the day as late as 6:00 or 7:00 in the evening. By comparison, a teacher may seem to have relatively good work hours, often from 8:00 A.M. to 3:00 P.M., Monday through Friday, but must take work home or stay after 3:00 P.M. to prepare for the next day. And remember, those hours of teaching are pressure packed and require continuous contact with young people of various ages and mental capacities, thus putting a different type of working strain on the professional. Important as they may be, the hours you work are just one feature of the working conditions that you can anticipate.

What will be your work setting? Retail store buyers may operate regularly on the floor of their department store but also may frequently make trips to other cities to purchase merchandise for the store. Thus, much travel is involved. Restaurant or hotel managers may spend a large part of the day on their feet operating within one segment or another of their business. An interior designer, on the other hand, may spend a day largely confined to small offices or drawing boards, where most of the work takes place. A child psychologist may interact daily with various clients in an office setting and may move very little from that one setting from day to day. Obviously, then, the environmental conditions of your work are important. Do you want to be in an office every day, or do you want to move from one area to another, constantly changing your environment?

Careers also vary in the level of responsibility you have for the success of your organization and the amount of authority you have to accomplish the organization's goals. As your career advances, so will your responsibilities and authority to make decisions. Some careers can also exert a great deal of pressure to perform. Careers in business are very performance oriented. Goals and objectives will be set, and you will be expected to meet them. This can create a very exciting environment and one in which you will quickly see the progress of your efforts, but it will also increase the amount of tension you feel as you work.

Many other working conditions may influence your career choices. Do you want flexible working hours and the freedom to choose your hours? What about dress—is there a uniform or professional way of dressing that is expected in your career? How much work will you take home with you each night? Many careers require a substantial amount of work at home; so expect this as a part of professional employment.

What about your social obligations after work? Does your business expect you to entertain clients as a part of your work? Will civic and community obligations be a part of your career? What are your vacation needs, and what vacation opportunities will you have? Finally, who are the people you will be working with on a daily basis? Are they the type of people with whom you will enjoy working? Do you enjoy meeting the public, if that is your responsibility. Do you enjoy working with peer co-workers, or do you prefer to work with a staff under you? Do you prefer to work alone? You must feel comfortable with your co-workers.

In the literature of the 1980s and 1990s much has been written about these and other working environments, as well as the idea of corporate cultures. Indeed, all work settings, corporate or otherwise, have their cultures—standard ways of doing things, a hierarchy of roles (bosses, workers, leaders, followers, associates, peers), daily routines, political affairs, specialized language, and so on. It is necessary to think of your job from this total perspective as a culture when seeking a career that has the right culture for you. You must especially keep the culture in mind in adapting to it when you begin working. Every organization has some unique formal and informal environments and ways of working, and it is absolutely necessary to become a part of this to become an effective professional. Learn about these environments, starting with your first part-time jobs and internships.

Now let us help you make the decisions leading to your professional choice.

Clarifying Your Specific Career Preferences _____

This book is designed to help you analyze professional opportunities in family- and consumer-oriented careers and to help you clarify your professional preferences. Undoubtedly you are reading this book partly because you are already interested in considering a family- or consumer-oriented career. Maybe you have already formed a preference, perhaps even a very strong one, for a specific career in a field such as fashion retailing, child development, dietetics, or teacher education.

But what if you are undecided or uncertain about your choice or are having second thoughts? You could be interested in becoming an interior designer but unsure of this choice. Unless you wake up at night thinking about being a designer, unless your every waking hour is committed to that single goal, the chances are that you are undecided. The next pages will help you to continue your decision making.

Although it is interesting and exciting to learn about the many possible careers open to you, it is also hard work. You will need to apply a lot of time, energy, self-motivation, and thought to seeking a profession, It may take you months or years to choose, accompanied by doubts and frustrations. However, think about the great rewards you will receive—you are making a lifelong plan and a major commitment that if properly executed will lead to great satisfaction and productivity.

Read All You Can About Careers

First, read this entire book, especially those chapters on specific careers. Keep an open mind to all possiblities, even if you now feel committed to a specific field. Also recognize the number of options in any given general career area. For example, specialists in fashion retailing may find careers in merchandising, store management, marketing, advertising, or personnel relations, among others. Similarly, students in education may become classroom teachers, but they may also find opportunities in many other fields to which education-oriented and communicative skills are important: Public relations, consumer affairs, and governmental and human service organizations offer many such opportunities for students in education.

For more details about specific careers, go to your library and find books about the fields of your interest. Many books are written on child development, nutrition, education, fashion retailing, interior design, and human services. If you are looking for general careers, look for general books. For instance, if you are interested in retailing, look for an introductory textbook on retail management or retail merchandising. And do not overlook the literally hundreds of trade publications and professional journals that are published in various professional areas of interest. For example, *Stores* magazine reports on merchandising, store management, and sales practices in the retailing business. The *Journal of the American Dietetic Association* and the *Journal of Nutrition Education* are professional journals for dietitians and educators in the field of foods and nutrition. *Child Development* and *Young Children* are professional periodicals of interest to child development specialists. The *Cornell Hotel and Restaurant Administration Quarterly* serves the interests of the hospitality industry. *Interiors* and *Home Furnishings Daily* serve contract designers and residential interiors business. *Forecast for Home Economics* and the *Journal of Home Economics* are publications for teachers and other communicators in all fields of home economics. Ask your college professors and librarians for information on other periodicals and journals in your field.

The United States government, especially the U.S. Department of Labor, publishes much information about occupations. The *Dictionary of Occupational Titles* (referred to as D.O.T.) lists literally thousands of specific job titles and occupations that can be relevant to family and consumer professionals. It also gives basic information on educational requirements, the skills required, and the working conditions for various occupations. It is well worth some time. Also of interest are the *Occupational Outlook Handbook* and the *Occupational Outlook Handbook for College Graduates*. These review certain general careers and expected opportunities for employment in the future.

Self-Analysis

Reading all you can about different career options is only the first step in career planning. Now you should turn to what many authorities consider the main part of life and career planning, self-analysis. By self-analysis, we mean trying to discover who you really are. This is one of the most difficult, but necessary, activities in your career planning. There are many kinds of self-analysis, ranging

SELF-ASSESSMENT EXERCISE 3–2

Important Activities

Find at least four helpful references in your library that discuss a career that interests you. List them below for future reference.

1. _____

   _____

2. _____

   _____

3. _____

   _____

4. _____

   _____

from the very formal to the relatively informal. We suggest that you go through the following process: First, go back to the section "General Criteria for Choosing Your Career" earlier in this chapter. Write a one-page essay about yourself on each topic subheading of that section. Start by listing your single greatest skill, capability, or area of expertise. Do the same thing with your second greatest skill, third greatest skill, and so on. Other important topics are your preferred life-style, your preferred geographic preferences, your personal interests and priorities, and the working conditions under which you function most effectively and happily. What is the result of all this? You have just produced a short autobiography consisting of several chapters about your professional self and what you are now as a preprofessional. This essay is a self-portrait that you can use to plan your future professional development.

There are other informal and formal ways of self-assessment. Richard Bowles, in his popular book *What Color Is Your Parachute?* suggests short essays and tests for assessing one's professional skills, interests, capabilities, and orientation. Nancy Folse and Marilyn Henrion, in their book *Careers in the Fashion Industry,* provide scales by which you can rate such things as your personal qualities, abilities, accomplishments, and values related to your work. And Howard Figler's *The Complete Job-Search Handbook* has short,

Self-Analyses for Careers Include

- Writing a short autobiography
- Identifying your educational goals
- Knowing your personal values
- Knowing your desired life-style
- Identifying skills you have
- Identifying skills you need
- Assessing your career-oriented values

thought-provoking exercises to assess your values, skills, creativity, and even your views of reality ("reality testing"). Many other books and career programs offered by your college provide similar exercises for self-analysis.

Professional Associations

Professional associations such as the American Home Economics Association, the American Society for Interior Designers, and the American Dietetic Association have active student programs on many campuses. You may also find clubs and interest groups such as a fashion industry club or a consumer relations board operating on your campus. The activities of these organizations are practical and focus on careers. They invite career speakers and working professionals as their guests at meetings. They may also plan field trips or other experiences in the actual careers you are seeking. Often they receive discounts on publications and books in your field of interest. Finally, participation gets you contacts—people who will work with you professionally in later years.

Now is a good time to support your professional association. See your major professor, academic adviser, or student group on your campus for information.

Career Programs

Look for career-oriented programs offered by your university, department, or professional organizations in your field. High schools and colleges often have career days when they bring professional speakers in various fields to campus for open discussions and visits. Professional associations and trade associations also offer career seminars, especially at the annual conferences that most profes-

SELF-ASSESSMENT EXERCISE 3–3

A Worksheet for Self-Analysis

List three or more items under each heading:
My most valuable personal characteristics:

1. _____

2. _____

3. _____

Personal characteristics I should improve:

1. _____

2. _____

3. _____

Favorite hobbies or leisure activities:

1. _____

2. _____

3. _____

Things I enjoy doing the most:

1. _____

2. _____

3. _____

Things that I try to avoid:

1. _____

2. _____

3. _____

Characteristics of my ideal job:

1. _____

2. _____

3. _____

sional associations have. For information on these programs, see your college placement office and student chapters of professional associations.

Talking with Professionals in the Field

What could be better than talking with some people who are currently working in your profession of interest? You will find that many professionals, even though they are busy and active in their fields, will take time to talk with you. Don't hesitate, don't be shy — call on them for information and advice. Talk with many people and get different viewpoints and perspectives on the field. Also talk with people in different positions of the organization in which you may be interested in seeking employment. For instance, if you're going into a retail environment, talk with salespeople, retail store buyers, general merchandise managers, and even the vice-president and president if possible.

Here is how to conduct this type of conversation. Telephone the individual you wish to talk with, or his or her secretary, and request an informational interview (remember, this is not a job interview; make that explicit). Tell the person that you want to talk for only about ten to fifteen minutes *maximum,* and stick to that when you actually conduct the interview. Some of the questions you may want to ask are the following:

1. What activities do you perform on a typical day?
2. What education and specific courses are important to obtain an entry-level position in this field?
3. What types of training programs or on-the-job training does your business or organization offer?
4. What are the good or bad points about your profession?
5. What is the future for advancement in this field?
6. Will this field be a good one to be employed in for the future?
7. What work experiences should I have to make myself more employable?
8. Where can I get more information about this profession?

Ask for references to trade publications, books, and other people in the organization with whom you might talk.

Sampling Your Career

Absolutely the best way to learn about a profession is actually to work in it. You need to obtain actual work experiences to learn more about your chosen career and to decide whether you like the

SELF-ASSESSMENT EXERCISE 3–4

What Do You Do Best?

List those subjects or courses in which you earn your highest grades.

1. _____

2. _____

3. _____

4. _____

List your special skills or abilities that are best developed.

1. _____

2. _____

3. _____

4. _____

In the past several years, what have been your greatest accomplishments?

1. _____

2. _____

3. _____

4. _____

work activity, daily routines, and skills required. Your work experience might simply be part-time work after school or between school hours, or it might be in a more formal internship program offered by your major, including fashion retailing, dietetics, interior design, and restaurant and hotel management. If you cannot find a paid employment position, do volunteer work for a company at which you hope to find employment. It might also be a co-op program between a particular employer and your university or perhaps a work-study program. The particular content or format of the work experience is not as important as is the fact that you will have gained the work experience. Many students have been attracted to a career or have decided *not* to pursue a career because of such work experiences. Try to get experience, even at the most elementary or low level in your organization, as early as possible in your college career.

Career Counseling and Guidance

Wouldn't it be great if you could hire a professional counselor or employment adviser to decide your career for you? Your counselor would look deep within you, see all your skills, strengths, interests and limitations, and proclaim that you are destined to be an interior designer (for example). Rarely are things so easy. Thus we start with the modest proposal that only you can be an expert on yourself. Only you know your strengths, weaknesses, values, goals, objectives, and desires. And only you can make the self-analysis necessary for intelligent career planning and decision making.

Nonetheless, there are many advisers, counselors, career planners, employment specialists, and the like to help you with your career selection and professional development. Should you use them? The answer is, in some cases, an emphatic yes. We especially recommend that you consult the career counseling and placement office at your school or university and watch your student newspaper or other campus information sources for their current activities. Many also offer their services to graduates as well as to current students.

If you go to a guidance counselor at your university or school, what can you expect? Counselors use a variety of approaches, from informal discussions to formalized testing and measurement of vocational capabilities or interests. Quite often counselors may give you tests, such as the Kuder Preference Record (Vocational) or the Strong-Campbell Interest Inventory. These tests measure vocational interests or aptitudes and will give you general guidance. Rarely will counselors name a specific career or field for you to pursue. Instead, they will point out the areas for which you appear to have an aptitude, such as using mathematics, working with people, or pursuing an art. A counselor may also point you in new directions where you can find information about the career right for you.

What about choosing a paid career counselor or adviser? There are thousands of such specialists going under such names as career counselors, employment advisers, and executive recruitment specialists. Some of these people may be helpful, but a word of caution is appropriate. Choose a paid counselor in the same way you would make any other expensive consumer purchase—with care and with your self-interest in mind. Most counselors offer a free or low-cost initial visit at which you can determine what services will be offered, what the expectations for success are, and what the cost will be.

SELF-ASSESSMENT EXERCISE 3–5

Your Work-Related Interests

This exercise helps you identify what working situations are important to you as you consider different careers. Identify which ones on this list are "very important" to you, and look for professions that match your "very important" interests.

Working Situations	Very Important
Being the leader at work	_____
Being a worker, not leader	_____
Having opportunities to advance	_____
Holding a steady job with defined responsibilities and activities	_____
Being a decision maker	_____
Working as a team with others	_____
Working mainly alone	_____
Writing memos and reports	_____
Communicating a lot in person and on the phone	_____
Working regular hours	_____
Working whatever time it takes to do the job (e.g., nights, weekends)	_____
Working with numbers and math	_____
Doing creative work	_____
Working in a scientific laboratory	_____
Reading scientific articles and reports	_____
Working with high technology (e.g. computers)	_____
Working in an office	_____
Working outside	_____
Traveling to different working locations	_____
Visiting with customers or clients	_____
Changing jobs or responsibilities regularly	_____

Working with a socially responsible employer ⎯⎯⎯

Trying innovative, unusual ways of doing things ⎯⎯⎯

Feeling I am helping others ⎯⎯⎯

Being able to see major accomplishments ⎯⎯⎯

Having a friendly working environment ⎯⎯⎯

Making a high salary ⎯⎯⎯

Making enough to get along ⎯⎯⎯

Having much free time for friends and family ⎯⎯⎯

Working full time ⎯⎯⎯

Working part time ⎯⎯⎯

Working in jobs requiring high energy ⎯⎯⎯

Seeing that my business is profitable ⎯⎯⎯

Continually learning new things ⎯⎯⎯

Working on long, involved tasks ⎯⎯⎯

Quickly moving from one activity to the next ⎯⎯⎯

Doing designs, drawings, sketchings ⎯⎯⎯

Counseling and helping people with problems ⎯⎯⎯

Teaching students, co-workers, or others ⎯⎯⎯

Selling products and services to consumers ⎯⎯⎯

Protecting the rights of others ⎯⎯⎯

Setting my own work hours ⎯⎯⎯

Working at home or outside of an office setting ⎯⎯⎯

Doing research ⎯⎯⎯

What Will All This Accomplish?

All these activities may not give you the answer to the single "best" career. What you will probably find is at least one potential match, or several potential matches, between you and a career. This will get you started toward a profession, by organizing your thoughts and preferences regarding your professional life. When completed, you can set more informed goals, both for the short term and for lifelong growth in your profession.

Questions and Exercises

1. Conduct an aptitude inventory of yourself by listing your specific skills (things that you are good at doing). These may include your academic, social, and physical skills.
2. Conduct a values inventory of yourself by listing those things that you value or consider to be important in life (e.g., family life, leisure time, fame, material possessions, freedom, social activities, power, personal creativity, success).
3. Get acquainted with the professional journals for your chosen specialty. Briefly list for each one the following:
   • Nature of the journal (research or popular literature)
   • Advantages of reading it
   • Contributions to the profession
   • Relevance to your career interest
4. Find out about a professional association for one of the family and consumer professions (see Chapter 19). Write a brief description of this association and include the following information:
   • Purposes of the association
   • Local student chapter activities
   • Requirements for membership
   • Benefits of membership
5. Conduct a ten- to fifteen-minute interview with a currently practicing professional in a career of interest to you. Include the following information in a brief report:
   • Qualifications for the career
   • Advantages and disadvantages
   • Typical daily activities
   • Advancement potential
   • Future demand for the career
6. Attend an orientation or introduction to career counseling given at your college's placement center. Write a brief report including the following information:
   • Services offered by the placement center
   • Career counselors available for student counseling
   • When and how to set up a placement file
   • How to use the career library
   • Availability of career placement tests (e.g., Kuder Preference Record, Strong-Campbell Interest Inventory).

7. Arrange to spend some time observing or assisting in a professional work environment related to your chosen career. Write a diary that includes your observations, activities, opinions, attitudes, and insights gained from this experience.
8. Create an "I Like Me" file for yourself. Use a three-ring binder or separate file folders to organize your personal file in the following manner:
   - Personal accomplishments (e.g., achievement awards)
   - Work experience records
   - Educational experience records
   - Special activities or memberships
   - Aptitude inventory (from question 1)
   - Values inventory (from question 2)

Update your "I Like Me" file regularly to use for your résumé.

Bibliography

Bolles, Richard N. *What Color Is Your Parachute?* Berkeley, CA: Ten Speed Press, 1990.

Coulter, Kyle Jane, Marge Stanton, and Norma Bobbitt. *Employment Opportunities for College Graduates in the Food and Agricultural Sciences—Home Economics.* Washington, DC: U.S. Department of Agriculture, November 1987.

Discovery for Colleges and Adults. Hunt Valley, MD: American College Testing Program, 1989.

Evans, Rupert N., and Edwin L. Herr. *Foundations of Vocational Education,* 2nd ed. Columbus, OH: Merrill, 1978.

Figler, Howard. *The Complete Job-Search Handbook.* New York: Henry Holt, 1988.

Flanagan, William G. "Choosing a Career—The Agony and the Ecstasy," *Forbes,* 129 (March 15, 1982), 138–144.

Hewes, Dorothy W. "From Home to Worksite: New Arenas for Home Economics," *Journal of Home Economics* 76 (Fall 1984), 33–37.

Hoeflin, Ruth, Karen Pence, Mary G. Miller, and Joe Weber. *Careers for Professionals: New Perspectives in Home Economics.* Dubuque, IA: Kendall/Hunt, 1987.

Holland, John L. *Making Vocational Choices: A Theory of Careers.* Englewood Cliffs, NJ: Prentice-Hall, 1973.

Hopke, William E. *The Encyclopedia of Careers and Vocational Guidance: Planning Your Career,* 7th ed. Chicago: Ferguson, 1987.

Hoyt, Kenneth B. "The Changing Workforce: A Review of Projections—1986 to 2000," *The Career Development Quarterly* 37 (September 1988), 31–39.

Jolly, Laura D., Renée A. Daugherty, and Peggy S. Meszaros. "C.H.E.C.K.ing into Home Economics Careers: A Computerized Approach," *Journal of Home Economics* 81 (Summer 1989), 15–19, 59.

McFadden, Joan R. "Decades Ahead: Opportunities and Challenges for Home Economics," *Journal of Home Economics* 76 (Fall 1984), 14–16.

Mencke, Reed A., and Ronald L. Hummel. *Career Planning for the '80's* Monterey, CA: Brooks/Cole, 1984.

Morf, Martin. "Eight Scenarios for Work in the Future," *The Futurist* 17 (June 1983), 24–29.

"Occupational Employment," *Occupational Outlook Quarterly* 33 (Fall 1989), 30–37.

Olney, Claude W. "The New Job Outlook: Preparing for the Years Ahead," *Journal of Employment Counseling* 25 (March 1988), 7–13.

Powell, C. Randall. *Career Planning Today.* Dubuque, IA: Kendall/Hunt, 1981.

Sargent, Jon. "A Greatly Improved Outlook for College Graduates: A 1988 Update to the Year 2000," *Occupational Outlook Quarterly* 32 (Summer 1988), 1–6.

Shaevitz, Marjorie Hansen. *The Superwoman Syndrome.* New York: Warner Books, 1985.

Westoff, Leslie Aldridge. "How to Capitalize on Hidden Talents," *Money*, 11 (November 1982), 151–155.

White, Martha C. *The 1988-89 Job Outlook in Brief.* Washington, DC: Superintendent of Documents, U.S. Government Printing Office, 1988.

CHAPTER 4

The Career Market of Today — What to Expect

It is important to have a realistic perspective on the career market. For example:

1. What are employers looking for in a qualified candidate? (It isn't just your major and grades.)
2. How are jobs and careers changing today? (How will you adapt to the many changes that are coming?)

This chapter offers some general answers to these questions. Our objective is to encourage "future-oriented" or "anticipatory" thinking so that you can think about what your future career environment will be like and how to plan for it.

What Do Employers Want? _____

First, you must know what employers expect of professional employees. Employers' expectations are high, because professional employees are responsible for the success of their organization—the accomplishment of their objectives and the satisfaction of their clientele.

Every profession has its own set of skills, qualities, and personal characteristics sought by employers. In general, these fall into seven categories: knowledge; thinking and problem-solving skills; creativity, innovativeness, and imagination; communication skills; human relations skills; positive character traits; and commitment. Notice that these are general skills that transfer from profession to profession. To enhance your potential for success in any profession, develop a broad range of these general professional skills.

Knowledge

Professions are built on specialized knowledge. Indeed, many professions are identified by their claim to a special kind of knowledge that no other profession possesses. The therapeutic dietitian, for example, combines a specialized knowledge of nutrition, biochemistry, human development, and consumers' cultural preferences for foods. The interior designer combines a unique knowledge of art, human engineering, physical engineering, materials, and current tastes in home fashions. The child psychologist synthesizes knowledge of childhood development, human development, family interaction patterns, and child physiology.

Employers look for professional employees who have the relevant academic skills, aptitudes, and knowledge. You should obtain as many of these as possible within the constraints of your learning resources and academic programs. In later chapters, we describe those skills that are desirable for each major of family and consumer professions.

Thinking and Problem-Solving Skills

It may seem obvious, but the one characteristic that all employers look for is an ability to think. Can you logically and analytically reason through a problem? Do you have critical thinking skills, the ability to see all sides of a problem? Can you defend your reasoning? Problem solving requires a series of logical steps, including identifying the problem, thinking of alternative solutions, analyzing the advantages and disadvantages of each, deciding on one solution, and formulating a plan of action to achieve it. Your ability to engage in such thinking is invaluable to all employers.

What Employers Expect of You

- Knowledge of your field
- Problem-solving skills
- Creativity
- Communications skills
- Human relations skills
- Positive character traits
- Professional commitment to your career

A second part of thinking is a willingness to learn new approaches, techniques, and knowledge in your field. Are you willing, and is your mind able, to do the necessary research to create new perspectives and new ideas? Will you regularly read journals, books, professional periodicals, and other publications in your field? Do you appreciate new ideas and new ways of doing things? All this is a part of the thinking and problem-solving process. If you can adapt to changes in your field, your adaptability can be one of the most important qualities leading to lifelong professional success.

Creativity, Innovativeness, and Imagination

The ability to conceive new and creative ideas or plans of action are highly valued qualities in an employee. Originality and innovativeness are obviously crucial to the success of, for example, new product designers, fashion designers, and interior designers. But original thinking and creativity can be equally important to solving the problems faced by business, government, and human service organizations. For example, the lifeblood of advertisers is new and different themes or messages that capture the audience's attention. Using similar creative approaches, educators experiment with new teaching techniques to improve the effectiveness of education. In sum, virtually all careers have a creative or innovative dimension that separates the truly successful professional from the average one.

Communication Skills

Employers want people who are skilled communicators of facts, ideas, and viewpoints. Employers often complain that today's visually oriented young people, raised on television and movies, cannot read and write. Ask yourself honestly, "Is this true of me?" If your skills of communication are less than you desire, work on improving them. Communicating is necessary in all careers and determines success or failure. For example, educators are inherently speakers and writers, but perhaps you would be surprised to learn that in business, employers frequently require professional communications, including presentations, reports, memos, files, briefs, papers, and other written or oral communications that range from the short to the lengthy and complex.

One of the most neglected communication skills is listening. Are you a good listener? Do you hear and understand what others are saying, or do you merely wait until it is your turn to speak? This important facet of communication is often overlooked, much to the distress of every speaker. Make sure you hear what is said and interpret it correctly.

Human Relations Skills

Effectiveness in social interactions is an important professional skill. Some of us naturally enjoy social interactions. We love to lead meetings and be the center of attention. Others are more introverted. Working with small groups and interacting with one or two colleagues is their characteristic pattern of social relations. Which of these are you? Employers look for these skills and attempt to match personal social styles to job requirements.

Getting along with people is central to positive human relations. But it is not the only part. Other special human relations skills that are sought by employers are leadership and the ability to negotiate. A good leader can attract and encourage others to perform successfully. A good negotiator is one who communicates information, viewpoints, or opinions that influence others. Such skills can be developed through a human relations course, a social skills course, or other professional courses to improve your communication and interaction with others.

Positive Character Traits

Employers are interested in your character, personality, and ability to cope with the working world. They want to know about your motivation. They are looking for self-starters, achievers, and reliable people with good work habits. Other desired traits include enthusiasm for work and a positive attitude toward work. Maturity and self-control are important to many occupations, particularly the human services. Willingness to take carefully calculated risks are sought in business. Your successful projection of such character traits can in fact determine whether you will be considered for employment.

SELF-ASSESSMENT EXERCISE 4–1

Taking a Closer Look at Potential Careers

Choose a specific career or job title (e.g., financial planner, interior designer, family counselor, consumer affairs professional, or teacher). What do you think employers will look for in their employees in the following key areas?

Career or Job Title: _____

Knowledge and Skills: _____

_____

_____

_____

Personal Character Traits: _____

_____

_____

_____

An often-overlooked influence on your professional acceptance is appearance and self-presentation. The recognized importance of dress and self-presentation has resulted in the recent growth of "wardrobe engineers," dress consultants, and other clothing analysts who promise to improve your professional image by means of your appearance. In most situations of life, including the professions, dress and self-presentation are important. For example, your appearance creates first impressions and says something about your status, social background, self-image, and even capability. Although many other factors influence professional success, never forget that dress and appearance are crucial to your professional image.

Commitment

Employers look for people with a true interest in and commitment to their field. This is true in business, education, government, and human services. All employers look for loyalty to their organization and its goals, for people who regard their work as a lifelong career and not just a job. They want people who have long-term goals, who want to be with the organization five, ten, or more years into the future. This does not mean that you must commit your life, body, and soul to the organization, but it does mean that you must want the organization to be an important part of your life.

One way to show your commitment to your organization is by your experiences. Have you worked in that type of organization or activity previously? Another way is by taking related courses or joining professional organizations. Of course, in the end, your good work, punctuality, and reliability best show your professional commitment.

The Changing Characteristics of Today's Career Market

You are preparing not just for a job lasting a year or two but for a career that will span many decades. Careers are fluid and ever changing, which requires you regularly to adapt your skills to the changing job market and to your changing career. You will likely hold a variety of jobs during your career. Indeed, many people will hold a variety of *changing careers* as the needs of the job market change.

Perhaps most important is that career markets offer an almost overwhelming number of varied and specialized opportunities for professionally oriented careers in the consumer and family sectors. Although some areas may now have fewer opportunities, trained professionals in family and consumer specialties should continue to find varied professional opportunities in their chosen field. You will have the most opportunities if you develop transferable skills, those that are important in many differing careers. Examples include human relations skills, the ability to write, and a willingness to work with numbers, all of which are transferable skills valued in widely differing careers.

One characteristic of all professions is the continuing explosion of knowledge and information. Thus you will need to continue your education beyond college. In some cases, obtaining an advanced degree will be necessary, whether it be a master's or a Ph.D. degree. However, in many careers, a bachelor's degree will be satisfactory provided that you keep abreast of new developments. This can be done through continuing education courses, short courses, journals, and a host of other approaches.

In many fields, knowledge grows especially fast. We all are aware of the rapid growth of scientific knowledge and the applications of such knowledge during this century. This explosion of knowledge has touched many consumer fields, especially foods, fabrics, and furniture. We are also assured of rapid increases in the application of technology to such fields as computerization and automation (e.g., robotics, or automated manufacturing using robots). In particular, the need for computer literacy—an ability and willingness to work in a computer-assisted environment—is mandatory. These trends will cause major changes in business practices and work settings. Examples are computerized management of retail stores, computerized design of apparel, computerized work at home for businesses and service organizations ("telecommuting"), computerized design of consumer products, and perhaps the "electronic cottage" forecast in Alvin Toffler's *The Third Wave*. As the world changes, we also are required to learn new skills and approaches. The globalization of today's economy requires new skills in international business, trade relations, politics, and cultural understanding. (It is impossible to do business with other nations without cultural literacy and language skills in particular.) Finally, it has become a given that we now live in a service economy, and new knowledge is being created daily on how best to function in this postindustrial society.

Another important trend is that careers are becoming more and more formally professional. For example, there may be expected minimum standards for admission to a field, such as specific degree requirements. This is currently the case in dietetics. You may also expect certification requirements, such as those required in primary and secondary education, as well as newer programs for certified financial planners and certified home economists. Some fields will expect you to continue your education to maintain your certification or license.

The professional work force of today is already demonstrating more sophisticated knowledge and skills. This is partly caused by the explosion in the knowledge of most fields and partly because more college-educated professionals are entering careers aimed toward families and consumers. Thus, the competition is more substantial, particularly in regard to advancement in your profession. Coping with the competition requires adaptability skills, the ability to adjust and respond appropriately.

The typical workweek is also changing. The idea of the forty-hour workweek appears well engrained in the American work culture; however, there are some trends worth mentioning. First, more people are choosing part-time, free-lance, or temporary professional employment, especially those running their own businesses or service activities. Second, there is a small but possibly growing trend toward job sharing, in which two people share a single full-time job, each on a part-time basis. Third, "flextime" or flexible work hours are growing. Fourth, many professionals work more than the standard forty-hour workweek. Professional careers usually require time and commitment, particularly those that are business oriented or self-run.

Finally, the career market of today is increasingly client centered and service oriented. Greater and greater efforts are being made to serve the needs of families and consumers. In the past, some businesses assumed that their main activity was to produce products efficiently, that whatever they produced would sell. Now the trend is to take a consumer orientation, that is, to identify the needs of individual consumers and families *first. Then* successful modern businesses organize their production and marketing activities toward serving those needs. The idea is that you will be more successful if the consumer is your central focus. It may seem obvious, but it is remarkable how many organizations, whether businesses, education, government, or human services, sometimes lack this client-centered focus.

Be ready for change, and be ready to adapt. Change is inevitable, and there is little you can do to stop it. Indeed, perhaps you will be one of the *change agents* in society, a person who encourages and leads the change.

Questions and Exercises _____

1. List some of the changes that have occurred within the last twenty years in the following categories:
   • Social
   • Economic
   • Political
   • Environmental
   • Technological
   a. Discuss how these changes have interacted (e.g., how a technological change has related to or caused a social change).
   b. What changes on your list do you think should be encouraged, and what changes do you think should be discouraged? Why?
   c. How will these changes affect family- and consumer-related careers?
2. Respond to the following questions in terms of your chosen career:
   a. What special knowledge must I possess to be successful in this career?
   b. How might I develop problem-solving skills for use in this career?
   c. How might I use my creativity in this career?
   d. How will this career use my writing, speaking, and listening skills?
   e. What human relations skills must I possess to be successful in this career?

f. What positive character traits do I possess that will enable me to excel in this career?

g. How might I show my commitment to this career?

3. What general qualifications do employers seek in professionals?

Bibliography _____

Bennett, Robert L. *Earning and Learning: A Guide to Individual Career Development.* San Mateo, CA: Action Link, 1980.

Bolles, Richard N. *The Three Boxes of Life, and How to Get Out of Them.* Berkeley, CA: Ten Speed Press, 1981.

Burgess, Sharon L. "Home Economics and the Third Wave," *Journal of Home Economics* 75 (Fall 1983), 10–13.

Carey, Max L. "Three Paths to the Future: Occupational Projections, 1980–90," *Occupational Outlook Quarterly* 25 (Winter 1981), 3–11.

Cetron, Marvin J. "Career Direction During the '90s," *Journal of Career Planning and Employment* 50 (Winter 1990), 29–34.

——, "Getting Ready for the Jobs of the Future," *The Futurist* 17 (June 1983), 14–20.

Cetron, Marvin J., and Thomas O'Toole. "Careers with a Future: Where the Jobs Will Be in the 1990's," *The Futurist* 16 (June 1982), 11–19.

Coulter, Kyle Jane, and Marge Stanton. *Graduates of Higher Education in the Food and Agricultural Sciences: An Analysis of Supply/Demand Relationships.* vol. II *Home Economics.* U.S. Department of Agriculture, Science and Education Administration, Publication Number 1407, February 1981.

Coulter, Kyle Jane, Marge Stanton, and Norma Bobbitt. *Employment Opportunities for College Graduates in the Food and Agricultural Sciences—Home Economics.* Washington, DC: U.S. Department of Agriculture, November 1987.

Dun's Marketing Services. *The Career Guide 1990: Dun's Employment Opportunities Directory.* New York: Dun & Bradstreet, 1990.

Erdlen, John D. *Where Are the Jobs?* New York: Harcourt Brace Jovanovich, 1982.

Figler, Howard. *The Complete Job-Search Handbook.* New York: Henry Holt, 1988.

Flanagan, William G. "Choosing a Career—The Agony and the Ecstacy," *Forbes* 129 (March 15, 1982), 138–144.

Foegen, J. H. "The Menace of High-Tech Employment," *The Futurist* 21 (September-October 1987), 38–40.

Fraser, Bryna Shore. "Preparing for Careers in the Computer Age," *Journal of Career Planning and Employment* 49 (Spring 1989), 34–38.

Gallup, George, and William Proctor. *Forecast 2000: George Gallup, Jr. Predicts the Future of America.* New York: Morrow, 1984.

Goodman, Leonard H. *Current Career and Occupational Literature.* New York: Wilson, 1984.

Hallet, Jeffrey J. "The Workplace of the Present Future," *Journal of Career Planning and Employment* 50 (Winter 1990), 43–46.

Haney, Peggy H. "Where Have All the Home Economists Gone?," *Illinois Teacher* 31 (September/October 1987), 9–12.

Henderson, Carter. "Exploring the Future of Home Economics," *Journal of Home Economics* 72 (Fall 1980), 23–26.

Hewes, Dorothy W. "From Home to Worksite: New Arenas for Home Economics," *Journal of Home Economics* 76 (Fall 1984), 33–37.

Holland, John L. *Making Vocational Choices: A Theory of Careers.* Englewood Cliffs, NJ: Prentice-Hall, 1973.

Kimmel, Karen. *Career Resource Centers.* Columbus, OH: National Center for Research in Vocational Education, 1982.

McFadden, Joan R. "Decades Ahead: Opportunities and Challenges for Home Economics," *Journal of Home Economics* 76 (Fall 1984), 14–16.

Mencke, Reed A., and Ronald L. Hummel. *Career Planning for the '80's.* Monterey, CA: Brooks/Cole, 1984.

Miller, Lawrence. *American Spirit: Visions of a New Corporate Culture.* New York: Morrow, 1985.

Morf, Martin, "Eight Scenarios for Work in the Future," *The Futurist* 17 (June 1983), 124–29.

Murray, M. Eloise, and Virginia Clark. "International Concerns of American Home Economics: A Quarter Century Perspective," *Illinois Teacher* 25 (March/April 1982), 185–190.

Naisbitt, John. *Megatrends: Ten New Directions Transforming Our Lives.* Chicago: Nightingale Conant Corp., 1984.

Norback, Craig. *Career Encyclopedia.* Homewood, IL: Dow Jones–Irwin, 1980.

"Occupational Employment," *Occupational Outlook Quarterly* 33 (Fall 1989), 30–37.

Powell, James. *The Prentice-Hall Global Employment Guide.* Englewood Cliffs, NJ: Prentice-Hall, 1983.

Rees, Jane, Margaret Ezell, and Francille Firebaugh. "Careers for Home Economists in the United States," *Journal of Home Economics* 80 (Summer 1988), 30–32.

Selmat, Nevaleen Joy Schmitz. "Changing Role of Women," *Illinois Teacher* 25 (November/December 1981), 82–84.

"Some Trends to Watch For," *Journals of Career Planning and Employment* 50 (Winter 1990), 34–36.

Exploring Career Choices

Part II provides in-depth career profiles and descriptions of family- and consumer-oriented professions. Included are introductions to careers, specific job titles, and discussions of responsibilities and qualifications of practicing professionals. Part II divides the family- and consumer-oriented professions into six categories, as follows:

- **Careers in Arts and Sciences (Chapter 5)**
- **Careers in Business (Chapter 6)**
- **Careers in Education and Extension (Chapter 7)**
- **Careers in Human Services (Chapter 8)**
- **Careers in Government and Public Policy (Chapter 9)**
- **Developing an Innovative Career Path (Chapter 10)**

These categories are based on the types of skills and qualifications required for each profession. For example, artistic and scientific professions such as interior design and human nutrition are included in "Careers in Arts and Sciences" (Chapter 5). Likewise, careers to which business skills are important come under "Careers in Business" (Chapter 6). The final chapter of Part II looks at innovative career choices, how you can tailor a career to your special qualifications and interests.

Careers in the Arts and Sciences

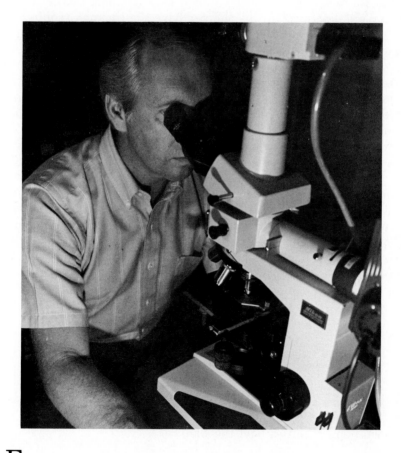

Exciting and well-established careers serving families and consumers pertain to the design and development of consumer products.
In this chapter we begin our exploration of the many careers serving
families and consumers by looking at specialized careers dealing
with each of the following consumer needs:

1. Foods and human nutrition
2. Clothing, textiles, and fashion
3. Interior design, furniture, and home furnishings
4. Housing and household equipment

Some of these careers are artistically oriented and thus require diverse artistic skills in drawing, color, graphic design, and art history. For example, the arts are the foundation of fashion design, textile design, and interior design. Other careers require strong foundations in sciences such as chemistry, physics, and biochemistry. These fields include foods, human nutrition, and textile science. All careers described in this chapter have the common requirement that the professional have a thorough, scientific understanding of the consumer's needs and an ability to translate those needs into well-designed, functional consumer products.

To enter these careers, education is required in various arts, sciences, technology, product development, and other design-oriented subjects. Because understanding consumers and their needs is also important, courses in consumer sciences such as consumer economics, consumer decision making, consumer behavior, advertising, human factors engineering (ergonomics), and environmental psychology are useful. These courses help the professional to understand what motivates consumers to choose products and how consumers actually use the products in their daily lives. And this in turn contributes to the professional's most important task: the design and development of consumer products to serve human needs and desires. The principle for success in this field is always keeping the consumer at the center of attention.

In this and the next three chapters, each major field of family- and consumer-oriented careers will be described in a *career profile,* in the following general format:

- Typical job titles
- Responsibilities
- Qualifications
- Special personal qualities
- Other factors (special working conditions, unique features, unusual opportunities, and the like)

CAREER PROFILE

Dietetics _____

Dietetics is one of the best known and most popular choices of careers among students in nutrition and foods. Dietetics is concerned with many scientific and practical aspects of foods, nutrition, diet, and human health. Professionals in dietetics work in many foods-related settings planning diets, planning menus, educating clients, doing research, and managing. Professionals in dietetics often enter careers in institutional foods service management and are responsible for directing food services in cafeterias and other eating facilities in institutions such as schools, hospitals, and nursing homes.

Typical Job Titles

Dietitian is the basic job title in this profession. Specialized job titles include the following:

- Registered dietitian
- Therapeutic dietitian
- Clinical dietitian
- Educational dietitian
- Administrative dietitian
- Consulting dietitian
- Food services director
- Food services manager
- Cafeteria supervisor
- Restaurant manager
- Gerontological nutritionist
- Weight management specialist
- Nutrition counselor
- Community nutritionist

See Chapter 6 for related careers in hotels, restaurants, and resorts.

Responsibilities

The general responsibilities of professionals in dietetics include preparing diet plans for client groups, preparing menus, promoting good eating habits, and ensuring the health and sanitation of foods.

Responsibilities, such as planning menus or choosing special diets, depend on the type of organization with which the dietitian is employed, whether a hospital, school system, cafeteria, or public restaurant.

Dietitians are also responsible for managerial and supervisory activities. They supervise the preparation of menus, which includes ordering, storing, and preserving foods, buying in bulk, ensuring that meals are balanced from day to day as well as within days, and overseeing staff. This can involve a substantial amount of records management and preparation of written materials, including weekly menus, recipes, and analyses of diets.

Dietitians can be educators as well. Dietitians are often employed to evaluate individuals' diets and recommend ways in which to improve them. This requires a sensitivity to human needs and a knowledge of the foods preferred by various cultural or ethnic groups. The dietitian's responsibility is to recommend diets and convince the clients of their importance, which requires positive human relations and persuasive skills as well as a sensitivity to individual needs, especially when the recommended diet must differ substantially from the one to which the individual is accustomed—for example, when a heart patient must accept a lower-cholesterol and salt-free diet.

Clinical dietitians often work with health-care teams of physicians and nurses, their role being to assess patients' nutritional status. The nutritional assessment of individuals having specific illnesses is an extremely important task and requires considerable knowledge of health, physiology, and human nutrition as well as basic dietetics. In such situations, the dietitian is an essential part of the health-care team, for no other member (not even the physician) is as well trained in human nutrition and foods.

Qualifications

Entry into dietetics requires a bachelor's degree in human nutrition and dietetics, the completion of a one-year internship in dietetics, and a passing score in the registered dietitian (RD) examination. Such a curriculum includes courses in foods, nutrition, chemistry, physiology, bacteriology, institutional management, and other scientific and clinical subjects. Continuing education is also required to maintain one's registration as a registered dietitian.

Work experience in various types of food services, particularly institutional food services, can also be helpful. You will also gain experience in your internship, and this is the most important work experience and professional credential you will obtain.

Special Personal Qualities

Dietetics is a scientific field, which means that you will spend a great deal of time reading scientific literature and expanding your scientific knowledge. You must also have a strong interest in science, particularly biochemistry, human biology, and nutritional sciences.

Those people working in institutional settings will also need managerial and supervisory skills. Those working in clinical settings, such as hospitals, and those working with private clients will need skills in dealing with people and influencing them to accept new dietary habits.

Other Factors

Because of the public's great health consciousness today, there are many new and exciting opportunities for dietitians, such as consulting in a private practice or for a hospital or medical clinic. Dietitians are also employed by supermarket chains and health food stores in the retailing of foods and nutritional products. This creates a unique, business-oriented opportunity for a dietitian who is also interested in consumer marketing or retailing. There is also a growing awareness of the nutritional needs of hospitalized or institutionalized patients, and so there may be openings in hospital nutrition.

Most dietitians work in food service management of all types. The majority of dietitians enter careers in school systems, cafeterias, nursing homes, the military, day-care centers, health-care facilities, and restaurants.

Concern with malnutrition in other countries is also resulting in opportunities for dietetics professionals. The Peace Corps is particularly interested in promoting health, sanitation, and dietary improvement in underdeveloped countries. The U.S. government, the United Nations, and international service organizations such as CARE also hire dietitians.

Dietitians also enter careers in business and industry, particularly with food-processing companies or firms making nutritional products such as diet foods and supplements. For careers in the foods industry, education and experience in foods sciences and human nutrition can be desirable and are discussed in the career profiles that follow.

CAREER PROFILE

Food Science _____

The profession of food science is concerned with all aspects of the storage, processing, preservation, and safety of foods. It is responsible for ensuring that foods are aesthetically pleasing, nutritionally adequate, and healthful. Professionals in this field ensure that the quality of food is protected as it moves from producer to consumer. This is a scientific and technical field and requires training in sciences and engineering.

Typical Job Titles

Typical job titles are the following:

- Food scientist
- Food technologist
- Research scientist
- Director of quality control
- Plant manager
- Director of research
- Process engineer
- Equipment designer
- Consultant

Responsibilities

Professionals in food science have many career options in such fields as research, teaching, industry, the Peace Corps, and consulting. Their responsibilities vary.

Some food scientists do research on the processing, preservation, and safety of food, on such topics as the freezing of foods for optimal preservation, sanitary handling of foods, packaging techniques, and appropriate processing machinery. Their research may also include the testing of foods to determine how much quality is maintained by different food processing or handling techniques.

Other professionals may be involved in engineering and technological aspects of food science, including the design, development, and testing of food-processing equipment for manufacturers or food service establishments (cafeterias, restaurants, institutional food services). This involvement requires considering human factors in the effective use of equipment. A food scientist may even train the personnel who will operate the equipment and facility.

Food science professionals may also obtain management and marketing positions with major food companies like General Foods or Kraft, or they may work with food retailers. Some may enter careers in journalism and communications and write about foods.

Food chemists, biochemists, and technologists also study the biochemical aspects of nutrition, such as food composition (vitamins, minerals, protein, fat, sugar, starch) and the nutritional adequacy of foods. In such careers a knowledge of scientific testing procedures, scientific instrumentation, and statistical analysis of data is important.

Qualifications

An undergraduate degree in food service, dietetics, or related areas may lead to various careers in food sciences. Your education should include some of the subjects required for dietetics as well as courses in food processing, sanitation, equipment engineering, quality control, and chemical testing of products. For those students with managerial goals, courses in institutional management, marketing, general business, and human factors are required.

Food science is a scientific field, and so a master's or a Ph.D. degree may be desirable or even necessary, particularly for positions in research or process engineering, which require advanced knowledge of the sciences and research design. Many scientific subspecializations can be studied in depth at the graduate level—for example, microbiology, food chemistry, quality control, and sanitation.

Useful work experience before graduation can include internships, part-time work, work with professors in nutrition labs at a college or university, and work with restaurants, supermarkets, or food-processing companies.

Special Personal Qualities

The personal skills and qualities required in food science differ, depending on whether one is seeking a scientific or a managerial career in food sciences. For the scientifically oriented person, it is most important to have an objective, analytical, scientific mind. Someone looking for managerial positions needs human relations skills as well.

Other Factors

There are also careers in food science in what is termed *sensory science*. Test kitchens in which recipes are developed and evaluated using human subjects (consumers), recipe development kitchens, or other testing facilities employ sensory science in their work. In such professional activities, the food scientist tests and evaluates new ideas for food products, emphasizing their sensory acceptability (taste, appearance) and their marketability. Such consumer and market research can lead to new, brand-name, packaged and processed foods. Careers in this field require a knowledge of food science, sensory science, psychology, experimental design, market research, and techniques of report presentation.

Careers in food communications and journalism are also available. Foods journalists write articles about food preparation techniques, new recipes, and ways for handling and storing foods. They may write on selecting cooking equipment and utensils. They are often involved with food photography, which includes finding the best or most aesthetically pleasing ways to display and picture food. For such professions, a broad knowledge of food science, writing, photography, and current trends in consumer preferences is required.

Food scientists are employed by government and industry as food inspectors to ensure safety and quality. Such professionals have a knowledge of product standards, product rating, and safe handling techniques for foods. They see that standards of food quality are met and report violations.

Food scientists have opportunities to interact with such food specialists as plant geneticists, animal scientists, plant breeders, and others involved in developing new foods. As biotechnology becomes more important to the production of foods, the food scientist will work with specialists in new product development and marketing as well. Food scientists and food engineers who can work with professionals from agricultural sciences have special opportunities and advantages in their careers. Likewise, food scientists who can translate their scientific and technical knowledge into business terms can find good positions in the marketing, selling, and technical service areas of the foods professions. Being able to work with the customers who buy a company's food products is the main skill.

Perhaps the most innovative career for the food scientist is developing totally new technologies and food preparations, or new food products for consumers. Such professionals find new and different ways to please consumers and to satisfy the customers' needs for good human nutrition. These can be among the most exciting careers for food scientists.

CAREER PROFILE

Human Nutrition _____

Human nutrition is a basic biological science. Nutritionists study how the body digests and uses foods. Thus it is a science concerned with human physiology and biochemistry and their relationship to human health and well-being. Most professionals in human nutrition do research on the nutritional composition and adequacy of the vitamins, minerals, and other components of foods.

Typical Job Titles

Typical job titles include the following:

- Nutrition research specialist
- Nutrition consultant
- Public health nutritionist
- Food chemist
- Biochemist
- Food scientist
- Biotechnologist

Responsibilities

The main responsibility of nutritionists is to find out more about the nutritional adequacy of various foods. This research requires expertise in biochemistry, biotechnology, microbiology, chemistry, human physiology, and scientific laboratory methods.

Human nutritionists often focus on the nutritional aspects of diseases such as heart disease, cancer, and even the common cold. Their objective is to identify any roles that diet may have in either causing or curing such diseases. Some nutritionists also look at how people's activities, such as exercise, alcohol consumption, or cultural preferences for particular foods, interact with nutrition. For instance, nutritionists may ask such questions as "Does following a particular ethnic diet (for example, Chinese foods) lead to a particular level of nutritional adequacy?" or "What is the relationship among exercise, diet, and blood chemistry?"

Human nutritionists often work with dietitians, food scientists, physicians, public health nurses, and others in health care. Their responsibility is to conduct research when needed into special nutritional aspects of a case or to report to the health-care team research relevant to individual cases. Thus the highly trained nutritionist becomes an important consultant when nutrition is essential to health care.

Nutritionists also have an educational responsibility. That is, they translate complex scientific research findings into terms that other professionals (dietitians, physicians) can understand and use. They often are also responsible for public education programs and client education.

Qualifications

As a scientific field, nutrition requires substantial education, often including graduate education through the Ph.D. degree. This is especially true for those students planning to enter research careers. However, some careers require only a bachelor of science or master of science degree in human nutrition, dietetics, food science, or a related field.

A strong background in biology is necessary, including human physiology, microbiology, and biochemistry. Chemistry (particularly organic chemistry), mathematics, physics, and scientific laboratory methods, including instrumental methods, are also essential. Courses in food, science, dietetics, and the cultural aspects of foods are valuable.

Some nutrition specialties require courses on other topics, such as toxicology, immunology, and pathology, specialized biological sciences in which some nutritional researchers must be well versed in order to conduct research into such fields as cancer, heart disease, allergies, or other environmental diseases that might be related to food intake. Such course may also be necessary when studying the effects of food additives on humans.

Special Personal Qualities

Nutritionists need to be objective, systematic, and inquiring. They also should enjoy working in a laboratory. Nutritionists must be willing to spend many hours working on complex and lengthy experiments.

Other Factors

Nutritionists work with many special populations, such as pregnant women, drug abusers, alcohol abusers, or those with particular diseases of nutritional interest. They many specialize in a particular area of research or in a particular health problem, such as obesity. Recently nutritionists have entered a new field: sports sciences and physical conditioning as they relate to human nutrition. The great current concern for health and physical fitness is responsible for the growth of this new career. Another new field is gerontological nutrition, which focuses on the foods and nutritional needs of aging populations.

Nutritionists may analyze fad diets and develop new diets for special populations. Or they may analyze health food diets, vegetarian diets, or highly specialized diets designed to reduce weight. Because dieting is a central part of our life-styles, nutritionists can find opportunities to apply their special knowledge of the nutritional adequacy of foods to identify appropriate diets and inform the public about dieting.

Majors in human nutrition may work in the applied fields of dietetics and food science as well. Refer to the earlier career profiles for more information on those opportunities.

CAREER PROFILE

Fashion Design

Fashion designers are experts in developing new styles of dress for consumers, including drawing, constructing models of new styles, designing patterns, overseeing production, and promoting styles.

Typical Job Titles

Typical job titles include the following:

- Fashion designer
- Costume designer
- Assistant designer
- Production assistant
- Designer trainee
- Fashion illustrator
- Fashion artist
- Sketcher
- Stylist
- Production manager

Responsibilities

A fashion designer is responsible for all activities related to the design of new styles, from their conception through their marketing. Specific activities include drawing sketches of new styling concepts, presenting sketches for approval, making models (prototypes) of selected styles, designing patterns, choosing fabrics and accessories, and supervising the construction of samples. Thus a successful designer is not only a creative artist but is also responsible for translating ideas into finished products.

Successful designers must keep up with existing trends in fashion, forecast new trends, and develop new styles. Therefore, fashion designers do not simply create new ideas for apparel. Rather, they must interpret trends in consumers' tastes and life-styles and then design new fasions that are in tune with current tastes. No matter how exciting, innovative, or elegant a design may be, it has little value unless consumers accept it.

Designers also design apparel that can be manufactured and sold at a reasonable price. They must make sure that their designs are comfortable and functional as well as fashionable. Finally, designers must make certain that their apparel is correctly sized and that it meets standards of quality and safety or health (e.g., fabric flammability, allergic or health elements of dyes, fabrics, and finishes). Therefore, designers must take into account many practical as well as artistic qualities of the garments they design.

Qualifications

Graduation from a program in fashion design, apparel design, apparel technology, or clothing and textiles is necessary to enter the field of fashion design. Many courses are important, such as art, design, fashion illustration, and photography. In addition, designers must be familiar with the mechanics of clothing construction, which includes pattern making, production, and assembly-line techniques.

Designers must be familiar with the history of fashion and textiles and general art history as well. Thus a wide range of courses in art and art history is helpful.

Most designers are also experts in each step of clothing construction. Although designers may have assistants who actually construct the models, designers must create clothes that are not too difficult to cut, sew, and finish. Designers must often instruct assistants in appropriate construction and style techniques, and so a technical knowledge of construction is mandatory.

It is also necessary for designers to know marketing techniques and business procedures in the fashion industry. Increasingly, designers are entering the business management of organizations. The result is that designers are finding that much of their time is devoted not only to designing and manufacturing new styles but also to managing their businesses. Another new area in which designers must gain expertise is in computer techniques. Computerized fashion design is used in many businesses today. Some manufacturers also use computers in all steps of manufacturing, from pattern design to actual sewing processes. Computers are also central to merchandising (see Chapter 6 for more on fashion merchandising).

Special Personal Qualities

The principal personal qualities that a successful designer must have are creativity and originality. The fashion design business thrives on innovation and dies without it. Fashion designers also must have a feeling for clothing, a sense of current and future trends in styling, and an understanding of color. And they must be able to materialize their ideas. Furthermore, the designer must be able to do this—successfully—year in and year out, for a few bad seasons can be the end of a career in fashion design.

Other Factors

Some special opportunities are open to fashion designers. Some designers become specialists in fashion illustration, fashion photography, and other journalistic aspects of fashion. In such occupations they never actually design and make garments but, rather, illustrate the works of others.

Another, growing area is designing clothing for special needs. There are successful fashion businesses designing clothing for handicapped persons, for those needing special sizes (e.g., tall sizes, large sizes, maternity wear), or for special applications (functional clothing items such as runners' bras, spacesuits, sportswear). Such examples point out that fashion design is more than a high-fashion or high-glamour business; it means serving needs of many consumers and audiences.

Designers can develop opportunities in many apparel-related businesses. The majority of jobs are with the smaller apparel and accesories manufacturers, of which there are thousands. Fashion designers can also start independent businesses as free-lancers or perhaps work out of their home, designing and making one-of-a-kind styles for a local clientele. Some designers also enter retailing, perhaps supervising apparel alterations or running a custom tailoring service for a store. Some even end up in creative business areas such as advertising or display departments. Designers thus have opportunities well beyond what is traditionally thought of as the fashion designer's career.

Another special career for the fashion designer is in costume design. Costume designers create wardrobes for movies, plays, or traveling entertainment groups (such as rock bands or touring theater companies). Theatrical costuming is a specialized art that requires an extensive knowledge of both historical costume design and contemporary design. Entry into theatrical costuming can be difficult, but there may be starting jobs with local civic theaters or other community playhouses that need costume work for the stage.

CAREER PROFILE

Textile Design

A career in textile design is similar to one in fashion design. Textile designers are involved in all aspects of designing knit, woven, and nonwoven fabrics, including the design of yarns, fabric construction techniques, and the coloring of fabrics.

Typical Job Titles

Typical job titles include the following:

- Textile designer
- Assistant designer
- Textile artist
- Colorist
- Stylist
- Textile technologist

Responsibilities

The textile designer is a creative artist who designs fabrics. Textile designers identify fashion trends in fabrics, illustrate designs for fabrics, and plan the manufacturing of fabrics. They must be able to put their designs on paper. They must also be able to turn creative fabric designs into practical ideas that can be produced at a competitive price.

Fabric design is far more complex than is sometimes realized. For example, special fabrics and yarns are often designed for specific fabrics or specific end uses (e.g., shirts, suits, lingerie, outerwear). Because of the technical problems in knitting, weaving, dyeing, printing, and finishing fabrics, the designer must understand manufacturing processes and take these into account when designing. In addition, all fabrics must be created with a particular end use in mind and must be constructed accordingly. For example, the weight, texture, and strength of a fabric must fit the intended consumer use. Therefore, textile designers are sometimes specialists in fibers, fabrics, coloring, finishing, or market analysis. In such cases the textile designer is one member of a team of designers.

Qualifications

The main qualification for a textile designer is creative ability combined with an ability to illustrate designs; that is, the designer must have artistic skills. A wide range of technical skills is also required in fiber science, textile science, color chemistry, and color matching. Most of these skills are taught in courses in textile science, textile technology, apparel technology, clothing, textiles, and general textile design.

Other desirable courses are art, art history, history of costume, history of textiles, and business subjects. Computers are a big part of the textile design business, and so an understanding of computer-assisted design and drafting is necessary.

A special qualification that is absolutely necessary is a good sense of color. Color is the main ingredient in all textile products, and it is what is most responsible for the sales of textile and apparel items. Therefore, the most sucessful textile designers have a special feel for trends in color, and they design with color foremost in mind. In addition, the successful designer must know how to coordinate colors. Finally, an awareness of colors in fashion trends is considered helpful, for fashions in colors change just as do fashions in apparel design.

Other Factors

Fabric designers have a variety of opportunities. They can become specialists in a particular type of fabric, for example, prints, woven fabrics, or knits. They can also become specialists in custom designing fabrics for specific applications, for example, fabrics for the NASA space program, industrial fabrics, tent and awning fabrics, or fabrics for sportswear. Some designers also become specialists in color, becoming color coordinators, color matchers, color consultants, or color stylists, and they must have expertise in a variety of subjects related to the dyeing of fibers, yarns, and fabrics. This is a complex field, and a knowledge of textile chemistry and textile design is necessary.

Textile designers can also be involved in the engineering and manufacturing of textiles. They may develop new processes for knitting, weaving, coloring, and finishing fabrics. A knowledge of textile machinery and technology is necessary in this specialized career.

Designers in the textile and apparel fields often create hundreds of styles yearly. Therefore, they must be able to generate many ideas for new styles. To succeed at this, the typical work life of a designer is exploring new ideas through drawings or sketches and research (perhaps on art history, current life-styles, and current media) and by talking with others in various design fields. Although designing may appear relaxed and flexible on the surface, designers feel a lot of pressure when so many new designs must be produced. Furthermore, there is pressure to meet deadlines, because new seasonal offerings are brought out several times each year. Thus, all successful designers need to meet creative demands and the seasonal pressures of deadlines.

CAREER PROFILE

Apparel Technology

Apparel technology includes many careers in apparel construction and apparel manufacturing. Technical careers are found in apparel design, apparel illustration, pattern design, pattern grading, apparel production (cutting and sewing), management, employee training, supervision, product testing, and quality control.

Typical Job Titles

There are many jobs in apparel technology, and each phase of apparel construction and manufacturing has career possibilities. Some of the typical titles include the following:

- Apparel designer
- Apparel technologist
- Manager of production
- Pattern drafter
- Pattern maker
- Pattern grader
- Quality control specialist
- Manager of quality control
- Clothing construction specialist
- Consumer education consultant

Responsibilities

Specialists in apparel technology have varied responsibilities in such areas as pattern design, pattern drafting, pattern grading (sizing), cutting, sewing, assembly-line management, quality inspection, and packing and shipping the final product. They also participate in product testing and quality control, ensuring that quality is maintained at each step of production.

A major responsibility in apparel production is to ensure that all steps of the assembly and manufacturing are well organized and operate efficiently. Specialists in apparel technology often train employees in the use of the quickest and most efficient assembly procedures. This requires the specialist who is supervising production to be familiar with each step of the construction.

To analyze production and make improvements, apparel technologists often conduct time and motion studies to determine how long it takes to do each production task. Using these data, the technologist, production manager, or production engineer can design better work methods and help manufacturing employees to improve their performance on the job.

Apparel technologists may also plan production schedules, assign tasks to each person in the assembly line, and ensure that the flow of goods through each manufacturing step progresses smoothly, efficiently, and on time.

Another responsibility is cost management. Apparel technologists must see that the production is done at the least possible cost. This involves careful materials management, such as making sure that all fabric is used without waste. It also means ordering the correct amount of fabric. Other aspects of cost management are choosing appropriate hourly salary or piece rates for each step of production and seeing that the production tasks are assigned to those employees most qualified for them.

Qualifications

Education in apparel design, apparel manufacturing, and quality control is essential. The apparel technologist must understand each step in apparel production. Other valuable skills are in mathematics, computer-assisted design, computer-assisted drafting, supervision, production management, and cost accounting. Courses in human factors engineering and production management are helpful. Finally, because apparel technologists train and educate other employees, a background in education is necessary, especially when apparel technologists must teach employees with little education many assembly techniques and working procedures.

Special Personal Qualities

Apparel technologists spend much of their day on their feet, sometimes in uncomfortable physical surroundings. Thus, physical stamina and energy are a special requirement in some jobs. Another personal quality is patience, particularly when educating employees in techniques of sewing machine operation or other technical skills. Because the technology of apparel production is changing rapidly with the introduction of computerized techniques and automation such as robotics, the technologist must also keep up to date on new techniques of manufacturing and help introduce them into the work place.

Another special quality is organizational ability. Apparel production requires several steps from start to finish, and the only way an apparel production plant can be successful (profitable) is if each step is carefully organized and waste is minimized. The technologist must also work well under stress, for there are times when the production line may stop or be slowed by the poor performance of a few employees. In such situations, the supervisor is under a great deal of pressure to restore production without undue stress.

Other Factors

There are career opportunities related to apparel technology in the home sewing industry and in consumer education for cooperative extension service (discussed in Chapter 7). In addition, apparel technologists often start their own clothing design and production businesses, using limited amounts of capital and perhaps sewing at home. Many successful small businesses have been started by people who are expert in both the design and the production of apparel.

Apparel technologists also have careers in textile or apparel testing and quality control departments. These departments exist not only in apparel and textile companies but in retailers and other consumer-oriented businesses as well (magazines, consumer testing services, private testing organizations). Quality control is an important part of the apparel and textile business and is a worthwhile and growing opportunity in the field.

Because the apparel business in foreign countries is growing, students with an interest in international trade and development may find positions abroad. Much apparel is being made in Asian countries (Hong Kong, Korea, Taiwan, and so on) as well as in Europe and Latin America. Analysts of the apparel industry forecast that in the future much apparel will be produced in Asia, and special opportunities may be available for those apparel specialists with language skills or a knowledge of other cultures.

Apparel technologists can also work at the retail level. They have particularly good opportunities in retail fabric stores as the owners of stores or as sales associates. Developing programs of consumer information, helping customers select patterns and fabrics, answering customers' questions, and a variety of other merchandising management functions can be undertaken in such a sales management career in retailing (see Chapter 6 for more details).

CAREER PROFILE

Textile Science

The profession of textile science involves many activities pertaining to fibers, fabrics, dyes, and textile finishing, including product development, product testing, quality control, and technical service to clients. In addition, textile scientists conduct scientific research on new textile products. A career in textile science requires a knowledge of such areas as textile chemistry, physics, and processing of textile products (dyeing, printing, finishing, yarn and fabric manufacturing, and textile testing).

Typical Job Titles

Textile scientist is the general term designating a professional in this field. Professionals often have specialized titles. Examples are the following:

- Product development specialist
- Research specialist
- Textile laboratory technician
- Textile designer
- Quality control specialist
- Manager of textile testing
- Textile chemist
- Textile physicist
- Technical service representative

Responsibilities

Textile scientists entering careers related to textile chemistry may develop new synthetic fibers or new dyeing and finishing techniques and test these new products and techniques. This work requires a knowledge of chemistry, physics, and other physical sciences as they relate specifically to fibers, dyes, and finishes. It also requires a knowledge of laboratory testing procedures and analysis of data derived from scientific experiments.

Some textile scientists enter process engineering and must be familiar with all the steps in manufacturing textile fibers, yarns, and fabrics. These steps include synthetic fibers manufacturing, yarn manufacturing, weaving, knitting, and fabric finishing. Each of these manufacturing steps takes place in modern, automated, computerized factories, and knowledge of these often complicated processes is essential.

Professionals may enter the areas of textile testing, quality control, and technical services to clients. Professionals in testing and quality control perform standard laboratory tests that determine the quality of products during and following manufacturing. Testing is done to ensure that their quality meets the manufacturing organization's standards. Such quality testing is also used to determine when manufacturing is out of control and needs to be corrected. Another related area is in providing technical service to clients. Major manufacturers of synthetic fibers (polyester, nylons, and the like) send experts to textile mills and finishing plants to help the plants set up processes for manufacturing products. Such technical service representatives must make certain that an organization's products are used effectively and efficiently by their customers.

Some important consumer-oriented careers are found in textile science. Some major retailers and manufacturers hire textile testing specialists to evaluate the relative qualities of clothing and textile products for consumer use. These professionals evaluate products from the consumers' perspective to ensure that the textile products meet their requirements.

In some positions, textile scientists also have educational responsibilities. For example, some textile scientists may do research on caring for fabrics and garments, the results of which will be printed on the products' labels and tags. Thus the textile scientist is responsible for translating technical scientific information into practical information that consumers can use in their decision making and care of products. Sometimes textile scientists work with marketing teams in designing the technical aspects of products. For example, if it is found that consumers want a fabric with very fine fibers, textile scientists may become a part of the design team identifying the best fiber and manufacturing techniques for making the product. Here textile science combines with consumer science, and the textile scientist must know not only the scientific and technical aspects of the product but also the consumers' needs and use of the product.

Textile scientists work with other members of textile and apparel design teams. They must be acquainted with the jobs of textile designers, apparel designers, apparel technologists, or other artists and scientists in the business. Thus, an appreciation of the artistic as well as the scientific aspects of the textile product is a requirement of this field.

Qualifications

Many schools offer undergraduate programs that include study in textile science as part of the clothing and textiles curriculum. In addition, some schools offer programs specializing in textile chemistry, textile design, and apparel technology (discussed in the preceding profiles). All these can lead to a career in textile science. In general, students interested in careers in textile science should obtain a foundation in chemistry, physics, and mathematics, as well as some engineering. Courses should be taken in areas such as textile chemistry, weaving, knitting, dyeing, textile finishing, and textile evaluation. It is also desirable to take consumer-oriented courses to learn about consumer needs and demands, for it is ultimately the consumer that all scientists serve.

Education in business and design is desirable as well. Art, design, graphics, engineering drafting, and related courses can be helpful. Finally work experience in the textile and apparel production industries is a definite advantage.

Advanced degrees are appropriate for those graduates entering research-oriented careers. However, many do enter textile science careers if they have completed a program that has a strong science background, including many of the courses just mentioned. In only a few career fields of textile science, such as polymer science or textile engineering, are advanced degrees a necessary qualification for entry into the profession.

Special Personal Qualities

The most important personal quality is a scientific attitude. Textile scientists often engage in research projects for which objective scientific approaches are necessary. They must also enjoy working in laboratories. For those interested in the design and manufacturing aspects, a knowledge of art principles in the design and engineering of textile production is appropriate.

Other Factors

Many professionals in textile sciences seek careers in textile testing, textile evaluation, and consumer aspects of textiles. However, often overlooked are opportunities in the manufacturing industries, including companies producing textile fibers, dyes, finishes, textile fabrics, and apparel. Thus, textile scientists should think of opportunities in their areas of special interest.

Perhaps the most exciting new opportunities are in the area of computerized design, analysis, and processing of products. Students in this field should be familiar with computer use in the textile science field and computer applications for the design and processing of textiles. Finally, many textile scientists can find positions in the business and marketing aspects of textiles.

CAREER PROFILE

Residential Interior Design _____

Residential interior design is a specialized profession that designs functional and beautiful interiors for all types of family housing. Residential interior designers work with single-family detached houses, townhouses, condominiums, cooperatives, mobile homes, and all types of multifamily housing (apartments, planned communities). A major activity of residential designers is selecting furniture, home furnishings, and household textiles for their clients. Some interior designers also custom design their products, for example, furniture designers.

Typical Job Titles

Job titles in the career field of residential interior design include the following:

- Interior designer
- Space planner
- Kitchen designer
- Graphic artist
- Furniture designer
- Home lighting consultant
- Urban renewal consultant
- Public housing consultant
- Environmental designer

Responsibilities

Responsibilities of the residential interior designer vary depending on the size and needs of the client. Jobs differ depending on whether one is providing a comprehensive design plan for a large house or merely furnishing one room of a small apartment. In general, interior designers for all types of residential housing clients perform two services: (1) making a plan of the interior space and all its components (furniture, accessories, carpet, wallpaper, paint) and (2) actually purchasing and overseeing the installation of the components for the client. In the planning stages the designer draws scaled floor plans showing the placement of all items, illustrates these for the client (often in perspective or three-dimensional form), and selects appropriate color schemes. The designer may also choose brands or manufacturers and estimate the costs of the materials used. Sometimes the interior designer's responsibility ends here, and the client takes over in the actual purchasing of the required items. But often the interior designer obtains the best bids from suppliers (furniture manufacturers, dealers, wallpaperers, painters, carpet retailers, and the like). Then the designer oversees delivery and installation to ensure that the quality is maintained and the plan is followed.

The special responsibility of a residential interior designer is to ensure quality control in all aspects of the design plan. This function includes finding the appropriate color coordination, choosing the best products for the price paid, and seeing that the product's health and safety aspects are maintained (e.g., avoiding flammable fabrics, checking to see that products are well built and do not have hazardous surfaces).

Interior designers also coordinate the activity of many independent suppliers, such as furniture dealers, painters, upholsterers, wallpaperers, and lighting specialists. Therefore, one of the interior designer's special skills is working with all these tradespeople and turning them into a team working for the client.

Perhaps the designer's biggest responsibility is identifying the client's special needs and life-style and choosing the appropriate products. The designer cannot impose his or her tastes on clients but must work within the client's particular situation and budget. Each client will have different needs and tastes, and the residential designer must adapt accordingly. The designer's responsibility, of course, is to educate the client in good taste and design for the circumstances, but in the end it is the client, not the designer, who must be served and satisfied.

Qualifications

Interior design is a highly specialized profession, and a bachelor's degree is becoming necessary for entry. Education for interior design should include professional subjects such as drawing, drafting, rendering, space planning, color analysis, computer-assisted design, architecture, landscape design, art, and art history. Because interior design is a business, courses in accounting, business writing, marketing, business relations, and ethics are recommended. Experience in such areas as estimating costs of jobs, preparing bids, developing budgets, writing specifications, and preparing contracts is also helpful.

Interior designers work as teams with colleagues and with clients, and so it is important to have good interpersonal working skills and an appreciation for other people's viewpoints. Other needed qualities are organization, the ability to meet deadlines, and a willingness to stay within clients' budgets. Design is also a competitive field with qualified professionals competing for jobs. The ability to operate in a competitive environment is imperative.

Special Personal Qualities

The interior designer must have a variety of artistic skills, including expertise in drawing, graphic arts, and rendering. It is also necessary to be familiar with a variety of styles and designs in furniture and home furnishings. A thorough knowledge of art history is necessary. Finally, that elusive quality of good taste and an understanding of the trend in home fashions are mandatory for the successful residential designer. A knowledge of products and how they fit customers' life-styles is essential.

Other Factors

Interior designers can work in a variety of business settings: large firms, major retailers (department stores, furniture specialty stores), small design firms, or their own privately operated businesses. Specialized careers also exist in fields related to interior design and furniture design. Specialized training is necessary for all these careers. Industrial designers are involved in the functional and aesthetic design of a wide range of consumer products, often including furniture and household products. Environmental psychologists are involved in the human factors aspects of design, ensuring that buildings and interior spaces meet their inhabitants' psychological and social needs. They attempt to find the most pleasant color schemes, spatial arrangements, lighting, furniture designs, and the like. Set designers prepare settings for theatrical productions and movies. Finally, furniture designers create furniture styles for manufacturing. They sketch designs, prepare specifications of materials for designs, and oversee construction of the finished product.

Free-lancing in interior design is very popular. Operating one's own business as a free-lancer can be very rewarding, and it includes all aspects of planning and executing designs for clients. The satisfaction of doing the whole job from conception through completion can be great. As a result, operating their own business becomes a goal of many professional designers.

CAREER PROFILE

Commercial Interior Design

Commercial interior designers work in all kinds of nonresidential settings, including restaurants, offices, schools, and other public spaces. They are involved in all types of commercial design for businesses, industry, government, and school systems, and their activities range from planning public space through actually choosing and placing design products.

Typical Job Titles

Typical job titles found in commercial interior design include the following:

- Commercial designer
- Commercial interior designer
- Contract designer
- Public space designer
- Interior designer

Responsibilities

The responsibilities of a commercial designer are similar to those of a residential designer. The client differs, however, because it is a business, public building, or similar public facility. The contract designer plans a space and its furnishings on the basis of the needs of the organization and often selects and places the materials. The types of materials, aesthetics, and functional purposes of the objects used in commercial design differ from those for residential interiors, however. The designer has to be familiar with the types of color schemes, quality levels of furniture and furnishings, and environmental psychology that works best in various institutional settings. The design of public space can be quite different from the design of private homeowners' environments, for the tastes of the many different people who will use the public spaces must be considered.

Contract designers are responsible for meeting their clients' budgetary requirements. Businesses and school systems often work within extremely tight budgets, and the designer is responsible for getting the most for the client's budget. This means that jobs must be carefully planned, materials and suppliers researched in detail, and costs controlled. Contract design is very competitive, for there are many firms anxious to receive lucrative business contracts. Therefore, the specifications and bids (prices) for a job must be prepared accurately and in detail.

Contract designers offer two services to their clients, preparing design plans and implementing the final plan chosen (supervising the work of painters, carpet layers, furniture deliverers, and so on). A contract designer may perform any or all of the services necessary to execute a plan according to the contract. The contract between the designer and the client spells out the designer's responsibilities. Once the contract for a job is signed, the designer must carry out all parts of the contract exactly as it specifies.

Qualifications

A degree in interior design is becoming mandatory for entry into contract design. As in residential design, a contract designer needs a broad range of courses in drawing, graphic arts, rendering, space planning, computer-assisted design, and architecture. Business skills also are necessary, even more than for a residential specialist. The contract designer must have a broad knowledge of bidding, specification writing, business planning, and contract writing. A knowledge of competent and reliable subcontractors (furniture dealers, painters, carpet layers) is also required, for many subcontractors are used in contract design and they can influence the designer's reputation.

Special Personal Qualities

Competitiveness is a special quality that commercial designers need, for there are many competitors for public and business design jobs. The ability to meet deadlines and to prepare complete bids on time is also paramount in this profession. Commercial designers must enjoy working with figures and specifications and be willing to adjust work schedules to suit the clients' needs. There are times when business may be slow and other times when there is immense pressure because of the clients' demands and needs. Thus, work routines can be irregular and sometimes long in this career.

CAREER PROFILE

Housing

Housing careers can offer interesting opportunities for a wide variety of majors in family and consumer fields. The provision of satisfactory family housing for all Americans is an important goal of our society. Our society has many housing arrangements: detached single-family houses, apartments, condominiums, townhouses, planned communities, and so on. There are many career opportunities in the housing field, from the development of new family housing projects (building and construction) and management of housing communities through the development of government policy for providing satisfactory housing alternatives to subgroups of society.

Typical Job Titles

Typical, and various, job titles in housing careers include the following:

- Housing analyst
- Housing consultant

- City planning consultant
- Urban renewal consultant
- Public housing consultant
- Real estate property manager
- Real estate sales associate
- Real estate broker

These jobs are available in many organizations in government and with home builders, real estate firms, and other housing businesses. In addition, housing-related job titles discussed elsewhere in this book include interior designer, appliance specialist, utility consultant with a gas or electric company (see the following career profile on household equipment), or energy efficiency adviser.

Responsibilities

As the preceding job titles suggest, responsibilities in housing careers can be as diverse as the job titles themselves. In general, employees of a governmental agency administer various local, state, or federally funded housing programs or projects. Housing is often constructed for special needs populations, for example, low-income groups or minorities experiencing cultural readjustment (as was recently the case with new Vietnamese immigrants). Governmental agencies also administer social and economic programs to benefit different segments of American society, such as development of housing communities, financing, rehabilitation of declining neighborhoods, and management of family housing projects.

Employees of builders or developers of housing and planned communities also have varied responsibilities. Some housing experts plan communities to serve various social and income groups. Other aspects of development include architectural design and interior design, careers requiring specialized degrees in those areas. There are also opportunities in marketing new housing developments, and there are jobs in resorts, retirement communities, nursing homes, and urban renewal and rehabilitation programs (for example, center cities). And because of the current interest in the renovation of existing housing, there can be opportunities in home-building organizations, businesses, and local governmental rehabilitation agencies.

People in real estate have different responsibilities. Real estate brokers advertise property for sale, show property to potential buyers, write contracts for sales, and follow up to ensure that the sales have been completed (closed) according to the contract. One starts in this field as a real estate sales associate and progresses into the management or ownership of a business as a real estate broker. Some brokers specialize in residential real estate (private homes, condominiums, townhouses), whereas others specialize in commercial and business properties.

There also are positions in real estate property management. Multifamily housing developments such as apartments, condominiums, and townhouses need property managers to oversee rentals, property maintenance, and other business affairs of the property. Property management can also mean creating social, educational, and recreation programs for tenants. And a new career field in leisure activities in real estate (e.g., resort management) is starting.

Another new career is in energy management. The energy crisis of the 1970s spawned considerable interest in energy-efficient housing systems, solar energy, and retrofitting houses to be more energy efficient (for example, installing insulation, caulking, storm windows, and other products to promote energy conservation). Conservation of energy in housing may be even more valued in the 1990s, given world constraints on supplies. Thus there are new employment opportunities in government agencies promoting conservation, companies manufacturing energy-conserving products, and public utilities (gas and electric companies) interested in sponsoring energy management programs.

Qualifications

The qualifications for entering housing careers differ. Only a few colleges and universities offer four-year degrees with majors in housing, but many schools offer courses that are relevant to housing and that can help prepare for a housing career. Most majors in family- or consumer-oriented fields can lead to one or more of the housing careers we have discussed. Majors such as interior design and consumer affairs can be especially valuable.

To enter a housing career you should have a broad background in the social sciences, including sociology, psychology, economics, and political science, because the field of housing is involved to a considerable extent with social policy and must serve human needs. In addition, it is important to understand the artistic and design aspects of housing and its components. For this you should have courses in chemistry, physics, and interior design (spatial design, layout, structure, and building materials). It is also valuable to have a knowledge of housing systems, including heating, electrical systems, plumbing, solar energy and appliances. Other professional courses to consider include housing alternatives, environmental psychology, urban renewal, social policy, problems of the aging, and barrier-free design of houses (for those with physical handicaps or other special housing needs).

Special Personal Qualities

The personal qualities of persons successful in housing careers include an interest in the welfare of other people and a concern for human needs. Houses are for people and should be developed with the needs and personalities of their inhabitants in mind. Housing careers in some areas also have special requirements. For example, workers in government programs for needy citizens must have empathy for the clients' problems. Real estate brokers must have energy and enthusiasm for working face to face with clients, often for days and weeks at a time. Developers of housing must be organized people who work well with schedules and the pressure of deadlines.

Other Factors

Other careers related to housing may be of interest. Financial services related to housing, such as mortgage loans and insurance, may offer opportunities. The home-remodeling industry also offers opportunities, particularly because our society is now taking a greater interest in programs of urban renewal. There also are jobs in family services involved with housing, for example, homes for unwed mothers, halfway houses, camp programs that include housing, and nursing home facilities. So many aspects of our society touch on housing that there can be no limit to the opportunities you may find by using a little imagination.

Housing is a career for people with many different family- or consumer-oriented degrees. It is not just for majors in housing, equipment, or interior design. All those with degrees in home economics and family studies have expertise relevant to housing. But housing careers may be considered nontraditional for such majors, and it will be necessary to sell your qualifications to potential employers. Employers welcome talented and qualified individuals, but when a major is thought of as nontraditional, you must make a more careful presentation of yourself through your résumé, portfolio, and personal experiences.

CAREER PROFILE

Household Equipment and Appliance Technology ____

Household equipment and appliance technology includes many specialized jobs in the design and marketing of major equipment systems and appliances for the home, including heating and cooling systems, solar energy, laundry systems, refrigerators, stoves, home computer systems, home entertainment systems, and other major appliances. Related opportunities also exist in home lighting systems, home security systems, communications systems such as intercoms, and various aspects of interior design (home furnishings, carpeting, draperies, and wall coverings).

Typical Job Titles

There are many careers in marketing and in providing consumer information in all areas of household equipment and appliance technology. Job titles in these areas include the following:

- Appliance information specialist
- Utility home economist
- Utility consumer information specialist
- Appliance consultant
- Appliance marketing manager
- Manager of training and demonstrations
- Industrial designer
- Human factors engineer
- Product designer
- Technical service representative
- Sales representative

Responsibilities

For those graduates employed by manufacturers or distributors, the major positions in household equipment and appliance technology are in marketing and providing consumer information through activities such as advertising, promotion, writing informational materials, and custom designing systems to meet clients' needs. If you have such a job, you call on major clients (retail stores, housing developers, government offices), demonstrate products, write sales orders, and follow up on sales. Thus your responsibilities are partly educational, partly engineering, and partly selling. They require a thorough knowledge of all components of the product and all its possible applications, as well as a knowledge of competitive products and the advantages your product has over its competitors.

Employees of retail stores have a similar set of responsibilities, but their primary contact is with the consumer. They set up displays of products, write orders for sales, and follow up on the delivery of completed sales. Teaching consumers to use products safely and effectively is also part of the job. Some jobs require explaining manuals or operating instructions to consumers, and others may require the actual rewriting of instructions. Obviously a technical knowledge of the product is central to success.

Public utilities such as gas and electric companies also employ specialists in household equipment and appliances. The major responsibilities of such professionals are (1) designing home systems such as heating, cooling, cooking, or laundry and (2) presenting informational programs on energy conservation and energy-conserving equipment. Such consumer advisers must be familiar with the design and use of appliances and equipment. They also provide information on how consumers can choose and use more efficient products.

Qualifications

Some universities offer majors in household equipment. Related majors include housing, interior design, and general home economics. Students interested in a career in equipment and appliance technology must have a strong background in science (physics and chemistry), industrial design, engineering graphics, product development, and product testing. In addition, knowledge of such areas as consumer affairs, consumer education, foods, nutrition, human biology, public relations, and sales management is desirable.

Because much of the work in this career area is marketing and consumer education, a successful professional must have excellent teaching and human relations skills. It also is helpful to be an outgoing, enthusiastic person who works and communicates well with others. A good speaking voice and pleasant appearance are assets as well.

Special Personal Qualities

To succeed in this career, you must have two special personal qualities. First, a scientific mind and thorough understanding of the design and engineering of the appliance or household systems you are involved with is mandatory. Equipment systems and appliances can be quite complicated, and consumers may ask difficult questions regarding their design, operation, safety features, and use. Second, because teaching is involved, successful professionals must possess teaching skills, particularly an ability to give customers demonstrations and hands-on experience with the product; they must be thoroughly experienced in all uses of the product and have the patience to lead consumers through all aspects of its use.

Other Factors

Opportunities are available with commercial kitchen equipment suppliers, home heating and cooling suppliers, kitchen designers, and appliance specialty stores. There are opportunities in free-lancing in such areas as teaching specialized courses (e.g., cooking by microwave, using food processors) or writing instruction manuals for the equipment's use. The area of energy efficiency continues to draw attention as well, and there are opportunities in solar energy and the retrofitting of existing homes to make them more energy efficient. Such positions are with governmental organizations and businesses involved in equipment and appliances.

Questions and Exercises _____

1. Choose a career in one of the following areas:
   • Foods and human nutrition
   • Clothing, textiles, and fashion
   • Interior design, furniture, and home furnishings
   • Housing and household equipment
   Interview a currently practicing professional in that career to find out the following information:
   • Typical job titles
   • Responsibilities
   • Qualifications
   • Working conditions
   • Advancement potential
   • Advantages and disadvantages
2. Conduct a minisurvey of the local market to find career opportunities in your city related to the career you chose in question 1.
3. Discuss how future life-styles and attitudes might influence the careers in the field you chose for question 1.
4. Discuss how future technological changes might influence the careers in the field you chose for question 1.
5. How might a professional in the area you chose for question 1 contribute to the health, welfare, and well-being of consumers and their families?

Bibliography

Ball, Victoria Kloss. *Opportunities in Interior Design Careers*. Lincolnwood, IL: VGM Career Horizons, 1988.

Brooks, Dorothy L., and Marie C. Dietrich. "Student Selection in Dietetic Internship Program," *Perspectives in Practice* 80 (April 1982), 355–359.

Caldwell, Carol C. *Opportunities in Nutrition Careers*. Lincolnwood, IL: VGM Career Horizons, 1987.

Calvert, Susan, Henry Y. Parish, and Karen Oliver. "Clinical Dietetics: Forces Shaping Its Future," *Perspectives in Practice* 80 (April 1982), 251–354.

Dun's Marketing Services. *The Career Guide 1990: Dun's Employment Opportunities Directory*. New York: Dun & Bradstreet, 1990.

Dunphy, Rose Marie. "Weight Reduction Specialists," *Chronicle Guidance* (Brief 571) (March 1987), 3–6.

Folse, Nancy and Marilyn Henrion. *Careers in the Fashion Industry*. New York: Harper & Row, 1981.

Guyette, Wayne C. "The Executive Chef: Manager or Culinarian?" *Cornell Hotel and Restaurant Administration Quarterly* 22 (November 1981), 71–78.

Hardy, Dorothy, and Marjorie Kriebel. "The Interior Design Profession: Qualifying Factors of Competent Professionals," *Journal of Interior Design Education and Research* 10 (Fall 1984), 3–6.

Johnson, Willis L. *Directory of Special Programs for Minority Group Members*, 4th ed. Garrett Park, MD: Garrett Park Press, 1986.

Lewis, Robert C. "Hospitality Education at the Crossroads," *Cornell Hotel and Restaurant Administration Quarterly* 23 (August 1982), 12–15.

McComber, Diane R. "Food Industry Job Functions Reported by Recent Graduates," *Journal of Home Economics* 82 (Fall 1990), 26–30.

Michael, Carol M. "Support Relationships in the Career Development of Home Economists in the Home Equipment and Related Product Industries," *Home Economics Research Journal* 16 (March 1988), 163–172.

Michael, Carol M., and Fern E. Hunt. "Opportunities for the Advancement of Home Economists in the Home Equipment and Related Product Industries," *Home Economics Research Journal* 16 (September 1987), 36–45.

Myers, Cheryl. "Entry Level Competencies Needed by Interior Designers," *Journal of Interior Design Education and Research* 8 (1982), 19–24.

Null, Roberta. "Environmental Design for the Low-Vision Elderly," *Journal of Home Economics* 80 (Fall 1988), 29–35.

Rutherford, Denney G. "The Evolution of the Hotel Engineer's Job," *Cornell Hotel and Restaurant Administration Quarterly* 27 (February 1987), 72–78.

Sheldon, Gwedolyn J., and Cynthia L. Regan. "Computer-Aided Design in Higher Education," *Journal of Home Economics* 82 (Fall 1990), 35–40.

Shields, Rhea, and Anna K. Williams. *Opportunities in Home Economics Careers*. Lincolnwood, IL: VGM Career Horizons, 1988.

Sneed, Jeannie, and Carole M. Herman. "Influence of Job Characteristics and Organizational Commitment on Job Satisfaction of Hospital Foodservice Employees," *Journal of the American Dietetic Association* 90 (August 1990), 1072–1076.

"The Supermarket Home Economist," *Journal of Home Economics* 66 (May 1974), 68–69.

Wayman, Wilbur S., Jr., and Patricia S. Wayman. "What Students in Accredited Interior Design Programs Learn about Business," *Journal of Interior Design Education and Research* 8 (1982), 25–27.

Zelnik, Martin, Lenore M. Lucy, Arnold Friedmann, and James Wines. "Interior Design and the Profession," *Interior Design* 59 (August 1988), 202–203.

CHAPTER 6

Careers in Business

Many family- and consumer-oriented careers, such as fashion merchandising, interiors merchandising, consumer affairs, and restaurant and hotel management, require both a knowledge of consumer products and business skills. Students with educational backgrounds in textiles, fashion, interior design, housing, consumer studies, food service management, general home economics, and many others have never before had such a variety of business-related career options. There are also opportunities in business for those students with other family and consumer specializations, for example, family studies and home economics education. In no other area of the occupational world are new and growing opportunities more abundant.[1]

Business-oriented careers serving families and consumers vary, yet all require similar basic skills and personal qualifications. This is true whether the field is housing, consumer affairs, fashion, restaurants, or others described in this chapter. The skills common to all business careers are in four categories:

Knowledge of the Product or Service. You need knowledge of the composition and characteristics of a well-designed, functional product. For example, in clothing what determines fashionability, durability, serviceability, or other attributes of quality? How is the product designed, engineered, and produced?

Understanding the Market for Your Product or Service. Who buys the product? Young people, women, men, a particular occupational group, or a particular group like working mothers? What people need the product? What motivates buyers to patronize your restaurant, store, business?

General Managerial Skills. Every business has its own business practices and operating procedures. You need to know the standard business practices in your field, which may include such technical skills as accounting, computer use, marketing research, or other business skills.

Positive Human Relations. Many "people skills" determine your success: how to present yourself professionally, your ability to communicate effectively with others, and how you lead and motivate others.

In this chapter we describe some of the most firmly established family- and consumer-oriented careers requiring business skills. We also mention many special opportunities in each field to help broaden your views on the numerous opportunities for family and consumer professionals.

CAREER PROFILE

Fashion Buying and Merchandising

A career in fashion buying and merchandising means forecasting new trends in fashions, buying merchandise from manufacturers, ensuring that the merchandise is delivered on time, and advertising

[1]Many of the careers described in Chapter 5 have a business orientation as well but stress artistic or scientific knowledge rather than business skills.

and promoting fashions to consumers. Successful merchandising requires not only a knowledge of and an interest in fashion but also many business and organizational skills including organizing the store, making budgets, keeping records of the inventory of fashions, and motivating sales associates.

Typical Job Titles

Fashion buying and merchandising careers have many different job titles and opportunities. For example, the following are typical job titles found in department stores (similar titles are used by other retailers):

- Executive trainee
- Management trainee
- Assistant buyer
- Buyer
- Merchandising analyst
- Department manager
- Divisional merchandise manager
- General merchandise manager
- Vice president for merchandising

Responsibilities

Let's look at the general responsibilities of the fashion buyer, which apply also to assistant buyers, department managers, inventory managers, and the other individuals whom the buyer supervises. The first responsibility is planning the fashion merchandise assortment, that is, studying current fashion trends and forecasting trends in consumer buying. Often it means studying customer preferences and what sold well in the past. From these data, buyers identify the types of merchandise that the particular clientele of their stores are most likely to buy. Then the buyer draws up a budget indicating how much merchandise in dollars and units will be in the store each month during a fashion season and an assortment plan specifying the styles, sizes, and prices of merchandise to be offered.

Once these plans are established, the next task is to go to markets to obtain the merchandise needed. Buyers travel to markets all around the United States and in foreign countries to obtain the necessary merchandise. Markets are where manufacturers and wholesalers meet to sell their products to retail stores. There are major markets in New York, Los Angeles, Atlanta, Dallas, and Chicago. The major foreign markets are in London, Paris, Milan,

Hong Kong, and Montreal. Buyers visit manufacturers and whole-salers in the cities nearest them or in cities that offer the best selections of merchandise. There they negotiate with manufacturers to buy the merchandise desired at the best prices and delivery schedule. Finally, the buyer writes orders with the manufacturers for the items selected.

Once the merchandise has been ordered and delivered to the store, the next task is to sell it. This involves advertising, setting up displays, and holding fashion shows and special events promoting the merchandise. Here creativity and ingenuity are required to find the best ways to present the merchandise to consumers and to make the final sales.

The last major task is in department management and supervision. The buyer is responsible for the day-to-day operation of his or her department, which includes many functions: managing the inventory, replenishing stock, seeing to the neatness and cleanliness of the selling area, and making sure that displays are well presented. Another responsibility is to train and supervise sales associates (salespeople). The success or failure of a store depends on its sales associates, who are in daily contact with customers and who establish the store's image and reputation. The buyer must train salespeople in such areas as presenting the merchandise to the customers and completing the sale. These functions of store operations and sales are increasingly performed by a separate managerial group; see the "Store Management" Career Profile that follows.

Qualifications

A degree in fashion merchandising, fashion retailing, or consumer studies is desirable for a career in fashion buying. Your education for a buying and merchandising career should include a wide range of fashion and merchandising courses: fashion concepts, textiles, history of fashion, clothing and human behavior, buying and merchandising, retail management, accounting, consumer behavior, consumer studies, marketing, computer science (management information systems), and advertising. In addition, the ability to communicate is important to this profession, and courses in human relations, English, business writing, journalism, public speaking, and public relations can be helpful.

Another qualification is experience in retailing. Recently, larger retail stores have based many of their hiring decisions on the applicants' previous experience in retailing. Thus the best candidates are those who have had experience in such occupations as sales associate (salesperson), stock control clerk, unit control clerk, merchandising assistant, or assistant department manager. Such experience shows that you have an interest in retailing and wish to continue your career on the basis of that experience. The more experience you have, the more valuable you will be to a potential employer.

Special Personal Qualities

You must possess other personal qualities to succeed in retailing. Retailing is a fast-paced, high-pressure business. Fashion trends and changes in consumer demand can happen overnight, and you have to react quickly. The day-to-day operations of retail departments can be hectic and mean long hours. Because many workdays are spent on your feet, physical stamina is an asset. And because you deal daily with customers and employees, you also have to be personable, warm, and effective in human relations. Maybe even more important, you have to enjoy interacting with people. To operate in such an environment, it is necessary to have communication and leadership skills and the ability to motivate other employees to work toward the goals of your department.

The personality characteristics that will help you are aggressiveness, assertiveness, positive attitudes toward human relations, optimism, and a willingness to take risks. This last quality is especially important, because you have to make a lot of decisions regarding new fashion trends, new merchandise, and when to mark down old and unsalable merchandise. All this requires a willingness to take risks in order to succeed. Finally, decisiveness is important. You have to be able and willing to make many decisions on a daily basis, often with only a limited amount of information and time.

Other Factors

Today fashion buying and merchandising are increasingly done through computerized management information systems. All areas of accounting, budgeting, purchasing management, inventory control, and floor management go through computerized systems. Therefore, those persons who succeed will be those who can deal with mathematical reports and computerized systems. Retail merchandising is not for those who hate math or fear computers.

The daily routine deserves special note. Retailing is not a nine-to-five occupation. Indeed, retail stores often are open until late in the evening and through weekends (some operate twenty-four hours a day, seven days a week). Therefore, in retailing your work schedule must be flexible.

There are also career opportunities for fashion buying and merchandising professionals in supporting business. For example, jobs for buyers can be found in resident buying offices, fashion consultants' offices, marketing services (market research, consumer research, advertising), and customer services. Excellent opportunities in the wholesaling of apparel, as a sales representative ("rep") for a manufacturer, are also obtained by experienced buyers.

Several other attributes of the retail profession require brief mention. Often there is a lot of travel in retail buying. At times there will be extensive paperwork, such as establishing merchandise budgets, preparing assortment plans, and managing inventory (much of this is now being done on computers, but this still involves paperwork for input and daily management). One final consideration is that retail management has well-defined career paths: There is a progression from assistant buyer to buyer and then to higher levels of management, including divisional merchandise manager, general merchandise manager, and vice-president. Retail buying and merchandising can also lead to other areas in the organization, for example, store management, store operations, personnel, advertising and promotion. Thus, retail merchandising is a career that has a variety of positions.

CAREER PROFILE

Store Management (Apparel) _____

A career path growing in popularity is in the area of store management. Many students who first enter careers in apparel and related areas, pursuing careers as buyers, later enter management. Store management is overseeing the day-to-day operations and control of a store. Often this includes many activities related to merchandising fashions or other products offered by the store, such as management of personnel, inventory control, advertising, and promotion. As large centralized stores have grown, store management has become a growing career path for students interested in retailing and fashion.

Typical Job Titles

The better known titles in this career path are the following:

- Assistant department manager
- Department manager

- Merchandising manager
- Group manager
- Store manager

As this sequence of titles implies, there is a progression of opportunity in store management; you may start managing a small department or area of a store but can rise to the top in managing the largest retail stores.

Responsibilities

As in the case of retail buying and merchandising, the scope of responsibilities in store management depends on the level in the organization at which you work. We shall outline some of the responsibilities that are common to all levels of store management. In general, store management encompasses all activities related to the store's day-to-day sales and merchandising operations, including stocking inventory on the shelves, making sure that the floor is neat, and seeing that all merchandise is presented in the most favorable manner. It means hiring and training of employees, scheduling work times for employees, and ensuring that the proper staffing is on hand for all store hours.

In addition to merchandise management and supervision of employees, managers in retail stores are responsible for the store's physical environment (fixtures, lighting, utilities, heating), cleanliness, sanitation (janitorial services), security, and loss prevention (protection from theft, protection of employees' physical security). In many cases the store management carries out merchandising functions such as advertising, display, and special promotional events that were once controlled by buyers. Managers also oversee the promotions of their employees, their professional development, and demotions or firings.

Qualifications

Many students enter store management careers with fashion merchandising or related degrees. Courses in management, merchandising, general business, personnel, public relations, supervision, and communications are helpful. The most successful store managers also have a knowledge of the products or services that they oversee, such as fashion, clothing, interior design, foods, household equipment, and appliances. Thus taking product-oriented courses gives the management person an advantage.

Special Personal Qualities

It takes special personal qualities to succeed in store management. As in the other areas of retail merchandising, store management requires a great deal of stamina, enthusiasm, optimism, and ability to deal effectively with other people. Successful managers are leaders, motivators and organizers of people. They are also decision makers and must make many decisions under stress. Thus self-confidence, decisiveness, and a positive self-concept are necessary. The successful manager also must be a self-starter who is able to set goals and delegate the responsibility and authority for accomplishing them.

One of the most important qualifications is a strong consciousness of the business's profitability. Retailing is a very competitive field in which success is measured by profits. Store managers are under continuous pressure to increase the store's sales and profitability. This pressure applies to buyers and lower-level department managers as well, but the greatest burden falls on upper management. The pressure to perform and to succeed in sales and dollar profits is continuous.

Other Factors

Because managers are organizers and leaders of many people with many different jobs, they must know the content of many jobs. They must understand what is going on in the advertising department; they must know the responsibilities of a buyer; they must be familiar with sanitation engineering; they must deal with personnel matters. Therefore, managers require a knowledge of all aspects and details of a business. The broader one's knowledge is, the more chance of success one will have.

Managers also may work in many areas within store management, some of which are store operations, personnel, advertising, and promotion. They may also work in various product areas, such as fashion apparel, interiors furnishings, housewares, consumer electronics, and gifts. Therefore, the opportunity to have an ever-changing career with new and interesting subject matter to deal with is always present. People who like variety will enjoy store management.

Store management is another career that has substantial advancement potential. There are many steps up the ladder of retail management, and for the upwardly oriented individual there is perhaps no better career in all fields of family and consumer professions.

This, of course, is truest in the largest cities and the largest retail organizations.

Those skills required of managers are the ability to deal with mathematics, statistics, and computers. The ability to scan and quickly interpret figures is especially important. Finally, a desire to succeed in a competitive and fast-paced business is mandatory.

Entry into careers in store management, as well as fashion buying and merchandising, is often through the executive training programs or executive management programs offered by the larger stores. In general, these programs may last ten weeks or more and may be a combination of formal training by the store and on-the-job experience. Following graduation from training programs, the professional enters either merchandising or store management. Typically people who are in store management transfer back and forth into merchandising and other aspects of the business to gain the broadest possible experience. Seeking out programs that offer the broad training and rotation among different functional areas of the organization is recommended. Creativity is helpful for success because store managers must come up with new ideas for selling merchandise and keeping employees motivated and enthusiastic about their daily activities. Organizations fail when their people lack motivation and excitement, and the most successful organizations are those whose jobs are creative, keeping the daily activities lively and exciting.

A person in store management may start his or her own business. Knowledge of the product, business, and store operations is required, and one's knowledge and stamina are tested to the extreme. The rewards, both financial and personal, are also among the highest. See Chapter 10 for more information on entrepreneurship—starting one's own business.

CAREER PROFILE

Fashion Consulting

Fashion consulting is one of the glamorous careers in the fashion business. Fashion consulting is monitoring changing fashion trends, keeping up with what is new in fashion design, and carrying out a variety of activities to promote consumer acceptance. Some of the jobs in fashion consulting are with retail stores, and others are with manufacturers, fashion illustrators or photographers, or private agencies. A new type of consultant, the image consultant, is also growing in popularity as a result of the "dress for success" movement of the 1980s.

Typical Job Titles

Typical job titles in retailing are the following:

- Fashion director
- Fashion coordinator
- Fashion consultant
- Fashion adviser
- Image consultant

Responsibilities

Depending on one's specific position with a store, manufacturer, or agency, a job in fashion consulting can have a variety of responsibilities, including keeping up with changing fashion trends, identifying what is new and exciting, and picking the winners and losers. The latter is an important part of the job, for a fashion consultant or fashion director must be well informed about fashion trends and be able to predict their progress.

A major responsibility of fashion directors working with retail stores is to develop and maintain the store's fashion image, or reputation. To do this, the fashion director advises the store's buyers and managers on current fashion trends and how to present them in the most effective way in each department. Thus the director provides a consulting or advisory service and also is ensuring that various departments of the store present a consistent image in relation to the store's objective and particular customers.

A fashion consultant or fashion director spends a great deal of time visiting fashion markets, reading fashion trade periodicals, traveling to fashion centers, attending fashion shows, and visiting with designers and manufacturers. All this research is aimed at gathering information on the new style offerings and identifying the dominant trends. Fashion consulting requires extensive knowledge of the market, the various brand names and designer labels, their quality levels, and how they will sell in the market.

Fashion consultants may also be involved in promotional activities, such as planning fashion shows, arranging for appearances of famous designers, preparing advertising, or supervising fashion displays. In these and other merchandising activities, the director works closely with merchandising managers and buyers. Therefore a successful fashion consultant or fashion director needs to understand the merchandising process and the needs of buyers and store managers.

The term *image consultant* is used for people who advise consumers in various ways of dressing to meet particular personal goals, for example, professional dress or color coordination.

Qualifications

For a career in fashion consulting, a background in clothing, textiles, and fashion is mandatory, including studies in fashion design, major designers, fashion illustration, photography, textiles, and consumer motivation. Other desirable courses are in areas such as visual merchandising, display techniques, art, art history, merchandising, communications, journalism, and public relations. A degree in any field of clothing and textiles is desirable.

Work experience is also important, particularly in retail stores. Work as a displayer, stylist, clothing construction specialist, or in other technical areas dealing with the product is valuable.

Other qualifications include creativity, coordinating abilities, ability to communicate one's views to others (clients, store buyers, managers), good taste, and an understanding of artistic excellence. People in fashion consulting are applied artists and must have artistic ability as well.

Other Factors

Fashion consulting may seem to be a glamorous career field, but it is also high pressured and competitive. It is a hard field to enter because there is a limited number of jobs, and it draws many candidates because of its perceived glamour. However, opportunities do exist for those who possess the necessary creativity and fashion sense.

To be successful, a fashion consultant must be able to sell ideas to buyers or personal clients. A fashion director or coordinator cannot dictate his or her views but must convince buyers or managers that these views are correct. Persuasive communication therefore becomes paramount, and those who are not tactful in their presentations are less likely to succeed.

Today there are special opportunities for careers in fashion consulting in such areas as image consulting for customers or other clients of stores, color consulting, or operating one's own business as a fashion consultant. Such consulting has become popular in the 1980s and 1990s; in fact for some stores it is considered good business to employ a fashion consultant or image consultant. Consumers enjoy using these services, and these consultants often become personal shoppers who help consumers plan, coordinate and purchase their wardrobes. However, there is always uncertainty as to how long such career opportunities will last. Therefore, building a career in fashion consulting should be done cautiously although there will always be opportunities for those consultants with the highest qualifications and personal skills in communicating.

CAREER PROFILE

Sales and Sales Management (Wholesale) _____

A relatively new career for specialists in clothing, textiles, fashion, and other consumer products is working at the wholesale level of sales and marketing. Here one works with a product's manufacturer, developing and implementing strategies for selling it to retail stores. There are positions not only in apparel and textiles but also in textile fibers, furniture, home furnishings, appliances, consumer electronics, and other major consumer products. This is truly a growth area for the consumer-oriented professional.

Typical Job Titles

Like other professions, sales and sales management have a variety of job titles. The best known are the following:

- Sales representative
- Manufacturer's representative
- "Inside" salesperson
- Showroom salesperson
- "Outside" salesperson
- Traveling salesperson

Often these titles are all referred to by the abbreviated term *rep* (for *representative*). Successful sales representatives can also grow into such higher-level jobs as the following:

- Sales manager
- District manager
- Vice president of sales

Historically most of the employees in sales have been men, but today women are entering in ever-growing numbers, and there now are many opportunities for women at all levels of wholesale sales management.

Responsibilities

The major responsibility of a sales representative is to present the various styles of merchandise offered by his or her firm to clients (typically buyers from retail stores or other retail organizations), show the most favorable qualities of the merchandise, indicate why this merchandise is the best for the client, and close the sale. Sales representatives work from showrooms that their companies own or lease or travel directly to retail stores and present samples of their merchandise there. Whether inside sales (showroom sales) or outside sales (traveling sales) is involved, the salesperson has samples of the styles offered by the firm and shows these to the client. From such samples clients make their decisions to purchase merchandise.

But the job of a sales representative is not merely showing merchandise and writing orders for sales. The clients' accounts must be serviced by following up on orders, ensuring that deliveries are made on time, and helping clients learn the best ways for presenting and selling merchandise. Often this sales assistance and follow-up are the key to success. Therefore, the major task of all sales personnel is supporting the client in every way possible.

The sales representative also must do a considerable amount of paperwork, beginning with writing up orders and ending with planning future calls on clients. Between these are telephone communications with clients and letters or memos indicating all follow-ups and delivery schedules. Salespeople also extend many courtesies to their clients, for instance, invitations to dinner or the theater or other entertainment.

Qualifications

People in sales have the widest variety of background and qualifications. Obviously a degree in an area related to the product you are selling will be helpful, for example, fashion, interior design, foods, housing, or equipment. People in the wholesaling of clothing must know clothing design, clothing quality, styling, and textiles. The same is true for selling furniture, furnishings, and appliances. Degrees in these areas are an advantage.

Experience in sales and past success in sales are important. Work as a retail sales associate is one kind of experience many students can acquire, and experience in wholesale channels is even better.

Special Personal Qualities

It takes a special personality to succeed in sales. It is absolutely necessary that you be optimistic, outgoing, enthusiastic, and extroverted. You must enjoy talking and listening to others. You must be able to lose a sale without becoming discouraged. Furthermore, you must be ambitious and a self-starter. All these characteristics require a great deal of emotional maturity.

Successful salespeople also must be able to communicate ideas, to sense a client's needs (and clients' needs differ rather dramatically), and then to show each client that the salesperson's products best fits the client's needs. Finding this fit between the client's needs and the products separates the good salesperson from the average one. The salesperson must be able to empathize with the client.

Work in sales requires a great deal of personal stamina. Traveling salespersons, particularly, must have considerable energy, for there are long hours on the road, and carrying samples can be equally demanding at times, particularly at the times of year when major markets are held. Buyers converge on sales offices all at the same time, during the weeks scheduled for markets, and work can be extremely demanding then.

Another important quality of successful salespeople is that they know the product well. Often they must know the competition's products equally well. This knowledge of products is the most valuable part of the salesperson's personal armada of sales techniques. No amount of glib talk or gift of gab can overcome a lack of understanding of the product and its market.

Other Factors

Because many salespeople work on commissions, sales can be a profitable occupation. However, salaries at first can be relatively modest until a salesperson gets established as productive in selling to and servicing clients.

Successful salespeople can move into upper positions of sales and showroom management. In addition, some successful salespeople become independent sales representatives, operating their own businesses as sales representatives for several manufacturers. Many independent sales representatives operate in apparel and other fields today. These people operate their own businesses and can be regarded as entrepreneurs. This is an especially rewarding opportunity in the sales field and is highly recommended. Of course, considerable experience and expertise in all fields of sales and sales management are necessary before one can independently run one's own business in wholesale sales.

CAREER PROFILE

Interiors Merchandising _____

Interiors merchandising is a special subcareer of residential interior design and contract design (see Chapter 5). The professional in interiors merchandising is involved in all aspects of the marketing of interiors products, at both the retail and the wholesale level. Interiors merchandising is less a design field and more a business and marketing field, although some specialized knowledge of design is required.

Typical Job Titles

Job titles in interiors merchandising include the following:

- Interior designer
- Design specialist
- Design consultant
- Marketing representative
- Merchandising representative
- Merchandising analyst
- Sales associate

These job titles and opportunities are found in department stores, furniture stores, wholesale organizations, and with manufacturers of many interiors products.

Responsibilities

The principal responsibility of professionals in this field is selling interiors. Interiors merchandising professionals who work in department stores and furniture stores advise customers on their household design and decorating plans. But their main task is to show

how the organization's particular products, brands, and services can fit into the customer's home. Unlike residential or contract designers, the professional in interiors merchandising is often working with particular lines and brands of products and must emphasize these products in his or her selling. In some cases, the designer orders products from outside or independent sources, but the primary responsibility remains to sell the store's particular merchandise.

Interiors merchandising professionals who work as manufacturer's representatives for manufacturers of interiors products have special responsibilities. Their job is to call on residential interior design firms, department stores, furniture stores, and other design businesses to present the manufacturer's products. This means selling designs to designers rather than to the final client. The responsibilities of this job are similar to those for sales management careers. It is necessary to know the product thoroughly and be able to present it to clients satisfactorily. Then the client's account must be serviced by following up on the delivery of orders, answering questions of clients, and generally making sure that the client is satisfied in all business dealings with the company.

Interiors merchandising professionals have a lot of contact with their clients and must be able to deal with many different kinds of people. The job requires much travel and many housecalls and presentations. The merchandising professional is also responsible for such business details as preparing estimates, writing orders, and making bids. Often they also oversee the final installation of products and ensure that the job is completed to the client's satisfaction.

Qualifications

Education in interior design, often with a bachelor's degree, is desirable. A broad knowledge of art, drawing, coordinating styles, and space planning is helpful. The merchandising specialist also must know the qualities of many different design products and be able to present them to customers. Business courses are also important, especially merchandising, advertising, salesmanship, and sales management. An accounting course can be useful as well, because of the necessity to write bids and specifications for clients.

Special Personal Qualities

The interiors merchandising professional is a specialist in building positive human relations. Building a positive rapport with clients is necessary but is not always easy. The continuous selling is stressful, and the successful merchandiser must be prepared to cope with this challenge. One needs a charming, outgoing, warm personality to get along in this career.

Other Factors

The advancement potential for people in interiors merchandising is good. Successful sales representatives can advance into upper levels of sales management. Developing one's own free-lance business as an interior design consultant is also possible, and here it is necessary to be well versed in both the design and the merchandising aspects of the interiors profession.

CAREER PROFILE

The Hospitality Industry

The hospitality industry — including restaurants, hotels, and lodgings — offers an interesting opportunity for people-oriented professionals. In the restaurant field, professional careers exist as executive chefs, restaurant managers, and owners. In the lodging field, excellent opportunities exist in managing small and large hotels, resorts, and motels. The hospitality industry is one of the largest and most widespread employers in the entire American economy.

Typical Job Titles

In the restaurant business, typical job titles include the following:

- Dining room manager
- Storeroom manager
- Executive chef
- Restaurant manager
- Restaurant owner
- Menu planner
- Food production manager

In hotels, there are executive and managerial careers such as the following:

- Hotel manager
- Front office manager
- Services manager

- Recreation director
- Food and beverage manager
- Wine steward
- Kitchen manager
- Housekeeping manager

Responsibilities

Restaurant management has many and varied responsibilities. You must deal with a complex, multifaceted product: a meal comes in many courses—salads, beverages, main course, desserts, and so on. Similarly, the clientele differs in different restaurants, and foods range from family-style cooking to gourmet. The most important task of a successful restaurant manager is to identify and meet consumers' special tastes for foods. Consumers' needs and desires vary, and styles of service change from smaller to larger establishments and from elite to average clienteles.

One of the most important tasks in restaurant management is to ensure the quality, safety, and healthfulness of the restaurant's food. Restaurants must provide nutritious and safe as well as tasty meals. Indeed, there is a legal as well as moral obligation regarding the customers' health, and restaurants are regularly inspected for violations of health codes.

Restaurants must also keep up with changing food tastes, appropriate aesthetics of restaurants (interior design, tables, furnishings, and so on), and new trends in consumer demand (for instance, the growth of new markets and the decline of established markets). Consumers' tastes are continually changing, and even the most traditional restaurants, such as those offering well-established Continental or French menus, have to adjust to new tastes and styles of cuisine.

Restaurant managers are responsible for many managerial activities, including hiring employees, training employees, supervising restaurant operations, purchasing foods, purchasing kitchen equipment, planning menus, pricing menus, supervising maintenance, and keeping records. Management also means being in the restaurant every day, working directly with employees, meeting clients, overseeing cash management, handling complaints, and creating a positive atmosphere. In larger restaurants, the manager has a staff to manage, perhaps including a food manager, a food and beverage manager, and an executive chef.

Operating a restaurant can be a demanding business, for at least two, and often three, meals a day are served (sometimes requiring a fifteen- to eighteen-hour day), and restaurants usually operate six or seven days a week. This creates responsibilities for staffing and scheduling, constant supervision during all open hours, and attention to day-to-day affairs. Restaurant management is a full-time profession.

Hotel management is an equally interesting and varied occupation. There are many types of hotels and lodgings: commercial hotels, residential hotels, motels, resorts, inns, boarding houses, and campgrounds. All need qualified on-site managers. There are many activities in operating a lodging facility. Management extends beyond the rooms and bedding facilities to the housekeeping staffs, bellhops, front office, registration office, guest accounts office, shops, restaurants, cocktail lounges, nightclubs, discos, newsstands, laundry facilities, transportation services, accounting department, secretarial services for businesses, fax/photocopy services, business meeting facilities, conference planning, beauty shops, health clubs, and other facilities demanded by clienteles. A hotel is more than a place for people to sleep; it is a recreational and entertainment facility, a "home away from home" for travelers. People expect more than merely a bed; thus the term *hospitality industry.*

Hotel managers are responsible for the efficient, smooth and timely operation of all components of a hotel facility. They must see to the pleasantness of the surroundings, including cleanliness, interior decoration, and comfort of furniture, bedding, and heating or air conditioning. Like restaurants, hotels serve many different consumer needs, ranging from small or intimate inns with their special personalized character to large hotels aimed at business travelers. Like restaurants, hotels also have to keep up with changing consumer tastes. Because a hotel is a labor-intensive business, the staff must be supervised, and so managerial skills are paramount. And hotels, like restaurants, are responsible for the health, safety and security of their clientele. Larger hotels often have special staffs for maintaining the security and safety of their facilities.

Depending on the type of hotel, managers may have separate staffs to manage housekeeping, accounting and bookkeeping, maintenance, security, conferences, meeting facilities, recreational and leisure activities, or other services operated for the benefit of customers. These specialized departments offer excellent training for the aspiring hotel professional.

Qualifications

There are undergraduate programs in restaurant and hotel management, food service management, and institutional management on many campuses. In addition, majors in other fields of family and consumer careers, such as merchandising, consumer affairs, and home economics, can qualify for entry into the management training programs offered by some hotels. The courses required for hotel and restaurant careers include accounting, marketing, and management. Specialized professional courses in food service management, nutrition, lodging management, and facilities management are also important.

One of the most valued qualifications is experience in a restaurant or hotel business. In restaurants one can start as a busperson and work up through various kitchen responsibilities, culminating in a mid-level managerial position. The more a persons knows about the many jobs required in a restaurant, the more successful a manager that person is likely to be. Similarly, in hotels, experience working the front desk, night audits, accounting, housekeeping, food and beverage management, and other services of the hotel is all important. In the hospitality industry one cannot overemphasize the value of hands-on experience. Many programs offer experience or internships, but if not, one can always gain experience through part-time work.

Special Personal Qualities

Hotels are twenty-four-hour-a-day, seven-days-a-week businesses, and restaurants are not far behind in their long hours of operation. Therefore, a willingness to work erratic hours is necessary to becoming a successful hotel or restaurant manager. Physical energy is also required, for a hotel or restaurant manager may be on his or her feet for long hours every working day, and the physical strains can be significant. Other helpful personal qualities include the ability to get along with people, an outgoing personality, and ability to withstand pressure in interpersonal relations. Supervising a large staff of employees is a challenging activity that requires positive human relations and is where one's tact and ability to get along come into play.

Another special quality is the willingness to meet regularly with customers. Restaurant managers and hotel managers are called on to meet and greet customers from time to time. Sometimes this is handling unpleasant personalities or customer complaints, and it is necessary to be skilled in handling these encounters positively and effectively to ensure repeat visits.

Other Factors

The variety of hotels and restaurants offering careers is substantial. Opportunities exist not only in traditional "sit-down" restaurants but also in fast-food restaurants, cafeterias, and major chains (for example, national chains like Denny's, McDonalds, and Furr's Cafeterias). There may also be jobs in the food and beverage facilities of airports, resorts, institutions (nursing homes or prisons), and institutional food services such as those for schools and hospitals (related careers in dietetics are described in Chapter 5). Executive chefs may also have interesting careers. In hotels, the career prospects are equally varied, depending on the size, location, and type of the hotel and the variety of its facilities.

CAREER PROFILE

Leisure, Recreation, and Travel

Careers in the leisure services industry pertain to all types of leisure pursuits, recreation, vacation, travel, and tourism for families and consumers. This is not a traditional career field for family and consumer majors because few programs offer majors with such specialization. However, students with majors in such fields as merchandising, consumer affairs, home economics, and family and consumer studies have transferable skills for these fields. Those students majoring in restaurant and hotel management have a more direct entry into leisure-oriented positions, especially those with resorts.

Typical Job Titles

Typical job titles include the following:

- Recreation director
- Camp counselor
- Supervisor of recreation programs
- Educational specialist
- Merchandising assistant
- Travel agent
- Travel consultant
- Sports consultant

There are also jobs in many recreation-related businesses, such as resorts, retail stores, travel companies, and equipment manufacturing firms. The job titles outlined in earlier career profiles are frequently found in these businesses.

Responsibilities

The responsibilities of leisure services positions vary, and such positions may be found in resorts of all types, including golf, tennis, skiing, and beach, and in hotels and restaurants at resorts. In most localities there are various types of golf clubs, tennis clubs, health and fitness spas, or other membership organizations. These all employ managers, program directors, nutritionists, and merchandising specialists.

There are job openings with sportswear manufacturers, leisure-wear manufacturers, retailers emphasizing leisure or sportswear, amusement parks, theme parks, camps, and campgrounds. The responsibilities in all these are diverse but in general include the management of the organization's various functions, knowledge of the product or service offered, and contact with customers.

Qualifications

There is no set educational direction for this field, and people enter it from virtually all backgrounds. A knowledge of consumer and family needs gained in many consumer- and family-oriented majors is a good credential. A knowledge of merchandising, consumer services, and positive human relations is also desirable. Courses in leisure studies and travel are offered by some community colleges and universities. Entry also requires work experience, usually working from the bottom up and into middle-level or higher-level managerial positions.

Special Personal Qualities

Obtaining a position in the recreation and leisure industry is extremely competitive. The work hours are long, often including all seven days of the week and all hours of the day. Some people are attracted to recreation and leisure careers because of the pleasantness of the surroundings and the activities, but this increases the competition for positions and lowers the salaries paid. But balancing these deficiencies is the satisfaction of working in a leisure-oriented profession and in providing such services to families.

These careers require constant contact with clients, considerable tact, an outgoing personality, and concern for positive human relations. An attractive appearance and pleasant personality are required because meeting people in person or by telephone is a daily activity. Successful people also become well versed in the particular area in which they specialize. For example, successful management in a golf resort requires a considerable knowledge of that sport.

Although the foregoing discussion may suggest that there are limitations to this career, it is wise to think of your career prospects as a family and consumer professional in the broadest professional terms. This career path thus has been included here because of the importance of leisure, recreation, and travel to the life-style of the modern family.

CAREER PROFILE

Consumer Affairs

Several careers deal with consumer and family financial matters, from marketing and consumer advocacy to family financial services such as insurance, banking, consumer credit, and investments. Well-established careers exist in such areas as consumer affairs, customer service, and consumer education and information (also discussed in the next chapter). Specialists in consumer affairs and family finances are employed by consumer-oriented businesses (product manufacturers, retailers), governmental agencies offering consumer protection programs, and educational organizations and extension services.

Typical Job Titles

The term *consumer affairs professional* covers many consumer-oriented professions. Typical job titles include the following:

- Consumer information specialist
- Consumer service representative
- Director of consumer services
- Consumer relations manager
- Consumer advocate
- Consumer and market analyst
- Consumer researcher
- Consumer educator
- Consumer product manager

In the related field of consumer financial services, typical job titles include the following:

- Loan officer
- Financial planner
- Credit counselor
- Financial counselor
- Insurance representative
- Banking officer (consumer affairs)
- Director of consumer relations
- Account executive for investments

People with expertise in both consumer affairs and business may enter the retailing careers mentioned in earlier career profiles, in jobs such as merchandising analyst, manufacturer's sales representative, and retail buyer.

Responsibilities

Professionals in consumer affairs view themselves as advocates of consumers' interests. Their responsibility, whether they are employed by businesses, government, or human service agencies, is to represent the consumers' interests to their employer and serve the consumers' needs. Specifically, their job is to make sure that their organization thinks of itself as an advocate of the consumer and tries to resolve the problems or difficulties that the consumer may experience in dealing with the business. This means promoting positive consumer relations by offering consumer services and prompt and fair handling of consumers' complaints. Research has shown that businesses that respond positively to consumers and that handle consumers' problems or complaints fairly and efficiently have repeat business. Many businesses, especially retailers and those who manufacture widely distributed consumer products, believe that this consumer advocacy orientation is crucial to their success.

Consumer affairs professionals hold many other positions benefiting consumers. Many oversee consumer education or consumer information, that is, teaching consumers about the use, safety, and economy of their products. In fact, consumer education and information has become one of the bigger fields of consumer affairs. The major responsibility in such a career is preparing informational materials, including brochures, instructional manuals, advertising copy, promotional campaigns, dealer training, consumer self-educational aids, personal demonstrations, and teaching programs aimed at consumers. The information specialist also has to know how to communicate effectively, not only in person but also through the various media and informational services that consumers use.

Many businesses and governmental agencies have established consumer affairs offices. Such offices exist to make sure that the consumer is represented and that the consumers' viewpoints are heard by the corporation's middle and upper management. Likewise, these offices ensure that the business is sensitive to the consumers' needs and that safer and more efficient products are offered in the market. A special goal of such departments is to see that safety, health, and personal well-being are considered by the manufacturer and retailer of products. And when products have deficiencies, such departments are also the centers for handling complaints and resolving disputes.

Consumer affairs professionals also participate in market analysis, market research, and product development. Often they are a part of the business team that plans products, in the case of manufacturers, or buys products, in the case of retailers. Thus the responsibility goes from advocacy to managing the business's buying and merchandising.

Consumer affairs professionals working in governmental agencies, labor unions, and human service organizations must be familiar with the laws regarding consumer interests. They are advocates in both the legal and the moral sense. Such professionals often influence the enactment of new laws and regulations in the consumers' interest and make certain that the laws are followed. Often these professionals lobby for consumer interests and become active in grass-roots consumer groups and political action groups. The consumer advocate is an agent of change, and many such advocates have been influential in the creation of consumer affairs offices, passage of laws, and identification of unsafe or ineffective products on the market. Thus they have helped improve the quality of the marketplaces and have performed important social functions.

The field of family financial services also employs a wide range of consumer affairs specialists and others trained in family finances or resource management. Careers exist in such financial fields as banking, consumer credit, insurance, and investments as well as in the relatively new fields of family financial planning and counseling; these careers are discussed in Chapter 8. Such careers require a broad-based knowledge of consumer affairs, family economics, financial analysis, investing, family relations, and counseling techniques.

Qualifications

Academic majors for this profession include consumer studies, family resource management, home management, consumer economics, family economics, and human ecology. These are specialized majors that deal with many aspects of consumer affairs and family financial management. Newer programs also focus on family financial counseling and include training in family finances, budgets, investments, insurance, and banking. In addition, general majors in home economics and family relations can provide access to these careers. Whatever major is taken, the courses should include consumer affairs, consumer behavior, consumer and family economics, consumer education, family resource management, family economics, accounting, family finance management, investments, banking, and insurance. Specialized consumer courses such as consumer relations, consumer advocacy, consumer public policy, and consumer information can also be valuable (much of their content is often covered in other broader courses such as consumer economics). Other more general courses that are helpful are personal finance, marketing, communications, public relations, advertising, and political science. Courses in educational techniques and evaluation can assist those students who are interested in careers in consumer information, education, or customer relations. Because this career also involves considerable contact with individual consumers and families, a sensitivity to human and family relations is required.

Special Personal Qualities

Students entering careers dealing with consumer advocacy, especially when it involves legislation and politics, must have a great deal of enthusiasm and stamina to succeed. It takes a lot of hard work to accomplish such goals as passing consumer legislation. Politics are involved, and it can take time to gain support from constituencies.

To succeed in business, the consumer affairs professional must appreciate both the needs of the business (to make a profit) and the needs of the consumer. The successful professional represents consumers' interests but at the same time must be aware of the business's needs. Thus the professional must balance the interests of both his or her employer and the consumer patronizing the organization. This is a large challenge, one that requires professional responsibility and a sense of ethics.

The successful consumer affairs professional must also have expertise in the particular area of consumer or financial matters in which he or she is employed. Education tends to be general in the field of consumer affairs, but employees of a specialized organization such as a cosmetics firm must have an extensive background in the product and its marketing strategies. Similarly a specialist in retailing must understand a variety of retail-oriented products and how to deal with many types of retail consumers (some being less than friendly or perhaps even hostile). Sensitivity to consumer concerns and positive human relations come to the forefront here.

Other Factors

The consumer movement of the 1960s and 1970s held much promise for careers in consumer affairs. In the early 1990s this profession is accelerating in growth. Today there are many opportunities for consumer affairs professionals in business and for family financial experts. Specialists in this field are employed by product manufacturers, retailers, banks, insurance organizations, credit counseling firms, government agencies, and utilities. Often such positions are found in a merchandising department or a customer service department, rather than a department designated as "consumer affairs" or a related consumer title. Thus, to find careers in this field one must dig below the organization's surface and sometimes may even need to convince the organization that it needs a consumer affairs professional. The important point to remember is that careers are available but that sometimes one must look hard for them and be flexible about where one works.

The newer area of family financial planning and counseling is offering opportunities to professionals in this field as well (see Chapter 8 for details). Many people think that consumer financial services such as credit counseling, insurance counseling, and retail banking are among the better opportunities for professionals in this field. Every person interested in consumer and family financial careers should be well versed in consumer and financial subjects.

CAREER PROFILE

Personnel Management _____

A career in personnel management includes recruiting employees, forecasting labor market trends, hiring new employees, and many other activities dealing with the employees of an organization. Students majoring in family and consumer subjects can find interesting opportunities in personnel, although this is considered a nontraditional career path. For example, a student with training and experience in fashion retailing might find excellent opportunities in the personnel department of retail stores. Students in consumer affairs, family studies, and other majors that have a "people orientation" may equally find interesting opportunities.

Typical Job Titles

Typical job titles follow:

- Recruitment specialist
- Executive recruiter
- Personnel manager
- Human resources specialist
- Personnel management specialist
- Labor relations specialist
- Director of training
- Director of human resources

Responsibilities

The personnel department of an organization, whether it be a business, government, or human service organization, performs a variety of functions. Its biggest task is recruiting employees for the organization. Related responsibilities are forecasting labor market trends, forecasting the organization's needs, taking formal applications, screening applications, interviewing, and, finally, hiring. Choosing employees is the most important decision that organizations make.

The personnel department also performs other important functions, such as educating and training of employees or running an on-the-job education program. Sometimes personnel managers retrain employees for new jobs or assist in their professional development to improve their existing job skills. Personnel managers also formulate personnel policies, establish standard pay scales in various skills and jobs, conduct performance evaluations, counsel employees, keep employee records, inform the organization about labor laws (equal opportunity, occupational safety and health regulations, and so forth), negotiate contracts with the unions, and maintain good relations with the unions.

Writing job descriptions has also become an important part of personnel management. In some businesses the personnel department also writes up the formal contracts for the employees, particularly for the professional employees or consultants to the organization. Finally, the personnel office is often responsible for terminating and firing and for developing retirement programs.

The personnel department provides many services to employees as well, including benefits such as insurance and pensions, social activities, recreational facilities, discounts for purchasing consumer products, and other fringe benefits. In this way the personnel office contributes to the health and welfare of all employees.

Qualifications

A degree in a family and consumer major can gain an entry level position in personnel management. But personnel management is becoming a specialized professional field, and so it is desirable also to take courses in personnel management, labor relations, human relations, human motivation and personality, psychological testing, and educational techniques.

Some of the important skills of personnel management are a sensitivity to human needs, an ability to evaluate an employee's character during brief encounters such as interviews, an ability to speak easily, effective writing skills, and a desire to recruit actively and sell the organization to potential employees. The job also requires considerable paperwork and the management of written files for each applicant and employee of the organization. Because keeping accurate and up-to-date files on each employee is so important, the personnel specialist must be efficient and organized.

Other Factors

To gain an entry into a personnel career and to succeed, you need to be familiar with many of the activities of the organization or businesss for which you are responsible. For example, a personnel specialist in a retail store must be familiar with the store's diverse jobs, such as sales associate, inventory clerk, store security officer, advertising copywriter, management information specialist, merchandising analyst, buyer, and department manager. Therefore, a person with an educational background and experience in fashion merchandising has some of the most important credentials for a job in personnel. Similarly, a person experienced in family relations has excellent credentials for a position in personnel with a human services organization. The best way to sell yourself as a family and consumer major is to point out these special qualifications and how they make you a desirable evaluator of personnel for your organization.

Several areas in personnel management are of interest to family and consumer professionals, such as drawing up programs of equal opportunity and affirmative action or counseling employees on family problems or related job problems. Another area for which a family and consumer major may have special qualifications is in retirement counseling, which is becoming an important activity of many personnel offices. Here one's training in such subjects as geriatrics, personal finance, human relations, and the needs of senior citizens can give the family-oriented professional an advantage in the employment office. And some employment offices offer counseling, loan services, or related financial services to employees that may present a unique opportunity for specialists in consumer affairs or family financial planning (see Chapter 8).

CAREER PROFILE

Public Relations

The principal goal of public relations is to build a positive image of and favorable reputation for a business or organization. Public relations specialists present to the public positive information about their clients and see that the public has a positive view of the business or organization. This is done by means of all the media. Although this career may be thought of as nontraditional for family and consumer professionals, there are positions open to these professionals. For example, many jobs in consumer information and education with businesses, utilities, trade associations, and product manufacturers are carried out through the public relations department.

Typical Job Titles

Typical jobs titles follow:

- Public relations agent
- Public relations specialist
- Consumer information specialist
- Consumer education specialist
- Public affairs specialist
- Publicity representative
- Educational director
- Director of public relations

For related career information, see the consumer affairs career profile in this chapter and the related educational career profiles in Chapter 7.

Responsibilities

The major responsibility of public relations professionals is to build and maintain in the public's mind a positive image of an organization. This requires knowing the organization and its activities and presenting them to the public. The public relations specialist gives this information to the public through press releases, informational brochures, programs, radio, television, magazines, and newspapers. The objective is to highlight the organization's strengths and to cope with its weaknesses when necessary.

Public relations specialists in consumer education and consumer information must accurately portray the organization's products, services, or activities. They may have a tendency to overpromote the organization, but overzealousness will surely be recognized and do more harm than good. Therefore, although the responsibility of public relations professionals is to put the organization in a favorable light, they also must be fair and honest or risk damaging the organization's reputation.

Frequently, public relations experts recommend coordinated campaigns of many public relations activities, which requires creating a series of related rather than separate activities promoting the organization. A campaign may include coordinated press releases, educational programs, speeches presented by executives of the organization, advertisements in commercial media, and other activities. Public relations also involves measuring public opinion and attitudes on issues. Thus it is valuable to have research skills, especially in conducting large statistical surveys of the public (e.g., public opinion polls).

Qualifications

Employers in public relations emphasize a broad education, including courses in English, writing, journalism, psychology, sociology, economics, business, research methods, humanities, and, of course, public relations. In addition, a family or consumer major offers expertise in a specific consumer product or family service, which can be attractive to organizations specializing in that family- or consumer-oriented field. To succeed in public relations, one must have an in-depth knowledge of the organization's products or services, which favors the family- or consumer-oriented major in a particular area of expertise.

Special Personal Qualities

Special personal qualities are needed to succeed in public relations. An outgoing, enthusiastic, warm personality is necessary because a public relations specialist meets with many different media representatives and segments of the public. All types of communication skills are important, including public speaking, effective writing, and visual communication through slides and posters. First and foremost, the public relations professional is a communicator, and the ability to communicate well separates the successful from the merely adequate.

Public relations is regarded as a desirable job, and the competition for employment can be great. The willingness to be mobile and to work in the largest cities will increase the opportunity for a career in public relations. Substantial knowledge of a particular product or service area and experience working in that field are other requisites for entry into this career.

Other Factors

In addition to the usual educational and public relations positions, people with expertise in communications may find interesting jobs in merchandising and advertising, including jobs such as those discussed in earlier career profiles as well as those in marketing services, which are discussed next. There are also interesting, related opportunities in communications and journalism, a career profile described in the next chapter.

To gain entry into this field, one must be able to show one's creative skills in a dramatic way by using effective letters of application, interesting résumés, and creative portfolios. The ability to write clearly, concisely and creatively is one of the best ways to be noticed and gain entry. In public relations the effective use of language is of paramount importance.

CAREER PROFILE

Marketing Services _____

Marketing services is a general term denoting highly specialized staff careers dealing with all aspects of marketing, including product development, market research, consumer research, advertising, promotion, and display. Some of these opportunities are investigating consumers' needs, developing products to meet those needs, and devising new advertising and visual merchandising (display) techniques. Students with family or consumer majors can qualify for specialized positions in marketing services, for example, majors in fashion merchandising, apparel design, interior design (display), textile science, consumer affairs, and family economics and home management.

Typical Job Titles

Typical job titles include the following:

- Market researcher
- Consumer researcher
- Marketing analyst
- Product development specialist
- Merchandising analyst
- Research scientist
- Technical affairs manager
- Advertising manager
- Account executive
- Publicity manager
- Promotions director
- Display director
- Visual merchandising director

Note that each of the job titles refers to a relatively narrow specialty of marketing services. Each requires special expertise and training, and no single major is good for all these careers.

Responsibilities

The responsibilities of marketing services jobs are as diverse as the job titles imply. In general, however, all marketing services positions have one responsibility in common: to support and assist all activities in the merchandising of products for the consumer. All these jobs promote the effectiveness and efficiency of a business's marketing.

Specialists in product development study consumers' needs and formulate new products to serve those needs. Market and consumer researchers study the actual consumers and users of products to learn more about what motivates consumers to buy products and how they use them. This information is then used to design new products and to create marketing programs such as advertisements, promotions, or displays. Merchandising analysts gather data for a store on trends in consumer buying and sales; this information is then used to identify successful products and to weed out those that are not. Advertising workers carry out many parts of an advertising program, including selecting the themes of advertisements, preparing scripts, doing the artistic work for advertisements, and selecting the media (television, newspapers, magazines, radio) for the advertisements. Visual merchandising and display workers are involved in all aspects of interior design. They are the artists who create a display, choose its components, and then construct the display.

As you can see, the responsibilities in marketing services vary. Each specialist is a part of the marketing team for the organization and performs a particular function. Some professionals gather and interpret information (e.g., product development specialists, merchandising analysts, marketing researchers). Others center on creative and artistic skills, (e.g., advertising specialists, copywriters, and display designers). Product developers require scientific and engineering knowledge as well as information about consumers' needs and tastes.

Qualifications

The qualifications required for entering marketing services are as diverse as the jobs themselves. However, many students majoring in fashion merchandising, design, and consumer affairs have entered many of these careers. Experience is often required for these positions, and courses in the appropriate areas (such as market research, art, design, or whatever the specialty may be) offer an advantage. All of these jobs can be technical and specialized, and additional education may be needed later.

Special Personal Qualities

Experience is a great asset to marketing services. By working as an assistant in any of these areas you gain background, contacts, and entry into the field. Because some of these areas are very competitive, especially those in advertising, experience often is the variable that will make you stand out from others. Gain experience by working in the entry-level jobs while you are in college, and this will give you leads into jobs when you graduate.

Other Factors

To succeed in marketing services, you must be creative and be able to respond quickly to change. For some fields such as market research and merchandising analysis, you must have mathematic skills, as interpreting statistical information is mandatory in these jobs.

In some of these jobs you will compete for advancement with business majors. To gain a competitive advantage over them, find jobs in product areas with which you are familiar. For example, if you majored in foods, use your knowledge of foods to secure a position in the foods industry. There are similar advantages for fashion majors, interior designers, and household equipment specialists. Your product knowledge, especially of its design and engineering, gives you an advantage over all other competitors (business or otherwise) in the field of marketing services. However, it is still necessary to be able to speak the language of business, and training in your specialized area (advertising, research, and so on) is still desirable.

One disadvantage of marketing services positions is that they are "staff" rather than "line" positions. Staff positions are advisory and rarely have final decision-making authority. Therefore, some professional do not look at staff positions as long-term careers but, rather, as stepping stones to line positions that will lead to upper management. Despite this bias against staff positions, marketing services careers do have good long-term prospects for family or consumer experts.

Questions and Exercises _____

1. Interview a manager in a business like a large department store or a small specialty store. Assess this career in terms of the following:
   - Typical job titles
   - Responsibilities
   - Qualifications
   - Working conditions
   - Advancement potential
   - Advantages and disadvantages
2. Describe the best personality for a successful manager.
3. How might the personal characteristics, skills, knowledge, and educational background of a successful retail buyer differ from those of a successful retail store manager?
4. Imagine yourself as a sales representative for an apparel manufacturer.

What steps would you follow in order to make a successful sale and ensure future success with your client?

5. How does a career in interiors merchandising differ from one in interior design (see Chapter 5)?

6. Using the help-wanted section of a local newspaper or a major newspaper like *The New York Times*, conduct a minisurvey of the local job market for persons interested in a career in any field described in this chapter. Include the following information:
   - Names of potential employers
   - Positions available
   - Procedures for employment application

7. What are some possible employers of consumer studies graduates, and what type of work could they find?

8. What human relations skills should graduates possess for success in a public relations career?

Bibliography _____

Arpan, Jeffrey S. *Opportunities in International Business Careers.* Lincolnwood, IL: VGM Career Horizons, 1989.

Ball, Victoria Kloss. *Opportunities in Interior Design Careers.* Lincolnwood, IL: VGM Career Horizons, 1988.

Barkley, Margaret V., and Elizabeth A. Monts. "Career Exploration in Hospitality and Recreation." *Illinois Teacher* 23 (March/April 1980), 207–208.

Burton, John R. "Employment Opportunities for Consumer Affairs Professionals," *Journal of Consumer Affairs* 10 (Summer 1976), 72–85.

Caldwell, Carol C. *Opportunities in Nutrition Careers.* Lincolnwood, IL: VGM Career Horizons, 1987.

Cohen, Harlow, and Eric H. Neilsen. "Finding and Developing Tomorrow's Top Managers," *Cornell Hotel and Restaurant Administration Quarterly* 29 (May 1988), 34–41.

Dahm, Ralph M., and James Brescoll. *Opportunities in Sales Careers.* Lincolnwood, IL: VGM Career Horizons, 1988.

Deen, Robert. *Opportunities in Business Communications.* Lincolnwood, IL: VGM Career Horizons, 1987.

Dolber, Roslyn. *Opportunities in Retailing Careers.* Lincolnwood, IL: VGM Career Horizons, 1989.

Dun's Marketing Services. *The Career Guide 1990: Dun's Employment Opportunities Directory.* New York: Dun & Bradstreet, 1990.

"Employment Firm Workers," *Chronicle Guidance* (Brief 402) (February 1988), 8–10.

Ethridge, Veree. "Consumer Education Outside the Classroom," *Illinois Teacher* 24 (March/April 1981), 184–187.

Folse, Nancy, and Marilyn Henrion. *Careers in the Fashion Industry.* New York: Harper & Row, 1981.

Fry, Ronald W., ed. *Marketing and Sales Career Directory,* 2nd ed. Orange, CA: Career Publishing, 1988.

Garman, E. Thomas. "Careers in Consumer Affairs," *Advancing the Consumer Interest* 2 (1990), 31–33.

Goss, Rosemary Carucci, Helen Wells, Savannah S. Day, and Robert J. Thee. "Residential Property Management: Potential for Career Opportunities," *Journal of Home Economics* 79 (Summer 1987), 46–48.

Guyette, Wayne C. "The Executive Chef: Manager or Culinarian?" *Cornell Hotel and Restaurant Administration Quarterly* 22 (November 1981), 71–78.

Hackett, Carole. "The Woman Food and Beverage Manager," *Cornell Hotel and Restaurant Administration Quarterly* 22 (November 1981), 79–85.

Haney, Peggy H. "Where Have All the Home Economists Gone?," *Illinois Teacher* 31 (September/October 1987), 9–12.

Henkin, Shepard. *Opportunities in Hotel and Motel Management Careers.* Lincolnwood, IL: VGM Career Horizons, 1985.

"Hotel or Motel Managers," *Chronicle Guidance* (Brief 350) (November 1987), 7–9.

"Image Consultants," *Chronicle Guidance* (Brief 625) (November 1989), 2–6.

Jackson, Gregg B., and Francine H. Meyer. *Evaluations of Firms and Professionals Who Provide Consumer Services.* Washington, DC: Washington Center for the Study of Services, 1981.

Johnson, Willis L. *Directory of Special Programs for Minority Group Members,* 4th ed. Garrett Park, MD: Garrett Park Press, 1986.

Key, Rosemary J., and Francille M. Firebaugh. "Family Resource Management: Preparing for the 21st Century," *Journal of Home Economics* 81 (Spring 1989), 13–17.

Lewis, Robert C. "Hospitality Education at the Crossroads," *Cornell Hotel and Restaurant Administration Quarterly* 23 (August 1982), 12–15.

Maresca, Carmela. *Careers in Marketing.* Englewood Cliffs, NJ: Prentice-Hall, 1983.

Mason, Jerry, and Bud Poduska. "Financial Planner or Financial Counselor: The Differences Are Significant," *The Journal of Consumer Affairs* 20 (Summer 1986), 142–147.

"Merchandise Displayers (Visual Merchandisers)," *Chronicle Guidance* (Brief 127) (November 1989), 10–13.

Myers, Cheryl. "Entry Level Competencies Needed by Interior Designers," *Journal of Interior Design Education and Research* 8 (1982), 19–24.

Nelson, Debra L., Karen L. Peterson, and A. Sherrill Richarz. "Child Care as a Consumer Issue," *Journal of Home Economics* 79 (Winter 1987), 5–8.

Oliverio, Michael A. "The Homemaker Rehabilitation Counselor," *Illinois Teacher* 24 (November/December 1980), 98–100.

O'Toole, Patricia. "Picking the Right Financial Planner," *Money* 13 (March 1984), 131–138.

"Personnel Administrators," *Chronicle Guidance* (Brief 258) (October 1987), 11–14.

Powell, James. *The Prentice-Hall Global Employment Guide.* Englewood Cliffs, NJ: Prentice-Hall, 1983.

"Probation and Parole Officers," *Chronicle Guidance* (Brief 277) (February 1987), 12–15.

"Public Opinion Researchers," *Chronicle Guidance* (Brief 583) (November 1987), 2–5.

"Public Relations Specialists," *Chronicle Guidance* (Brief 172) (April 1987), 10–12.

Rotman, Morris B. *Opportunities in Public Relations Careers.* Lincolnwood, IL: VGM Career Horizons, 1988.

Rutherford, Denney G. "The Evolution of the Hotel Engineer's Job," *Cornell Hotel and Restaurant Administration Quarterly* 27 (February 1987), 72–78.

Schmelzer, Claire D., Patricia S. Costello, S. Lynn Blalock, and Peggy S. Meszaros. "Baccalaureate Hotel, Restaurant, and Institutional Management Programs in Home Economics Units," *Home Economics Research Journal* 18 (September 1989), 53–60.

Shields, Rhea, and Anna K. Williams. *Opportunities in Home Economics Careers.* Lincolnwood, IL: VGM Career Horizons, 1988.

Steinberg, Margery. *Opportunities in Marketing Careers.* Lincolnwood, IL: VGM Career Horizons, 1988.

Traynor, William J. *Opportunities in Human Resources Management Careers.* Lincolnwood, IL: VGM Career Horizons, 1989.

Wayman, Wilbur S., Jr., and Patricia S. Wayman. "What Students in Accredited Interior Design Programs Learn About Business," *Journal of Interior Design Education and Research* 8 (1982), 25–27.

CHAPTER 7

Careers in Education and the Cooperative Extension Service

There are many well-established and important opportunities for graduates with degrees in home economics education or related educational majors like extension education, vocational education, family life education, and early childhood education. The principal careers are as vocational home economics teachers, adult education teachers, extension home economists, family life educators, and secondary home ecomomics teachers. In addition, there are many related educational careers as Head Start teachers, community aid home economists, consumer educators, curriculum specialists, daycare school administrators, educational material writers, elementary school teachers, 4-H youth development leaders, nursery school teachers, Peace Corps volunteers, rehabilitation educators, handicapped recreation specialists, VISTA workers, youth counselors, directors of senior citizen programs, child care consultants, and directors of drug and alcohol centers.

Your education degree is versatile and can lead to job opportunities in noneducation fields as well. Many of these are described in other chapters of this book, in such areas as child development, store management, real estate, insurance, consumer affairs, customer services, banking, food and appliance demonstration, public relations, social welfare services, financial counseling, and volunteer work. With additional schooling you can also become a guidance counselor, community college teacher, junior college teacher, university professor, rehabilitation specialist, research specialist, school administrator, vocational director, or state or school district supervisor of home economics education. These latter positions may require one to five years of classroom teaching experience, depending on the particular requirements in your state.

In this chapter, we discuss specific education-oriented possibilities, but these jobs are only suggestions of the many directions that a career in education and extension may take.

CAREER PROFILE

Preschool and Nursery School Education

One career path available to people with home economics education degrees is in preschool and nursery school education. In some states, home economics education certification is for grades K through 12. Home economics educators are best prepared to teach children good food habits, proper nutrition, sanitation, proper clothing, safety in the home, and to understand their changing bodies.

Typical Job Titles

As a preschool or nursery school educator, a person with a degree in home economics education is eligible for the following jobs:

- Private preschool teacher
- Kindergarten teacher

- Head Start teacher
- Handicapped or special needs teacher
- Preschool or nursery school manager
- Preschool or nursery school director
- Preschool or nursery school supervisor

Responsibilities

The role of the preschool teacher is to give children new learning experiences. Some of the topics taught are cooperation, punctuality, numbers, color, science, language, social studies, art, music, confidence building, personal hygiene, and self-care. The teacher must create an environment that encourages learning and studying.

The typical workday is from 8:00 A.M. to 3:00 P.M., Monday through Friday, for ten months. However, some school districts are implementing year-round educational programs. Some preschool programs have a morning session and an afternoon session with different students attending each. Much time is spent in parent conferences and in evaluating the students. Other outside-the-classroom responsibilities are preparing lessons and activity sheets and grading papers. Teachers spend much time standing, walking, kneeling, sitting, and moving about the room.

The preschool routine is structured, with the tasks and activities planned and precisely executed. Teachers look for creative ways of helping children learn, through class trips, speakers, and projects. They are responsible for the children's education and well-being in the classroom but help them learn new concepts and ideas.

A nursery school program is slightly different from a preschool program. Parents may bring their children to the nursery school and pick them up at their convenience. During the day, nursery school teachers have a routine, and the children begin the scheduled activities after arriving at the school. Nursery school teachers' responsibilities are similar to those of preschool teachers. However, the children are younger, as young as two months to five years. The majority of nursery school teachers' time is spent in the same room. Such teachers also work with other adults, university students, members of the community, parents, and other teachers and administrators.

Teaching in either a preschool or a nursery school is not routine. Every day is different. One may treat a skinned knee one day and be a referee between two or more children the next. This is an enjoyable career for those who like working with small children.

A nursery school or preschool director supervises the program, including ordering supplies and equipment, preparing and balancing the budget, counseling parents, hiring personnel, conducting staff meetings, planning meals and snacks, and working with the children.

Qualifications

To be a preschool or nursery school teacher, you need a bachelor's degree from an accredited institution in early childhood and child development. The courses generally taken for this major are from many fields, including math, science, English, art, child development, educational psychology, teaching methods, reading, educational foundations, and student teaching. If the preschool is part of a public school system, you must meet the state's certification requirements. Certification is not always necessary to teach in a private or parochial school or in a nursery school.

Volunteer experiences in the YMCA or YWCA, Girl Scouts, Campfire Girls, Boy Scouts, churches, schools, and day-care centers are helpful for entry into this career. After spending some time teaching in a preschool or nursery school, the teacher with administrative abilities may advance to principal, teaching supervisor, or to a community college or university position. All these positions require education beyond the bachelor's degree.

Special Personal Qualities

The personal qualities required include a genuine interest in and liking for children, the ability to get along well with children, patience, self-discipline, firmness, authority, self-respect, sense of humor, flexibility, a sense of fairness, a positive attitude toward learning, creativity, a fun-loving attitude, dependability, and competency in classroom management. One of the most important qualities a teacher must possess is a love for teaching and learning and the ability to communicate this love to the students. Equally important is the ability to see children as individuals with likes and dislikes, strengths and weaknesses.

Other Factors

The job prospects for teachers look promising through the late 1990s, with more openings than qualified applicants. The major source of job openings will be vacancies created by resigning and retiring teachers. However, stabilizing enrollments in some parts of the country may limit the number of new openings in those schools. There will be a growing need for nursery school and preschool teachers as the number of dual-career families grows. There are also more single parents today, and child-care and preschool programs for these children are a must. In addition, many businesses are becoming interested in or have already established child-care facilities on their premises for the children of their employees. Therefore, nursery and preschool teachers will be hired by these firms.

CAREER PROFILE

Elementary Education

Career options in elementary education are available to a person with a degree in home economics education or specialization in early childhood or child development education. Many elementary schools welcome home economics educators, and many schools are now hiring full-time home economists to teach in the primary grades. These teachers may teach in grades 1 through 6 and in a variety of subject matters. It is a truly versatile opportunity for an educator.

Typical Job Titles

Careers in elementary education include the following:

- Elementary teachers
- Elementary curriculum specialist
- Audiovisual consultant
- Health specialist
- Elementary home economics teacher

Responsibilities

Many of the requirements for and responsibilities of elementary teachers are the same as those for preschool and nursery school teachers. Elementary teachers work with students in kindergarten through sixth grade. Some schools have departments that allow teachers to teach specific subjects. A person with a home economics education degree is best qualified to teach good food habits, nutrition, sanitation, safety in the home, grooming, clothing and clothing care, decision making, responsibilities in the home, and to help children understand their changing bodies.

Elementary teachers cover more subject areas and are able to use more teaching strategies and media as childrens' attention span and knowledge increase. In addition, elementary teachers help children master the basic skills of reading, writing, spelling, speaking, and arithmetic. The emphasis is on personality and character development. Elementary teachers also participate in indoor and outdoor activities and work with other teachers and parents.

Many activities are carried out outside the classroom, including planning lessons, writing, grading papers, attending faculty meetings, supervising extracurricular activities, serving on faculty committees, and participating in workshops and in-service activities. One advantage for the elementary teacher is that aides and parent volunteers are available to assist in clerical work, prepare teaching aids, read to children, supervise lunch and playground activities, and assist with school projects.

The typical classroom environment is physically and personally demanding. Class sizes vary from twenty to thirty-five children, all of whom require more or less constant attention. Elementary teachers are constantly walking around the room and are on their feet most of the school day. Teachers are constantly communicating with their students. Generally teachers are in the same room with the same students throughout the school day. However, in some schools teachers teach a specific subject to all students in a particular grade and the teacher changes classrooms. In other schools, the students will change classrooms.

In addition to preschool teachers' responsibilities, elementary teachers counsel students regarding academic problems; prepare and administer tests; possibly teach many subject areas; supervise play, rest, and lunch periods; confer with other teachers; and participate in in-service education.

Like preschool teachers, most elementary teachers work from nine to ten months, with typical workdays from 8:00 A.M. to 3:30 or 4:00 P.M., Monday through Friday. Many work additional hours preparing the activities for the next day or grading their students' work. Parents want to know the progress of their children, and thus parent reports and conferences must be arranged. Schools also have open houses and other special events in which teachers participate. During the summer, many teachers take university courses to renew or upgrade their teaching certificate.

Qualifications

To qualify for certification in elementary education, you must have a four-year bachelor's degree from a teacher's education program in home economics education or education with a specialization in early childhood, elementary, or child development. You must also have satisfactorily completed student teaching and the prescribed education courses. Some states also require teachers to complete a program of graduate courses for certification.

The courses generally taken for this major are from many fields, including all the home economics subjects, art, science, math, English, reading, history, educational psychology, music, teaching methods, educational foundations, teaching skills in reading, writing, and communication, and student teaching.

After one to five years of experience in the classroom and additional university coursework, teachers may seek positions as principals or other positions in the school system. In addition, there are teaching careers in community colleges and universities.

Special Personal Qualities

Elementary school teachers must have a genuine interest in children, an ability to get along with them, patience, self-discipline, self-respect, a sense of humor, flexibility, a positive attitude toward learning, creativity, dependability, a desire to be part of children's educational and emotional development, and competence in classroom management.

Other Factors

Because of rising enrollments, opportunities for elementary school teachers are expected to increase over the next decade. Another source of job openings will be the replacement of resigning or retiring teachers.

CAREER PROFILE

Secondary Education _____

Most opportunities for home economics educators are at the secondary-school level. In secondary education, a vocational home economics teacher can teach general home economics (grades 7 to 12), vocational home economics (grades 9 to 12), or occupational home economics (grades 11 to 12). Also, there are opportunities in special education and working with handicapped students.

Typical Job Titles

There are many careers and job titles in this profession, as follows:

- Vocational home economics teacher
- Home economics teacher
- Occupational home economics teacher
- Guidance counselor
- Reading specialist
- Special needs or education teacher
- Educational therapist
- Vocational guidance counselor
- Home economics state supervisor

Administrative opportunities include the following:

- Department chairperson
- Vocational director
- Assistant principal
- Principal
- Assistant superintendent
- Superintendent
- Dean of students

With additional coursework you may become one of the following:

- Community college teacher
- Continuing education teacher
- University professor
- Educational researcher
- Curriculum specialist
- Curriculum researcher

Positions are also available in the national professional associations such as the American Home Economics Association and the Cooperative Extension Service (see the Cooperative Extension Service Career Profile in this chapter).

Responsibilities

Home economics educators teach in the specialized fields of clothing and textiles, interior design, child development, family life education, journalism, management principles and techniques, communication, foods and nutrition, housing and home furnishings, consumer education, and skills in professionalism and public relations. These courses are necessary to prepare young men and women for their future roles in society. Many teachers are also responsible for the important educational activities conducted through student clubs, including the Future Homemakers of America (FHA) and Home Economics Related Occupations (HERO)—the career-oriented dimension of home economics education.

Home economics educators engage in many classroom activities, home experiences, extracurricular activities, FHA and HERO youth organization events, simulated experiences such as those in day-care centers, and laboratory experiences—particularly in foods, nutrition, clothing, and textiles. They lead field trips, obtain guest speakers, and assign individual projects. They are responsible for either selecting or preparing many learning aids for classroom use, for example, filmstrips, manuals, computer-aided instruction, videotapes, study guide sheets, and worksheets. They also ensure that learning activities from the FHA and HERO are integrated into the classroom instruction.

Teachers must regularly update their skills through in-service education and college coursework. Thus, many teachers use their summers to attend college to upgrade their knowledge and skills or working or volunteering in businesses. The latter is being encouraged for certification renewal and also improves the community's relationship with the schools.

Because vocational home economics education is part of the vocational education program in most high schools and some junior high schools, the vocational home economics teacher may be employed on an extended contract to perform additional activities. Included among these activities are making home visits to view students' home projects, attending state and national education conferences, attending FHA or HERO activities, accompanying students to camps, and conducting leadership activities.

Most states have curriculum guides that outline the topics to be taught. The teachers prepare lesson plans and teaching activities based on these curriculum guides. Not only are the guides helpful in structuring the classes but they also are important because they outline the course content and competencies that students should achieve.

In addition to teaching assignments, there are many activities in which home economics teachers may participate. Among them are advising and counseling students; completing federal, state and local forms; grading and evaluating students; supervising extracurricular activities such as pep club, yearbook, prom committee, or cheerleaders; chaperoning dances or bus trips; selling or collecting tickets for sporting events; supervising study halls; speaking to community organizations; serving on community advisory boards and committees; assisting the county extension agent with such things as judging at the county fair and/or state fair; judging district and state FHA and HERO projects; serving dinner or food at various school functions such as school board meetings; consulting with other teachers, parents, and community members; preparing bulletin boards, displays, and exhibits; preparing for open houses; teaching minicourses in the school for several weeks on a specialized topic, such as financial planning or apartment and home renting versus buying; and shopping for classroom and laboratory supplies, particularly for the foods lab.

The home economics teacher's work varies from school district to school district. Some districts have split programs with a morning shift and an afternoon shift of teachers and students. Others have a rotating shift in which some start early; all are present from 10:00 A.M. to 2:00 P.M.; and a later group stays until 5:00 or 6:00 P.M.. To use the school buildings all year around, some schools are on a quarter system in which the teachers work for three quarters of the year. However, many work for the traditional nine to ten months.

Home economics education teachers may also teach adult classes in the evening. In most areas this is generally in addition to the school contract, and the teacher receives extra compensation.

Qualifications

To teach vocational home economics you must have graduated from an accredited four-year vocational home economics education program and received state certification. Certification programs vary among the states. Temporary certificates, good for one school year, are issued in an emergency or if a teacher is transferring with a valid certification from another state. Transferring teachers are generally given one year to obtain state certification. In addition, some states may require one year of graduate work before certification.

The typical courses for majors in home economics education cover a broad range of subjects. The general subjects are humanities, speech, chemistry, biology, and English. The specialized subjects are educational foundations, school law, educational psychology, teaching methods, student teaching, and concentrated courses in child development, family relations, clothing, textiles, housing, home furnishings, interior design, consumer science, foods, and nutrition.

If you are planning to teach in a different state from where you are attending college, you should find out the certification requirements. The *Manual on Certification Requirements for School Personnel in the United States* may be in the university library, or it can be obtained from the Superintendent of Documents, Washington,

DC. Another helpful publication is the *Requirements for Certification of Teacher, Counselor, Librarian, Administrator for Elementary School, Secondary School, Junior College* from The University of Chicago Press.

For some positions you will need additional university graduate courses or a master's degree. Administrative positions generally require one to five years of teaching experience, depending on the state's requirements, and advanced education is helpful or necessary.

Special Personal Qualifications

A secondary teacher needs special personal qualities: a desire to work with young people; an ability to motivate students; organizational, leadership, and administrative skills; communication skills; creativity; flexibility; adaptability; and patience. In addition, a teacher should be able to understand teenagers and how the adolescent mind works and have a caring personality. The teacher must work well with the other teachers and administrators.

Other Factors

In addition to teaching, secondary home economics teachers may diversify into related areas of education. These positions include educational therapist, special needs teachers, general guidance counselor, vocational guidance counselor, media specialist, curriculum specialist, and reading specialist. With experience and additional university coursework, you may seek any of the administrative or other positions listed in the Typical Job Titles section. There may also be openings for educational consultants who do a variety of activities such as writing curricula, leading workshops, helping a school district develop educational resources, presenting in-service education, or choosing equipment to purchase.

The number of people entering the teaching profession declined to record lows in the early to mid-1980s, probably as a result of the difficulties experienced by many teachers in the 1970s who were unable to find jobs and the teachers' low salaries. However, in the 1990s there will be a large demand for qualified teachers. National experts are predicting a general teacher shortage in the 1990s, and even now many school districts in some parts of the United States do not have enough teachers to begin or complete the school year. Clearly this means many job opportunities for qualified teachers.

CAREER PROFILE

Home Economics Occupations _____

Some vocational home economics education teachers teach occupational classes at the secondary level. In such a vocational program, teachers have primarily eleventh- and twelfth-grade students in specialized courses such as child care and food service. However, in some programs, tenth-grade students can enroll. These programs can be one, two, or three years in length. In addition to the classwork, students are placed in related jobs in the community. Thus they balance classroom instruction with an actual job.

Typical Job Titles

Some typical job titles follow:

- Occupational home economics teacher
- Food service teacher
- Clothing and apparel design teacher
- Human services teacher
- Child care teacher
- Home health aid teacher
- Housing and interior design teacher

The titles listed in the "Secondary Education" section are also relevant to an occupational teacher, including the service personnel and administrative positions.

Responsibilities

In addition to normal classroom responsibilities (see the Secondary Education Career Profile), occupational teachers visit potential employers, place students, and supervise students in work environments. Occupational teachers usually begin work a week before the school's starting date to make these visits and locate positions for the students. They often receive extra compensation for such additional responsibilities.

Some schools have more than one vocational home economics occupational program, for example, both child care and food service. In addition, the teacher advises the Home Economics Related Occupations (HERO) club. These activities are related to course content and integrated into the classroom. Students participate in this club to obtain relevant career experiences, leadership skills, and enriched classroom experiences.

Qualifications

Occupational teaching may require additional certification beyond the vocational home economics education certificate described in the Secondary Education Career Profile. To qualify for this certification you may need to complete the occupational education courses at the university and a specified number of working hours in the field or pass an Occupational Competency Exam. The specific requirements vary from state to state. For your state's requirements, see your home economics education professor or write your state's department of education certification office.

CAREER PROFILE

College and University Education _____

There are various career paths available as an educator in community colleges, technical colleges, four-year colleges, and universities. Persons in this career work with young adults who have elected to continue their education. They teach a highly specialized subject matter that requires advanced education and experience. This career also includes the opportunity to do research in one's field.

Typical Job Titles

Typical job titles include the following:

- Lecturer
- Instructor
- Assistant professor
- Associate professor
- Full professor

With some experience in the classroom, an educator may proceed to department chair and other administrative positions.

Responsibilities

The responsibilities of college teaching are varied. Typically, professors at colleges or universities teach six to twelve credits or units per semester or quarter, depending on whether they have an instruction appointment or a part-instruction and part-research position. A community college teacher may teach from twelve to sixteen credit hours per term. The college teacher teaches the students through lectures, demonstrations, laboratory periods, field trips, and other instructional settings.

In addition to teaching, other responsibilites are serving on committees, offering service to the community, serving on advisory boards, preparing radio or television spots, attending professional meetings, and keeping up to date by reading current literature.

For the university faculty members to be effective, they must also keep up with research and new developments in their fields. In research-oriented universities, faculty members become actively involved in conducting and publishing research. Such universities usually offer graduate programs as well, and research is conducted by teams of faculty members and graduate students.

Qualifications

A master's degree is required, and preferably a doctorate, to enter nearly all positions in higher education. In four-year colleges and universities, a doctorate in one's specialized field is required except in special situations. To advance into administrative positions, additional graduate work in administrative subjects, accounting, and higher education is helpful.

Some states have minimum requirements for two-year college teachers. For specific requirements, write to the director of two-year college education in the relevant state. This information can also be obtained from the latest edition of the *Community, Junior and Technical Directory.*

Special Personal Qualities

College and university professors must be able to present up-to-date information and explain its value to their students. Considerable intellectual ability is required to master this knowledge and the research techniques in most family and consumer disciplines. Being an effective teacher also requires many communication skills and the use of differing teaching strategies for each course and level. The job of a professor requires considerable time to prepare courses, read journals, conduct research, and write articles. Therefore, it is a demanding career that requires a wide range of skills that take years to learn.

CAREER PROFILE

Adult and Continuing Education

Adult education and continuing education programs offer adults opportunities to update and upgrade themselves. Adult education courses are informally offered by a wide range of community organizations, local government, and private groups. Usually these are non-credit courses. Continuing education is more formal and is offered by four-year colleges, universities, and some two-year institutions. These courses are often offered for credit and are attended by both degree-seeking and nondegree students. Programs encompass many subjects based on community needs or preferences. Among these are popular family- and consumer-oriented courses, ranging from personal finance and parenting to restaurant management and apparel store entrepreneurship.

Responsibilities

Careers are available for instructors in many subject areas. Courses usually deal with a specific subject matter such as child development, gourmet cooking, or a particular art form. Most adult and continuing education teachers are part-time teachers for their specific courses, although some have full-time jobs in their specialty. Responsibilities vary, similar to those for other teaching careers described in this chapter and depend on needs of the program as well as whether the teacher is a full-time or part-time employee.

Qualifications

Qualifications can be similar to those in the College and University Education Career Profile. A master's degree is desirable. However, note that advanced degrees are not mandatory to teach in this area—experience and expertise are more important. The teacher should enjoy teaching, be good at it, and be familiar with a subject area that is in demand by adult learners who are not necessarily seeking a degree.

CAREER PROFILE

Cooperative Extension Service _____

The Cooperative Extension Service is jointly administered and funded by federal, state, and county government. Its purpose is to communicate practical information to the public on a wide range of subjects, including home economics. Employees of the Cooperative Extension Service have expertise in many family and consumer subjects, such as clothing, personal finance, household equipment, child development, foods, nutrition, and family relations. They provide information and assistance to families through formal programs, the mass media, and personal contacts.

Typical Job Titles

Typical titles in the Cooperative Extension Service are

- Cooperative extension service agent
- County extension service director
- Regional extension service director
- Extension service program director
- State extension service specialist (for specific program areas)

In most cases extension service professionals specialize in one field, such as clothing, foods, or family relations.

Responsibilities

The Cooperative Extension Service provides information on the entire field of home economics, such as foods, nutrition, child development, child care, family relations, textiles, clothing, housing, and consumer science. The primary function of extension professionals is to plan, conduct, and evaluate educational programs on home economics and 4-H youth development. The objective is to help people enhance their quality of life. The agent brings to rural and urban families the latest information from home economics research. This information is disseminated through public programs, conferences, videos, news releases, bulletins, leaflets, brochures, pamphlets, and other literature. In addition, extension service agents answer questions or resolve problems through direct contacts with clients, either by phone or personal visits.

The activities of extension service agents are many and varied. Some agents lead youth programs of 4-H youth development or day camps for young people. Some present programs to homemakers on nutrition, financial planning, and child abuse. They may suggest economical menus, solutions for home-canning problems, ideas on buying and preparing foods, and answers to consumers' questions. An agent may be asked to visit an individual in the home to help solve a problem. Agents may also provide information in their area of specialization through a weekly newspaper column or a report on radio and television shows.

Extension service work is not a nine-to-five job, and the jobs are not boring, monotonous, or routine. There is no set pattern of tasks. A typical day may include a speech on consumer information, another speech on child care available in the community, answering questions that come in by telephone, advising a 4-H youth development club, taping a radio or TV program, and teaching a class. One day may be entirely in the office and the next entirely in the community. The job also carries responsibilities for helping volunteer groups, clubs, and other organized groups in the community.

Extension agents are located in both small towns and large cities. But their real office is in all the surrounding communities they serve. Agents may meet in a home, church, school, or community building where they present their demonstration or program. Although the work of the extension service has traditionally been in rural areas, urban and suburban residents now are calling for assistance. This need is creating new opportunities and clientele for the Cooperative Extension Service professional.

Qualifications

The qualifications for this field are similar to those for home economics secondary education. A bachelor's degree from a four-year institution is required, with an emphasis on home economics education, home economics extension, or a more specialized home economics major like family relations or clothing. Most agents concentrate on one subject area such as clothing, foods, or family economics. Experience in working with the public is worthwhile. Courses on program planning, communications, the media, and educational work with families are also desirable. Work experience in planning, delivering, evaluating, and reporting educational programs is useful.

Most states require extension directors and agents assigned to multicounty and state staffs to have at least one advanced degree.

University cooperative extension faculty members generally need a doctorate. Cooperative extension agents may also qualify for positions in the federal government with advanced education.

Special Personal Qualities

Cooperative extension agents need to be able to speak, write, and teach effectively. They are asked to analyze situations and solve problems. Keeping up to date on the latest research on one's subject is also important.

Cooperative extension agents must be organized and responsible, and they should be sympathetic, understanding, patient, and have a sense of humor. Finally, because they are continuously in contact with the public, good health and a neat appearance are desirable.

Other Factors

For a person who does not wish to live in a large city, extension work may be an ideal career. Most agents are assigned to a county and travel throughout that county, which means that much of the work is in suburban or rural areas. Depending on the county's population, several agents may be employed, and each may specialize in one or two areas of home economics.

CAREER PROFILE

Communications and Journalism _____

Can you express yourself clearly? Then maybe communications and journalism are for you. Career options in this field are available for individuals with degrees in home economics education and other family or consumer majors. Careers are found in the media as well as in business and governmental organizations. Because communications and journalism are often an educational activity—conveying information and knowledge—this can be the perfect career option for home economics educators.

Typical Job Titles

Typical job titles include the following:

- Advertising copywriter
- Assistant editor
- Public relations specialist
- Consumer affairs editor
- Newspaper feature writer
- Newspaper feature editor
- Educational materials writer
- Advertising account executive
- Educational television specialist
- Free-lance journalist
- Educational consultant

Responsibilities

All areas of communications and journalism have common responsibilities. Such specialists must communicate with their clients. They work with marketing specialists and researchers to analyze consumers' needs and wants. They demonstrate the use of their organization's product, and they may inform salespersons, market researchers, and others about their products. They communicate with others through many outlets and may be consulted for suggestions regarding the design of all communications by their organization.

Home economists with expertise in communications are employed by radio and television stations, advertising agencies, newspapers, magazines, government, publishing companies, public relations agencies, wire services, and professional journals. They prepare a variety of communications in the areas of interior design, foods, nutrition, textiles, clothing, budgeting, home management, housing, fashion, and home decoration. They convey to the public the new and current trends and how these may affect the individual and the family. They introduce new products, arrange products for photographs, prepare educational materials, write articles for the news media, travel as a representative of the company, design product packaging, prepare promotional strategies, and present programs such as children's story hours, forums, demonstrations, and talk shows. In addition, they may promote products, represent the consumer's viewpoint, recommend actions to the firm, and evaluate results. They also may be asked to supervise photography sessions.

To succeed in communicating, the specialist must be aware of the target audience and prepare scripts carefully. To hold an audience's attention, communications must be creative, dynamic, colorful, attractive and especially informative. Visual communications are particularly important, for example, giving demonstrations, showing samples of products, and providing illustrated resource materials or brochures.

Family- and consumer-oriented professionals also work in advertising for agencies, the media, manufacturers, retail firms, trade associations, and government. Their primary interest is to keep a product or service before the consumers and to present the consumers' interest to their business. They may be asked to develop a promotional campaign for a new or established product.

Those professionals who enter public relations may often travel to promote the company's product and use many communication strategies. Large companies generally have full-time public relations personnel, and the smaller companies may hire a public relations person on a part-time basis when it is time to introduce a new campaign or a new product.

As a specialized communicator, the educational television specialist combines education and broadcasting. This job requires planning and writing programs, developing television classes, and writing and presenting materials. Clearly this is a career in which a background in both education and communications is an asset.

Educators often make good copy editors because of their experience in writing and thinking clearly when presenting information to their learners. Some home economics teachers have full-time teaching positions and work part-time as editors for publishers, local newspapers, or radio or television stations.

Qualifications

A bachelor's degree and sometimes graduate work is desirable for a career in communications and journalism. Typical courses include English, history, speech, art, chemistry, radio and television, journalism, education, and technical writing. Specialized courses include child development, nutrition and food science, family relations, clothing, textiles, merchandising, home furnishings, household equipment, interior design, and consumer science. The broader your education is, the larger will be the range of subject matter in which you can be an effective communicator.

Other assets are practical experience in areas such as writing for your college or local newspaper, assisting with recruitment flyers, or providing career placement information. Experience in all types of communications ranging from drama groups to classes in public speaking is valuable as well.

Special Personal Qualities

Professionals in communications must express themselves clearly both orally and in writing; that is, they must have a good command of the English language. Other qualifications are organizational skills and creative and artistic abilities. These professionals are expected to combine subject matter competencies with communications skills when researching, planning, organizing, illustrating, exhibiting, and writing. Most firms have incorporated computer technology, thus communications specialists need to be experienced in word processing.

Communications specialists constantly deal with people and thus need good human relations skills. A pleasant and animated speaking voice is also desirable; audiences do not enjoy monotonous, boring voices.

Other Factors

People in journalism or communications must constantly meet deadlines, resolve urgent problems regarding their audience, handle all situations gracefully, and be able to attract an audience's attention. Night and weekend work may be required. Working hours can be long and variable, and the pressures to perform successfully are continuous.

Questions and Exercises _____

1. Choose a career in one of the following areas:
   - Preschool and nursery education
   - Elementary education
   - Secondary education
   - Home economics occupational education
   - College and university education
   - Adult and continuing education
   - Cooperative Extension Service
   - Communications and journalism

   Locate a practicing professional in that career and interview him or her to find out the following information:
   - Working conditions
   - Advancement potential
   - Advantages and disadvantages
   - Typical job titles
   - Responsibilities
   - Qualifications

2. Compare and contrast the work of a preschool teacher and an elementary teacher in terms of the following information:
   - Responsibilities
   - Qualifications
   - Working conditions
   - Advancement potential
   - Advantages and disadvantages
3. Observe a typical day in a secondary home economics classroom at a local high school. Compile an anecdotal record of your observations, including the following information:
   - Student activities observed
   - Teaching strategies observed
   - Student-teacher interaction observed

   Reflect on what you observed in the classroom in terms of the following:
   - Insights into teaching careers
   - Insights into yourself as a future teacher
   - Insights into human relations
4. Look up the certification requirements for secondary education in your state. Include the following information in the list of certification requirements:
   - Formal education needed
   - Experience required
   - Testing procedures for certification
   - Circumstances for temporary certification
   - Time required to obtain certification
5. How do the career responsibilities of a vocational home economics teacher, an occupational home economics teacher, and a general home economics teacher differ in secondary education?
6. Compare and contrast the work of a classroom home economics teacher (at any educational level) and a home economics extension agent in terms of the following:
   - Responsibilities
   - Qualifications
   - Working conditions
   - Advancement potential
   - Advantages and disadvantages
7. What are some possible employers of graduates with a communications and journalism emphasis, and what would they do in these organizations?
8. Discuss the issue of teacher testing for competency.

Bibliography

Beard, Marna L., and Michael J. McGahey. *Alternative Careers for Teachers.* New York: ARCO, 1985.

Bell, Camille G., and Sue Couch. "Workshop for Teachers of Occupational

Programs: A Model for Teacher Education," *Illinois Teacher* 25 (January/February 1982), 131–134.

Carlson, Jean B., and James R. Lockwood. "Human Service Educators in the Business World," *Journal of Teacher Education* 31 (September–October 1980), 27–30.

Coleman, Mick, and Chrystal Barranti. "Family Life Extension in the Twenty-First Century: Program, Operational, and Identity Challenges," *Journal of Home Economics* 80 (Winter 1988), 11–16.

Compton, Cheryl W., and Alyce M. Fanslow. "Entrepreneurship: A Career Opportunity for Home Economics Students," *Illinois Teacher* 24 (May/June 1981), 207–210.

Dohner, Ruth E. "Alternative Careers of Home Economics Education Graduates: A National Survey," *Journal of Vocational Home Economics Education* 4 (Spring 1986), 1–9.

————. "Home Economics Teacher Education: Preparing Graduates for Alternative Careers," *Journal of Vocational Home Economics Education* 4 (Spring 1986), 10–18.

Dun's Marketing Services. *The Career Guide 1990: Dun's Employment Opportunities Directory.* New York: Dun & Bradstreet, 1990.

Ethridge, Veree. "Consumer Education Outside the Classroom," *Illinois Teacher* 24 (March/April 1981), 184–187.

Evans, Rupert N., and Edwin L. Herr. *Foundations of Vocational Education,* 2nd ed. Columbus, OH: Merrill, 1978.

"Financial Aid Administrators (Education)," *Chronicle Guidance* (Brief 486) (March 1988), 8–10.

Fine, Janet. *Opportunities in Teaching Careers.* Lincolnwood, Ill.: VGM Career Horizons, 1989.

Gunn, Barbara A. "The Possible Dream: Older Americans and Home Economists—Year 2000," *Journal of Home Economics* 78 (Summer 1986), 18–21, 26.

Hall, Helen C., and Sandra W. Miller. "Home Economics Teacher Education into the 21st Century," *Journal of Home Economics* 81 (Summer 1989), 7–14.

Hawks, Leona K. "Day Centers for the Homeless: A Role for Home Economists," *Journal of Home Economics* 81 (Fall 1989), 33–37.

"Home Economists," *Chronicle Guidance* (Brief 105) (April 1987), 7–10.

Jackson, Gregg B., and Francine H. Meyer. *Evaluations of Firms and Professionals Who Provide Consumer Services.* Washington, DC: Washington Center for the Study of Services, 1981.

Johnson, Willis L. *Directory of Special Programs for Minority Group Members,* 4th ed. Garrett Park, MD: Garrett Park Press, 1986.

Kellett, Carol E. "Home Economics Education: Changes as We Approach the 21st Century," *Illinois Teacher* 32 (January/February 1989), 98–102, 106.

Lambert, Maureen S., and Kermeta "Kay" Clayton. "Preparing Home Economics Education Majors for Career Alternatives," *Journal of Vocational Home Economics Education* 3 (Spring 1985), 32–41.

Meszaros, Peggy S., Elaine Jorgenson, and Beverly Crabtree. "Home Economists as Educators: Linking Cooperative Extension and Vocational Education Systems," *Illinois Teacher* 25 (November/December 1981), 58–61.

Miller, Sandra W., and Karen Busch. "'Fresh Approach': Cooperation Between Home Economics and Vocational Rehabilitation," *Illinois Teacher* 31 (September/October 1987), 15–17.

Nelson, Debra L., Karen L. Peterson, and A. Sherrill Richarz. "Child Care as a Consumer Issue," *Journal of Home Economics* 79 (Winter 1987), 5–8.

Nelson, Linda. "International Dimensions and the Secondary Home Economics Program," *Illinois Teacher* 31 (November/December 1987), 64–65, 72.

Nies, Joyce I. "Faculty Development: An Imperative for the Nineties," *Journal of Home Economics* 82 (Fall 1990), 11–15.

Oliverio, Michael A. "The Homemaker Rehabilitation Counselor," *Illinois Teacher* 24 (November/December 1980), 98–100.

O'Neill, Barbara M., and Rita T. Wood. "Extension Home Economics: Past, Present, and Future," *Journal of Home Economics* 81 (Fall 1989), 38–40.

Osborn, Barbara L., and Linda H. Lewis. "Home Economics Education for Adults: Then and Now," *Journal of Home Economics* 75 (Fall 1983), 18–20, 60–61.

Parker, Frances J. *Home Economics: An Introduction to a Dynamic Profession*, 3rd ed. New York: Macmillan, 1987.

"Peace Corps Volunteers Combine Home Economics Skills to Address Third World Needs," *Journal of Home Economics* 79 (Summer 1987), 28–29, 51.

Peterat, Linda, and Linda Eyre. "Charting a Career Path—Voices of Home Economics Educators," *Illinois Teacher* 33 (March/April 1990), 158–160.

Powell, James. *The Prentice-Hall Global Employment Guide*. Englewood Cliffs, N.J: Prentice-Hall, 1983.

Rossmann, Marilyn Martin, Joanne Hunter Parsons, and Deborah Holman. "Career Alternatives for Home Economics Educators," *Journal of Home Economics* 75 (Spring 1983), 12–15.

Sain, Carol Akkerman. "Preparing Students to Teach Young Children, Adults and Special Needs Groups Through Preservice Education," *Illinois Teacher* 25 (January/February 1982), 128–130.

Selmat, Nevaleen Joy Schmitz. "Changing Role of Women," *Illinois Teacher* 25 (November/December 1981), 82–84.

Shields, Rhea, and Anna K. Williams. *Opportunities in Home Economics Careers*. Lincolnwood, IL: VGM Career Horizons, 1988.

Teemer, Gini. "Rationale for Family Life Education," *Illinois Teacher* 31 (March/April 1988), 164–168.

Thomas, Ruth G. "Home Economics in Secondary Education and the Development of Human Competence," *Journal of Home Economics* 77 (Fall 1985), 2–6.

Thomson, Joan S., Sue Buck, and Marilyn Herman. "Perspectives on the Future of Extension," *Journal of Home Economics* 81 (Spring 1989), 9–12.

Ware, Barbara Ann. "Vocational Home Economics: Preparation for Work as a Basic," *Illinois Teacher* 22 (May/June 1979), 276–282.

CHAPTER 8

Careers in Human Services

The twentieth century has proved to be a time of turbulence and rapid change for the American family. Consider all the trials and challenges that many families have had to face: economic uncertainty, unemployment, financial difficulties, marital problems, family violence, divorce, remarriage, aging, care for the handicapped, care for the disadvantaged, welfare for the indigent, and management of the stresses of daily life. Along with these ever-present problems of family life, new challenges continually surface: the homeless, AIDS, dual-career families, "latchkey" children, displaced

174

homemakers, and the growing "age wave" of senior citizens to name a few. Being a humanitarian nation, the United States has created many institutions to serve these needs and solve these problems: service agencies, hospitals, nursing homes, hospices, child-care centers, halfway houses, camps, and numerous other service facilities. From these human services have been born some of the most rewarding and satisfying career opportunities for family-oriented professionals.

A variety of college majors can lead to these careers. In this chapter we focus on how established programs in such majors as child development, human development, family relations, family economics, family studies, and home economics can be springboards to careers in the human services. Keys to a successful career in human services include obtaining (1) a foundation of courses in family and child studies; (2) supportive general courses in the behavioral sciences, especially psychology and sociology; (3) specialized education in humanitarian subjects such as human relations, counseling, family financial management, rehabilitation, social welfare, cultural diversity, and the design of products for the disabled (clothing, housing, interior design); and (4) work experiences and volunteer assignments in service-oriented professions. In addition, for some family professions such as clinical practices or marriage and family counseling, graduate education is necessary.

Eight general career areas are included in this chapter: child development, adolescent services, marriage and family counseling, family financial planning and counseling, social welfare, rehabilitation, international development, and the administration of human services. The services provided in each of these careers differ dramatically, but they all have the common thread of being "helping" professions, professions dedicated to giving assistance to those with special problems and needs.

CAREER PROFILE

Child Development

A career in child development can include many different specializations dealing with the health, education, and welfare of children of all ages. The goal of all occupations in this field is to improve children's physical, emotional, and educational well-being.

Typical Job Titles

Typical job titles in child development include the following:

- Child welfare professional
- Child psychologist
- Youth programs director
- Preschool director
- Preschool teacher
- Elementary school teacher
- Child mental health specialist
- Camp director
- Day-care center director
- Day-care teacher
- After-school program director
- Childlife therapist
- Guidance counselor
- Recreational specialist

As these titles indicate, there are opportunities in schools, public service agencies, camps, churches, community organizations, YMCA and YWCA, Boy Scouts, and Girl Scouts.

Responsibilities

The responsibilities are varied in these careers. In general, specialists in educational careers help children in their early social, physical, and intellectual development. Children need to learn to appreciate their bodies, eat regularly, enjoy relaxing, rest when necessary, and play with other children. Teaching social skills such as cooperation, friendship, and communication is also an important task of the specialist. In the early school years, reading, writing, arithmetic and an introduction to the arts and sciences are the modern curriculum. Educators must understand the world from the child's viewpoint, explain the world in words that children can understand, and help children develop their abilities.

Child psychologists and child mental health specialists have different responsibilites. They identify problems faced by children, counsel them, and advise parents on child rearing. This is a complex profession that requires special tasks and training. In some cases these specialists must deal with emotionally disturbed children and neglected or abused children, and often they must refer children and parents for appropriate therapeutic or psychological assistance.

Professionals participating in day-care programs or related service programs for children have their own responsibilities. Day care involves such routine activities as managing the eating, sleeping, health care, and recreational needs of young children. In addition, day care has an educational function, including learning activities and games in which children need to be involved. Day care is more than the custodial care of children; it is an important part of their intellectual and personal development. The best day-care programs are those catering to the full range of children's intellectual and emotional needs.

Careers in children's services can also be as a youth program director (e.g., with the YMCA or YWCA), camp director, or recreational specialist. The major task in directing such services is to plan and execute meaningful activities for young children. This task means identifying the ages and aptitudes of client groups and devising activities appropriate to each level of social and personal development. It requires a knowledge of both the physical and mental capabilities of children. Because the contact with many children is almost continuous in this occupation, it also requires the ability to understand children and communicate with them in a warm and pleasant manner. Finally, it requires a knowledge of children's games, sports, activities, current reading interests, and other aspects of children's lives.

Qualifications

Education in child development is extremely valuable for this career. Other appropriate majors are family relations and home economics. For certain specialized careers such as child psychology and therapy, advanced education is needed as well. Recommended courses include human development, child development, preschool education, early childhood education, educational psychology, personality psychology, and human motivation. A solid background in other behavioral sciences adds to these credentials. For those students headed toward administrative or managerial careers in such settings as day-care centers or service agencies, a background in management and accounting can also be helpful. Finally, courses in recreation, counseling, and rehabilitation are helpful.

Special Personal Qualities

One quality that is essential for the child development specialist is having empathy and love for children. As in all the helping professions, the specialist must also have that special desire to help others. It is also necessary to have a high degree of maturity, patience, and persistence. Learning and development occur at varying rates in children and often very slowly. This is when patience and maturity are needed.

At times the psychological demands of careers in child development can be substantial, especially in situations in which children have serious social or emotional difficulties. Successful professionals overcome this distress by knowing that they are contributing to the children's health and welfare.

It is also necessary to get along well with children and communicate well with them. Creating a warm and human environment, an environment in which children know they are wanted and appreciated, is the key to success.

Other Factors

There are career opportunities beyond the traditional professions of child development. For example, you may consider creating children's toys, educational games, and educational materials, or retailing children's products. Many stores have children's departments that sell products besides clothing and toys. And a growing range of specialty stores focus on the retailing of books, toys and other products strictly for children.

There are also opportunities to start businesses such as child-care centers and day-care programs. Other opportunities are developing educational programs for parents with young children. Or one may start a career by volunteering time to support a children's service agency, a crisis center for children, a Girl Scouts or Boy Scouts program, Big Brothers/Big Sisters, or other community program for children. Not only does volunteering offer personal self-satisfaction, it can also lead to a career serving children.

CAREER PROFILE

Adolescent Services _____

Growing up is more difficult than ever before. Perhaps you remember all the challenges of your adolescent years: succeeding at your school education, forming a positive self-image, making friends, avoiding the temptations of drugs and alcohol, learning to deal with sexual relations, discovering the adult world, taking greater responsibility for your life, and making decisions for yourself. Such are the makings of many problems in adolescent life, but fortunately there are many professional services to help teenagers and young adults solve their problems.

Typical Job Titles

Among the typical job titles in adolescent services are the following:

- Guidance counselors
- Therapists
- Social welfare workers
- Human relations specialists
- Adolescent service specialists
- Youth service workers
- Program directors

Programs specializing in the problems of adolescence exist in such places as government service agencies, hospitals, and counseling agencies such as adolescent care centers, pregnancy centers, Planned Parenthood centers, and halfway houses. There also are programs for adolescent problems such as juvenile delinquency, alcoholism, drug abuse, and pregnancy.

Responsibilities

The responsibilities of a career in adolescent services are similar to those of child development specialists. However, there is one important exception. The stage of development known as adolescence is characterized by considerable turbulence that is created by both the adolescent's changing physical body and the new responsibilities and decisions that are a part of modern adolescent life. It takes special empathy and understanding of such problems to achieve success in any adolescent service.

Careers in educational services for adolescents require a knowledge of the stages of adolescent growth and development. In early adolescence (typically the early teens), physical changes and entry into a larger social environment dominate an adolescent's life. In later adolescence come thoughts of adult life, testing of adult roles, and socialization in the adult world.

Professionals in counseling programs help young persons to understand themselves better—their personalities, characteristics, interests, achievements, educational needs, and career opportunities. Specialists in counseling offer advice on these and many other developmental activities. Counselors must also recognize problems and refer adolescents to the appropriate agencies when such a course is warranted.

Many adolescent services have specialists in handling juvenile delinquency, teenage pregnancy, drug abuse, alcohol abuse, educational difficulties, and employment difficulties. Their primary duty is to understand the particular problem and the methods for preventing or solving it. Such specialists must be able to recognize the causes of these problems. For example, what encourages the high rates of teenage pregnancy in some populations? Is it peer pressure, escapism, a desire to make a statement of personal maturity, or something else?

Although specialized knowledge is important to each adolescent service, some general responsibilities apply to all occupations in this field. First, perhaps the biggest challenge is to help the adolescents recognize that a problem exists. This can be the largest challenge because it can be difficult to convince an adolescent that he or she has a problem with, for example, drugs, alcohol, school, pregnancy, or peer relations. A second task is to gain the adolescent's respect by communicating and showing empathy. A third responsibility is to help find a solution, and finally, to monitor the adolescent's progress toward this solution.

Qualifications

A degree in child development, family relations, or a related area is desirable for entry into adolescent services. Courses in child development, adolescence, human relations, and counseling and guidance are important. Specialized courses in such areas as rehabilitation, criminal justice, and substance abuse may be necessary for certain careers. Graduate education, although not mandatory for all occupations, can be helpful. For those students interested in school guidance and counseling, teaching certificates or other certifications may be required. Check with your state and local school districts for their requirements.

Experience can also help. Internships in human service agencies are valuable, especially if your experience is with adolescent groups. If internships are not available, you can still make voluntary work experiences part of your school education and perhaps earn credits in independent study or other special credit courses.

Special Personal Qualities

Patience and the desire to help are paramount in this occupation. Understanding and concern for adolescents, particularly their emotional problems, are necessary. The ability to motivate adolescents is also needed. Often it helps to have a forceful personality, given the reluctance or defiance of some adolescents. Indeed, many adolescents who need help do not want it and may even resist it (sometimes violently). Being able to deal with such situations constructively is crucial.

Working in adolescent services also means working with others — with the family, employers, welfare service agencies, and perhaps law enforcement agencies. Thus, communication skills and enjoyment of working with others are useful.

Other Factors

The emphasis in adolescent services is often on preventing problems as well as on solving them. Thus, there is a growing demand for educational programs devoted to discouraging problems such as dropping out of school, delinquency, alcohol abuse, and drug abuse.

There are jobs for youth services workers in vocational schools, middle schools and high schools, children's homes, substance abuse hospitals or facilities, homes for teenage mothers, residence halls, and other living facilities. Opportunities can also be found in working with the retarded and handicapped, a subject covered in a career profile later in this chapter.

CAREER PROFILE

Marriage and Family Counseling _____

Professional counseling in marriage, family life, and child development has become an important helping profession in our society. Marriage and family counselors are professionally trained in understanding, explaining, and resolving personal problems, social problems, marital problems, family violence, and educational development. Some counselors may concentrate on economic and financial matters, as explained in the later career profile on family financial planning and counseling. The goal of family counseling is to increase the quality of family life and the stability of the family unit. Many counselors also specialize in leading individuals and families into more productive life-styles, thereby avoiding problems before they occur.

Typical Job Titles

Typical job titles in counseling include the following:

- Marriage counselor
- Family life counselor
- Marriage and family counselor
- Child psychologist
- Counseling psychologist
- Counseling therapist
- Teen parent educator
- Family therapist

These are professional positions for which advanced education is necessary. In addition, there are paraprofessional positions in counseling. Paraprofessionals assist professional counselors, such as those just mentioned. These assistants' job titles include the following:

- Mental health assistant
- Psychiatric assistant
- Psychological technician
- Social services assistant
- Human relations specialist

Many of these jobs are found in government, service organizations, and counseling agencies.

Responsibilities

Counselors' and therapists' major responsibility is to identify their clients' problems, help them understand these problems, discuss alternative solutions with them, and lead them to a solution. Clients range from couples with marital problems to young children with problems with their parents.

A second task is to conduct educational and training programs. Many counselors advocate this proactive approach to counseling as a way of avoiding problems. Program counselors may offer premarital counseling, parent education, or occupational or vocational training. Many counselors are interested in family financial and economic counseling (see the next career profile).

Some of the family problems that counselors confront are serious, such as child abuse, spouse abuse, divorce, emotional problems in children, substance abuse, and financial difficulties. Such problems threaten the very existence of the family and the lives of its members. Therefore, the professional counselor must help the individual or family members understand their difficulties and arrive at a solution in the best interest of all. This outcome can be accomplished only by the most sensitive, empathetic, and persuasive of counselors.

Qualifications

The starting place for education in counseling is in child development, family relations, psychology, sociology, and related areas. A degree in child development, family relations, or home economics is among the credentials for entry-level positions as paraprofessionals or professional aides. For professional positions and to obtain necessary professional certifications or licences as counselors, clinicians, or therapists, a master's or Ph.D. degree is usually necessary. However, a professional without a doctorate can qualify for some positions in community organizations, agencies, and social service programs run by government or private service groups.

In addition to courses in child development, family relations, and related behavioral sciences, training in counseling, guidance, educational psychology, human relations, personnel management, and family finances is desirable. Those students wishing to specialize in a particular area, such as child psychology or financial advising, should take courses in that area.

Special Personal Qualities

Counseling requires a special personality that includes extreme patience, maturity, empathy, understanding, an even temper, and emotional control. A counselor must be able to build positive relations with clients and adapt his or her personality to the situation at hand in whatever way is necessary to obtain the client's confidence. This may require seriousness at one time, a sense of humor at another, and forcefulness of personality at yet another.

Counseling is a communicative profession. Counselors have to be able to express themselves in words that people with different educational levels, cultural backgrounds, and mental abilities can understand. They have to be experts at persuasive communication and at helping the client understand their viewpoints. A counselor also must be a good listener. The counselor must induce clients to express their problems and then interpret them. This ability requires concentration and mental stamina.

Good counselors create a feeling of security, comfort, and safety in their clients. Those who establish this rapport are likely to have satisfied clients who act on the counselor's advice.

Other Factors

In some fields of counseling, such as clinical or counseling psychology, it is necessary to meet certification or licensing requirements. To obtain such certifications, advanced education leading to a doctorate in psychology is required.

Counselors work in a wide range of settings, from social service agencies and governmental organizations to private practices. Some specialize in a particular area, such as child guidance, school counseling, marriage, or financial counseling. Some write newspaper columns, magazine articles, and books for the general public on marriage, family life, family finances, personal development, lifestyles, stress, and sexual relations. Some companies have written self-help software for use on personal computers; these programs counsel individuals on their personal computers in the privacy of their homes. Other applications of computers to counseling are personality or vocational counseling tests that give clients instant feedback during their counseling. These examples indicate that counseling can be a varied occupation that may appeal to many professional interests.

CAREER PROFILE

Family Financial Planning and Counseling _____

A new and growing field for careers is in the general area of family financial services. Two careers in this field are family financial planning and family financial counseling. Students who find this field to be of interest should also consider the related field of consumer affairs (see the Consumer Affairs Career Profile in Chapter 6).

Typical Job Titles

There are two general job titles in this profession, as follows:

- Family financial planner
- Family financial counselor

Professionals in this field can also become one of the following:

- Investment advisers
- Insurance representatives

- Credit counselors
- Loan officers
- Family financial specialists
- Financial consultants
- Bankruptcy trustees
- Rehabilitation program advisers

Responsibilities

A family financial planner assesses a family's financial needs and goals and then helps them decide on financial strategies to achieve their goals. Often this means drawing up a financial plan for the family that spells out the means of reaching these financial goals, such as investments, savings programs, trusts, retirement income programs, insurance, consumer credit, and banking.

Financial planners must have expertise in many financial services in order to advise families. Often they will be licensed or have specialized training in one or more specialities, for example, stock investments, insurance, and credit counseling. The most successful financial planners have a general knowledge of many financial investments and management practices in order to advise clients on the wide range of alternative financial strategies. However, some planners specialize in a particular area, such as insurance, tax shelters, or mutual funds. They sell only the product in which they specialize, and in such cases planners have an ethical obligation to ensure that the particular product they are selling is appropriate to the client's needs and goals.

A family financial counselor is different from a planner. Counselors deal with families' financial problems, such as difficulties with consumer credit and debts. In many respects a financial counselor is similar to a marriage counselor: a professional who helps families solve their problems.

A family financial counselor needs many skills. Not only must the counselor understand the family's financial problems but he or she must also be familiar with many areas of general family crisis counseling. The reason for this is that families' economic and financial problems often become entangled with other problems such as family disagreements, violence, and divorce. Indeed, financial counselors face some of the most serious problems of family life, for many of the problems that families face today have economic or financial roots.

Professionals in family financial planning and counseling must gather data on all aspects of family finances (assets, liabilities), identify goals or problems, and assist the family to reach these goals or resolve these problems. The successful family financial adviser must balance the family's needs with its financial ability to obtain income and manage its financial resources effectively. Planners and counselors must understand the family's financial constraints and help the family to work within them.

Qualifications

Academic majors in such areas as consumer studies, family resource management, home management, family economics, and consumer economics can lead to careers in family financial services. Some universities offer courses on family financial planning and counseling, including training in family finance, budgeting, investments, insurance, and banking. In addition, majors in home economics and family relations can be useful for entering this career.

Whatever the major, courses should include consumer affairs, consumer behavior, family economics, consumer education, family resource management, accounting, investments, banking, taxation, estate planning, and insurance. Concentration in such fields as personal finance, family financial management, and counseling is helpful, as are courses in human relations, family relations, and economics.

Special Personal Qualities

Because financial planning and counseling require much face-to-face contact with clients, such specialists must have good interpersonal skills. They must be able to communicate effectively with clients and to show them how various financial management strategies can help them. Most of the special personal qualities discussed in the marriage and family counseling career profile are also relevant to this field.

The ability to work with numbers is essential to success in this field. Planners must be able to calculate a variety of financial statistics, using basic arithmetic such as ratios and percentages. In addition, they must be able to explain financial data to their clients.

Other Factors

The careers of family financial planning and counseling have been growing rapidly in the 1980s and 1990s, as have spin-off services such as credit counseling, insurance counseling, tax planning, and retirement and estate planning. The field is becoming increasingly professional as organizations such as the International Association for Financial Planning develop standards for professional practice.

For the broadest range of career opportunities, it is desirable to become well versed in many financial and economic subjects. Therefore, students interested in a career in family financial services should take courses in economics, accounting, personal finance, investments, banking, consumer credit, insurance, and tax policies. This broad knowledge will open careers either as a general financial planner or counselor or as a specialist in a particular area such as banking or insurance. Also, this is a career for which regular updating and refinement of skills will be necessary, for the financial investment strategies for families are always changing. What is appropriate strategy for financial management today can be totally inappropriate tomorrow.

CAREER PROFILE

Social Welfare

Social welfare is a generic term for many careers in the social services devoted to helping people with special needs. These services include the specialized professions of child development, adolescent services, and family counseling described earlier, and many others as well, such as aid to families with dependent children, employment counseling, unemployment compensation, displaced homemakers, senior citizens, child abuse, family violence, meal services for the needy or handicapped, community recreation, community charity, and a host of others. All offer career prospects for the socially concerned professional.

Typical Job Titles

Careers in social welfare include professional and paraprofessional opportunities. Typical job titles include the following:

- Health and welfare aide
- Social service aide
- Psychiatric aide
- Recreational worker
- Community service worker
- Human relations specialist
- Employment counselor

- Program services director
- Gerontologist

Positions can be found in youth groups, community action groups, senior citizen groups, retirement homes, adult day-care centers, convalescent homes, hospitals, youth homes, rehabilitation centers, mental health organizations, employment offices, schools, education centers, and orphanages.

Responsibilities

The principal responsibility of social welfare professionals is to help individuals with special needs or problems. Usually professionals work with a particular group of clients such as displaced homemakers, the unemployed, or senior citizens. The variety of activities can range from helping families cope with psychological or interpersonal problems to teaching individuals about health, nutrition, child care, and money management.

Social welfare professionals frequently assist clients in their psychological and social development to build a positive self-image, self-esteem, and social competence. These results are achieved through counseling or educational sessions with clients and by joining with professionals such as psychologists and social workers when professional interventions or consultations are indicated. Social welfare paraprofessionals must be sensitive to their clients' needs and call for assistance from other professionals when appropriate.

When working with other professionals, social welfare professionals often supervise programs for clients. For example, if a professional financial counselor recommends a program of money management as a solution to family economic problems, a social service assistant might work with the client on actual budgeting, checkbook management, shopping, or other money management skills.

Qualifications

A degree in such fields as child development, family relations, social welfare, or home economics provides excellent credentials for social welfare professionals. Majors in consumer affairs, family economics, nutrition, and dietetics also offer needed skills.

Education for a social welfare career should include courses in psychology, sociology, communications, counseling, education, child development, family relations, gerontology, personal finance, family economics, and human relations. Advanced degrees can be an asset as well. Graduate degrees in social work or the ministry may be necessary in some situations.

It is useful to gain experience in this field while in college, either through volunteer work or internships. Good jobs for volunteers can be found in social service agencies, mental health agencies, youth organizations, orphanages, and the social service programs of local government.

Special Personal Qualities

The same personal qualities mentioned in the preceding career profiles are appropriate to all social welfare workers. The desire to help, empathy, and an ability to communicate are important. Maturity, patience, and understanding are also needed.

Human service and social welfare workers may work under great pressure, because the number of human problems is large, and some problems may seem unsurmountable. This is not an occupation for the easily discouraged but for optimistic people who truly wish to help. It can be a satisfying profession.

Other Factors

In the past, social service agencies have sprung largely from government or community organizations. However, businesses and labor unions may be important supporters of social welfare programs in the future. Certainly businesses and unions have an interest in the welfare of their employees or members and an increasing awareness of their social responsibilities as providers of social services. Perhaps one of the greatest contributions a social welfare professional could make is to inspire the development of new programs in these settings. For example, many businesses provide such family services as day-care centers, fitness centers, financial planners, and courses in time and stress management.

We are continually recognizing new social needs in our society. For example, social welfare specialists have recently noticed the growing problems of displaced homemakers and "latch-key" children. Another emerging field is gerontology, including such diverse specialties as gerontological nutrition, adult day care, and retirement planning. Social welfare is the profession responsible for identifying problems and helping provide solutions.

Social problems that should grow in the future are those dealing with senior citizen services (senior citizens are a growing percentage of the population), retirement programs, and employment counseling for persons seeking new careers (e.g., people laid off in a declining industry and those requiring job retraining). Finally, more social programs will be aimed toward the healthy and well, for example, adult education programs and recreation and leisure programs.

CAREER PROFILE

Rehabilitation

Rehabilitation is a specialized subarea of social welfare. Professionals in rehabilitation carry out a wide range of specialized activities to help disabled or disadvantaged individuals lead as normal a life as possible. Professionals work with the physically handicapped, mentally handicapped, low-income groups, or other client populations that require special help to overcome a handicap. Such activities may be counseling, physical therapy, and the design of special clothing to fit the needs of people with physical handicaps or deformities.

Typical Job Titles

Specialists in rehabilitation work have a variety of titles, including the following:

- Rehabilitation counselor
- Occupational therapist
- Psychiatric technician
- Home economist in rehabilitation
- Educational therapist
- Corrections officer
- Youth services director
- Product designer — clothing for the handicapped
- Product designer — barrier-free interior design
- Probation officer
- Parole officer

Some careers require special licensing or special education.

Responsibilities

In general, a rehabilitation professional works with other professionals such as physicians, counselors, and psychologists to solve problems of the handicapped or disadvantaged individual. Each member of the team has a specialized role and is considered the expert to whom others of the team look for advice and leadership. The problems of the disadvantaged and handicapped are usually complex, and no team member alone can resolve them.

A rehabilitation counselor is usually the first to make contact with clients needing assistance. Counselors explore clients' needs, determine what professional specialists may be needed, and develop rehabilitation programs. Sometimes counselors work exclusively with a particular type of client, for example, the blind, mentally ill, alcoholic, or drug addicted. Another type of rehabilitation counselor, the parole officer or correction officer, counsels those who have been released after being incarcerated for crimes. These counselors give assistance in locating jobs, obtaining necessary educational skills, developing positive family relations, and adjusting to a new life-style. This assistance requires having regular meetings with the client (parolee) and ensuring that he or she is making a satisfactory and socially desirable reentry into society.

Some specialists focus on certain aspects of a rehabilitation program. A psychiatric technician works with patients and families to help individuals understand themselves and take charge of their lives. An educational therapist identifies an individual's educational needs through counseling and testing and develops a program to fit that person's educational needs. An occupational therapist identifies particular aptitudes or skills that individuals can use to get a job and helps individuals learn new job skills. A home economist in rehabilitation might specialize in teaching family living skills such as budgeting, nutrition, and family relations. Learning such skills is important to rehabilitating the disabled and the disadvantaged into being successful individuals in society.

New opportunities in rehabilitation serve the physical needs of the handicapped. Designing clothing and barrier-free interiors and furniture for the handicapped are examples. Professionals with backgrounds in such fields as apparel design, interior design, and housing are well qualified. The major responsibility of these professional designers is to recognize that the handicapped and disadvantaged individuals want products similar to those in the larger society about them. Products need to be designed with these special needs or disadvantages in mind but at the same time must not single out or identify the handicapped and disadvantaged persons as being different from others. The handicapped want to live as the non-handicapped do, and the responsibility of rehabilitation specialists is to help them achieve this goal.

Qualifications

Education in child development, family relations, home economics and other family- or consumer-oriented majors can lead to careers in rehabilitation. A broad selection of courses in the behavioral sciences, counseling, guidance, human relations, special education, mental health, abnormal psychology, and the physiology of physical disorders is required. Each field of rehabilitation may also have its own educational requirements.

In addition, advanced education may be required in some specialties, especially in the counseling professions and in mental health rehabilitation. Licenses or certifications may also be required in some states. Check into these requirements for any specialization that interests you.

Special Personal Qualities

A career in rehabilitation requires the special qualities of human services workers that we have seen in previous career profiles. Most important, rehabilitation specialists must be emotionally stable and patient, for they work with clients who are in desperate circumstances or who have severe physical or mental disabilities. Balancing this strain, however, is the pleasure of helping people in need and seeing them achieve greater self-sufficiency and satisfaction.

Other Factors

Some rapidly growing rehabilitative services are creating new career opportunities. Examples are clinics that help drug abusers, alcohol abusers, smokers, and dieters. These rehabilitative programs are run by community service agencies, hospitals, and private groups. Today there is a great demand for self-help and self-improvement programs, and this demand can lead to new opportunities for people with backgrounds in rehabilitative services.

Other rehabilitative services include groups serving war veterans, research institutes developing products to meet the needs of the physically handicapped, and businesses specializing in products for the handicapped. In addition, new industries are springing up to provide for the needs of the handicapped in recognition of the fact that the handicapped and disadvantaged are a large proportion of our population and that their needs can be served effectively by businesses as well as public service agencies.

CAREER PROFILE

International Development _____

There are opportunities for human services professionals to work in international development throughout the world. There is a great need for human services and human welfare on all continents but particularly in the Third World countries, the less-developed nations. The same human services needed in the United States are needed in other countries as well and often more desperately. The settings in which international development specialists work can be far different from those in the United States and approaches to solution of human problems can also be different, given cultural and language differences. These differences should not be considered drawbacks; a job in international development is a chance to expand one's awareness of the world while helping others.

Typical Job Titles

Typical job titles for international development specialists are the following:

- Peace Corps volunteer
- Foreign service officer
- Foreign government consultant
- Development specialist
- Government liaison officer
- International consultant

There also are positions in merchandising or international relations with businesses and trading companies that export or import consumer products. Many of the jobs described in Chapter 6 may be available in these branches of international business.

Responsibilities

Because careers in international development can be diverse, it is hard to typify the profession as a whole. Volunteering for the Peace Corps is one of the most challenging positions a person can choose. Peace Corps volunteers work in villages and rural areas in underdeveloped countries and attempt to improve the people's health, education, and personal welfare. The volunteers' specific tasks range from setting up public health projects and teaching cooking skills and nutrition to encouraging better health practices, teaching child development skills, and training villagers in crafts and gardening. Volunteers may also train other paraprofessionals, or change agents, who will take over when the Peace Corps volunteers have left. Often Peace Corps volunteers coordinate their activities with local governmental agencies or village or community leaders. Peace Corps volunteers must understand, appreciate, and respect the cultural heritage of their host country and conduct all activities within its cultural and legal boundaries.

Responsibilities of a different sort are required in other international development careers. For example, consider those employees of a major governmental body such as the U.S. Department of State or an international organization such as the United Nations or the World Bank. The common goal in these international organizations is to promote effective and open relations among countries through educational exchanges, economic development programs, scientific exchanges, trade programs, and cultural exchanges. Many of these programs call for human services professionals, particularly for programs in such areas as human development, family life education, and human foods and nutrition. Perhaps the greatest responsibilities are held by workers in the areas of foods and agricultural policy; the provision of such basic needs is among the most important international activities of this nation.

There are interesting opportunities for consultants, advisers, and specialists in family or consumer programs. For example, many countries need family-planning specialists and consultants in clothing, housing, recreation, nutrition, care for children, family financial management, and general home economics. Consultants advise in their special areas as requested by the client, which is often the country's government. Professionals in international development need to remember that their major responsibility is educational, to help a country and its citizens learn particular skills and to help themselves. Much of international development is building goodwill among countries, and that should never be forgotten.

Qualifications

A degree in nearly all family- and consumer-oriented majors can lead to careers in international development. Degrees in such areas as child development, family relations, dietetics, nutrition, and general home economics are in especially high demand. A working knowledge of one or more foreign languages is also a plus, and courses in cultural anthropology and political science are appropriate as well. Supporting courses in international relations, international marketing, and international politics are also useful. A knowledge of a particular country's culture, history, political and economic systems, and language is important.

Special Personal Qualities

To succeed in the international arena, one needs understanding, patience, and a respect for other cultures. Nowhere is one exposed more to diversity than in an international development career.

The ability to communicate in a foreign language is also paramount in this career. Working and living in foreign countries can be difficult. The cultural amenities and life-style one may be used to in the United States may not be available in many other countries. Can you give up your favorite activities—movies, tennis, dancing, or visiting with friends? If not, international development may not be for you. But if you love traveling, learning about new cultures, and seeing new places, certainly there is no more exciting adventure than to be in international development.

Other Factors

The difficulty of international development careers is getting started. Many professionals have started as Peace Corps volunteers, but this is not the path for all. Another starting place is in such international organizations as the United Nations, the U.S. Department of State, the U.S. Department of Agriculture, the Food and Agricultural Organization, the World Health Organization, CARE, and the Agency for International Development. Some state governments have international relations divisions. Large international companies also may have openings.

CAREER PROFILE

Administration of Human Services _____

All the careers discussed in this chapter involve direct help of clients in need, usually on a face-to-face basis. Behind the scenes supporting this important contact with clients there must be administrative support and management, which is sometimes provided by the helping professionals themselves. However, increasingly there is a separate staff of professional administrators responsible for management, particularly in the larger organizations or governmental agencies with many programs. And this separate staff provides another career path for the professional in human services.

Typical Job Titles

Job titles in the administrative field include the following:

- Agency manager
- Program director
- Program administrator
- Program coordinator

These types of general managers carry out the many duties needed to operate an agency or organization. In addition, special administrative positions may perform one activity for the organization. Job titles for such specialists include the following:

- Fund raiser
- Director of development
- Director of professional staff
- Director of volunteer services
- Public relations manager
- Operations manager

Responsibilities

A general administrator, like an agency manager or program director, does many things to support the organization. The main responsibility is to set objectives for the organization (e.g., What does the organization want to accomplish?). A second responsibility is developing the policies and procedures for meeting these objectives, which involves such activities as identifying needy clients, managing the organization's relationships with clients, and dismissing clients whose problems have been solved.

Another important administrative task is communicating with the board of directors or other bodies that guide the organization. Typically, community service agencies, community foundations, and most other service groups have a board that establishes objectives, policies, and procedures. Administrators communicate and coordinate with these governing bodies and see that their decisions are carried out.

Managing the organization's finances is another important activity and requires establishing budgets and developing accounting procedures for keeping track of all funds. Another financial activity for many service organizations is fund raising. Here the administrator becomes a director of development, a person who seeks funds from individuals, government, local businesses, or philanthropic foundations. This process requires writing proposals describing what the organization intends to do with the money raised and selling the proposals to the appropriate sponsors.

There are many other areas of management: the management of operations, or the day-to-day routines; and personnel management, or determining needs, hiring professionals, assigning responsibilities, supervising employees, providing for professional development of employees, and making promotions. Administrators also become involved in public relations with the community, clients, and financial contributors to the organization.

Staying abreast of changing public policy is also important to human service organizations. Many laws and regulations govern human services, and these are constantly changing. Especially important are laws and regulations regarding clients' rights to privacy, safety, health, and information.

The final responsibility is to measure the effectiveness or success of the services provided, which requires devising appropriate measures of success such as the number of clients served, the number of problems solved, and the satisfaction of clients with the outcomes. Administrators are accountable for the results of programs they manage.

Qualifications

Education for a career in the administration of human services requires a large range of courses. The starting place is education in an undergraduate major such as child development, family relations, human development, general home economics, home economics education, institutional management, or food service management (the latter careers are specialized administrative careers in institutions and food services—see Chapter 5). This education provides the foundation needed for a career in human services. In addition, this career requires courses in such areas as business, public administration, and educational administration. A knowledge of accounting and bookkeeping systems is also helpful. Other valued courses are personnel management, supervision, public relations, and political science.

Experience is valuable in all areas of human services and is important to entering administrative careers as well. Experience should be gained working as a helping professional or paraprofessional in jobs described earlier in this chapter. A student must know the perspective of those who actually deal with clients, and that knowledge must be gained firsthand. After obtaining this experience, the graduate can seek entry-level managerial positions. In most cases employees start at lower administrative levels and work up to higher levels of management.

For some careers in human services administration, a master's or doctorate may be required. This is often the case in hospital administration, public health administration, and educational administration. Be sure to learn the requirements in your state if you have a particular area in which you wish to specialize.

Special Personal Qualities

To be an administrator is to deal in human relations. Administrators manage people and thus need to be sensitive to their needs and demands. Many different administrative styles for successful management are taught in courses on supervision or business management.

Administrators must be fact gatherers as well as decision makers. They must be willing to gather all facts relevant to a situation, make informed decisions based on those facts, and then communicate these decisions to the employees.

Leadership, too, is an important attribute of an administrator. The administrator sets the tone of the organization and, in many ways, is its role model. People in the organization look to their leader to set an example and show the way. The importance of providing a positive role model can never be overstressed.

Other Factors

One of the well-established administrative careers for family and consumer professionals is in institutional management, specifically institutional food service management. Many colleges and universities have programs of study in institutional management or food service management. These programs prepare students for careers in food services at schools, nursing homes, cafeterias, restaurants, and many other human service organizations. These careers are described in two career profiles, "Dietetics" (Chapter 5) and "The Hospitality Industry" (Chapter 6).

Administrative positions are found in all types of human service organizations: community service agencies, public health agencies, religious organizations, government offices (federal, state, and local), businesses of all types, counseling services, hospitals, nursing homes, retirement homes, resorts, recreation centers, day-care centers, rehabilitation centers, youth centers, jails, and educational institutions. Although most programs of study in human services emphasize the helping aspects of this profession, they also offer an opportunity to go into administration.

Questions and Exercises

1. Choose a career in one of the following human service fields:
   - Child development
   - Adolescent services
   - Marriage and family counseling
   - Family financial planning and counseling
   - Social welfare
   - Rehabilitation
   - International development
   - Administration

   Find a practicing professional in that career and interview him or her to find out the following information:
   - Working conditions
   - Advancement potential
   - Advantages and disadvantages
   - Typical job titles
   - Responsibilities
   - Qualifications
2. Consider the technological, economic, political, environmental, and social changes that have occurred in the United States in the past twenty years. How have these changes influenced the development of careers in human services?
3. What is the most important personal quality for human services professionals to possess, regardless of the specific area in which they work? Why is this characteristic necessary for success in any human services field?
4. What are some possible employers of graduates with degrees in marriage and family counseling or family financial planning and counseling?
5. In what ways are the careers of a child development specialist and an adolescent development specialist different? In what ways are they similar?
6. Interview a professional working in social welfare in order to find out the following:
   - Private or public organizations needing professionals to work in social welfare

- Positions available
- Procedures for employment application

7. In what settings do rehabilitation home economists work? Discuss the specific responsibilities of rehabilitation home economists in each of these settings.
8. Interview a Peace Corps recruiter to find out the following information:
   - Qualifications for acceptance into the Peace Corps
   - Positions available for family and consumer professionals
   - Procedures for applying for employment
9. Outline the responsibilities of an administrator for a human service organization, and discuss the educational qualifications, experience, and personal characteristics that would enable one to carry them out.

Bibliography

Balkwell, Carolyn, Roberta Null, and Audrey Spindler. "Health Care, Hospice, and Home Economists: A Programmatic Response to Demographic Trends," *Journal of Home Economics* 78 (Summer 1986), 27–29, 46.

Barkley, Margaret V., and Elizabeth A. Monts. "Career Exploration in Hospitality and Recreation," *Illinois Teacher* 23 (March/April 1980), 207–208.

Butler, Robert N. "Helping the Elderly," *Journal of Home Economics* 71 (Fall 1979), 33–34.

Dun's Marketing Services. *The Career Guide 1990: Dun's Employment Opportunities Directory*. New York: Dun & Bradstreet, 1990.

Everts, Joanne. "From Generalist to Specialist—Child Care Needs It All," *Illinois Teacher* 25 (January/February 1982), 116–119.

Gardner, Bill F. "Homemaker Rehabilitation: A Career Possibility," *Illinois Teacher* 24 (November/December 1980), 95–97.

Gunn, Barbara A. "The Possible Dream: Older Americans and Home Economists—Year 2000," *Journal of Home Economics* 78 (Summer 1986), 18–21, 26.

Hanson, Doris, Edna Page Anderson, Peggy Meszaros, Ruth Norman, Louise Woerner, and Marjorie Wybourn. "Training Home Care Workers," *Journal of Home Economics* 72 (Spring 1980), 27–30.

Ittig, Kathleen Browne. "Consumer Participation in Health Planning," *Journal of Home Economics* 70 (January 1978), 21–24.

Jackson, Gregg B., and Francine H. Meyer. *Evaluations of Firms and Professionals Who Provide Consumer Services*. Washington, DC: Washington Center for the Study of Services, 1981.

Johnson, Willis L. *Directory of Special Programs for Minority Group Members*, 4th ed. Garrett Park, MD: Garrett Park Press, 1986.

Kazda, Kraig, and Marilyn R. Bradbard. "Professional Employment Opportunities for Family and Child Development Graduates at the Master's and

Doctoral Levels, 1974–1984," *Journal of Home Economics* 78 (Winter 1986), 18–23.

Kocher, Eric. *International Jobs: Where They Are; How to Get Them.* Reading: MA.: Addison-Wesley, 1988.

Lind, Robert W. "Jobs for Family Life Majors," *Journal of Home Economics* 68 (January 1976), 60–62.

Magnet, Myron. "What Mass-Produced Child Care Is Producing," *Fortune* 108 (November 28, 1983), 157–174.

Mason, Jerry, and Bud Poduska. "Financial Planner or Financial Counselor: The Differences Are Significant," *Journal of Consumer Affairs* 20 (Summer 1986), 142–147.

Miller, Sandra W., and Karen Busch. "'Fresh Approach': Cooperation Between Home Economics and Vocational Rehabilitation," *Illinois Teacher* 31 (September/October 1987), 15–17.

Mitchell, Joyce Slayton. *College Board Guide to Jobs and Career Planning.* New York: College Entrance Examination Board, 1990.

Montgomery, James E. "Quality of Life for the Aging: Home Economics' Role" *Journal of Home Economics* 70 (Fall 1978), 12–14.

Morris, James, and Harvey Joanning. "Marriage and Family Therapy: A Growth Area for Home Economics," *Journal of Home Economics* 78 (Summer 1986), 36–37.

Murray, M. Eloise, and Virginia Clark. "International Concerns of American Home Economists: A Quarter Century Perspective," *Illinois Teacher* 25 (March/April 1982), 185–190.

Oliverio, Michael A. "The Homemaker Rehabilitation Counselor," *Illinois Teacher* 24 (November/December 1980), 98–100.

O'Toole, Patricia. "Picking the Right Financial Planner," *Money* 13 (March 1984), 131–138.

Parker, Frances J. "Needed: Home Economists in the Peace Corps," *Illinois Teacher* 21 (January/February 1978), 166–168.

"Peace Corps Volunteers Combine Home Economics Skills to Address Third World Needs," *Journal of Home Economics* 79 (Summer 1987), 28–29, 51.

Peterson, David. *Career Paths in the Field of Aging.* Lexington, MA: Lexington Books, 1987.

Plihal, Jane. "Sensitivities and Sensibilities for International Work," *Illinois Teacher* 31 (November/December 1987), 55–57, 63.

Powell, James. *The Prentice-Hall Global Employment Guide.* Englewood Cliffs, NJ: Prentice-Hall, 1983.

Prehm, Marilyn S., and Eloise Comeau Murray. "Implications of the Interface of Home Economics and Women in Development," *Home Economics Research Journal* 18 (September 1989), 19–31.

Schwab, Lois O. "Independent Living for the Handicapped: New Opportunities for Home Economists," *Journal of Home Economics* 71 (Fall 1979), 31–32.

Shields, Rhea, and Anna K. Williams. *Opportunities in Home Economics Careers.* Lincolnwood, IL: VGM Career Horizons, 1988.

Story, Marilyn D. "Home Economists and Hospice: A Needed Combination," *Journal of Home Economics* 75 (Summer 1983), 29–33.

Traynor, William J. *Opportunities in Human Resources Management Careers*. Lincolnwood, IL: VGM Career Horizons, 1989.

Williams, Ellen. *Opportunities in Gerontology Careers*. Lincolnwood, IL: VGM Career Horizons, 1987.

Williams, Herma, Ruth Harris, and Betty Harrison. "Home Economists and the Displaced Homemaker," *Journal of Home Economics* 71 (Spring 1979), 30–31.

Williams, Sally K., Dorothy L. West, and Eloise C. Murray, eds. *Looking Toward the 21st Century: Home Economics and the Global Community*, Mission Hills, CA: Glencoe/McGraw-Hill, 1990.

Wittenberg, Renée. *Opportunities in Child Care Careers*. Lincolnwood, IL: VGM Career Horizons, 1987.

————. *Opportunities in Social Work Careers*. Lincolnwood, IL: VGM Career Horizons, 1988.

Yost, Anna Cathryn. "The Rehabilitation Home Economist," *Journal of Home Economics* 72 (Spring 1980), 50–53.

CHAPTER **9**

Careers in Government and Public Policy

The message of this chapter is that virtually every career described in Chapters 5 through 8 exists somewhere in the federal, state, county, and city governments. The challenge is to find the jobs and their specific job titles, which often differ from those listed in the preceding chapters. This is a vast, "hidden" job market, in which you may find opportunities in your professional field.

Learning About Government _____

When you seek a career in public policy and government, begin by taking courses in civics and political science. Learn how the government is organized. For instance, the federal government has three branches, the legislative, executive, judicial. Within these branches are many agencies (e.g., the Agency for International Development), administrations (e.g., the Administration on Aging, the Food and Drug Administration), commissions (e.g., the Federal Trade Commission), offices (e.g., the Office of Consumer Affairs), and bureaus (e.g., the Bureau of Indian Affairs). The number of governmental units may seem overwhelming, and finding opportunities sometimes seems like seeking buried treasure, which is why a course in government is so important.

Next, learn to understand and appreciate the goal of government, which is to render public service and to respond to the needs of its constituents. In general, government serves the following five areas of human needs:

1. Health
2. Safety
3. Social welfare
4. Economic welfare
5. Education

Goals are accomplished by passing laws and regulations, such as those regulating fair business practices or the quality of food, and by providing financial grants to governmental bodies or other interest groups so that they may solve their problems independently. Government is particularly responsive to those groups that bring the most attention and public support for their special interests. Recently, the government's attention has been focused on public health problems (e.g., drug abuse, smoking, diet, AIDS, quality of the food supply), groups with special needs (the handicapped, minorities, the homeless), low-income families, senior citizens (e.g., Medicare and Social Security programs for retirees), the unemployed, and the educationally disadvantaged. Such governmental activities are among the central interests of family and consumer professionals.

Professionals from family and consumer specializations have entered many of these areas. For example, professional home economists promote the passage of laws and regulations governing the health, safety, and informational aspects of consumer products. Likewise, professional associations such as the American Home Economics Association and the American Vocational Association (see Chapter 11) actively support legislation and public policy related to the interests of families, consumers, and vocational home economics in general.

Federal Government Careers _____

The federal government employs many administrators, program officers, project managers, information specialists, and researchers in family and consumer professions. Sometimes the job titles are similar to those listed in earlier chapters, but often they are different, and so it is necessary to do a bit of research to find the appropriate titles for your profession. There are job opportunities in Washington, DC, as well as in the major cities where regional offices are located (including Atlanta, Boston, Chicago, Dallas, Denver, Kansas City, New York, Philadelphia, San Francisco, and Seattle). Smaller governmental units are also located throughout the United States, and their addresses are in the *U.S. Government Manual*.

The following are the government departments that have positions for family and consumer professionals:

1. *U.S. Department of Agriculture:* This department has subdivisions focusing on foods, textiles, consumer services, international programs, marketing services, research, and education. Considerable research is done on foods, nutritional aspects of foods, textile fibers (especially cotton), marketing processes, and consumer demand for products.

2. *U.S. Department of Commerce:* This department focuses on the development of business and industry. It provides specialized information and assistance to local businesses, including new businesses, retail stores, and minority-owned businesses. The National Bureau of Standards develops standards and testing procedures for consumer products and is an important consumer-oriented agency.

3. *U.S. Department of Education:* This department focuses on all levels of education but mainly on primary and secondary education. It is concerned with the educational quality of programs and conducts research to assess their quality and to develop new programs of instruction meeting the nation's needs. Vocational home economics education and consumer and homemaking education are good backgrounds for working here.

4. *U.S. Department of Energy:* This department conducts research on energy utilization and efficiency. It also offers informational programs on consumer use of energy. In the 1990s energy policy and the relative roles of oil, gas, nuclear, and solar energy will be debated, and the future energy supplies will be shaped by governmental decisions.

5. *U.S. Department of Health and Human Services:* This department deals with the broadest range of human and social welfare services. Important administrations within this agency include the National Institutes of Health and the Food and Drug Administration. Activities of the Department of Health and Human Services include research, education, and consumer safety and setting quality standards for foods, cosmetics, and other consumer products. The agency is also the home of the Social Security Administration, which administers retirement and disability programs.

6. *U.S. Department of Housing and Urban Development:* This department plans housing programs and the development of urban areas. It employs experts in urban planning, social aspects of housing, economic aspects of housing, and housing needs of disadvantaged populations.

7. *U.S. Department of Labor:* This department is concerned with the health and safety of the labor force. Special areas of interest include employment programs, training programs, occupational safety, and occupational health.

8. *U.S. Department of State:* This department is concerned with all foreign relations. Of special interest to some family professionals is its Agency for International Development, which administers aid programs to other countries, particularly Third World nations.

9. *U.S. Department of Transportation:* This department is concerned with all forms of transportation. Of special interest to consumer-oriented professionals are those programs dealing with auto safety and consumer information regarding automobiles.

10. *Federal Trade Commission:* This commission is involved in consumer protection and administers laws relating to consumer interests. It employs many lawyers but needs some consumer affairs professionals as well.

11. *Small Business Administration:* This administration assists entrepreneurs in starting new businesses. It has local offices in major cities throughout the country and runs programs on establishing business plans and obtaining finances for new businesses. Many retailers, crafts stores, and other consumer-oriented businesses have started from SBA programs.

12. *U.S. Customs Service:* This service supervises the importation of consumer products. Because importing has become an important part of some industries, particularly clothing and textiles, this may be a place with employment opportunities for some consumer specialists.

13. *Veterans Administration:* This administration provides assis-

tance for veterans of military service. It has an extensive system of hospitals, clinics, and nursing homes and needs human services professionals, nutritionists, and dietitians.

14. *Military Services:* The Army, Air Force, Navy, and Marines offer opportunities for family- and consumer-oriented professionals. Human services professionals are needed as family counselors, financial counselors, and therapists for service personnel. Managers of retail stores ("post exchanges") that are operated on military bases are needed, as are dietitians and managers of cafeterias and other military food services. The military services also have specialized research subdivisions that focus on military clothing, foods service, housing, and other consumer-oriented needs of the military.

15. *Various Regulators of Financial Services:* The Federal Deposit Insurance Corporation insures families' savings. The Securities and Exchange Commission regulates the trade of securities (stocks, bonds, and other related financial instruments). Such financial services protect consumers and families. Financially oriented professionals may find interesting career opportunities here.

16. *Volunteer Agencies:* The best-known volunteer program sponsored by the government is the Peace Corps. The Peace Corps provides international services to countries in need, usually in less affluent and underdeveloped countries, including Eastern Europe. The government has sponsored other volunteer programs from time to time, such as the Foster Grandparents Program, Senior Companion Program, Volunteers In Service To America (VISTA), and the National Student Volunteer Program. Volunteer programs offer opportunities for home economics professionals, human service professionals, dietitians, and nutritionists.

State, County, and City Government Careers _____

State, county, and city governments also offer many career opportunities. The following are some areas in which opportunities for family and consumer professionals can be found in most local government agencies or units:

1. Human services (child welfare, senior citizens programs, handicapped programs, food services for the needy)
2. Human relations

3. Community development
4. Employment and job training programs
5. Recreation programs and centers
6. Parks departments
7. Public housing programs
8. Home health services
9. Consumer affairs (complaint handling, attorney general's office, consumer information offices)
10. Consumer services (trash collection, fire protection)
11. Public health
12. Public assistance (welfare, food stamps, employment programs)
13. Local government credit unions
14. Cooperative Extension Service
15. Adult education programs
16. City management planning
17. Public safety departments
18. Rehabilitation services
19. Community hospitals
20. Family social services and counseling offices
21. Youth programs
22. Probation and parole departments
23. Courts
24. Veterans affairs offices
25. Volunteer services
26. Detention centers
27. Substance abuse programs
28. School systems
29. Minority business offices
30. Arts and crafts programs
31. Nutritional consulting programs

Special Opportunities in Public Policy _____

There are several other means by which you can turn your interest in public policy into a career. You may find jobs in political action committees (PACs), public interest groups, political parties, consumer coalitions such as the Consumer Federation of America, lobbying groups, public policy divisions of professional associations (e.g., American Home Economics Association, American Vocational Association, and other political associations), or other organizations at grass-roots levels. All these organizations try to influence the legislation, regulation, and formulation of public policy.

Some of these organizations take political positions on issues regarding families and consumers. The following are some of their activities:

1. Communicating with legislators on specific family and consumer policies
2. Writing family impact statements or consumer impact statements regarding legislation and public policies
3. Doing research on the effect of laws and regulations on families
4. Writing legislation regarding consumer and family issues such as child welfare, nutritional quality, product safety, and family welfare
5. Lobbying for the passage of laws
6. Mobilizing others to pass new laws and regulations
7. Following up to see that laws and regulations are enforced
8. Participating in workshops, forums, and public meetings

Such political activities have become an important part of family and consumer careers. Several businesses and organizations have formed PACs, lobbies, and offices in Washington to influence public policy. They have large staffs and spend a lot of money on the causes they support.

A career in public policy, whether in government or in political action organizations such as those just described, can be a satisfying profession. For those professionals who believe in serving families and consumers, there certainly can be no better way than to determine the public policies that affect us all.

Questions and Exercises _____

1. Choose one of the major government agencies offering employment to professionals in any family- or consumer-oriented field and find its address in the *U.S. Government Manual*. Write to this agency to find out its employment opportunities.
2. Visit the Federal Job Information Center in your area and interview an employment specialist about federal government career opportunities in your area(s) of interest. Find out the following:
   • Names of agencies for potential employment
   • Positions available
   • Procedures for application
3. Using the government sections of your city's telephone directory, find the government units that may offer employment for family and consumer professionals. Contact the unit that most appeals to you and obtain the following information:

- Positions available
- Procedures for employment
4. Conduct a minisurvey to find out the employment opportunities for professionals interested in a public policy career serving families and consumers. Your search might include the public policy divisions of the following organizations:
   - American Home Economics Association
   - Consumer Federation of America
   - Political action committees
   - Congress Watch
   - Democratic party
   - Republican party
   - Local political organizations

Bibliography

Amidei, Nancy J. "Home Economists in Public Affairs: Making a Difference," *Journal of Home Economics* 71 (Spring 1979), 16–18.

Baxter, Neale. *Opportunities in Federal Government Careers*. Lincolnwood, IL: VGM Career Horizons, 1987.

————. *Opportunities in State and Local Government Careers*. Lincolnwood, IL: VGM Career Horizons, 1985.

Dun's Marketing Services. *The Career Guide 1990: Dun's Employment Opportunities Directory*. New York: Dun & Bradstreet, 1990.

Durgin, Rod W., ed. *Guide to Federal Jobs,* 2nd ed. Toledo, OH: Resource Directories, 1988.

Gardner, Bill F. "Homemaker Rehabilitation: A Career Possibility," *Illinois Teacher* 24 (November/December 1980), 95–97.

Hanson, Doris, Edna Page Anderson, Peggy Meszaros, Ruth Norman, Louise Woerner, and Marjory Wybourn. "Training Home Care Workers," *Journal of Home Economics* 72 (Spring 1980), 27–30.

Ittig, Kathleen Browne. "Consumer Participation in Health Planning," *Journal of Home Economics* 70 (January 1978), 21–24.

Jackson, Gregg G., and Francine H. Meyer, *Evaluations of Firms and Professionals Who Provide Consumer Services*. Washington, DC: Washington Center for the Study of Services, 1981.

Johnson, Willis L. *Directory of Special Programs for Minority Group Members,* 4th ed. Garrett Park, MD: Garrett Park Press, 1986.

Levering, Robert, Milton Moskowits, and Michael Katz. *The 100 Best Companies to Work for in America*. Reading, MA: Addison-Wesley, 1987.

Lind, Robert W. "Jobs for Family Life Majors," *Journal of Home Economics* 68 (January 1976), 60–62.

Montgomery, James E. "Quality of Life for the Aging: Home Economics' Role," *Journal of Home Economics* 70 (Fall 1978), 12–14.

Murray, M. Eloise, and Virginia Clark. "International Concerns of American Home Economists: A Quarter Century Perspective," *Illinois Teacher* 25 (March/April 1982) 185–190.

Parker, Frances J. "Needed: Home Economists in the Peace Corps," *Illinois Teacher* 21 (January/February 1978), 166–168.

Phihal, Jane. "Sensitivities and Sensibilities for International Work," *Illinois Teacher* 31 (November/December 1987), 55–57, 63.

Powell, James. *The Prentice-Hall Global Employment Guide.* Englewood Cliffs, NJ: Prentice-Hall, 1983.

Schwab, Lois O. "Independent Living for the Handicapped: New Opportunities for Home Economists," *Journal of Home Economics* 71 (Fall 1979), 31–32.

Shields, Rhea, and Anna K. Williams. *Opportunities in Home Economics Careers.* Lincolnwood, IL: VGM Career Horizons, 1988.

Waelde, David E. *How to Get a Federal Job,* 7th ed. Washington, DC: FEDHELP Publications, 1989.

Williams, Herma, Ruth Harris, and Betty Harrison. "Home Economists and the Displaced Homemaker," *Journal of Home Economics* 71 (Spring 1979), 30–31.

CHAPTER 10

Developing an Innovative Career Path

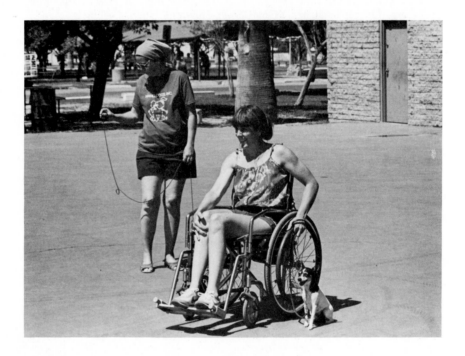

The last five chapters described established, well-known, and popular careers for consumer and family professionals. But what about people who want to do something special, creative, and completely out of the ordinary? Certainly there are those of us who wish to avoid the well-worn path in pursuit of greater adventure, risk, challenge, and reward. For such a person, this chapter on innovative career paths offers some answers.

This chapter is not just for the fearless or the risk taker, however. Rather, the theme of this chapter is that you can create your own careers to meet your own interests. Many people have already done so. Perhaps the greatest thing about family and consumer careers is that there is always room for people with newer, better ideas or ways to serve consumers and families.

A Perspective on Innovative Careers _____

There are many ways to design a career that meets your special interests. The following are some areas in which family and consumer professionals may do well:

1. *Entrepreneurship:* Start your own business.
2. *Free-lancing:* Be an adviser, consultant, writer, communicator, educator, or whatever your client wants.
3. *Cottage industry:* Do you have special skills for fashion design, interior design, macramé, lace making, French cooking, or some other such thing? Become a manufacturer in your own home.
4. *Volunteering:* Do you want to work in a particular field, but there is no job exactly where you want? Volunteer yourself into a career.
5. *Create a job:* Do you have a better way of doing things for Company X? Create the job and sell yourself to the company.

Do you have the skills and personality needed to pursue one of these innovative career paths? These careers are not for everyone, but many of us are more qualified to pursue a unique angle on careers than we realize. If you have a technical skill, such as design, household equipment, financial counseling, consumer research, or microwave cooking, it can be an entree into an innovative career. If you are good at self-discipline, perseverance, organization, and management, you may find an innovative career path. If you are a venturesome, risk-taking person, one who is less concerned with personal security than with the potential for success, start thinking about this opportunity now.

However, do not be blinded by the excitement of these careers. Recognize the obstacles against success. There will be long hours of hard work and frustration when your expectations are not fully met. It can take years to establish a successful career. For many people, it may be necessary to spend years working with others to learn more about your chosen field before you are ready to branch out on your own. Such obstacles keep less dedicated people from even trying, but for the right person, the rewards and satisfaction of an innovative career outweigh the obstacles and risks.

Special Qualities of Innovative Career Seekers

- Desire to be independent, to be one's own boss
- Not concerned with job security
- Great self-confidence
- Willingness to work long hours
- Not afraid of taking risks
- Has a better idea for doing something

Entrepreneurship — Starting Your Own Business _____

Becoming an entrepreneur by starting your own business is the American dream and the American way. Literally thousands of new businesses are started each year in the United States, and today tens of thousands of entrepreneurs have established successful businesses. Although you may be most familiar with big companies, such as Levi Strauss, General Foods, or Holiday Inns of America, it is the thousands of smaller and unknown businesses that give our economy its strength.

Entrepreneurship frequently begins in college. Perhaps you have noticed businesses such as the following that your friends have started:

1. *Airline representative:* This student sells package ski tours to students for their spring vacations.
2. *Student subscription service:* This student collects orders for subscriptions to major national magazines and earns commissions from those subscriptions.
3. *Balloon bouquet service:* This student makes decorative displays of balloons, called Balloon Bouquets, which are delivered to various clients on campus and in the local community.
4. *Color analyst:* This student does part-time color analysis for friends and referrals from friends.
5. *Cake baker:* This student bakes, decorates, and delivers birthday cakes at the university and even sings "Happy Birthday" to the recipient.
6. *Party service company:* This group of entrepreneurs caters food

and drinks and supplies bartenders, chauffeurs, waiters, and waitresses for all kinds of social functions.

7. *Calendar designer:* These student entrepreneurs created a calendar featuring pictures of the best-looking men on campus.

These all are serious careers pursued by serious students. Some may seem a bit frivolous, but such are the makings of successful, innovative careers.

Entrepreneurs generally start with a traditional business. Examples of such traditional, consumer-oriented businesses are fashion apparel stores, interior design services, restaurants, or other retail establishments specializing in a consumer product. For family professionals, business practices are started in such areas as marriage counseling, family therapy, and family financial counseling. A host of other family services may be candidates for the entrepreneur, including child-care or day-care services or care for other populations with special needs or problems. Opportunities may be limited only by the ability to turn the imagined into an organized and carefully planned reality.

Your new business need not be a traditional retail store, counseling service, or child-care service. There are many high-growth areas that you could choose. For example, ready-made gourmet food stores, used clothing stores, and housekeeping and housecleaning services appear to be popular fields. Or you might consider developing a new business. For example, *Forbes Magazine* identified several businesses started by entrepreneurs: a woman who sells quality educational toys through home demonstrations (similar to Tupperware), one who teaches marketing (a consumer-oriented subject) to banks, one who provides sanitation checks and bacterial measurements for food service organizations, and one who formed a mail-order company to supply household renovation products. These are excellent examples of the unusual professions that one can develop.

What does it take to become a successful entrepreneur? The surest way to success is to offer a product or service that no one else has. In addition, there must be a genuine need for it. Success can come if you have a better idea, something special, different, or of a higher quality than anything else on the market.

Without a better product or service, a new business is at a disadvantage and may not beat the competition. But other factors determine success as well. Especially important is having a business plan, which establishes the operating procedures for your business. A complete business plan includes such things as accounting and financial statements, a plan for merchandising and advertising your business, a plan for managing the personnel of the business, and procedures for the daily operations and management of your business. And you will need money to finance your business. Setting up a new business can be very costly. We hear success stories of people who started new businesses in garages or lofts for small sums, perhaps several thousand dollars, but it is more likely that you will need $50,000 or more to start most businesses. Start-up costs vary depending on the type of business, but if you are under-financed you will have difficulty paying your bills, and the business may quickly fail.

There are other keys to starting a successful business. Do you have a special knowledge of your product or service, or do you have a knack for that enterprise? Can you get a good location, one where many consumers can easily find you? Can you capture a large share of the possible customers for your type of product? Will the name of your store, its appearance, and its advertising capture the imagination and attention of your potential customers? And do you have the personality to be successful? The experts say you must have a great desire for accomplishment, self-respect, freedom, independence, ambition, and aggressiveness. Accent such qualities with an excellent product and your desire to serve others, and you will greatly enhance your prospects for succeeding.

Your new business will offer many risks and rewards. The risks are that it may be years before you make a profit. Customers may not beat down the doors to buy from you at first. Weathering such disappointments requires perseverance and patience. But the rewards, especially over the long term as your business develops, may be great. You will have achieved freedom and control over your destiny. You will be the leader and the major decision maker of your organization. You will do things the way you want them done, not the way others tell you to. Ultimately, a successful business will yield financial rewards, which is certainly not to be overlooked.

To start a business you must do several things. First learn more about what you need to do to build a business. Talk with successful entrepreneurs in your field, read books on entrepreneurship and small businesses, and take an entrepreneurship course. Colleges and universities offer these courses, as do private organizations (check the credentials of private teaching organizations before spending a lot on such courses). You can also get assistance from the Small Business Administration, which sponsors seminars and provides expert advice from former entrepreneurs. From such sources you will learn how to formulate a feasible business plan for your venture. You will learn how to obtain necessary legal and accounting advice, how to apply for the necessary business licenses, and how to determine the financial requirements for your business as it grows.

Our discussion of entrepreneurship is an introduction to whet your appetite and perhaps build your enthusiasm. Entrepreneurship requires extensive study, thought, planning, and time. If you are thinking of becoming an entrepreneur some day, now is the time to begin your investigation of this most fascinating profession.

Cottage Industry — Working Out of Your Home _____

A cottage industry is really nothing more than a special case of entrepreneurship. You are starting a business that you intend to operate from your home. Obviously it will be a small business, at least at first. Small businesses at home offer all the rewards of entrepreneurship, including self-satisfaction and knowing you can serve others. The additional reward is that your small business may one day lead to a larger and larger business and a permanent career.

In all likelihood your business at home will based on some special skill or interest. For instance, you may be expert at a craft such as macramé, gourmet cooking, tailoring dresses, refinishing furniture, or repairing small appliances (use your imagination—what special things can you do?). Such are the diverse underpinnings of a cottage industry.

A cottage industry thrives on several qualities: pride, high quality, attention to detail, uniqueness, and personal attention. The personal service given to customers is particularly important because word-of-mouth referrals are the best advertising. The quality of the product or service is equally important. Finally, being on time and keeping promises to your clients are essential because they impress clients and make them regular customers.

A cottage industry is well suited for the person who is less business inclined or who finds the management of a larger business a chore rather than a delight. By keeping your business small and working at home, you avoid many of the difficulties of managing a larger business and a staff. The obvious sacrifice, of course, is that your home-oriented business cannot grow substantially and may not yield the greatest financial rewards. Financial reward usually comes only to larger businesses.

There are special problems inherent in a cottage industry. How much will your business at home interfere with your normal family life? Will family members be supportive, or will they feel threatened? Other problems are local laws governing businesses operated at home, local zoning restrictions, and relations with neighbors. You need to be aware of laws or local restrictions and abide by them. In some communities it is illegal to operate businesses in residential neighborhoods, and these local restrictions must be respected. Neighbors often object to increased traffic in the neighborhood and unknown visitors. Communities often restrict the amount of your house that can be devoted to business (perhaps to one room or to one-fourth of the square footage), and you may not be able to post signs or provide special parking for clients. In such situations it may become necessary to rent commercial space in a separate location to operate your business.

Although the problems we have mentioned can be serious, all can be overcome with a little care and thought on your part, and a successful business in your home can be established.

Free-Lancing as a Career

Free-lancing is surely the most diversified of all the innovative career paths one can take. Free-lancing is, by definition, taking on a career involving many different odd jobs for many different clients. In this career it pays to be a generalist—to be knowledgeable about many subjects and to apply your knowledge to the diverse needs of clients. One assignment may require your expertise as a nutritionist, the next as a consumer affairs professional, and the next as a writer and editor. The successful free-lancer may work with businesses, school systems, public service agencies, major corporations, newspapers and other media. Truly it is a career for the person who loves variety and change in assignments from day to day, week to week, and year to year.

Here is a sampling of the jobs and special assignments that a free-lancer might undertake for different clients:

- Writing special articles or columns for magazines, newspapers, newsletters, or other publications
- Editing books for publication
- Writing extension service publications
- Reviewing books for publication
- Teaching short courses or evening courses in community colleges or universities
- Teaching major university courses
- Teaching nutrition to food service workers in cafeterias or other food services

- Teaching nutrition education to senior citizen groups and other clients
- Reporting consumer affairs on television
- Organizing demonstrations of consumer products (microwave manufacturers, food processors, and other makers of consumer products typically demonstrate their new lines)
- Testing recipes for food companies or magazines
- Acting as a consumer information distributor, by taking consumer information to retail store buyers and managers on behalf of manufacturers
- Teaching crafts such as sewing, jewelry making, or whatever your skill
- Public speaking and guest lecturing
- Designing your own products for consignment and resale (e.g., through art galleries, craft fairs, specialty stores)
- Investigating consumer problems and consumer complaints for major manufacturers, Better Business Bureaus, or professional and trade organizations
- Teaching consumer education to many different audiences (occupational groups, income groups, ethnic groups)
- Consulting with the state board of education or local school districts on the development of curricula in various home economics or vocational subjects
- Teaching parent education courses
- Teaching Lamaze or other birth delivery methods at local hospitals
- Training homemaker health aids for a state licensing program
- Working part time with local human services agencies
- Working as a research assistant on projects for research firms or universities
- Developing advertising or promotional plans for businesses
- Writing and evaluating computer programs
- Advising businesses on developing better relations with their consumers

This is just a sampling of free-lance jobs. The success of a free-lance consultant depends largely on his or her ability to meet the needs of many different clients and his or her expertise in a variety of areas. Often this requires special study, research in libraries, and discussions with other working professionals.

To get started in free-lancing requires several things. First it is necessary to build a business identity. You need a business card, stationery with your logo or letterhead on it, and a secretarial service or answering service. You also may need transportation. You need to contact potential clients to learn about their needs. This means telephoning, writing letters to, and visiting businesses. This makes your skills visible, and in free-lancing, visibility is everything. Creating an image as a professional, organized, and qualified individual is the end product of all these communications.

A number of personal qualities determine free-lancers' success. Besides an ability to communicate and present oneself, thorough and prompt attention to clients' desires is mandatory. Businesses and agencies expect results, and fast. Another characteristic leading to success is flexibility in dealing with different clients. Last, but not least, free-lancers must be able to accept the uncertainty of free-lancing. Particularly as one starts as a free-lancer, the jobs may be slow to come, but even after one is established work may come in irregular spurts. The result is that free-lancing lacks the security of a full-time job. These limitations aside, there are many successful free-lancers operating in consumer- and family-oriented careers today.

Consulting as a Career

Consulting is a special case of free-lancing. Consultants are often specialists in a narrow area of expertise, such as nutrition, vocational education, marketing, fashion design, consumer affairs, journalism, or human services. Consultants sell their expertise to

---

SELF-ASSESSMENT EXERCISE 10–1

Developing a Special or Innovative Career

Can you find one or more ways to develop a special or innovative career for yourself?

Idea 1: _____

_____

Idea 2: _____

_____

Idea 3: _____

_____

interested audiences in that area. Consultants are often affiliated with specialized businesses, such as a wardrobe consultant working with a department store or a dietitian working with a hospital. Often consultants are independent business persons operating out of their homes.

Consulting, like free-lancing, requires communication skills and flexibility. The most successful consultants have had extensive experience in their areas, and often they have advanced degrees or other education to strengthen their credentials.

Volunteering Your Way into a Career _____

What do you do if you've been looking for your chosen job but just haven't been able to find it? In some careers, there will be times when jobs are scarce, particularly during a recession or when employers' budgets are under pressure. At such times you may consider volunteering your way into a career. In fact, volunteering can be a better way of finding a career than many people imagine.

There are several approaches to volunteering oneself into a career. One way is to do volunteer work with human service agencies and public service organizations while you are in college. You can spend a few evenings a week or a few hours on the weekend to participate in these organizations. In return for your time you will make contacts with professionals in the field and get to show your capabilities. Nothing can be a better advertisement, not your résumé or a personal letter of recommendation, than other professionals seeing your talents in action. At the very least you will generate positive references for future employment, but more often the dedication and capabilities you show will lead to a permanent position once one becomes available. In effect, volunteering makes you the "insider" for job opportunities.

Another approach is to volunteer for a political party or a political action group. Here you will make political contacts and also contacts in businesses and local government. Participation in political organizations is particularly helpful in landing jobs in the local or state government. Opportunities in such areas as consumer affairs, the attorney general's office, or human service agencies are frequently found through these political contacts.

There are several other places at which you should consider volunteering your way into a future career. Businesses sometimes take short-term employees for training or intern purposes. The employees are paid, and the short-term job may lead to a longer-term job in the future. Another approach is to volunteer to help your professors with their research projects or consulting activities. And not to be overlooked are the many opportunities to volunteer that exist right on your own campus—the student newspaper, student government, or other student organizations

Where can you learn about volunteering opportunities? Newspapers publicize the needs of various organizations. Other sources are local employment agencies, chambers of commerce, and public service organizations such as the Kiwanis Club or the United Way. Or you may contact potential employers directly and indicate your interest in volunteering. And don't forget to check your campus placement office for job listings.

Creating Your Own Job

There may be many organizations or businesses that need your expertise but just haven't discovered that need yet! For example, in the 1970s, consumer affairs emerged as an important professional field. However, many businesses were unaware of how important a consumer affairs professional could be to their organizations. Students with degrees in such majors as family economics, home management, consumer studies, and general home economics found an opportunity to sell their knowledge of consumers to businesses. Once businesses recognized the need for consumer specialists, new positions were created in consumer services, consumer education, consumer information, and consumer relations. And now in the 1990s consumer affairs has grown into a substantial career, with thousands of professionals working in the largest corporations, retailers and service organizations in the United States and abroad.

Many other specialists have created careers in a similar manner. For instance, dietitians are becoming part of health teams in hospitals. Interior designers are increasingly accepted in architectural design firms. Educational specialists are being hired by the manufacturers of consumer products such as toys to apply their expertise to the design of educational products and to give consumers instructions about them. These examples show that you may be able to sell your skills to employers who currently do not hire in your area. Just a little creativity and personal initiative may open the door.

How should you go about creating your own job? Begin by writing your own job description, listing such things as the job title, the job's responsibilities, and what the job would do for the company or organization that is not done now. The latter is very important, for if the organization sees no benefit in the job you suggest, it is unlikely to give it to you. But if you can generate a convincing job description and show that you can do things that are needed but not presently being done, you just may talk yourself into a job.

Other Nontraditional Careers

Do not overlook the many nontraditional careers that you may be qualified to enter. For example, one clothing student secured an internship with a space suit engineering firm, which led to a job in the National Aeronautics and Space Administration (NASA). Another example is a home economics major with an interest in chemistry who went into industrial chemical sales on the basis of courses in both chemistry and home economics. And a fashion merchandising major entered a career in retail banking on the basis of expertise in related fields of consumer decision making, personal finance, and retailing. The point is that any major can transfer to careers that seem outside your training. Make employers aware of those transferable qualifications, and you too can find a nontraditional career.

A New Generation of Careers

Our economy is continuously creating new careers and jobs where none existed previously. Consumer affairs, mentioned earlier, is a recent example. Another example is color analysis, in which experts in color and fashion have generated careers in personal image and fashion consultation. For the future, the following are some new fields in which family and consumer professionals may find jobs.

Home Services. A variety of professional services may be established to aid families having two incomes and two working professionals (child-care services, senior services, housekeeping services, home management services).

Computer Graphics and Computer-Assisted Design (CAD). Computers are used to design fashions, interiors, appliances, and other consumer products.

Home Computer Training. This is perfect for the home economics generalist who is familiar with nutrition, housing, personal finance, and consumer affairs.

Systems Analysts. Systems analysts are sometimes thought of as computer experts, but there is more to it than this. For example, systems analysts are hired by retailers and others to analyze business procedures and write manuals on them.

Auditors. Auditors are not just financial analysts or accountants. In general they are people who investigate an organization's performance and recommend improvements. They are often hired by consumer-oriented businesses needing performance evaluation (for example, retail stores).

Videotex Services and Electronic Marketing. A new industry is currently being developed to deliver consumer information by cable and television directly to consumers' homes. Catalog mechandising, electronic banking, advertising, consumer information, and financial planning will be available through interactive home computer and video systems. Major companies such as IBM and Sears are joining forces to make this a reality.

Housing Rehabilitation. The remodeling and renewal of older neighborhoods, particularly in inner cities, has grown during the past quarter-century. This may become an even more important business in the future, given the demand for satis-factory housing.

Geriatric Services. As more of the population grows older, there will be an increased demand for products and services for the special needs of older citizens.

Telecommunications. Much of the communications and journalism of the future may use teleconferencing, telemarketing systems, Videotex, and other networks of telephones, computers, and video communications. Consumer and merchandising profes-sionals will fit right into these new networks.

Energy Analysts. Energy conservation will continue to be important, not only in residential housing and related consumer

---

SELF-ASSESSMENT EXERCISE 10–2

Innovative Careers

Can you name unusual careers of the future not mentioned in this chapter?

Career 1: _____

Career 2: _____

Career 3: _____

Career 4: _____

TABLE 10.1 Examples of Twenty-First-Century Careers for Family and Consumer Professionals

Career counselor	Home computer salesperson
Certified alcohol counselor	Human services director
Certified financial planner	Image consultant
Child advocate	Information broker
Child day-care service	Information coordinator
Communications specialist	Information manager
Complaints manager	Information research scientist
Computer-assisted design (CAD) technician	International marketing manager
Computer-assisted manufacturing (CAM) specialist	Licensed therapeutic recreation specialist
Computer systems analyst	New health foods
Consultant	New product manager
Database designer	Ombudsman
Database engineer	Oncology nutritionist
Database manager	Phobia therapist
Director of human resources	Public affairs psychologist
Divorce mediator	Rehabilitation housing technician
Documentation specialist	Sales trainer
Ecologist	Sex therapist
Employee relocations service director	Software salesperson
Energy auditor	Software writer
Environmental engineer	Solar energy consultant
Family mediator	Solar engineering technician
Fiber optic technician	Specialized food services
Financial consultant	Systems analysis manager
Financial planner	Technical services manager
Forecaster	Telecommunication salesperson
Free-lance writer	Training services
Halfway house manager	Tutor
	Videodating services

Source: Adapted from *Personnel Administrator* 28 (December 1983), p. 90.

products but in business and industry as well. Energy engineers and auditors may be needed to work with homeowners, utilities, businesses, and government.

Teachers with Special Expertise in Computer-Assisted Instruction (CAI). As computers become more a part of education, there will be a need for teachers who can develop computerized instructional materials and teach children how to use computers. For example, CAI can be used in many home economics areas such as interior design, budgeting, nutritional assessment, menu preparation, and home record keeping.

To conclude, Table 10.1 lists twenty-first-century careers for family and consumer professionals. In each case, realistic new opportunities exist for the consumer or family professional. Whenever new social institutions arise, or whenever new human services for special populations are needed, there will always be new careers created for the skilled and foresighted.

Questions and Exercises _____

1. What type of person is best suited to an innovative career? Consider the following aspects:
   - Personality
   - Self-concept
   - Values and attitudes
   - Social skills
   - Intelligence
2. Design an entrepreneurship career for yourself. Explain why you feel that you are suited for this type of career in terms of the following:
   - Your knowledge
   - Your skills
   - Your education
   - Your personality
3. Visit the Small Business Administration in your city, and speak to a consultant about beginning a small business, including the following:
   - Product or service offered
   - Financial planning (obtaining needed money)
   - Marketing strategies
   - Organizing the business
   - Advertising/promotional strategies
   - Choosing the best location
4. Interview a professional consultant or a free-lance home economist to find out the following:
   - The nature of consulting or free-lancing
   - Variety of working conditions
   - Special skills, aptitudes, knowledge, and personality needed
5. Select a business or service organization to which to volunteer your services. Keep a record of your volunteer activities: your observations, duties and responsibilities, and personal contacts. Write a summary of your experience, including what you learned and how this may influence your future career choices.
6. Write a job description for a career that you would like to create for yourself. Include the following:
   - Job title
   - Responsibilities
   - How the job will benefit the company or organization
7. Contact someone in an organization where you would like to work in

your career. Use your job description and salesmanship to sell yourself and your job.

8. List your skills that are transferable to nontraditional careers.

Bibliography _____

Bly, Robert W., and Gary Blake. *Dream Jobs—A Guide to Tomorrow's Top Careers*. New York: Wiley, 1983.

Compton, Cheryl W., and Alyce M. Fanslow. "Entrepreneurship: A Career Opportunity for Home Economics Students," *Illinois Teacher* 24 (May/June 1981), 207–210.

Creasy, Donna Newberry, "A Husband and Wife Business," *Journal of Home Economics* 67 (July 1975), 35–37.

Dun's Marketing Services. *The Career Guide 1990: Dun's Employment Opportunities Directory*. New York: Dun & Bradstreet, 1990.

Feingold, S. Norman. "Tracking New Career Categories Will Become a Preoccupation for Job Seekers and Managers," *Personnel Administrator* 28 (December 1983), 86–91.

Fortenberry, Sally L. "Entrepreneurship: A Viable Addition to Home Economics Curriculum," *Journal of Home Economics* 80 (Spring 1988), 3–6.

Goetting, Marsha A., and Gayle Y. Muggli. "Made in Montana: Entrepreneurial Home Economics," *Journal of Home Economics* 80 (Spring 1988), 7–10.

Levinson, Harry, ed. *Designing and Managing Your Career*. Boston: Harvard Business School Press, 1989.

Maineri, Sandra Bologna. "Free-lancing as a Career," *Journal of Home Ecomonics* 72 (Spring 1980), 56–57.

Maineri, Sandra C. "Creating a Career: How I Developed a Job Market as a Free-Lance Home Economist," *Journal of Home Economics* 68 (September 1976), 51–52.

Mathews, Kathy. *On Your Own: Ninety-nine Alternatives to a 9 to 5 Job*. New York: Random House, 1977.

McAdam, Terry W. *Doing Well by Doing Good: The First Complete Guide to Careers in the Nonprofit Sector*. New York: Penguin Books, 1988.

McConnel, Patricia. *Women's Work-At-Home Handbook: Income and Independence*. New York: Bantam Books, 1986.

Mitchell, Joyce Slayton. *College Board Guide to Jobs and Career Planning*. New York: College Entrance Examination Board, 1990.

Naisbitt, John. *Megatrends: Ten New Directions Transforming Our Lives*. Chicago: Nightingale Conant Corp., 1984.

Naisbitt, John, and Patricia Aburdene. *Megatrends 2000: Ten New Directions for the 1990's*. New York: Morrow, 1990.

Occupational Outlook Handbook. Washington, DC: U.S. Government Printing Office, 1990.

O'Toole, Patricia. *Corporate Messiah: The Hiring and Firing of Million-Dollar Managers.* New York: Morrow, 1984.

Powell, Janet. "Entrepreneurship," *Illinois Teacher* 33 (March/April 1990), 141–142.

Scollard, Jeanette R. *The Self-Employed Woman: How to Start Your Own Business and Gain Control of Your Life.* New York: Simon & Schuster, 1986.

Wilkins, J. *Her Own Business: Success Secrets of Women Entrepreneurs.* New York: McGraw-Hill, 1987.

Winston, Sandra. *The Entrepreneurial Woman.* New York: Newsweek Books, 1979.

Winter, Maridee Allen. *Mind Your Own Business, Be Your Own Boss.* Englewood Cliffs, NJ: Prentice-Hall, 1980.

Work, Clyde E., June H. Wheeler, and Jeanette V. Williams. "Guidance for Nontraditional Careers," *Personnel and Guidance Journal* 60 (May 1982), 553–556.

Professional Development for Careers

Part III is a comprehensive guide to the professional development for your career. It will help you choose a professional education and guide you through the steps of job seeking. It includes the following six chapters:

- **Your Lifelong Plan of Education and Professional Development (Chapter 11)**
- **Internships and Other Preprofessional Employment (Chapter 12)**
- **Developing Your Strategy for Job Seeking (Chapter 13)**
- **Your Professional Résumé and Portfolio (Chapter 14)**
- **How to Find Out About Desirable Employers (Chapter 15)**
- **How to Obtain Interviews and Offers of Employment (Chapter 16)**

Your Lifelong Plan of Education and Professional Development

Education is the centerpiece of your growth as a professional. Therefore, we open our discussion of professional development by looking at your education for family- and consumer-oriented careers. We believe that professional education is a lifetime process, beginning with undergraduate education and continuing with many types of professional development following college. First we look at the most important part of education opening the door to careers — your college education.

Your College Education

College is many things. It is a place to get an education leading to a career, and it is also a place of socialization, personal growth, and maturation. To help you achieve your goals for college, it helps to start with a realistic understanding of where your college life is going.

Your College Life

College life is four years of study in a major field, and it is also four years of continuous changing and adjustment in your life-style. Each year of college brings new courses, new things to do, and new events. Table 11.1 gives a year-by-year review of typical college ac-

TABLE 11.1   Career Planning While in College — A Year-by-Year Guide to Activities

---

Freshman Year — Beginning Your Attack

Adjusting to the campus and the university system takes all year.
- Attend an orientation session — it can help you ease into college life.
- Tentatively select a major field.
- With the help of your adviser, enroll in core courses.
- Take one or more courses in your major to learn more about it (and to see if it's right for you!).
- Take a course on career planning.
- Seek out a support group — dorm, social group, club, organization, peer counselor or adviser — people who can assist you with

The catalog	Preregistration
The schedule of classes	Where to go for what
The student handbook	Who to see for what

- Ask your department for handouts on career options and information related to your major.
- Make it a point to visit most places on campus your first year.
- Look around, and don't hesitate to ask questions.
- Summer vacation: Get a job. Earn money, get work experience, and learn to get along with people in a work environment. See the placement office for job announcements.

Sophomore Year — Assessment and Exploration

You hit the ground running this year, and so use the momentum.
- Complete the introductory courses in your prospective major field.

- Get to know some faculty, staff, counselors, and administrators. Ask for advice and information about student clubs and organizations and opportunities on campus to supplement your academic work.
- Join campus club and activities. Join a club focusing on your major field of study. Begin to develop your career.
- Enroll in a career planning course if you haven't already.
- Participate in a career planning workshop.
- Assess personal values, interests, and skills through vocational testing (student counseling service). Take self-administered exercises in career planning. Talk with counselors and advisers.
- Gather occupational information from the placement office, the university library, the student counseling center, and your departments.
- Attend career fairs and career seminars to talk with representatives from a variety of career fields.
- Summer vacation: Get a job. Earn money, develop skills, build a work record, develop maturity. Start pursuing positions early.

Junior Year — Career Decisions and Reality Testing

- In your chosen career field, take several courses in your major. Develop a portfolio of professional-quality, career-related projects from course assignments or independent study.
- Select electives from other academic areas to enhance your qualifications. Talk to placement advisers about your employability and goals.
- Analyze your career attitudes. Have you assumed responsibility for making decisions about your life's work? Do you have alternative career plans? Have you combined reality with your values and attitudes?
- Join campus clubs and organizations in your chosen field if you haven't done this yet.
- Read professional journals and newsletters to become acquainted with the jargon and events in your field.
- Develop a résumé and begin comparing your qualifications with the requirements listed on job announcements at the placement office.
- Seek out an internship, co-op program, or part-time field experience to try out your career. Reevaluate your interests, goals, and experiences in the summer after your junior year.

Senior Year — Developing Your Job Search Strategy

- Complete course requirements in your major field. Plan a job-seeking strategy, using Chapters 12 through 16 of this book.
- Discuss career opportunities and plans with faculty, counselors, and professionals in your field.
- Attend workshops on preparing résumés and planning for interviewing.
- Take advantage of any opportunities to interview employers on campus. Register early in your senior year to participate in the placement office's on-campus interviews.
- Select faculty and administrators to give references for you. Discuss your interests, skills, and personal strengths related to the positions you will be seeking.
- Conduct a thorough job search to obtain your desired position.
- Continue to evaluate your professional and personal development. Make lifelong adjustments to fine-tune for satisfaction. Consider graduate school if appropriate to your professional career.

Source: Adapted from materials from the Placement Office, The University of Arizona.

tivities and events. Freshmen and sophomores will find this table helpful in previewing their future in college, and juniors and seniors will find it helpful in recounting how far they've come and identifying what is yet to be done.

Choosing a Career-Oriented Major

Undoubtedly the most important decision in college is choosing a major. There are no simple tests or formulas that can tell you what major is best. No one is better equipped to make that choice than you are. If you remain unsure about your major and career, however, our advice is straightforward. Take the time now to explore the alternatives — by reading Chapters 5 through 10 and doing the end-of-chapter exercises. Only by exploring can you identify possible majors that match your interests, talents, and personality. Do some of the exercises in these chapters to help you sort out winning choices. Also see Self-Assessment Exercise 11–1, "Sorting Out Your Best Majors" to clarify your choices.

An extraordinary array of events and circumstances shapes students' choices of a major field of study: quality of the program, status of the program, job prospects following graduation, image of the school, facilities available, financial aid, workload in the courses, practical opportunities for learning (internships, work experiences, student clubs), helpfulness of the faculty, influences from others (friends, parents, employers), and even social opportunities or a pleasant campus life-style. Research suggests that all these things can be important, especially the content of the major, what you can do following graduation, and opportunities to help other people. Financial prospects and starting salaries are important to some students as well, but the prospects for long-term growth and personal success is the real priority for many. Education is also sought for self-enrichment and to seek a "better future," as students well recognize. Obviously, we are dealing with one of life's most demanding choices, one we want to make carefully with the most complete information available.

One way to tell whether your choice is a good one is to ask yourself, "Do the things I've done or experienced in this field bring me enjoyment and excitement?" For example, have you always enjoyed being with children, or do you often find yourself sketching out ideas for new fashions? At night do you wake up thinking about a particular field, or do you find yourself always wanting to learn more about it? These are sure signs of an interest that may lead to a major and a career. But don't pursue a career too far unless you feel some of this emotional attachment and excitement.

If you've explored various careers but your choice remains unclear, here are some things you can do. Take a sample of introductory courses in several fields such as merchandising, consumer studies, and family relations. Another helpful approach is to take part-time or volunteer jobs to preview careers. Undecided students may also consider a general major such as general home economics, human ecology, family studies, or other general majors that offer a broad selection of courses. General majors can lead to attractive career selections, particularly when you concentrate your electives in a few career areas.

Is it possible to choose the wrong major? Some students complete college only to decide their major was not necessarily the field in which they wanted to work. Was their degree a waste? Of course not! You can succeed in a variety of occupations and professions regardless of your major. It is true that employers want you to be

---

SELF-ASSESSMENT EXERCISE 11-1

Sorting Out Your Best Majors

Refer to the career profiles in Chapters 5 through 8. List the four that best match your interests, talents, and personality.

Ranks

1. _____ _____

2. _____ _____

3. _____ _____

4. _____ _____

From this list, rank the best, second best, third best, and fourth best in the right column above.

Now write the majors that are best for your top two or three choices (the career profiles note some of leading majors for each career).

1. _____

2. _____

3. _____

4. _____

These are among your best majors.

familiar with a particular field, but they also look for people with thinking skills, problem-solving skills, creativity, and the like (see Chapters 3 and 4). These general skills can be acquired from many well-planned programs of study. Therefore, the choice of your major does not irrevocably bind you to a specific career, because you will develop many transferable skills for other careers.

Of course, your best professional opportunities are in careers closely related to your educational background. Your career-oriented major gives you a head start. And for many family- and consumer-oriented careers, the right major may be essential to attaining an entry-level position. These are reasons that make selecting the right major important.

Once you have selected your college major, it is useful to take a close look at what your program includes. In general, college majors in all family and consumer fields offer (1) a liberal education constituting the foundation of the major and (2) professional training, including specialized, technical, and career-oriented courses. For example, let's look at an interior design major, which typically includes the following:

1. Liberal education in such subjects as English, literature, general history, art history, psychology, sociology, technical writing, communications, and math.
2. Specialized professional education in art, color, textiles, photography, furniture design, space planning, history of interiors, architecture, drafting, rendering, model making, and computer-assisted design. Additional courses can be taken in the related fields of merchandising, accounting, and management.

A useful exercise is to write down the courses you will take each semester (or each quarter) during your college years. Many colleges will do this for you, but it is a useful exercise that can increase your awareness of your major and its content. Complete Self-Assessment Exercise 11–2 (pages 238–239) for your chosen college major, using your college or university catalog as a guide. Your completed exercise will look like Table 11.2, which shows an example for a four-year, semester-by-semester program of study in fashion merchandising (this example shows course numbers and course names for each semester, which differ from school to school). Keep in mind that this is merely an example and that you'll probably find differences at your college or university. The important thing is to follow the planned sequence at your school because the courses build on one another in a carefully chosen plan.

TABLE 11.2   Fashion Merchandising Major—Plan of Study (By Semesters)

Freshman Year

First Semester	*Second Semester*
Subject:	Subject:
CT 114, Apparel Analyis	CT 145, Fashion Concepts
ID 115, Fundamentals of Design	Engl. 102, Composition II
Engl. 101, Composition I	Art 101, Studio Art
H.Ec. 129, Professional Development	Psych. 100, Introduction to Psychology
Soc. 100, Introduction to Sociology	Com. 102, Public Speaking
MIS 111, Introduction to Computers	

Sophomore Year

First Semester	*Second Semester*
Subject:	Subject:
Com. 112, Business and Professional	CT 284R, Textile Science
Communication	CT 284L, Textile Science Laboratory
Chem. 101, Chemistry I	Econ. 201b, Microeconomics
Chem. 102, Chemistry I Laboratory	Humanities Elective
Econ. 201a, Macroeconomics	Math or Science Elective
Humanities Elective	Acct. 200, Introduction to Accounting
General Elective	

Junior Year

First Semester	*Second Semester*
Subject:	Subject:
CT 325, History of Fashion	Marketing or Business Elective
Behavioral Science Elective	Humanities Elective
Engl. 307, Business Writing	CT 393b, Preparation for Internship
Business Elective	Behavioral Science Elective
CT 304, Merchandising Analysis	Mktg. 364, Creative Advertising
Mktg. 361, Introduction to Marketing	CT 445, Clothing for Special Needs

Summer—Junior Year

Internship Recommended

Senior Year

First Semester	*Second Semester*
Subject:	Subject:
Mktg. 458, Retailing Management	CT 444, Clothing and Human Behavior
CT 454, New Developments in Textiles	Marketing Elective
Family- or Consumer-Oriented Electives	CT 434, The Fashion Industry
CS 446, Consumer Economics	Family- and Consumer-Oriented Electives
Business Elective	General Electives
General Elective	

Several activities help start your college program of study. First, be sure that you are assigned to an academic adviser who specializes in your major, and talk with this person when you need advice on your studies. Your adviser knows the academic requirements of programs and the courses you need to take and can advise you on other professional career matters as well. Second, take a "Professional Development" or "Introduction to Careers" type of course early in your college career (the exact titles vary). This sort of course helps you to clarify career goals and encourages you to take charge of your program of study. Third, take one or more introductory courses in your major as early as possible, to learn more about the major. Finally, get the advice of successful students who are a year or two ahead of you, and the advice of working professionals in the field as well.

Will Your Major Lead to a Job?

Our discussion of your career-oriented major would not be complete without commenting on the job opportunities you may expect following graduation. In Chapter 3 we reviewed studies suggesting that there is substantial demand for well-educated students in all family- and consumer-oriented careers (review Chapter 3 for details). There is great public concern with these fields today, and the number of new opportunities for professionals is growing daily.

SELF-ASSESSMENT EXERCISE 11-2

Your College Plan of Study

Fill out this plan of study for your chosen major, semester-by-semester or quarter-by-quarter as appropriate to your program.

FRESHMAN YEAR

Semester 1/Quarter 1   Semester 2/Quarter 2   Summer School/Quarter 3

_____   _____   _____

_____   _____   _____

_____   _____   _____

_____   _____   _____

SOPHOMORE YEAR

Semester 1/Quarter 1	Semester 2/Quarter 2	Summer School/Quarter 3
_____	_____	_____
_____	_____	_____
_____	_____	_____
_____	_____	_____
_____	_____	_____

JUNIOR YEAR

Semester 1/Quarter 1	Semester 2/Quarter 2	Summer School/Quarter 3
_____	_____	_____
_____	_____	_____
_____	_____	_____
_____	_____	_____
_____	_____	_____

SENIOR YEAR

Semester 1/Quarter 1	Semester 2/Quarter 2	Summer School/Quarter 3
_____	_____	_____
_____	_____	_____
_____	_____	_____
_____	_____	_____
_____	_____	_____

There should be career opportunities for qualified graduates in all major areas, although some areas are more competitive than others. Attaining your chosen career will require much of you, as described in earlier chapters (see Chapters 3 and 4 and the following Chapters 12 through 16 for further information), but employment opportunities will be available in the future for the student who obtains the skills required and who remains flexible to choose from a variety of opportunities that each field offers.

Managing College Life _____

Attending classes, reading assignments, studying for tests, completing projects, and writing papers are the central activities of college students. Many other aspects of college life vie for your time as well: social organizations, student clubs, dating, relaxation, sports, and part-time work lead the list. Does all of this make you feel busy? Pressured? Not enough time in the day? Welcome to college!

Balancing all these activities, interests, and demands on time is probably the biggest challenge that college students ever face. Some students feel that they must do everything, but the wisest students recognize their goals and spend time on only what is really important to them. Of course your professors expect that the major commitment will be to your studies, and we would be the first to agree. At the same time, professors recognize that college life is more than studies, just as life after college is more than your work. In fact, to ignore the opportunities for socialization and extracurricular activities would diminish the value of your college education.

The important thing is to make sure that no one college activity dominates your college life. Be especially aware of the "traps" of college life. One is social life, and many schools provide more than enough fun and relaxation. Enjoy relaxing to shake off stress and get you ready for more work, but don't overdo it. Another trap is part-time work. We advocate part-time work, especially when it provides experience relevant to professional careers. But don't get overcommitted to work while you're in school. If financial needs require you to work, check your school's financial aid office to find ways to supplement your income and reduce the number of hours you work. It is not worth sacrificing the educational value of your college experience for work.

Extracurricular activities are another trap in which the overcommitment of time is a danger. Some people seem to major in fraternity, sorority, school newspaper, or student club. All these are desirable activities in moderation, but avoid letting them dominate your college life.

There are times when college life seems unmanageable. This is particularly true for freshmen, and when pressures start to build, seek help. Whatever the problem, do not let it grow. Talk it out with some of your friends, family, peer counselor, and head resident where you live (residence hall, fraternity or sorority house). Visit your academic adviser and talk openly. Help is also available at other places in your university, such as the guidance and counseling office, student placement service, student government, student union services, or the dean of students.

Some keys to successful college life may seem obvious but are worth repeating. Take care of yourself. Eat three balanced meals a day (nutrition is extremely important), don't abuse alcohol or other stimulants, get enough sleep, and take time for exercise and relaxation. Find moments to be alone, rest, think, read for pleasure, and clear your head. Get away from campus once in a while. Do a special favor for a friend. Whenever you do well, such as getting a good grade on a test or completing a term paper, give yourself a special reward like going out for dinner or a movie. All these little things add to your physical and mental well-being and make your college life an even greater pleasure.

Continuing Your Education After College _____

Graduation marks your transition to a new educational arena. In many ways, education never ends, and your education has not ended just because you have graduated. You will leave college, but there are many continuing education programs that all professionals take. For example, seminars, workshops, conferences, short courses, correspondence courses, and many other learning experiences may be offered to you after college. These are provided by the professional associations in your field. For example, associations like the American Home Economics Association, American Dietetic Association, National Council on Family Relations, National Retail Federation, American Society of Interior Designers, American Association of Textile Chemists and Colorists, and many others in family- and consumer-oriented fields offer programs for your continuing professional development. (We hope you joined student chapters of these or other professional organizations while you were in school.) The programs focus on the newest or best techniques in your profession and help you keep up to date with changing trends and practical applications in your field. Such continuing education builds on the education that you received in college. Professional courses are also offered by many businesses, consulting firms, and educational institutions.

Employers regard continuing education as essential to the growth of their employees. In fact, some offer their own programs of executive development or continuing education taught on the premises where the employee works. College courses may also be brought in to the employer. Employers often financially support your attendance at educational programs and short courses, knowing that they are making a good investment in your future and thus that of their organization.

Graduate School

You can also continue your formal education in a graduate program leading to a master's or doctoral degree. In general, master's degrees require thirty to fifty semester hours credit past the bachelor's degree and one to two years to complete. Doctoral degrees usually require sixty to ninety semester hours and four years beyond the bachelor's degree. Some professions require graduate degrees for entry or advancement. Professions such as marriage counseling, family therapy, textile science, and nutrition require graduate degrees. Teachers must have master's degrees in some school systems, although many are hired with only undergraduate degrees. A Ph.D or Ed.D. degree is required to teach and do research at the major universities because doctoral degrees are oriented toward research, and many of today's universities emphasize both research and teaching.

Attaining a graduate degree is no guarantee of a better job or a more successful career, but it is probably one of the more important building blocks. It may win you a promotion, and it certainly will show your supervisors that you are motivated in your career. And there is no question that where people are otherwise equally qualified, those who have the most impressive degrees or credentials will get the promotions. So, advanced degrees add to your opportunities for professional growth, not only because of the knowledge that you obtain but also because of the image they convey to your supervisors and coworkers.

When should you start your graduate study? People used to enter graduate school immediately following college, and some still do so today. However, many people now feel that some practical experience is good to have before entering graduate school. This is true for merchandising and design students, and it is probably true for other family-oriented professions as well. As a compromise, some individuals go to graduate school part time while working, but this is the slow route to getting a degree and requires sacrifices along the way. Overall, it appears that getting some work experience and then going to graduate school full time is the preferred route.

Once you are working, your employer may pay for some or all of your education. Many companies pay for courses that are related to their business. Some companies may even pay you while you are getting a degree, but this practice is limited to the larger companies and those with substantial financial resources. If your organization cannot financially support your graduate education, at least it may give you a leave of absence to return to school. Then, after completing your education, you can return to the job you left. And this might put you on a faster track toward promotion, although you will have sacrificed one or two years away from the job.

Choosing a graduate school is different from choosing an undergraduate institution. There are hundreds of undergraduate programs in family- and consumer-oriented professions throughout the country. A smaller number offer master's programs but there are only a handful of doctoral programs. In general, the best-known doctoral programs are offered at the state-supported universities in the United States and Canada. Look for graduate programs that have at least two or three established faculty members specializing in your area of interest. Also look for faculty members who have published well-received books and articles or who have had practical work experience in the field. In graduate education, the faculty members with whom you will work should be the basis for your choice of school.

The Role of Professional Journals and Trade Publications _____

During your college program you will be exposed to professional journals in your area of specialization, for example, the *Journal of Consumer Affairs,* the *Journal of the American Dietetic Association,* the *Journal of Marriage and the Family,* the *Journal of Retailing,* the *Home Economics Research Journal,* and others. You will also see many of the so-called trade publications, which report on practical activities in the field (e.g., *Stores Magazine* for merchandising, *Interiors* for interior design, *Forecast for Home Economics* for home economics education). These and many other periodicals offer some of the best information about your continuing education. One of the first things to do after graduation is subscribe to one or more of these publications, many of which come as a part of membership in professional organizations of your field. Join these organizations and get a free subscription.

Once you have selected the best journals and periodicals, read them regularly. Most of them have abstracts or executive summaries that preview articles and help identify the ones most useful to you. An hour spent once every few weeks reading these publications is a very small commitment in comparison with the information you may receive. And keep a file of back issues, for you'll refer back to them. In this way you will build your own professional library and have resources for doing your own research.

The Importance of Keeping Up to Date _____

Today information about everything is expanding exponentially. In some fields, such as computers and computerized information systems, our knowledge may be tripling every year, and maybe faster. The importance of keeping up to date on new information and new trends in your field cannot be overemphasized. In fact, if you do not keep up to date, you may quickly become obsolete. It takes as little as two or three years for today's professions to change dramatically. For example, just several years ago people in consumer affairs were not nearly so involved in family financial counseling as they are today. Similarly, specialists in fashion merchandising have also become experts in computerized inventory management as a result of the rapid growth of technology in that field. Your field can change just as quickly.

The message is clear—educating yourself is a continuing process that begins early and continues well past college. Use all the means necessary to keep yourself well informed about the changing trends affecting your career. Read widely, take the necessary courses, and always be prepared to revise the ways you practice your profession as better approaches become available.

SELF-ASSESSMENT EXERCISE 11-3

Keeping Up in Your Field

Choose several publications that will help you keep up to date in your profession. Check your library and write down the best ones for learning about new trends.

1. _____

2. _____

3. _____

4. _____

Questions and Exercises _____

1. Read at least two current professional journals associated with your career interests.
2. Write a statement describing your lifelong educational plans and objectives.
3. Write a college plan of study for your chosen major. List the courses you will take each semester/quarter for your entire time in school. Is this sequence of courses logical? For example, do the courses build on one another and become more advanced?
4. Look into the graduate programs at two universities of your choice. Will your college program of study qualify you for entry into a graduate program?
5. After graduation, how will you keep up to date with new knowledge in your field? Why is this important?

Bibliography _____

Azibo, Moni, and Therese Crylen Unumb. *The Mature Woman's Back-to-Work Book*. Chicago: Contemporary Books, 1980.

Carey, Max L. "Three Paths to the Future: Occupational Projections, 1980–90," *Occupational Outlook Quarterly* 25 (Winter 1981), 3–11.

Cetron, Marvin, and Thomas O'Toole. "Careers with a Future: Where the Jobs Will Be in the 1990's," *The Futurist* 16 (June 1982), 11–19.

Feingold, S. Norman. "Tracking New Career Categories Will Become a Preoccupation for Job Seekers and Managers," *Personal Administrator* 28 (December 1983), 86–91.

Fetterman, Elsie, Myra L. Lenburg, and Shirley A. Mietlicki. "Training the Home Enterpreneur," *Journal of Home Economics* 78 (Summer 1986), 40–45.

Gerken, Dumont, Robert Reardon, and Roger Bash. "Revitalizing a Career Course: The Gender Roles Infusion," *Journal of Career Development* 14 (Summer 1988), 269–278.

Harren, Vincent A., M. Harry Daniels, and Jacqueline N. Buck. *Facilitating Students' Career Development*, San Francisco: Jossey-Bass, 1981.

Hewes, Dorothy W. "From Home to Worksite: New Arenas for Home Economics," *Journal of Home Economics* 76 (Fall 1984), 33–37.

Hoyt, Kenneth B. "The Career Status of Women and Minority Persons: A 20-Year Retrospective," *Career Development Quarterly* 37 (March 1989), 202–212.

Jarvis, Phillip S. "A Nation at Risk: The Economic Consequences of Neglecting Career Development," *Journal of Career Development* 16 (Spring 1990), 157–171.

Mouat, Lucia. *Back to Business: A Woman's Guide to Reentering the Job Market*. New York: Sovereign Books, 1979.

Niles, Spencer. "The Effects of a Career Planning Course and a Computer-

Assisted Career Guidance Program (SIGI PLUS) on Undecided University Students," *Journal of Career Development* 16 (Summer 1990), 237–248.

Shaevitz, Marjorie Hansen. *The Superwoman Syndrome.* New York: Warner Books, 1984.

Winefordner, David W. *Career Planning and Decision-Making for College.* Bloomington, IL: McKnight, 1980.

CHAPTER 12

Internships and Other Preprofessional Employment

W_e often hear that experience is one of life's great teachers. During your college years, you will be involved in many experiences and activities — classes, clubs, social activities, sports participation — and all these will be valuable to you as a person. But no experience can count toward your future as can an experience in the working world, an experience in your chosen career or profession. Plan to obtain preprofessional employment experience as part of your college life.

Work experience can help your educational and professional development in many ways, as follows:

1. You will learn the procedures, policies, and daily activities typical of the work world.
2. You will learn how theories and concepts can be applied to real-world situations.
3. You will learn the values and expectations of our work-oriented society.

4. Your maturity, sophistication, and responsibility will grow.
5. You will build a network of contacts for future jobs, professional friendships that can be of lasting value.
6. You will show employers you are interested in your field, because you have worked in it, succeeded in it, liked it, and want to come back for more.
7. You will have obtained entry-level experience and be ready for higher or more skilled positions in your profession.

Popular ways for students to gain professional work experience include internships, cooperative programs, part-time employment, and volunteer work.

Internships

An internship is a formal work experience that is part of your college curriculum, directly related to your major and career interest. Formal internships have become extremely popular and are offered in many colleges and universities today. The best internships are those in which the employer creates a learning environment and emphasizes training and education rather than actual work. This does not mean that an intern is not a productive worker but, rather, that the educational experience comes first.

Internships are available from virtually all types of employers, including retail stores, interior design firms, human service agencies, social welfare organizations, communications media, and government

---

SELF-ASSESSMENT EXERCISE 12–1

Values of Work Experience

List three ways in which your work experience will be valuable to your future employer.

1. _____

2. _____

3. _____

at the federal, state, and local levels. The equivalents of internships also exist in home economics teacher education programs, in which teachers gain actual experience in classroom situations. Or you may be able to create an internship based on your interests and needs.

Your internship will usually be scheduled between the junior and senior year of college or in the first semester of your senior year. At this point you will have done most of your coursework and be familiar with the theories, concepts, and methods in your field of study. This is when learning through an internship is of maximum value. The internship may be a short experience of one hundred to two hundred hours, but more often it should be a long-term experience lasting ten to sixteen weeks. Internships usually earn college credit, based on the amount of time spent in and the extent of the educational experience.

There are entry requirements for many internships, such as the courses that must have been completed and the minimum acceptable grade point averages (usually a C+ to B− average minimum and often higher). In addition, before entering the internship you will need to prepare a résumé of your education and experience and a portfolio containing examples of your work or other qualifications. Many internships also require you to interview formally for your position. This is desirable for both you and the employer, because you will want to work with an employer that meets your interests and the employer will want to choose interns who might be hired after their graduation. Also note that preparing a résumé and having an interview gives you practice for when you seek a job after college.

Your internship will include a variety of activities before, during and after the actual work experience. Most internship programs have a "preinternship" course on the procedures for completing the internship. Frequently you will be asked to write a proposal for the internship, stating your objectives. During the internship you should keep a daily record of your experiences and achievements. You may be asked to interview with executives or other organizational managers at the firm where you are interning. When the internship is completed, you will be asked to write a report of your experience and accomplishments and an analysis of the organization where you worked. This review of your internship will be a permanent record and will also reinforce what you have learned.

What you will actually do during the internship will depend on how well planned your internship is, your initiative, and your employer's willingness to assign you to various learning experiences. Initially you will likely be involved in routine experiences, such as operating on the sales floor of a retail store, meeting clients at a social service organization, answering the telephone, or carrying out basic organizational and clerical activities. But your internship should involve much more than entry-level activities. It should take you through various divisions of the organization, to give you experience with the organization's various functions. This breadth should make you aware of how the many subjects of your field relate to real professional practice. The broadest practical experience should also help you find a position after graduation.

Cooperative Programs

Also gaining in popularity, although not yet as well known as internships, are cooperative programs, or "co-ops." Like an internship, a co-op program involves work experience. In a typical program, a student may work full time for a semester, return to school for a semester, and then return to work again for a summer or a semester. Sometimes co-op programs start much earlier in the student's academic career than an internship does, often as early as the freshman year.

Co-ops are most popular in the applied sciences, such as textile science, food science, housing, interior design, fashion design, or household equipment. They are especially beneficial to scientifically or technically oriented students because many of them offer hands-on work with the newest scientific equipment or computers. Another advantage is that some co-ops pay above-average salaries to participants, whereas an intern may not always be paid. Employers are willing to pay co-op participants well because they hope to retain them as employees after graduation. The one drawback of a co-op is that it may take participants five years to graduate, as compared with four years in a regular program. But this is a small disadvantage in return for the advantage in gaining the work experience.

If a co-op program is not available in your major, you may find an opportunity through the cooperative education director at your university. Many academic departments do not operate co-op programs, and it may be necessary to design your own. You may be able to sell your idea for a co-op program to a specific employer. To do this, send your prospective employer a proposal indicating your interests in a co-op, your credentials, and your hope for a long-term opportunity with the firm following the co-op. Many employers recognize the advantages of hiring and training young professionals early in their college career.

SELF-ASSESSMENT EXERCISE 12–2

Your Experiences

Can you identify your experiences, working or otherwise, that might be valued by an employer? Why would these be valued?

1. _____

2. _____

3. _____

Part-Time Employment _____

Regardless of whether an internship or a co-op program is available to you, you should consider obtaining some part-time employment during your college career. It is particularly valuable if you can find employment related to your career of interest. For example, merchandising students should find part-time work as sales associates or stock clerks with department stores or supermarkets. Human services workers could find assignments in camps, the YMCA or YWCA, or social service agencies. These part-time jobs give you an excellent introduction to your field of interest and can tell you if the field is really compatible with your interests. Thus, part-time employment becomes one of the determinants of your actual career choice — if you don't like the part-time work, you surely won't like it full time! Of course, in part-time jobs you should expect a larger-than-average amount of routine or clerical work, which can give you a distorted or inaccurate view of the profession. Nevertheless, such seemingly routine experiences actually become excellent credentials for your future employment.

Must your part-time work be in your area of interest to be valuable? Not necessarily. In any job, you learn some of the rules and styles of all jobs, which contributes to your professional growth. It may even broaden your view of work. However, first try to get part-time work in an area in which you see a potential for long-term employment.

For more information on part-time jobs, see the part-time placement service of your placement office or local employment agencies. In addition, one of the best ways to obtain part-time employment is to go personally to the employment office of prospective employers. When applying for part-time employment, be sure to look your best and to fill out employment applications neatly and completely. The impressions you create in both your appearance and application may determine whether you get the job.

The Value of Volunteer Work

In some professions, particularly the human services, volunteering is an accepted way to gain entry into the profession. We recommend voluntary experiences to all students, both for the experience and the entree. As a volunteer, your work can range from basic clerical duties to creative activities pertaining to the organization's goals, and management. Often you will work with a practicing professional such as a social service worker, retail store buyer, or an interior designer. Assisting such professionals is among the better experiences of volunteering.

Volunteers are needed at social service organizations, hospitals, retirement homes, child-care centers, and other human welfare organizations. Volunteers may also be accepted in retail businesses, YMCAs and YWCAs, government offices, political parties, churches, and local cultural groups (theatrical groups, historical societies). Volunteer even if you have only a few hours a week to share. And

SELF-ASSESSMENT EXERCISE 12–3

Key to Success

How will you add to your work experience? Describe ways that will contribute to your professional development.

_____

_____

_____

_____

_____

_____

remember that volunteering adds to your qualifications in the same way that any other work experience does.

Experience Counts

Look on getting experience as part of your college education. Plan early to acquire experience through whatever means is necessary. Whether you have only a few hours a week to volunteer or a semester for a full-time co-op program, your time will be well spent. But don't overdo it. Remember that the main goal of college is to get an education. Use your work experiences to complement and enrich your education.

Questions and Exercises

1. Conduct an informational interview at the office of an employer with whom you would like an internship.
2. Write a proposal for an internship or co-op position. Include a statement of personal objectives, assignments, or duties you expect, and how your work will be evaluated. Be specific.
3. List the businesses or organizations in which you would be qualified to be an intern.
4. Visit your school's intern or co-op coordinator, and discuss internship possibilities.
5. What ways other than through internships and co-ops can you gain employment experience before graduation?
6. Why is experience important to your job search, and what types of experiences are employers seeking in your chosen profession?

Bibliography

Berliner, Don. *Want a Job? Get Some Experience, Want Experience? Get a Job.* New York: Amalom, 1978.

Bennett, Robert L. *Careers Through Cooperative Work Experience.* New York: Wiley, 1977.

Directory of Washington Internships 1983–84: A Guide to Current Internship Programs and Placements in the Nation's Capital. Washington, DC: National Society for Internships and Experiential Education, 1983.

Hoyt, Kenneth B. "The Career Status of Women and Minority Persons: A 20-Year Retrospective," *Career Development Quarterly* 37 (March 1989), 202–212.

Hulse, Lisa S., ed. *1985 Internships: 3400 On-the-Job Training Opportunities for All Types of Careers.* Cincinnati: Writer's Digest Books, 1984.

Jobst, Katherine. *Internships, 1990.* Cincinnati: Writer's Digest Books, 1989.

Maineri, Sandra Bologna. "Free-lancing as a Career," *Journal of Home Ecomonics* 72 (Spring 1980), 56–57.

Maineri, Sandra C. "Creating a Career: How I Developed a Job Market as a Free-Lance Home Economist," *Journal of Home Economics* 68 (September 1976), 51–52.

O'Toole, Patricia. *Corporate Messiah: The Hiring and Firing of Million-Dollar Managers.* New York: Morrow, 1984.

Pare, Elizabeth. "The World of Work: A Family Affair," *Illinois Teacher* 32 (September/October 1988), 2–5.

Powell, James. *The Prentice-Hall Global Employment Guide.* Englewood Cliffs, NJ: Prentice-Hall, 1983.

Simmons, Philip, and Roseanne Haggerty. *The Student Guide to Fellowships and Internships.* Haggerty, NY: Dutton, 1980.

CHAPTER 13

Developing Your Strategy for Job Seeking

Today, advice for the job seeker abounds, from how to clarify your career preferences and how to prepare résumés to books recommending "guerrilla tactics" for the job market (creative approaches to finding jobs). Likewise, there are workshops, seminars, guidebooks, and manuals for job seekers. The next four chapters in this book describe the best ways of seeking a job. We shall consider such topics as developing a professional image, designing a professional résumé, making contacts with employers, interviewing for positions, and conducting yourself in your new job. This chapter is devoted to developing a strategy for job seeking, including a detailed, organized plan of action.

Developing a Strategy for Job Seeking _____

At the start let's recognize the obvious. It is not easy to find that all-important first job, the job "just right" for you. Finding a match between your qualifications and an employer who needs them requires time and hard work. But it should be a rewarding and exciting time, a time of discovery, learning, and adventure.

Two Keys to a Successful Career Search

- Self-Assessment—Knowing Yourself
- Defining Realistic Career Goals

Job seeking is far more than a telephone call to an employer or a résumé in the mail, and it is more than a casual contact with your university's placement service. Successful job seeking requires a strategy, a step-by-step plan of action. Figure 13-1 outlines such a strategy. Basically, job seeking has six steps, as follows:

1. *Self-assessment.* A useful starting point is to assess your interests, qualifications, and abilities. Some approaches to self-assessment were outlined earlier in Chapter 3, and this is a good time to review it. In particular, list such things as your capabilities, personal interests, priorities, life-style preferences, geographic preferences, financial expectations, educational background, and experience. This is a serious step in career planning, and you must carefully analyze each of these categories. They identify you, and will help you choose the right opportunity.

2. *Define your career goals.* In what type of organization do you wish to seek employment—business, government, school, human service organization? Can you be specific, for example, identify the type of business (department store, discount store, specialty store, chain store)? Can you identify the specialization you wish to pursue, such as design, merchandising, consumer education, high school teaching, writing, or working with disabled children? Can you identify appropriate job titles, such as retail buyer, contract designer, or resource teacher? And most importantly, can you state in a phrase or sentence your short-term goal for the next few years and your long-term goal for the next five to ten years?

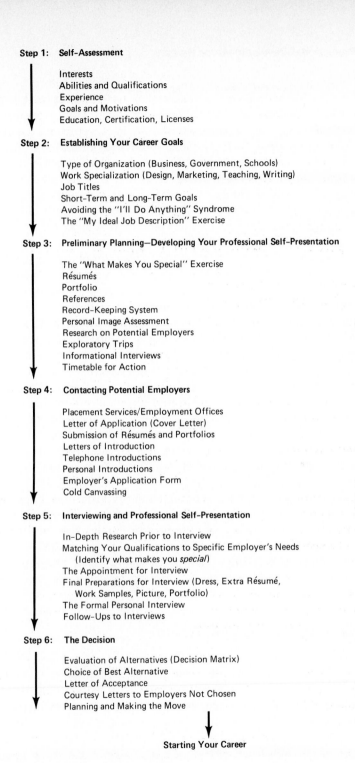

Step 1: Self-Assessment

Interests
Abilities and Qualifications
Experience
Goals and Motivations
Education, Certification, Licenses

Step 2: Establishing Your Career Goals

Type of Organization (Business, Government, Schools)
Work Specialization (Design, Marketing, Teaching, Writing)
Job Titles
Short-Term and Long-Term Goals
Avoiding the "I'll Do Anything" Syndrome
The "My Ideal Job Description" Exercise

Step 3: Preliminary Planning—Developing Your Professional Self-Presentation

The "What Makes You Special" Exercise
Résumés
Portfolio
References
Record-Keeping System
Personal Image Assessment
Research on Potential Employers
Exploratory Trips
Informational Interviews
Timetable for Action

Step 4: Contacting Potential Employers

Placement Services/Employment Offices
Letter of Application (Cover Letter)
Submission of Résumés and Portfolios
Letters of Introduction
Telephone Introductions
Personal Introductions
Employer's Application Form
Cold Canvassing

Step 5: Interviewing and Professional Self-Presentation

In-Depth Research Prior to Interview
Matching Your Qualifications to Specific Employer's Needs
    (Identify what makes you *special*)
The Appointment for Interview
Final Preparations for Interview (Dress, Extra Résumé,
    Work Samples, Picture, Portfolio)
The Formal Personal Interview
Follow-Ups to Interviews

Step 6: The Decision

Evaluation of Alternatives (Decision Matrix)
Choice of Best Alternative
Letter of Acceptance
Courtesy Letters to Employers Not Chosen
Planning and Making the Move

Starting Your Career

Figure 13-1   Strategy for Job Seeking

3. *Preliminary planning—Developing your professional self-presentation.* You will begin a series of activities that will produce your professional identity. Some are developing a professional résumé, compiling a portfolio of your accomplishment, devising a record-keeping system, doing preliminary research on potential employers, and establishing a timetable for action.
4. *Contacting potential employers.* Now it is time to take the initiative. There are a number of approaches to contacting employers and gaining interviews. In a later chapter we shall outline the standard approaches as well as some more aggressive approaches that successful graduates use.
5. *Interviewing and professional self-presentation.* Your goal is to secure an appointment for an interview and to conduct successful interviews with one or more potential employers. It is important to do research on the organization before your interview, and it is important to match your qualifications to the employer's needs. Professional self-presentation means identifying what makes you special and employable. There are also certain ethics and courtesies that distinguish the thoughtful candidate from others.
6. *The decision.* When you have had all your interviews, evaluate the alternatives and choose the best one. Send a letter of acceptance to the employer you choose and letters of regret to those not. Planning the move to your new job and your new location is the last step or activity in your decision making.

The foundation of your job-seeking strategy are Steps 1 through 3. At this point we assume you have finished Step 1, a comprehensive self-assessment of your personal interests, goals, and qualifications (if this is not the case, refer to Chapter 3 and complete your self-analysis before proceeding). We shall begin with a discussion of Step 2 in the job-seeking process, defining career goals.

Establishing Your Career Goals

One of the most important steps in career planning is to define your career goals in a statement, as specific as possible, of what you want to do. The following are some guidelines on alternative ways to state goals:

1. *Statement of desired professional specialty or job title.* You may state your objective in general terms or narrow it down to an

area of specialization within a job. For example:

    a. Interior designer
    b. Interior designer — residential interiors
    c. Residential interior designer — specialist in kitchen design
    d. Child-care specialist
    e. Child-care specialist — public service agency
    f. Child-care specialist — mentally retarded children

2. *Statement of career goals in terms of function or responsibilities.* Write a short phrase or sentence describing the responsibilities and activities that you seek in your career. For example:

"Position with responsibility for managing and controlling the operation of a fashion department in a large specialty store."
"Position involving daily interaction with young children, including teaching, supervising, and engaging in structured activities for the benefit of the child-client."

3. *Statement of goals in terms of skills.* State your special capabilities and make their application a part of your career goal. For example:

"Position involving analysis of consumer markets and requiring knowledge of such specialized subjects as consumer affairs, consumer decision-making processes, consumer education, retailing management, and general business management."
"Position requiring knowledge of nutritional assessment, physiological development, psychological development, dietary analysis, and individual personal counseling regarding diet and personal health."

4. *Statement of short-term and long-term goals.* This type of statement is usually effective for business-oriented students, because businesses like individuals who have both short-term and long-term goals. For example:

Short-term goal: Executive management trainee with a major retail store.
Long-term goal: Advancement to assistant buyer, buyer, and higher levels of management in the merchandising and marketing division of a retail store.

5. *Combined statement of goals.* In this type of statement you combine several of the categories that you have just reviewed. For example:

"Consumer information analyst with the U.S. Department of Agriculture, U.S. Department of Commerce, or major federal government agency. Position desired requires a knowledge of consumer needs for information, education, and protection through governmental agencies and governmental programs."

"Registered dietitian with a major teaching hospital. Position requiring knowledge of nutritional assessment, diet therapy, and personal counseling of clients. Desire to work with teams of doctors and other medical professionals making up a total health-care team."

On the basis of these examples, try writing your own career goals in each of the five formats.

SELF-ASSESSMENT EXERCISE 13–1

Important Activity

Write a "Career Goals" statement for your chosen career. Try to be brief yet specific.

_____

_____

_____

Establishing career goals is more than simply stating the type of work or job you want. Rather, it means thinking about where you want to work, the responsibilities you seek, the environment in which you work best, the hours you want to work, your salary requirements, relations with colleagues, relations with clients, and so on. In short, what is your ideal job? To answer this, we have developed a short exercise entitled "My Ideal Job Description" (Self-assessment Exercise 13–2). After doing this exercise, you will have created a more complete picture of your career objective and where you want to be going in the next several years.

There are some "don'ts" in establishing your career goals. Probably the most important is to avoid the "I'll do anything" syndrome. It may seem simple to say "I'll do anything" and let the employer decide which jobs you are capable of doing. Some job seekers even think this is the best way to increase their options. Unfortunately, employers do not agree but, instead, seek individuals who know their objectives and who state what they want to do. Another thing to avoid is making sweeping generalizations such as "I am seeking a position allowing creative expression or a chance to interact with people." Equally unappealing are statements such as "Desire rapid advancement to higher levels of management, culminating in a vice presidency or presidency of the organization." And last, never state a career goal unless that is what you really want.

Preliminary Planning

Once you have established your career goals, your planning for the job search begins in earnest. Start your preliminary planning early. It takes time to find the right job, perhaps six months to a year, and there is much to be done.

The first steps in the job search are setting up a record-keeping system, building files to help you compare employers, obtaining information about different employers, establishing professional refer-

---

SELF-ASSESSMENT EXERCISE 13–2

My Ideal Job Description

Instructions: Write in as much detail as possible what you think would be the best job for you (be realistic as well as optimistic). Although it may be hard to find the perfect job, this will help you rank your options.

Job Description: _____

1. Career goals:
2. Job title:
3. Responsibilities:
   Doing what in
     1 year:
     2 years:
     5 years:
4. Where (Location):
5. Environment of job (relations with clients, colleagues, organization's "personality"):
6. Hours, routines:
7. Salary:
8. Special personal satisfactions (what will make you "happy" with this job, for example, advancement, seeing that others are well served, seeing the business turn a profit, having responsibility over others, and having good relations with coworkers, power, security, travel, material rewards):

ences, and planning a timetable for your actions. But first decide what makes you special, what will make you stand out and be more "marketable" than the other job seekers competing with you.

What Makes You Special?

On any given day, recruiters and placement officials may see dozens of applicants for positions. Sometimes they receive hundreds of résumés or applications. On paper and in person, many people look the same. Therefore, one crucial key to successful job seeking is for you to avoid this sameness. To succeed, look different, and show the qualities you have that the other candidates do not. Self-assessment Exercise 13–3 tells you how to distinguish those qualities that make you the best candidate for employment. This is an important exercise because it is these advantages that you should emphasize in your résumé, portfolio, and interviews.

Here are some things that help you stand out. Your occupational experience is the most important credential to many employers. Your educational achievements, both academic and extracurricular, are also important. Major accomplishments such as projects completed at school or on the job are noteworthy. When you are interviewed, your professional image, ability to communicate intelligently, and knowledge of the organization (e.g., its products, services, philosophy, structure, personnel) will stand out.

Your Limitations and How to Cope with Them

We have limitations or deficiencies in our background, and these must be acknowledged. What if you have lower-than-average grades or no work experience? Will such things prevent you from getting a job? Not necessarily. Nevertheless, if there are weaknesses in your credentials, you must deal with them constructively.

Suppose you have little work experience or perhaps none at all. The obvious solution is to get some, but it may be hard to find the appropriate position. Why not consider volunteering, perhaps working with a political party or a public service group? Businesses will accept volunteers in some cases, as will professors at your school. Or perhaps your grades have been lower than average. In this situation, look for the brighter side: Were your junior and senior grades better than your freshman and sophomore grades? (If so, highlight this fact.) Or if you had especially good grades in a few subjects that are important to your career, highlight this fact.

Another approach to coping with limitations is to expand your

SELF-ASSESSMENT EXERCISE 13–3

What Makes You Special

A. List All Your Special Skills That Give You an Advantage:
Examples:
   1. A home economics education major has this combination of skills that no other major possesses:
      • General understanding of consumer and family issues, for example, clothing, foods, nutrition, housing, design, consumer problems, consumer buying, child development, and family relations
      • Proven humanistic interest in serving consumer and family needs as shown by selection of major
      • Skills and experience in communications and educating others
   2. A fashion merchandising major has this combination of skills that no other major possesses:
      • Knowledge of the product, including fashion and fabric trends, and determinants of product quality
      • An understanding of what motivates consumers
      • Understanding of how products are designed for specific target markets
      • Knowledge of fashion-merchandising processes and systems for various business settings
      • Understands the workings and relations of textile producers, apparel producers, buying offices, retailers, and other elements of the fashion business
   3. A dietetics major has this combination of skills that no other major possesses:
      • Knowledge of human nutritional requirements
      • Knowledge of the basic sciences, for example, physiology, biochemistry
      • Skill in food preparation and technology
      • Understands age and sex differences in human development and related nutritional needs
      • Recognizes differences in food tastes and preferences of various cultural and socioeconomic groups
      • Advocates nutritional adequacy as fundamental to health care and personal development

B. Write Down All Your Work Experiences and Transferable Working Skills:
Examples:
   1. A person who worked as a retail salesperson has had firsthand, hands-on experience with and knowledge of such retailing principles as
      • What motivates consumers to buy
      • Successful selling techniques
      • Meeting organizational goals
      • Managing daily inventories
      • Identifying faulty merchandise and recognizing when markdowns (sales) are needed
   2. A person who worked as a camp counselor may have these skills applicable to working in other human services (e.g., in other counseling offices,

public service offices, or even business areas such as customer services or sales to new clients):
- Ability to speak and communicate effectively
- Understanding of the other person's needs and wants
- Patience
- Maturity
- Ability to listen well and empathize
- Ability to interview customers
- Recognition of importance of schedules
- Ability to encourage positive behaviors in others
- Skill in working with and leading others

C. Give Concrete Examples of Your Accomplishments:
Portfolio showing your ability to get a job done
Projects completed
Samples of work

D. Write Down Your Best Personal Qualities:
Willingness to work hard
Belief in the organization
Honesty
Reliability
Common sense
Leadership
Optimism
Flexibility
Dependability
Punctuality/timeliness
Organization skill
Analytical ability

- Identify three to five of your personal qualities to emphasize
- Have concrete examples demonstrating each of your qualities

E. The Following Are Special Preparations for Job Seeking:
Becoming familiar with the organization in which you seek employment
Cultivating a professional image and appearance
Drawing up a résumé
Obtaining references and introductions from "significant others"
Presenting yourself through oral and written communications

F. List Your Licenses, Certifications, or Other "Testable" Skills:
Teacher's certification
Registered dietitian
Computer programming/computer skills
Computer-aided design
Experience with microcomputers
Knowledge of special laboratory equipment or procedures
Licenses—broker, real estate, sales, financial planner, and so on

---

education. Perhaps you can gain a new skill, such as accounting, human relations, or computer applications, or additional education in a field related to your major. For example, after graduation one fashion merchandising student attended a fashion design school to study for a year. He acquired new skills in design that complemented his merchandising skills and led to a career with a fashion store specializing in custom design.

If your weaknesses restrict your ability to attain a higher position in an organization, remember that it is all right to settle for a lower-level position initially. Then work your way up the organization, remembering that it is your performance that will count toward your advancement. Another approach is to seek jobs in less popular or fashionable companies, organizations, or areas of the country. The largest major companies have the most competition for jobs, and in such organizations even highly qualified students may not obtain employment.

Job seekers with a handicap or physical disability face a special limitation, but at no time in history has the job market so openly welcomed the handicapped. Employers have learned that people with a handicap make an extra effort to compensate for it. Furthermore, there are few careers in family- and consumer-oriented professions in which a handicap would be considered a serious limitation. The most difficult problem the handicapped face is what is commonly called "attitudinal barriers"—their co-workers' difficulty adjusting to the handicapped. Here a positive, collegial approach by the handicapped person can help. The employer also should encourage common courtesies and see that barriers restricting work activities are minimized. Cooperation among employers, co-workers, and the handicapped can overcome most limitations.

Whatever limitation you may have, be it experience, grades, a handicap, or whatever, find a way to cope. Don't let limitations lead to discouragement.

SELF-ASSESSMENT EXERCISE 13–4

Heal Thyself?

All of us have some limitations or things we may need to improve (or explain). Do you have any weaknesses (e.g., low grades, lack of experience, difficulty writing, math anxiety)? List them and comment on how you can cope with them when you seek a job.

1. _____

2. _____

3. _____

Setting Up a Record-Keeping System

Before you actually begin the job search, set up a complete record-keeping system documenting every contact you make with potential employers. Figure 13-2 shows a model form. You can use it or make your own, including all the categories of information that you deem desirable. Your form should at least include the following information: the employer's name and telephone number, the particular person contacted, and the nature and the dates of each contact.

Some people also like to have a summary of contacts with all employers. Figure 13-3 shows a form for this use. On one page you can see at a glance whom you have contacted and the status of those contacts. It is a useful form, and you can add columns as you see fit.

As your job search progresses, a comparison of opportunities becomes more complicated. To cope with this, it is useful to devise what may be called a "decision matrix" to help you compare one opportunity with another (see Table 13.1). The left column of the matrix lists the characteristics you may wish to compare: products or services offered, clientele or markets served, job content, and so on.

To use this matrix you will have to learn a lot about the different organizations you are considering. When you find out something, write it on the appropriate line. When the matrix is completely filled, you will be able to see at a glance the strengths and weaknesses of various job opportunities. This will serve you in two ways:

1. It will help you identify the best organizations at which you want to seek employment.
2. It will help you compare three or more job offers.

As part of your records, keep copies of employers' informational literature, application forms, newspapers or magazine clippings on the organization, annual company reports, and any other information you find helpful. And be certain you keep a copy of all correspondence that you send to or receive from each employer. Keep these in a separate file for each company you contact. Finally, whenever you have a contact with an employer, such as by telephone or interview, write a memo summarizing such things as the person contacted, the subjects discussed, your impression of the individual with whom you talked, and any actions you should take following the contact. This may seem cumbersome, but as your contacts and discussions with various organizations multiply, it becomes impossible to recall each conversation.

RECORD OF CONTACT WITH EMPLOYER

Name, address, telephone of employer: _____

Person(s) contacted, telephone: _____

Dates submitted
Preliminary inquiry: _____

Letter of application: _____

Résumé: _____

Portfolio: _____

Organization's application: _____

Following contacts: _____

Other correspondence, telephone calls (record dates, nature of contact,
results achieved or actions to be taken): _____

Interview scheduled: _____

Interview completed
List persons interviewed: _____

Topics of discussion: _____

Courtesy letters sent following interview: _____

Job offer or rejection received: _____

Letter accepting/rejecting offer sent: _____

Starting date of employment: _____

Actions prior to starting date
Physical exam by organization (when required): _____

Complete paperwork: _____

Contact employee benefits office if required: _____

Contact employer's relocation office for moving instructions if required: _____

Communicate with immediate supervisor as needed prior to arrival: _____
It is advisable to send a courtesy letter to your new supervisor
indicating the date and time you will arrive and your enthusiasm
for your new career.

Figure 13-2

Preliminary Research for Job Seeking

Another important activity is to prepare for your job search. The
following are some suggestions:

1. *Visit your placement service.* Check the schedule of organizations interviewing during the coming semester and obtain
copies of all information provided by employers who are visiting your campus.
2. *Visit your library.* Look up such things as company annual re-

SUMMARY OF ALL CONTACTS WITH ALL EMPLOYERS

Employer	Person Contacted	Inquiry or Application Letter Sent	Résumé or Portfolio Submitted	Interview Offer	Interview Taken	Job Offer/ Rejection Received	Offer Accepted or Rejected	Notes

Figure 13-3

TABLE 13.1   A Matrix for Comparing Job Opportunities in Different Organizations

	Organizations		
	A	B	C
Products or Services Offered	_____	_____	_____
Clientele or Markets Served	_____	_____	_____
Job Content:			
1. Specific responsibilities	_____	_____	_____
2. Project assignments	_____	_____	_____
3. Working conditions	_____	_____	_____
4. Professional exposure	_____	_____	_____
5. Travel	_____	_____	_____
Personal and Professional Development:			
1. Training program	_____	_____	_____
2. Performance review and guidance	_____	_____	_____
3. Possible career paths	_____	_____	_____
4. Educational assistance	_____	_____	_____
Opportunity for Individuality:			
1. Individual responsibility and authority	_____	_____	_____
2. Use of decision-making ability	_____	_____	_____
3. Leadership requirements	_____	_____	_____
4. Autonomy	_____	_____	_____
Earnings Potential:			
1. Salary	_____	_____	_____
2. Benefits	_____	_____	_____
3. Promotions	_____	_____	_____
4. Raises	_____	_____	_____
Geographic Locations:			
1. Possible work locations	_____	_____	_____
2. Entry-level choices	_____	_____	_____
3. Relocations	_____	_____	_____
4. Overseas possibilities	_____	_____	_____
5. Life-style, housing, cost of living	_____	_____	_____
Atmosphere of Organization:			
1. Reputation	_____	_____	_____
2. Financial strength	_____	_____	_____
3. Management attitudes	_____	_____	_____
4. Relations with coworkers	_____	_____	_____

ports, newspaper or magazine articles, or other reports on the organization.

3. *Attend placement service workshops.* Often workshops are offered on such topics as identifying potential employers, writing résumés, interviewing, and doing research on companies.

4. *Visit cities or geographic regions of potential employment.* This is especially valuable because it gives you a firsthand experi-

ence of what it's like to live in the area. You can visit potential employers, look at housing, and get a feeling for the area.

5. *Subscribe to magazines or local newspapers in cities where you wish to work.* City magazines and newspapers have useful "help wanted" sections. These publications also help you get a feeling for the area where you are to live, and they are good sources of general information.

6. *Read trade magazines and journals in your field.* The purpose of this is to keep up to date on the current trends in your field.

7. *Obtain informational interviews.* An informational interview is not a formal job interview but a chance to gather data on organizations you may with to consider later.

Professional References

As your job search begins, you need to establish professional references to give to employers. By professional references we mean individuals who can comment objectively on your qualifications and skills in the area in which you seek employment. References can include professors with whom you have had several classes, academic advisers, and past employers. Also include school administrators, school counselors, local business or community leaders, or other professional people if they know you well. However, do *not* include friends or relatives who know you primarily on a family or social basis.

In selecting your professional references choose, if possible, people who are themselves professionals in your field. You will be judged by your references as well as by what they may say about you, and so choose carefully (a letter of reference from Aunt Sally will carry no weight in the job search). And be sure your references have known you well preferably for a year or more. Most people who write professional references will start their letters with a statement about how they know you, for example, "I have known Joe for approximately two months, but only where he sits in my class." Obviously, you will want to choose references who could start with a statement such as "I have known Joe for two years. He has been in three of my classes and has performed much above the average of my other students."

How many references should you have? Employers usually ask for at least three, but you should have at least five to six to make sure you have enough. Be sure to ask people if they will serve as your references before submitting their names to employers. It will not help you to have an employer "surprise" your reference. We also recommend that you don't ask your references to write a "to whom it may concern" letter; most employers like a letter written directly to them. The main exception to this rule is placement files used by teachers, which are an accepted practice in many places.

A Timetable for Action

Establish a week-by-week schedule for each phase of your job search. At the start, designate several weeks for completing the preliminary planning we have just discussed. Then block out periods for interviewing, accepting a position, and starting work. It is good to have a starting date in mind, for many employers will ask when you will be available to start working. And here it pays to be flexible, for some employers may want you immediately, and others as much as several months later.

Remember that your job search may take months, often six months to a year or more. So schedule enough time to complete all activities. We recommend that you begin your preliminary planning and timetable for action in the second semester of your junior year or at the beginning of your senior year. This should give you a comfortable amount of time in which to complete your search.

Your Professional Image

There is no better time than now to assess and improve your personal image. A professional image is presented through appropriate dress, personal self-presentation (poise, self-confidence), and communications skills. You may have acquired many of these attributes during college, but you'll find that many will need to be revised as your career approaches.

Appropriate physical appearance, personality, and style are crucial to your acceptance in the working world. All create an image of who you are. Whether such impressions and images are right or wrong is immaterial, for employers' judgments are based on them.

What can you do to improve yourself? There are numerous "dress for success" books on the market today, some of which have become very popular. In general, they recommend conservatively designed and high-quality suits for professional wardrobes (note that this does not mean high fashion). Your wardrobe is only the starting point in creating a professional image. Improving social skills, human relation skills, and the ability to speak in public are equally important and can be learned in the courses you take in college. If you have not taken courses in human relations, public speaking, and technical or business writing, sign up for them.

There are other ways to acquire a professional image. Perhaps the best one is to visit the actual places of employment and see how the people there dress and interact with others. Talk with people and ask about the informal rules of dress and personal communications in the office. Observe the quality and styles of apparel, and note the degree of informality or formality in the office. Be sure you observe people in positions similar to those that you are seeking, for it is pointless to learn the standards of dress in the secretarial pool if you are looking toward the management suite. Also visit the placement center and see how students and interviewers dress. Presenting yourself similarly is a good approach, but try *not* to look like a clone of the other students who are interviewing. Be a little different, yet maintain a professional touch.

Norms of dress differ among professionals. For example, business dress is typically a conservative, good-quality, dark colored suit for both men and women. One exception exists in fashion fields in which stylish dresses may be desirable. Some fields may be innovative and informal in dress, especially those pertaining to art and design. In short, all fields have different dress codes.

SELF-ASSESSMENT EXERCISE 13–5

Professional Dress

Describe the current standards of professional dress in your profession. Consider the following:

Suits _____

Dresses/skirts _____

Shirts/blouses _____

Ties _____

Socks/stockings _____

Shoes _____

Hair style _____

Makeup/shave _____

Accessories (hats, gloves, purse, briefcase, jewelry) _____

Sorority/fraternity pin (and other items *not* to wear) _____

Questions and Exercises _____

1. Assess your interests, qualifications, and abilities (see Chapters 3 and 4).
2. Write a brief statement of your short-term and long-term goals for your (1) career and (2) personal life. Do these goals complement or conflict with each other?
3. Set up a timetable for your job seeking.
4. Practice writing career objective statements. Emphasize the following:
   a. Your functions
   b. Your applicable skills
   c. Both functions and applicable skills
5. Complete this chapter's "My Ideal Job Description."
6. Complete this chapter's "What Makes You Special."
7. List your limitations or deficiencies. How will you deal with them when questioned by a prospective employer?
8. Modify the record-keeping system, contact form, and decision matrix shown in this chapter to meet your needs.
9. Begin preliminary research on potential employers and jobs.

Bibliography _____

Beatty, Richard H. *The Complete Job Search Book*. New York: Wiley, 1988.

Besson, Taunee. "A Stalled Job Search Can Be Pegged to Attitude," *National Business Employment Weekly* (July 30, 1989), 9–10.

Bingham, Mindy, and Sandy Stryker. *More Choices: A Strategic Planning Guide for Mixing Career and Family*. St. Petersburg, FL: Ingram Publishing, 1987.

Bolles, Richard N. *What Color Is Your Parachute?* Berkeley, CA: Ten Speed Press, 1990.

Davidson, Jeffrey P. *Blow Your Own Horn: How to Market Yourself and Your Career*. New York: American Management Association, 1987.

Figler, Howard. *The Complete Job-Search Handbook*. New York: Henry Holt and Company, 1988.

Hillstrom, J.K. *Steps to Professional Employment*. New York: Barron's Educational Series, 1982.

Hopke, William E. *The Encyclopedia of Careers and Vocational Guidance: Planning Your Career*, 7th ed. Chicago: Ferguson, 1987.

Hoyt, Kenneth B. "The Career Status of Women and Minority Persons: A 20-Year Retrospective," *Career Development Quarterly* 37 (March 1989), 202–212.

Jackson, Tom, and Davidyne Mayleas. *The Hidden Job Market for the Eighties*. New York: Times Books, 1981.

Lombardo, Joseph, and Amy Lombardo. *The Job Belt: The 50 Best Places in America for High Quality Employment—Today and in the Future*. New York: Penguin Books, 1986.

McAdam, Terry W. *Doing Well by Doing Good: The First Complete Guide to Careers in the Nonprofit Sector.* New York: Penguin Books, 1988.

McConnel, Patricia. *Women's Work-At-Home Handbook: Income and Independence.* New York: Bantam Books, 1986.

Mencke, Reed A., and Ronald L. Hummel. *Career Planning for the '80's.* Monterey, CA: Brooks/Cole, 1984.

Mouat, Lucia. *Back to Business: A Woman's Guide to Reentering the Job Market.* New York: Sovereign Books, 1979.

Munschauer, John L. *Jobs for English Majors and Other Smart People.* Princeton, NJ: Peterson's Guides, 1986.

Nivens, Beatryce. *The Black Woman's Career Guide.* New York: Doubleday, 1987.

Patterson, Barbara, Nancy Meadows, and Carol Dreger. *The Successful Woman.* Englewood Cliffs, NJ: Prentice-Hall, 1982.

Powell, C. Randall. *Career Planning Today.* Dubuque, IA: Kendall/Hunt, 1981.

Westoff, Leslie Aldridge. "How to Capitalize on Hidden Talents," *Money* 11 (November 1982), 151–155.

CHAPTER **14**

Your Professional Résumé and Portfolio

Traditionally one of the first contacts employers make with prospective employees is not in person but through a written résumé. Increasingly, professionals are also adding a portfolio of accomplishments to supplement their résumé. Before beginning your job search, it is important to prepare an attention-getting, professional résumé and portfolio of accomplishments to present to employers. The résumé and portfolio help you sell yourself to employers—they are the not-so-subtle advertisements of your qualifications for employment.

Preparing Your Résumé _____

A professional résumé is the first and therefore the most visible part of your professional identity that you present to potential employers. A résumé is a short, selective summary of your education, abilities, special skills, work experience, and other accomplishments. It serves the following two closely related purposes:

1. It shows an employer what specific qualifications you have for specific jobs the employer needs to fill.
2. It advertises the qualities that you possess that make you employable.

The latter function cannot be overemphasized—the best résumé spotlights the outstanding things you have done and clearly shows you as special. Through a résumé you get your foot in the door, so to speak, which can lead to a job interview.

Typical Formats for Résumés

There is no standard way to write a personal résumé. Each of us differs in education, experience, and qualifications, and a good résumé should show these differences.

Some helpful guidelines for preparing and formatting your résumé are the following: First, remember that a résumé should be brief and to the point. For most students, a one-page résumé should suffice, although students with important experience and accomplishments might have two pages. But never exceed two pages, even if your accomplishments are extensive and varied. Instead, find a way to summarize and highlight those experiences that are relevant to the employers' needs.

Another important rule concerns the typing and visual presentation of your résumé. A résumé is most attractive and readable when professionally typed on a high-quality typewriter, using a carbon ribbon that will give a dark and sharp image. Many people have their résumés printed on a word processor; this is acceptable, but only if it is done on a letter-quality printer rather than a dot matrix printer. The letter-quality printer creates a much sharper, distinct, and professional appearance. Using a laser printer for your résumé is even better. Many computer labs on your college campus have laser printers available for student use. In addition, commercial photocopy facilities near campus have laser printers that can be used for this purpose. The résumé should be typed on high-quality white paper

(20-lb or 24-lb rag content), although some people in artistic areas may use high-quality colored paper or parchment. For the majority of résumés, however, we recommend plain white 20-lb watermarked paper.

What should you include in your résumé? The following is a list of some things that you may wish to include (not all have to be included):

Your Name and Address. Typically, your name is placed at the top center of the page. Underneath will be your address and telephone number. Some people put both a temporary or school address and a permanent home address in this section.

Career Objective or Goal. This is a short statement of the specific type of position you seek. Presenting a career goal is optional, and some authorities suggest not putting in a career goal at all. However, if you do have a well-focused direction for your career, as you should, the career goal is helpful.

Education. Describe your educational background with the most recent degrees first, working back in chronological order. State the degree (e.g, B.S., B.A., M.A., M.S., Ph.D., Ed.D.), college or university, graduation date, major area of study, and minor area of study. You may also include such things as honors, awards, and grade point averages, assuming that these will add to your credentials. In addition, some people list specific courses taken in school.

Experience. List relevant paid and voluntary experiences. This is one of the most important parts of the résumé. List your most recent job or experience first and then work backward. You should state the dates of employment or work experience, name of the employer, job title, and a short description of your responsibilities and accomplishments in that job or experience. Be concise, and show that you really accomplished something.

Related Activities. This section could also be called "extra-curricular activities," "college activities," or "related college activities." This is an opportunity to show experience you have had that may be relevant to your career, for example, offices held in student clubs, work on student newspaper, work in student government, experience in a consumer relations board, experience in leading social clubs or fraternities or sororities, and the like.

Honors and Awards. List scholarships, awards, and honors received.

Professional Affiliations. State information about membership in professional organizations or clubs related to your professional field. You also can list civic clubs and community organizations if you actively participated in them.

Professional Licenses, Certifications, or Skills. List such things as teacher certifications, registrations (e.g., registered dietician) and knowledge of special skills such as computer languages, foreign languages, or operation of specific scientific equipment.

Personal Data. This section might be called "other pertinent data" or "personal background" and includes facts you are willing to share with the employer. This is a good place to show your personal side, including hobbies, personal interests such as travel, and sports participation. Personal data also indicate potential skills to an employer that may be valuable to the job (e.g., interest in and willingness to travel).

References. Usually you should state that references are available on request. However, this may not be necessary because potential employers assume you will supply a list of names and addresses upon request. There is a more important and valuable use of this space in your short résumé than listing your references here.

Now let's discuss what you should *not* include in a résumé. First, never pad your résumé; do not put in things you have not done, and do not overstate your accomplishments. Employers check the accuracy of résumés; including fictional credentials will result in disaster. Second, put in your résumé only those facts that positively and clearly show a strength. For example, do not put in your grade average if it does not flatter you. Other questionable things are photographs (rarely included), high school education, salaries from previous jobs, reasons for leaving previous jobs, locational preference, and names of past supervisors. Nor is it required that you provide facts such as age, height, weight, date of birth, or marital status.

The overall organization and order of your résumé is a matter of personal choice. Some people prefer to present their credentials in reverse chronological order with the most recent work experience first. Another approach is to outline your functional experiences. That is, instead of chronologically presenting your experience, list general functions or job titles and achievements under each function. Employers like to see what you have accomplished, and this approach can be well received. Another effective strategy is to combine the functional and chronological approaches, reporting your

---

SELF-ASSESSMENT EXERCISE 14–1

For Your Résumé

List the most important points about yourself that would appeal to employers. Highlight these in your résumé or portfolio.

1. _____

2. _____

3. _____

4. _____

education in reverse chronological order but your experience by function. And we suggest placing the most important parts of your credentials early in the résumé and making them stand out through the use of boldface section headings (e.g., **Work Experience, Education**). Use spaces around major parts to make them stand out.

In the next several pages are four examples of one-page résumés using chronological and functional approaches. These résumés show how much information can be obtained on only one page. Also note how the section headings and format help the key parts stand out. As you prepare your own résumé, experiment with alternative wording and formatting to find the right combination. Remember that the résumés we have included are merely examples and need not be followed rigidly.

Custom-Tailored Résumés

It used to be that once your résumé was prepared, you would have fifty to hundred copies made, and it was then complete. But why not custom design your résumé for each job? The advantages are obvious. First, learn as much as possible about the job and employer, and then design your résumé accordingly. This would mean that every résumé you send out could be different. This procedure could require a lot of work and retyping, but one way to make this easier is to put your résumé on a word processor. You then edit and copy each version from the original master.

There are other ways to custom design your résumé. Some people like to have their résumés typeset to add an impression of high quality and visual appeal. With typesetting you also can obtain visual effects that are not possible with most typewriters. Some word

---

SELF-ASSESSMENT EXERCISE 14–2

Stand Out

How can you make your résumé stand out? Suggest ideas (but beware of gaudy or unprofessional gimmicks):

1. _____

2. _____

3. _____

4. _____

---

processing programs give the appearance of being typeset, particularly if a laser printer is used. Or you can add graphics, lines or symbols to illustrate your résumé and thus increase its visual appeal. To do this you must hire a graphic artist unless you have this skill yourself (in which case you can show the skill through your résumé). However, some computer programs can add these items for you.

The variety of styling details and artistic touches you can put into your résumé is endless. Properly done, these details add visual appeal and help your résumé stand out from the others. Such additions are especially appropriate for students in design fields or fields in which visual communication is important (e.g., journalism, communications, teaching, consumer relations, public relations). But adding novelty is not for everyone. There is a fine line between professionalism in résumés and mere "show business," and no one wishes to appear to be more "show" than qualified professional. Use custom design with restraint and good taste.

No matter what style of your résumé, keep in mind that your goal is to impress a potential employer with your qualifications to do a particular job. What employers want to know, indeed the only thing they want to know, is what you can do for them.

Preparing Your Portfolio _____

Another way to present your accomplishments, which is catching on in some areas of consumer and family professions, is through a portfolio. In fact, having a complete portfolio is critical to the job search for art and design fields, such as interior design, fashion

---

PATIENCE GOODTEACHER

9000 N. First St., Apt. 20
Tucson, Az 85700
(602) 581–6000

JOB OBJECTIVE: A teaching position in secondary home economics.

PHILOSOPHY OF EDUCATION: I favor a strong coordinated academic and vocational
program, with balanced teaching of concepts and skills. My goals for teaching include
individualization and integration of curriculum, creative planning, and analytical thinking.
My goals for my students are academic self-direction, creativity, social responsibility, and
emotional growth.

EDUCATION:

Bachelor of Science in Home Economics Education, The University of Arizona, May 1991.
Certified to teach Home Economics, Grades K–12.

SPECIAL SKILLS:

Curriculum Strengths:
- Education base in clothing and textiles, housing and interior design, foods and nutrition,
  child development, and family relations.
- Specialization in communications, public relations, and consumer science.

EXPERIENCE:

Student Teacher, Agave High School, Marana, AZ, 1991
  Taught one senior survival class, one semester class of child development, and three
  comprehensive classes representing grades 9–12. Developed and assessed home
  economics curriculum.

Girl Scout Leader, Tucson, AZ, 1987–1990
  Junior High School troop leader for two years and assistant leader for one year.
  Led all types of scouting educational activities.

Day-Care Assistant Director, Tucson, AZ, 1984–1986
  Planned and implemented day-care programs for children 3 to 6 years old, with emphasis
  on educational activities.

REFERENCES:

Available from the office of Career and Placement Services, The University of Arizona,
Tucson, AZ 85721.

Figure 14-1

design, textile design, and fashion illustration. But portfolios can be
just as useful for other professionals, and we recommend that all
applicants prepare one.

A portfolio is a representative sample of one's actual work and
accomplishments. For example, the portfolio of interior designers
could feature their actual designs of interiors, including photographs, color slides, or layouts. Their artistic skills could also be
displayed in line drawings and renderings of various architectural

MARTIN S. MONEYMAKER

University Address
3131 S. 1st Ave., Apt. 301
Tucson, Arizona 85000
(602) 900–1234

Permanent Address
400 Wilson Street
Beverly Hills, CA 90200
(213) 900–3030

EDUCATION

August 1986 to May 1990 The University of Arizona
Degree: Bachelor of Science
Major: Merchandising and Fashion Promotion

MAJOR COURSES

Management ● Marketing
Fashion Buying ● Human Relations
Apparel Analysis ● Fashion Industry
Computer Science ● Accounting Systems
Professional Development ● Interpersonal Communications

PROFESSIONAL EXPERIENCE

Retail Internship Fall 1989	Smith's Department Store, Los Angeles, CA Responsible for setting department goals, budgeting, planning merchandise assortments, buying, and analyzing data from the computerized merchandising information system.
Bookkeeper Summer 1989	Moneymaker Enterprises, Beverly Hills, CA Worked in the accounting department of family business, one of the largest in California. Assisted in account maintenance, banking, payroll, and analysis of profitability/return on investment.
Assistant Manager 1988–1989	Bestmerchandise of Arizona, Tucson, AZ Responsible for managing and organizing sales for the men's suits department. Assisted buyers in stock planning, pricing, markdown analysis and inventory control. Supervised three sales associates. Worked 20 hours a week while in school.
Sales Associate 1987–1988	Bestmerchandise of Arizona, Tucson, AZ Responsible for personal presentation of merchandise to clients, requiring considerable knowledge of products and skills in salesmanship. Assumed many managerial roles as well. Became top producing sales associate though working only twenty hours a week.

EXTRACURRICULAR ACTIVITIES

Organizer and Coordinator of Fashion Shows at Tucson Resorts
Fashion Industry Club
Fraternity Pledge Coordinator
Active Volunteer for Big Brothers Program
Hobbies include stamp collecting and physical conditioning.

Figure 14-2

FAITH CHARITY WARMHEART
2929 Smith Road
Anywhere, Arizona 85000
(602)900-3030

EDUCATION

Bachelor of Science in Child Development and Family Relations
The University of Arizona, May 1991

Supporting Courses

Child Development	Professional Writing
Family Relations	Personnel Management
Guidance Principles	Speech Communication
Human Relations	Health Education
Parent Education	Women and Health
Professional Development	Nutrition and Food Service

EXPERIENCE

Teacher The Children's Congregation, Tucson, Arizona
Responsibilities include coordinating and implementing an educational program
for first-grade students in a positive learning environment. Parent consultations,
seminars, and workshops were also included.
August 1987 to present (part time)

Youth Adviser United Youth, Tucson, Arizona
Position includes supervising, coordinating, planning,and conducting monthly
social and educational activities for 20 to 30 teenagers.
December 1986 to present (volunteer part time)

Division Head Camp Fun and Games, Phoenix, Arizona
Supervised and advised kindergarten through second-grade counselors, giving
direction and guidance in a social and educational camp curriculum. Included
conducting meetings and attending workshops and seminars.
Summer 1987

Sales Associate Smith's Department Store, Tucson, Arizona
Assisted clientele in sales capacity, with an emphasis on customer service.
Responsibilities included customer assistance, wardrobe coordination, and
cashiering.
Summers 1985, 1986

EXTRACURRICULAR ACTIVITIES

Vice-president, Child Development Student Club
Dormitory page, The University of Arizona
Member and participant in various student government programs
Active participant in sports, including tennis and aerobic exercise

Figure 14-3

I.M. BESTQUALIFIED

Local Address	**Permanent Address**
1011 N. Smith, Apt. 220	100 Williams Drive
Tucson, Arizona 85000	Small Town, Arizona 85000
(602) 900-8400	(602) 101–2001

CAREER OBJECTIVE: Seeking a career in business or government in consumer affairs, in areas including consumer relations, consumer information, and consumer products marketing.

EDUCATION:

B.S. May 1991   Home Economics majoring in Consumer Studies/Home Management. The University of Arizona. Courses: consumer behavior, consumer relations, communications, marketing, management, family economics, and general economics.

EXPERIENCE:

8/90–12/90   *Consumer Affairs Intern,* Attorney General of Tucson, Arizona. Analyzed consumer laws and policies of Arizona. Studied actual law enforcement regarding consumer matters. Completed case research on consumer complaints. Wrote and edited consumer information brochures.

5/88–12/89   *Research Assistant,* Market Research of Tucson, Inc. Coded information from consumer preference questionnaires. Tabulated data by computer. Helped design a study measuring consumer satisfaction with resorts in Tucson.

8/87–5/88   *Preschool Aid,* Kiddyfun Daycare Center. Aided three teachers in supervising playtime and art time. Sat in for absent teachers, planned activities. Responsible for 30 preschool children.

8/86–8/87   *Office Aid,* The University of Arizona. Duties involved general office management, file maintenance, and effective communications. Responsible to seven professors and their work for five to 200 students.

EXTRA CURRICULAR AND HOBBIES:

Member, *Kappa Omicron Nu,* professional honorary
Participant in various student government activities
Active leader and vice-president, American Home Economics Association, Student
   Member Section
Hobbies include swimming, reading, and working with children.

Figure 14-4

design concepts. One part of the portfolio should show one's ability to organize, plan, and execute a complete project, from its preliminary planning through each stage of development. Through the years of study, interior design students develop such materials and can make a complete portfolio showing their skills. Artists in other fields (textiles, fashion) can prepare similar presentations of their work.

Students from nondesign fields can also prepare portfolios. In such cases they compile actual projects, reports, papers, or even a work experience. Any tangible activity that one has completed can be a candidate for the portfolio, as long as it is in a presentable form. If any projects are not in good condition, they should be retyped on a high-quality typewriter with a carbon ribbon or be redrawn and redone as appropriate. Never submit a portfolio that is not neat and visually attractive.

How is the portfolio set up? Artists and designers usually present samples of their work in carrying cases, but just as acceptable is a high-quality slide or photograph collection of accomplishments. People in other fields may wish to use bound or loose-leaf notebooks. Make copies of your portfolio; you will rarely send out the original copy.

The following is an outline of the possible contents of a portfolio:

1. *Cover Page.* On the cover page, state your name and the title of the portfolio, for example, Mary L. Smith, Portfolio of Accomplishments and Qualifications. Area of Specialization: Residential Interior Design. Each line should be centered and displayed attractively in large type.
2. *Table of Contents* or *Summary of Contents.*
3. *One-Page Résumé* or *Short Biographical Sketch.* A narrative summary of your background and qualifications.
4. *Comprehensive Résumé.* This is optional and is for those applicants with extensive experience and qualifications.
5. *Illustrations and Photographs of Your Work.* A separate subsection illustrating each area of your qualifications and experience. For most designers this is the main and most important section of their portfolio.
6. *Written Projects.* Present projects by titles or objectives as appropriate (e.g., Project Title: Fashion Forecasting Techniques; Project Title: A Comparison of Marketing Techniques of Three Retail Fashion Stores).
7. *Work Experience.* Examples of projects you have completed at work, diary records of work experience, and letters of recommendation as appropriate.
8. *Special Recognitions and Honors.* Such things as actual copies

of commendations, awards, honors, or other documentation of significant recognition that you have received.

A portfolio should show your personality and ingenuity in presenting yourself. Be sure it is not a helter-skelter presentation of activities but, rather, a well-organized and focused presentation of your expertise and talents. Remember that a portfolio should sell you to an employer. As such, it should show your very best work but not things that are of modest quality or that do not represent your current level of skill. A well-prepared portfolio should give you an edge over most other candidates.

Using Your Résumé and Portfolio _____

Your résumé is nothing more than a "calling card" or "door opener" to initiate contact with an employer. If it says something memorable about you and thus stands out, it will receive attention leading to further discussions with the employer. In addition, your professional portfolio can complement your résumé by showing tangible evidence of your accomplishments.

But as important as your résumé and portfolio are, don't become overly dependent on them. It is all too tempting to send résumés to dozens of employers and then wait passively for the phone to ring. Likewise, a portfolio that lacks "personality" or the personal style of its creator will appear sterile and not speak for you. Résumés and portfolios are simply tools that support but do not replace a personal self-presentation.

Questions and Exercises _____

1. Experiment by writing your résumé in different formats:
   a. chronologically
   b. functionally
   c. a combination of chronologically and functionally
2. Think about ways to custom design your résumé. Draft several custom designs to see whether you like your résumé in a different format. Ask your placement officials, professors, and personnel managers to comment on your custom résumé.
3. Compile a portfolio and have it evaluated by your professors and working professionals before using it in your job search.

Bibliography _____

Beatty, Richard H. *The Résumé Kit.* New York: Wiley, 1984.

Berliner, Don. *Want a Job? Get Some Experience. Want Experience? Get a Job.* New York: Amalom, 1978.

Bolles, Richard N. *What Color Is Your Parachute?* Berkeley, CA: Ten Speed Press, 1990.

Croft, B. *Getting a Job: Résumé Writing, Job Application Letters, and Interview Strategies.* Columbus, OH: Merrill, 1989.

Hadary, Sharon G. "Job Hunting Tips From the Front Line," *National Business Employment Weekly* (September 3, 1989), 5–6.

Harcourt, Jules, and A.C. "Buddy" Krizan. "A Comparison of Résumé Content Preferences of Fortune 500 Personnel Administrators and Business Communication Instructors," *Journal of Business Communication 26* (Spring 1989), 177–190.

Jackson, Tom. *The Perfect Résumé.* Garden City, NY: Anchor Books, 1981.

Krannich, Ronald L., and William J. Banis. *High Impact Résumés and Letters: How to Communicate Your Qualifications to Employers,* 3rd ed. Manassas, VA: Impact Publications, 1990.

Marquand, Ed. *How to Prepare Your Portfolio: A Guide for Students and Professionals.* New York: Art Direction, 1981.

Matthews, Judith, and Joan Gritzmacher. "Preferred Content and Format for Portfolios and Review Criteria," *Journal of Interior Design Education and Research 10* (Fall 1984), 28–31.

Powell, C. Randall. *Career Planning Today.* Dubuque, IA: Kendall/Hunt, 1981.

Yates, Martin J. *Knock 'em Dead: With the Very Best Résumés,* 3rd ed. Holbrook, MA: Bob Adams, 1988.

CHAPTER 15

How to Find Out About Desirable Employers

Having established your career goals and prepared a résumé and portfolio, you are now well on your way toward seeking potential employers. But where will you look for them? Here are some answers.

Where to Look for Potential Employers _____

Some students think job seeking merely means stopping at their university or college placement service, where many possible employers for family and consumer professionals may visit. But searching for potential employers is much more than this—you should develop a job-searching strategy that employs many different resources and approaches to finding that best opportunity for you. The following are some sources you should look into when your job search begins in earnest. The more of the following sources you use in your search strategy, the greater the likelihood is of your finding a good job.

University Placement Service

For most students, the starting place for the job search is their college's or university's placement service. The placement service invites employers to visit the campus and schedules interviews with students that can lead to placement in jobs. The procedures used by placement services vary from university to university, but in general, graduating seniors are given first priority for interviews. Some placement services allow alumni to use their services for interviewing; others let underclassmen interview for part-time or summer employment with various companies.

Some placement services also offer additional aids to job seekers. For example, some teach seminars and short courses on employment-seeking skills: how to search for a job, how to write a résumé, and how to conduct oneself in an interview. Most placement services also keep a library of information on the organizations and businesses that recruit on campus, as well as books and other informational resources on careers. The placement service also distributes the *College Placement Annual* and may have other directories that list the names, addresses, and types of graduates sought by large employers. Every college student should obtain a copy of the *College Placement Annual* from the college placement service.

The types of companies and organizations that recruit on campus usually fall into the following two categories:

1. The major, large national companies that have high levels of employment
2. The larger local or regional companies from the major cities of your geographic region

Such employers hire large numbers of graduates, typically to enter their training programs to prepare for careers in their organizations. Therefore, some of the most interesting and engaging careers can be found through the placement service. However, an important point to remember is that only a small portion of the possible organizations at which you might find exciting careers will interview on your campus. Therefore, few students should rely on the placement service as their sole source of contact with potential employers. A more extensive search strategy is needed to find that exciting first job.

Governmental Employment Offices

Most state and local governments have employment services or job-finding services. In these offices employers list their job openings in specific areas in career fields. Of course, not all employers and not all professional career areas are listed with these job services at any given time, but some are, and so the source should not be overlooked. Governmental job services are free of charge, both to the job seeker and the employer who registers jobs with the service, and they are worth a call or visit.

Where to Look for Potential Employers

- Placement services
- Employment agencies
- Local newspapers
- Professional publications (newsletters, magazines)
- Directories
- Personal contacts (friends, family)
- "Legwork" — Leave no stone unturned.

Professional Employment Agencies

You may also think of using professional employment agencies that recruit particular occupational specialists or professionals, such as scientists, textile specialists, nutrition specialists, or other executives and professionals. The names of these agencies can often be found in trade publications.

Employment agencies work on a fee basis, the fee being paid by either the employer or the employee. Be sure you understand the fee arrangement in advance, for fees can be expensive. Other services that an agency performs, such as résumé preparation or seminars in interviewing skills, can also be expensive. Ask about charges. In some cases you may be requested to sign a contract with the employment agency. Be sure you understand all aspects of the contract, and do not sign one if it requires the payment of fees whether or not you receive placement. In general, we think that contracts between you and an employment agency are unnecessary and that any fees paid for using the employment agency should be paid by the employer, not you.

Newspapers, Magazines, and Other Publications

Many job openings are advertised in the help-wanted sections of many publications. Your local newspaper is the logical starting point. Look at both current and recent back issues, not only in the obvious places like the help-wanted section but also in news articles, the business section of the newspaper, and even the life-style section. In such sections of the paper you'll often read articles about local organizations and businesses, and such information may give leads to jobs. For example, a story about the opening of a new retail business in your city suggests a need for certain professional and managerial employees; likewise, the announcement of a new community service program signals a need for professionals to staff the program. The announcement of a new school building program may mean that new teachers and administrators will be hired soon.

Out-of-town newspapers are also a good source of potential employers. Newspapers from cities around the country are usually available in your university or public library. Virtually all libraries carry major national newspapers such as *The New York Times, Los Angeles Times,* and *The Wall Street Journal.*

There are also special-interest publications and trade publications in all family and consumer fields, whether restaurants, nutrition, textiles, child development, or retailing. These special-interest publications advertise job openings and professional careers pertaining to their specialized readership. For example, newspapers such as *Women's Wear Daily, Daily News Record,* and *Home Furnishings Daily* list openings in a wide range of wholesale careers in women's and men's fashions, furniture, and interior design. Similarly, *AHEA Action,* published by the American Home Economics Association, advertises career openings for college professors in home economics fields. Look for the trade and professional publications in your field of interest, and you will find similar opportunities.

The following are some other published sources of job openings that you might consult:

1. Academic journals in your area of specialization
2. General magazines
3. College alumni magazines
4. Newsletters in your area of interest
5. Placement newsletters circulated by your placement office, employment agencies, or governmental job services
6. Regional trade newspapers or newsletters
7. Job bulletin boards or other public places where announcements of jobs are posted

8. Directories of businesses, professions, or members in special-interest groups; these directories can give you leads to people who may have recommendations for your career search (the *Encyclopedia of Associations,* discussed in a later chapter, is an example).

Not all professional jobs are advertised through periodicals, but because of affirmative action and equal opportunity laws, most jobs must be publicized. Therefore, the more sources you consult, the more likely you are to discover something.

Directories

There are numerous directories of different organizations, associations, and potential employers in various fields. The *College Placement Annual* is an obvious one. Also, telephone directories, especially the Yellow Pages, can offer leads. Your library likely has telephone directories for all cities in your state or local region, as well as telephone directories from major cities. As the saying goes, "Let your fingers do the walking through the Yellow Pages" and find a variety of employers such as retail businesses, hospitals, fitness centers, government offices, child-care centers, public service organizations, or whatever type of organization you seek. The Yellow Pages and other parts of a telephone book can suggest employers you may never have thought of otherwise.

Other directories are those produced by trade organizations and professional societies. Your library may have a collection; inquire at the reference desk or information center. Also, be sure to look at "directories to directories." Such general directories as the *Encyclopedia of Associations, The Guide to American Directories*, and publications by the Standard Rate and Data Service list the many directories and periodicals published in nearly all fields.

Personal Contacts and Recommendations

You have undoubtedly heard that who you know counts in finding employment. This is true. The following are just a few of the personal contacts that may find job leads for you:

1. Relatives
2. Friends
3. Friends of your parents
4. Friends of relatives
5. Friends of your friends

6. Classmates
7. Co-workers
8. Former employers
9. Professors
10. Academic advisers
11. People currently working in the field
12. Guest speakers in your classroom
13. Your clergy
14. Neighbors
15. Staff of your college placement office
16. Staff of employment agencies
17. Staff of personnel offices with business and organizations

Think of all the people you know in these and other walks of life. Such personal contacts may provide the most promising leads to jobs. This network of contacts introduces you to the grapevine or the informal channels through which much of the job market operates in today's professional world. Do not hesitate to ask any personal sources for ideas and leads to employment. In some cases you can even go a step further by asking a particularly promising lead or "inside contact" in an organization to recommend you for employment. For example, many a job has been landed simply because a friend (or a friend of a friend) said a good word about you to the right person at the right time. Likewise, it pays to ask around about job offerings. The "who-you-knows" are the most popular hunting grounds in today's job market.

Some people feel a bit shy about asking professional or personal contacts for help, or they may even feel guilty about having the advantage of contacts. Do not let this prevent your asking for recommendations from others. Indeed, it is likely that people will be flattered that you thought enough of them to ask their advice or ideas about a job. Most people are willing to help a sincere and enthusiastic job seeker. On the other hand, do not overuse or abuse your personal contacts. Treat personal contacts and personal recommendations with respect, and acknowledge all assistance that these people give you, whether or not the contacts lead to employment.

Legwork and Prospecting

Thus far we've talked about sources of jobs published in the traditional media or obtained through traditional sources such as placement offices or professional contacts. Now let's look at how you can take the initiative and personally attack the job market. By this we mean getting out in the field, on your feet, making new contacts, and visiting sources of information and places of employment. It means calling local organizations or businesses, visiting the chamber of commerce, visiting places of employment to talk with employees, or doing whatever is needed "on foot." The goal is to have an up-close-and-personal look at the job market. After all, the job market doesn't automatically come to you, but with an investment of time and energy you can take yourself into the job market and introduce yourself to it personally.

One strategy to take is to visit those people with whom you would like to work, or those people whom you would like to emulate in your professional career. For example, a child development student can interview people who manage child-care centers, welfare programs operators, and human service organization professionals. A retail management student might interview buyers, store managers, sales managers, merchandise managers, and entrepreneurs who have started their own businesses. The idea is to visit with these working professionals on an informational interview basis. That is, the purpose of your visit is merely to gather information and make an initial personal contact (this contact may be used later in the actual job search if and when appropriate). You must understand that such professionals are busy but may be willing to share their experiences with promising employees and graduates.

SELF-ASSESSMENT EXERCISE 15–1

Key to Success

Where will you search for employers? List the best sources in your field (e.g., specific magazines, placement centers, friends, personal contacts):

1. _____

2. _____

3. _____

4. _____

5. _____

6. _____

7. _____

8. _____

Another way of prospecting for career opportunities is to visit the localities where there may be positions open. Spend a week or so in a city where you would like to work, and visit possible employers. Take this time to build contacts and to hold as many informational interviews as possible. Before your visit, you should make appointments with various organizations and companies when possible. Write letters requesting appointments, but because some of your letters will not be answered, be sure to telephone ahead to find out with whom you might talk. Another approach that works occasionally is "cold canvassing"—simply appearing unannounced at potential places of employment and presenting your interests. This approach takes a certain amount of assurance and aggressiveness and can lead to many disappointments because contact with the right people will not always be possible. But many employers look on such aggressiveness as a positive attribute in their employees. So, the cold canvassing approach should be included in the job search strategy of students who are comfortable with it.

What is a Successful Job Search?

To close this discussion, let's summarize several keys to success for the job seeker. The following are some things that may lead to job and career opportunities:

1. *Leave no unturned stones.* To uncover what is often called the "hidden job market," you should systematically investigate most or all of the preceding sources of job opportunities and information about careers. Make contacts with places, organizations, and people who have opportunities you seek. Build files of contacts and networks of persons.
2. *Cast a wide net in your job search.* Fishermen with the largest nets catch the most fish, and job seekers who fish the widest territory find the most opportunities. This means searching for opportunities in as wide a geographic range of regions or cities as possible and considering the broadest selection of potential employers as your market for employment.
3. *Consider employment at less popular or less fashionable places.* Want to work at a glamourous store in New York City, such as Bloomingdales? Equally excellent, though less-well-known stores exist in other major cities like Providence, Richmond, Tucson, Albuquerque, Charlotte, or Indianapolis. Want to work with a prestigious company like General Foods? Why not consider the less-well-known but equally successful smaller food-producing companies around the country. Competition for employment is

greatest in the "in" cities, and large companies have much to offer and should be considered. But don't limit yourself to a specific company or city without realizing that this limits your opportunities. Consider smaller cities, smaller companies, and smaller organizations—not only is the competition less severe but the opportunity for growth and advancement is greater.

4. *Be flexible.* Single-mindedness of purpose and goal is laudable, but a little flexibility in all aspects of the job search will increase your alternatives as well. We believe you should set your goals high but not too high—just equal to who you are and what your realistic goals for the start of your career are. A little flexibility or willingness to work around those goals, if not precisely toward them, is in order for every job search. Realize and accept that your first job may not be absolutely perfect. A good enough fit between the job seeker and a career has been the start for the majority who have gone before you.

5. *When a decision is near, contact the person or persons who have the ultimate responsibility to hire you.* When your job search is in progress, you may meet many individuals, including people in charge of a department where you want to work, a personnel manager, a department co-worker, and many others. One or two of these people have the authority to hire you. It may be the department head; it may be the personnel manager; and it may even be the co-worker with whom you will be most directly associated. Identify the decision maker, and put your greatest time and energy in persuading that person that you are right for the position.

Getting to Know Employers

Now that you have cast the wide net and caught a number of potential employers, you will want to find out more about each. What exactly does each do? What products or services does each offer? Who are the consumers or other clienteles that each serves (what type of person does this employer attempt to satisfy)? Where is the employer located? What are its successes or things it does well? Does it have notable failures? Is its financial condition satisfactory, or is it running out of money and perhaps going out of business? What are its employment and personnel policies? What is its "personality"—that is, what are the people and policies like, and would you fit in with them? What is the potential for your future with this organization? These and other questions cry for your attention, and getting the answers is part of the successful job search.

Here is where a little time spent in the library, at the placement service, and actually visiting the employer is in order. Your objective is to gather as much information as possible and to answer questions such as the preceding. When you identify an employer that looks good, further research then is necessary.

The following are some of the sources of information that will help you learn about companies or organizations:

1. *Annual reports.* Large, publicly owned companies such as Sears, Levi Strauss, General Foods, and many others prepare annual reports that describe their products and services and give financial information about the companies (current profitability, current sales, sales by different product lines). Smaller companies also prepare annual reports. Different types of annual reports are also prepared by a wide range of governmental and human service organizations; these differ from the annual reports but do state what the organizations are accomplishing or what their current goals are.

2. *Indexes.* To find articles on companies or organizations, search such indexes as the *Business Periodicals Index, The Wall Street Journal Index, The New York Times Index,* the *Magazine Index,* the *Education Index,* the *Art and Technology Index,* and others that may be relevant to your specialized field. There frequently are articles on larger- to medium-sized organizations. In addition, local newspapers and local indexes (where available) may be of help.

3. *Books.* In some cases you may be fortunate enough to locate a full-length book or perhaps a shorter booklet that has been written on a company or other organizations in government or human services. Many books have been written on the largest and most successful business corporations in the United States. Books have also been written on the major human services, such as the Peace Corps, the American Red Cross and government agencies.

4. *Printed materials from organizations.* Most organizations print brochures and informational flyers for public distribution. Some are especially tailored to the job seeker. Check your placement center to see if such printed matter is on file. Write the personnel office or the public relations office of organizations and request this information (better yet, telephone directly the public relations office or the personnel office and ask for these materials). You may obtain financial statements or financial docu-

ments on companies in this manner, such as the annual reports mentioned earlier and what is known as a "10–K" report, which documents a company's finances in considerable detail.

5. *Internal documents of organizations.* These documents are the nonpublic documents that are not available to most people but that you may find, given some luck or inside contacts. Such things as the printed policies or procedures of an organization, operating manuals, training documents, personnel guides, and other internal documents can provide interesting and informative reading on how an organization operates. In most cases such internal documents are not readily available, but it does not hurt to seek them.

6. *Local chambers of commerce, service clubs, and trade organizations.* Every city and community has professional trade and civic organizations in which members of the business and professional communities meet. Many have local chapters, and often you can attend meetings as a visitor. Also be sure to check the chamber of commerce and the Better Business Bureau.

7. *Personal visits to organizations.* Again, we reiterate the importance of actually visiting an organization to talk with people, to see the layout, to watch for interaction patterns between people, to note dress, and to get a general overall feeling for an organization. Remember, this is not a formal interview trip but merely an introductory, fact-finding mission.

8. *Information on cities and localities.* These next sources may not yield information on specific organizations or companies, but they can tell you about the locations where you are thinking of working. First, write or phone the visitor's information bureau (often also called the tourist information or the convention information bureau). Most medium-sized and larger cities have such an information bureau where you can learn much about their activities, climate, and environment. Also look for special sources of information on cities and localities that are available in your library: *Statistical Abstract of the United States, Quality of Life Indicators in U.S. Metro Areas, County Business Patterns* (and other documents of the Bureau of the Census and Department of Commerce), *National Atlas of the U.S.A., Directory of Shopping Centers in the U.S. and Canada,* and *Dun & Bradstreet's Million Dollar Directory.*

As you can see, many informational sources are available. The larger organizations are especially well covered. The medium and small organizations, however, may be more difficult to investigate. In such cases personal visits will be your most productive resource. Whatever type of organization or company you are seeking, there is information if you will take the time to find it. And remember that the well-informed job applicant makes a favorable impression on employers. So when an opportunity to interview arises, do the necessary research.

Where to Learn About Employers

- Company annual reports
- Personnel office brochures
- Articles on employers (see *Business Periodicals Index*)
- Chambers of commerce
- Local libraries — some keep files on local employers
- Personal visits — talk with current employees and keep your eyes open
- Actually checking out products, services, or clients of employer

What to Look for in an Employer _____

Now let's take a moment to reflect on everything you have done to this point. You have identified your career goals, developed a professional résumé, portfolio, and self-presentation, identified potential employers, and investigated some employers to gather information. In short, you are a well-prepared and well-informed job seeker. Now, perhaps for the first time, you have a precise idea of what kind of employer you want. You can determine the best employers from a number of vantage points. We judge an employer according to the following criteria:

1. Concern for high quality in the products or services it offers
2. Concern for satisfying the needs of the consumer or client
3. Concern for the health and welfare of its employees
4. A reputation as a good citizen of the community, exercising social responsibility in hiring and community relations.
5. A financially stable background, including a record of financial success and profitability where appropriate
6. A fit between your personality and professional interest and the employer's "personality" and professional needs
7. An atmosphere of positive human relations, teamwork, and pride among the employees

Just as your employer has every right to expect much of you, you have every right to expect much of your employer. You have your own standards and values too, and these should be satisfied as you make your final choices of potential employers. The message we intend here should be clear: Conduct serious interviews and job searches only with those potential employers that meet your standards and expectations.

Thus our objective in this chapter has not been just to suggest ways to find potential employers; we also think it is worthwhile to do the extra research and thinking to find the most desirable employers. These are the ones that both specialize in your professional field of interest and meet your expectations in other ways as well. Such employers may not be immediately recognized but can be discovered with persistent research on your part.

Some Employers of Family- and Consumer-Oriented Professionals _____

To close this chapter, we list some major types of employers with which family and consumer professionals in different specializations may find jobs. Virtually all of these employers offer entry-level positions.

Retail Merchandising—Fashions, Interior Design, Textiles, Household Equipment, and Home Furnishing

Department stores
Specialty stores
Chain stores
Discount stores
Off-price stores
Catalogs
Mail-order houses
Videotex/computer-purchasing services
Other shop-at-home services
Buying offices
Market research firms
Consulting firms
Fashion media
Sewing centers
Supermarkets

Fashion publicists
Travel agents and agencies
Shopping malls and centers

Consumer Studies and Family Financial Management

All types of retailers just listed
Retail banks
Financial counseling organizations
Credit unions
Savings and loans
Stockbrokerage firms
Loan companies
Any financial institution dealing with consumers
Trust companies
Investment companies
Credit bureaus
Media
Videotex services
Consumer information services
Federal, state, and local government
Insurance companies (life, health, medical, property, casualty)
Real estate firms
Computer firms (manufacturers, software writers)
Larger office buildings and apartment complexes
Utilities (telephone, electric, gas, cable television, Videotex)
Military services

The Hospitality Industry

Restaurants
Cafeterias
Institutional food services (schools, nursing homes)
Country clubs
Golf clubs
Resorts of all types (winter, summer, seasonal resorts)
Cruise ships
Major hotels
Major hotel chains
Smaller hotels
Private corporations and businesses (e.g., those with private clubs,
    dining rooms, or other facilities for employees and executives)
Health clubs
Spas

Dude ranches
Tennis clubs
Clubs for singles or older individuals (or others with special
  interests and needs)
National, state or local parks
Community recreation centers
Camps of all sorts (e.g., youth camps)
YMCA/YWCA
Free-lancing
Recreation centers
Health-care organizations
Rehabilitation centers
Senior citizen centers
Managed retirement communities

Foods and Nutritional Science

Major food-oriented corporations
Testing laboratories
Federal, state, and local government facilities
Research institutes
Universities
Institutional food services
Hospitals
Nutritional consultants
Nursing and convalescent homes
Health agencies
Emergency medical services
Senior citizen centers
Managed retirement communities
Weight management centers
Hospital supply and equipment manufacturers
Health insurers

Interior Design

Architects
Private design firms (large, medium, and small)
Starting one's own firm
Large restaurant or hotel chains
Real estate developers (private homes, commercial real estate)
Shopping malls
Major retail stores
Other major business firms employing designers of all types

Apparel and Textile Science and Design

Major chemical companies
Fiber producers
Textile producers (weavers, knitters)
Apparel manufacturers
Retail stores
Testing bureaus
U.S. government laboratories
Industrial fabric producers
Industrial designers
Engineering firms
Medical firms
Apparel-producing companies
Retail stores
Pattern companies
Home-sewing fabric companies
Fashion design houses
Fashion media
Fashion consultants

Education and Communications

Schools of all types (certification required for public schools and
  most private schools at the primary and secondary levels)
YMCA/YWCA
Human service agencies
Museums
Managed retirement communities
County extension services
Weight management centers
Community centers
Federal, state, and local government
The media (radio stations, television, cable television, newspapers,
  popular magazines, trade publications, advertising and public
  relations firms, market research firms, corporations offering
  consumer products, retail stores, public service organizations
  with public communications)
Businesses of all types
Human services organizations

Child Development

Human service agencies focused on children

YMCA/YWCA
Retailers with specialized children's departments
Day-care centers
Recreation centers
Camps
Hospitals
Rehabilitation centers
Social work organizations
Children's therapists
Community health clinics
Hospitals
Criminal justice organizations
Child development institutions
Schools
Preschools
Counseling organizations
Youth services
Museums
Libraries
Business and industry child-care centers
Abuse centers
Family shelters

Family Relations

Human service agencies
Federal, state, and local government
Private family therapists and counselors
Marriage and family counseling services
Community foundations
Businesses specializing in family-oriented products or services
Community service agencies
Housing agencies
Abuse centers
Family shelters
Managed retirement communities
Housing developers
Senior citizen centers
Recreation centers
Social welfare agencies
Religious organizations
YMCA/YWCA
Camps
Resorts

Child service agencies
Criminal justice organizations
Prisons
Hospitals
Mental health organizations
Rehabilitation centers
Public and private schools
Preschools
Child development institutions
Mental health institutions
Lobbyists and public interest groups
Political organizations
Employment agencies
Departments of human resources
Law offices
Personnel service organizations

This is only a partial listing of the organizations, businesses, and other sources of employment for family and consumer professionals, but it should suggest the breadth of opportunities that are open.

SELF-ASSESSMENT EXERCISE 15–2

Another Key to Success

Identify by name those organizations, businesses, or government agencies that need people with your abilities.

1. _____

2. _____

3. _____

4. _____

5. _____

6. _____

7. _____

8. _____

9. _____

10. _____

Questions and Exercises _____

1. Visit your university placement center to see what services it offers.
2. Visit and/or investigate other useful employment services, such as government employment offices, professional employment agencies, newspaper classified ads, professional journals, trade publications, and computerized "job banks" (a new type of employment service).
3. List personal contacts who could help you with your job search.
4. Do library research on a company or organization where you might like to work. Look up annual reports, articles in major publications (e.g., *The Wall Street Journal, Forbes, Fortune*), and stories in local newspapers where the company or organization is located.
5. List the companies and organizations that you intend to approach for employment. Learn all you can about them (see question 4).

Bibliography _____

Baron, Tony. "Using Your Connections," *National Business Employment Weekly* (August 13, 1989), 5–6.

Basta, Nicholas. *Top Professions: The 100 Most Popular, Dynamic and Profitable Careers in America Today.* Princeton, NJ: Petersons Guides, 1989.

Bolles, Richard N. *What Color Is Your Parachute?* Berkeley, CA: Ten Speed Press, 1990.

Dun's Marketing Services. *The Career Guide 1990: Dun's Employment Opportunities Directory.* New York: Dun & Bradstreet, 1990.

Erdlen, John D. *Where Are the Jobs?* New York: Harcourt Brace Jovanovich, 1982.

Fry, Ronald W., ed. *Marketing and Sales Career Directory,* 2nd ed. Orange, CA: Career Publishing, 1988.

Gaff, Sally Shake. *Professional Development: A Guide to Resources.* New York: Change Magazine Press, 1978.

Hadary, Sharon G. "Job Hunting Tips from the Front Line," *National Business Employment Weekly* (September 3, 1989), 5–6.

Helwig, Andrew A., Randy Hiatt, and Joe Louis Vidales. "Job Hunting: Critical Knowledge and Skills," *Journal of Career Development* 15 (Spring 1989), 143–153.

Hoyt, Kenneth B. "The Career Status of Women and Minority Persons: A 20-Year Retrospective," *Career Development Quarterly* 37 (March 1989), 202–212.

Jackson, Tom. *Guerrilla Tactics in the Job Market.* New York: Bantam, 1983.

Kimmel, Karen. *Career Resource Centers.* Columbus, OH: The National Center for Research in Vocational Education, The Ohio State University, 1982.

Krannich, Ronald L. *Careering and Re-Careering for the 1990's: The Complete Guide to Planning Your Future.* Manassas, VA: Impact Publications, 1989.

Lombardo, Joseph, and Amy Lombardo. *The Job Belt: The 50 Best Places in America for High Quality Employment—Today and in the Future.* New York: Penguin Books, 1986.

McAdam, Terry W. *Doing Well by Doing Good: The First Complete Guide to Careers in the Nonprofit Sector.* New York: Penguin Books, 1988.

Mitchell, Joyce Slayton. *College Board Guide to Jobs and Career Planning.* New York: College Entrance Examination Board, 1990.

Nivens, Beatryce. *The Black Woman's Career Guide.* New York: Doubleday, 1987.

Norback, Craig T., ed. *Careers Encyclopedia.* Lincolnwood, IL: VGM Career Horizons, 1988.

Occupational Outlook Handbook. Washington, DC: U.S. Government Printing Office, 1990.

Sacharov, Albert. *Offbeat Careers: The Directory of Unusual Work.* Berkeley, CA: Ten Speed Press, 1988.

Shields, Rhea, and Anna K. Williams. *Opportunities in Home Economics Careers.* Lincolnwood, IL: VGM Career Horizons, 1988.

Snelling, Robert O. *Jobs! What They Are—Where They Are—What They Pay.* New York: Simon & Schuster, 1989.

Stoodley, Martha. "Choosing the Right Tool," *National Business Employment Weekly* (January 14, 1990), 9.

Wilkins, Craig. "How to Use Your Local Library," *National Business Employment Weekly* (July 30, 1989), 17–18.

U.S. Government Manual. Washington, DC: U.S. Government Printing Office, 1988.

How to Obtain Interviews and Offers of Employment

This chapter discusses making initial contacts with employers through various communications, obtaining interviews, making preparations for interviews, conducting the interview, keeping in contact following the interview, and responding to a job offer. We also shall consider the protocols and ethics of job seeking. Finally, the chapter ends with three postscripts, on rejection shock (how to handle a rejection by an employer), mistakes job seekers make, and special procedures for government job seekers.

Contacting Employers — Professional Letter Writing and Telephoning

Armed with career goals, résumé, portfolio, professional image, and knowledge of employers, you have now arrived at the time to contact employers. Contacts are made in many ways: through placement services, employment agencies, friends and personal contacts, to name but a few. However, most contacts will not be through intermediaries but will be directly between you and the employer, by letter or by telephone.

Effective letter writing and telephoning are specialized communications skills in which all your accumulated skills and artistry with words come into play. You've learned to write expressively and creatively and to speak professionally and enthusiastically as a part of your college studies. The years you've spent developing these skills now come to the forefront. There is no ideal solution or standard format for making these contacts. The best letters and calls are brief and to the point, yet express some of the things special about you.

Most first contacts with employers are by letter. There are two basic types of letters; the letter of inquiry and the letter of application, or cover letter. A letter of inquiry is used to ask an employer about current vacancies or to request information about a company without necessarily seeking a specific position. Frequently a résumé is included with the letter, but rarely would a complete portfolio be included because employers are under no obligation to return it. The content of a letter of inquiry varies but usually includes a statement of the general area about which you would like information (for example, opportunities in sales, in child health services, in nutrition education), and a brief description of your qualifications. The letter also should mention how you can be contacted or when you will be contacting the employer. Often you should call after your letter has arrived, thus showing personal initiative in your inquiry (this is also the best way to get a response).

A letter of application is a direct response to a position that has been advertised or a vacancy that you know exists in the organization. The letter of application should include a résumé tailor made to that vacancy if possible. The letter of application will usually include the following parts:

1. The first paragraph identifies the position for which you are applying and may mention where you learned about the position.
2. One or more paragraphs should highlight your qualifications that are most relevant to the position. These paragraphs may also

state such things as training or prior experience related to this job and why you are interested in working with this employer.

3. One statement should indicate that a résumé of your credentials is enclosed. You may also state that additional credentials are available, such as your portfolio, a file of references, details on the résumé, or other items that may be of interest to the employer. Mention only things directly related to the position you are seeking.

4. The last paragraph should indicate how and when you may be contacted. Some people like to include a statement such as "I am interested in exploring this position with you further and will telephone your secretary for an appointment to discuss this during the week of ————." Or you might say something like "I will be in Boston the week of March 27. Could we get together and discuss the position sometime during the week?" Such statements as these show initiative and force you to take action rather than wait for the employer to respond to you.

Figure 16-1 shows a typical letter of application containing these points. All letters, whether of application or inquiry, should be professionally typed on bond paper. Never use a form letter, a mimeographed, or a photocopied letter. The letter should be addressed to a specific person in the organization who is involved in the hiring decision (this may be a personnel officer, but frequently it will be an executive or officer elsewhere in the organization). Finally, some experts suggest showing some of your creativity and personality in your letter (see Figure 16-1). If you choose to add these personal touches, do not go overboard. Restrict the letter to no more than one page of single-spaced typed copy.

Like writing letters, telephoning requires careful preparation, specifically, making up a script similar to a letter, including the following:

1. Who you are
2. Why you are calling (seeking an informational interview, applying for a specific position, or asking for additional information)
3. If applicable, your basic qualifications and why they are relevant to this employment
4. A request for an interview or an opportunity to discuss the position in greater detail

Your script should be short and to the point and should address the person in charge of the hiring decisions or someone closely con-

```
                                        129 University St.
                                        Tucson, AZ 85721
                                        February 4, 1991

Mrs. Barbara Smith
Employment Manager
Davison's Downtown Store
Atlanta, Georgia 30300

Dear Mrs. Smith:

The purpose of this letter is to apply for a position in the
management training program at Davison's.

I shall graduate in May from The University of Arizona, with a
Bachelor of Science degree majoring in Fashion Merchandising.
Determination and eagerness to enter into retailing enabled me to
graduate in three and one-half years, while maintaining a high
scholastic average. In addition to courses in fashion, merchandis-
ing, and retail management, I have a working knowledge of cloth-
ing construction and textile design. Weekly discussions of Women's
Wear Daily brought to mind the economic problems facing large
department stores and also how solutions were found by corporate
and noncorporate groups. I have had several jobs in various areas
of retailing: three years as a salesperson at a shoe boutique,
one year as a bridal consultant, and summer employment at a
local fabric center learning piece goods merchandising and textile
performance. I also learned about Davison's and its leading posi-
tion in the Atlanta retail market through these discussions.

By participating in several campus and community activities, I
have learned efficient time management, and I also have become
aware of the need for flexibility when working with different
types of people. I also served as the fashion representative on
campus for a major pattern company, where I enjoyed presenting
programs and collecting market data to be used in forecasting
fashion trends.

Enclosed is a résumé outlining my background and qualifications.
I will be visiting Atlanta from February 18 through February 25.
Could we arrange a meeting at your convenience during this time?
I will telephone your secretary next week concerning the arrange-
ment of such an appointment.

Sincerely,


Elizabeth M. Williamson

Enclosure
```

Figure 16-1

nected to it. The script should be conversational in tone; do not let it sound as if you are reading it. The following is typical:

Hello, Mr. Jones. My name is Lorraine Smith from The University of Arizona. I have been reading *The New York Times* and saw that you have an opening in retail management training. I would like to be considered for this position. I have worked for a store similar to yours, Dillard's in Tucson, and will receive my bachelor's degree majoring in fashion merchandising from The University next month. I'm very excited about a career in retailing, and based on my years of experience I believe I am a good candidate for your position. May we get together sometime next week and discuss this? [Here she pauses and allows Mr. Jones to respond.]

Try to anticipate the questions you might be asked. Frequently, questions will be used to screen out unqualified applicants. Such questions ask about your experience in an area of employment and the like. Do your homework in advance and know as much about the organization as possible. Another thing you can do is make "practice calls" to try out your prepared script on a friend or family member. Some people suggest tape-recording your script and playing it back to see how you sound. This may be helpful because when you have prepared a script it is easy to sound stiff rather than conversational.

Practical Exercises That Get the Job

1. Prepare a script for a telephone call to a potential employer.
2. Write an application letter to a potential employer.
3. Now evaluate these from the employer's viewpoint (have a friend or professional acquaintance do this also). If you were the employer, would you interview the person calling? Why or why not?
4. Now rewrite your script and application letter to correct the problems you discovered in Step 3.

Remember that the purposes of your letters and telephone calls are to (1) convince the employer of your qualifications and (2) obtain an interview. Be sure you are addressing the correct person in the organization and know this person's role and job title. Be positive about yourself and the organization, and especially how the two of you would complement each other. Give the person contacted alternative dates for interviewing and make yourself available. This positive and assertive approach has yielded many an interview to job seekers, and it can work for you too.

When the potential employer says yes to your request for an interview, a number of things must be done. First, be sure to get the correct day and time for the interview. Ask about the approximate duration of the interview, whether it will be an hour or an all-day series of meetings with various people. Also determine the exact location of the interview, and get directions on how to get there if you don't already know. If the interview is offered by telephone, confirm the details (date, time, and other facts) by mail.

The Interview—How to Prepare and What to Expect ____

Your work has paid off—you have been invited for a job interview. The first thing to do, if you haven't done it already, is to do research on the employer. This was discussed earlier and needs no elaboration here. Suffice it to say that you should get to know the employer as well as possible, using the sources reviewed in the last chapter. It is also useful to learn who will interview you. Know their names, job titles, departments, and responsibilities.

If you are preparing for an informational interview, you will want to make up questions to ask the employer. Such questions may include (1) what type of work is done at the place of employment, (2) what special skill or education is needed, (3) what experience will help in this job, (4) what is the daily work life like (routines, hours, etc.), (5) what travel is involved, and (6) what the prospects for this career are. Also be prepared to answer questions such as "Why did you come to this organization for information?" "What are your qualifications?" or "Would you be interested in working with this firm?" Finally, close the informational interview with a statement of appreciation and a request that you be allowed to call at a later time for further information.

Preparing for a formal job interview requires researching the organization and learning about the individuals with whom you will interview. It may mean refreshing your knowledge in many areas, possibly in courses that you completed years earlier. In some ways it is like studying for an exam. And again, it also requires preparing answers to questions that you might be asked by the interviewers.

Much of an interview's success is based on your personal style and self-presentation: how effectively you speak; how self-assured you are; and if you have a professionally appropriate appearance, a firm handshake, direct eye contact with those you meet, and a natural conversational style. A warm, sincere, enthusiastic, and honest personality and a willingness to listen when others are speaking will be appreciated. Your ability to answer all questions directly and intelligently will also be noticed. Employers especially want to hear positive answers to questions about how you would accomplish your job.

Typical questions asked in interviews are about educational background, employment experience, life-style, and goals. Indeed, the types of questions and their implications vary widely. Employers will ask many different questions, and you cannot anticipate all of them. However, certain questions are nearly always asked, and you should have answers for them prepared in advance. Here are questions often asked:

1. What are your long-range goals and career objectives?
2. What are your short-range goals for the next two to five years?
3. What would you like to be doing five years from now? What job title would you like to be holding, and how much responsibility would you like to have?
4. What are the most important rewards or benefits you expect in your career?
5. Why did you choose this career? And why did you choose this specific position?
6. Why did you choose this specific company (organization, human service agency, hotel)?
7. What qualifications do you have that make you the best candidate for this position?
8. What do you know about the products (services, clients) offered by this organization?
9. How would you describe yourself? What are your most important values? What are your most important or typical personality traits?
10. What are your greatest strengths? What are your greatest weaknesses?
11. How can you contribute to the success of this company (organization, hotel)?
12. What are your greatest accomplishments? Why were they important, and how did you achieve them?
13. Why did you choose your major area of study? What subjects did you like best and least?
14. Are your grades in college important indicators of your potential? Could you have achieved better grades? Do your grades indicate what you have achieved in college?
15. What were your extracurricular activities? What did you accomplish in them?
16. How would you describe your work experience? How is it related to this position?
17. How would you describe an ideal job?

18. What do you know about our organization?
19. How well do you work under stress or pressure?
20. How can you tell if a company or organization is the right one for you?
21. Are you willing to travel and relocate as part of your job?
22. Do you think you would like to live in this community where we are located? What do you know about it, its cost of living, problems, and life-style?
23. Describe a problem you recently faced and how you solved it.
24. What have you learned from your mistakes?
25. Why did you leave your job (or why do you want to change jobs)?
26. How do you like to spend your leisure or spare time? What are your hobbies?
27. Are you willing to work overtime? Weekends? Evenings?
28. After graduation, how do you expect to continue your professional development? By attending further classes? Participating in organizations? Taking short courses?
29. What have you done that shows your energy, initiative, and drive?
30. What do you want to do in life?
31. Why should we hire you?

Try to answer each question in a way that reflects your talents and how you can best serve the organization with which you are interviewing. Always be positive and diplomatic.

You should also prepare a list of questions. Employers expect you to ask questions and will be concerned if you have none. Such questions might include the following subjects:

1. Responsibilities and typical assignments of the position
2. Opportunities for advancement
3. Numbers and types of employees supervised
4. Travel required
5. Training programs and opportunities for on-the-job training
6. Working conditions and typical daily routines
7. Fringe benefits

Eventually salary will be discussed. In general, salary should be brought up at the later stages of the interview. To ask about salary too early is to look as though your priorities are centered more on money than on the job. Raise the salary issue if the employer does not, but do so later in the interview when the mutual interests of the employer and you have been established.

You should have a plan for conducting the interview so that you can control it as much as possible. You can prepare in the following areas:

1. Know your job objective.
2. Be familiar with the specific position or job title for which you are applying.
3. Know the people who are interviewing you and address them by name.
4. Show how your college training is relevant.
5. Show that your work experience is relevant.
6. Show that you have ambition and initiative.
7. Show your energy and enthusiasm.
8. Stress your positive qualities.
9. Do not dwell on negative points. Let them drop quickly (better yet, turn a negative into a positive).
10. Act poised, confident, warm, and personable.
11. Look professional and similar to those with whom you are interviewing.
12. Speak of your ability to take responsibility.
13. Be sensitive to the interviewer. Watch him or her for clues of pleasure, displeasure, excitement, or boredom with your statements, and respond appropriately.
14. At the end of the interview, summarize your credentials and what you learned in the interview. By doing this you can show that you fit the organization and its goals.

There are several other things to do. First, arrive early for the interview (do not risk being late). If the employer has some form of employment testing, perhaps a skills or personality test, take these willingly but carefully. Tests help employers find the right fit between you and the organization (you need not complete questions you find offensive or an invasion of privacy). Also realize that some interviews may not go as well as others do and that some interviewers may be disinterested or even hostile. And finally, if you are on an expense account for the interview, ask reimbursement only for fair and actual expenses incurred, and get receipts (transportation and hotel receipts are required in most instances). The fairness of your expenses is one measure of your ethical standards, and the employer is well aware of this.

When all interviews are complete, thank each person you have talked with. If possible, note the name of each person you talk with,

SELF-ASSESSMENT EXERCISE 16–1

Summary of Interview

Keep a record of each interview on a form such as the following:

Name/address of interviewer:

_____

Questions you were asked and your answers:

_____

Questions you asked and answers:

_____

Important information or facts gathered:

_____

Conclusion 1. Actions employer will take:

_____

Conclusion 2. Follow-up actions you will take:

_____

_____

his or her title, and the main points of discussion. It is a courtesy to write thank-you letters expressing your positive feelings about each interview and your further interest in the company. Also, for future reference, keep a complete record of your interview schedule and all the people you met (e.g., Figures 13-2 and 13-3). This record can be handy if you choose to accept a job offer with the organization.

What should you take to the interview? A number of items are mandatory. You should have extra copies of your résumé, and a portfolio of your accomplishments that are relevant to the particular job opportunity. It is also useful to take a list of your references and the names and addresses of your former employers and supervisors. Finally, take a pad of paper to record notes, appointments, and other tidbits of information gathered during the interviews. All items can be carried in an attaché case or small brief-case. Select a high-quality case; it is a part of your professional appearance.

Accepting an Offer of Employment _____

One of the most exciting days in your life is the day that you receive a letter offering you employment. Even more exciting is the day that you decide to accept. Congratulations come from friends, parents express their pride in you, and you recognize that all the years of work have finally paid off. Amidst this excitement are a few last things to do in making your final, formal acceptance.

First, send a formal letter of acceptance to your employer. It should verify the job title, salary, starting date, and other conditions and circumstances. Your letter also should express your appreciation for the offer of employment and your enthusiasm for the opportunity. Send the letter as soon as possible, but in any event be sure to meet the employer's deadline for acceptance. Before sending the letter, you may want to call the person to whom you are sending the letter to say that you are accepting and that the letter will be in the mail as of a certain date.

When your acceptance is certain, it is also good to write or call co-workers and individuals with whom you interviewed at the company. You should express your appreciation for their interest in you and indicate that you are looking forward to working with them. At this time it is especially important to contact your future supervisor, by both telephone and mail. This is a professional courtesy, but you will also want to discuss specific aspects of the job, your responsibilities, and what will be expected of you. This is a good time to begin showing that you will be a concerned, thoughtful, and motivated employee.

You should also contact the organization's personnel office to complete whatever employment forms and histories are needed in advance. Some organizations may require you to take physical or other examinations. Personnel offices in larger organizations may have relocation services to help you with moving your household goods, making travel arrangements, and apartment or house hunting. Moving can be difficult; begin planning it as soon as possible.

Protocols and Ethics for Job Seekers _____

As in other aspects of social life and human relationships, there is a certain etiquette and ethics in job seeking. By etiquette we mean common, accepted, and expected courtesies that you need to follow in the search. One of the most important is writing the various letters used in the employment process. We have already discussed your letter of inquiry and letters of job application. The following are other letters that professional protocol requires:

1. *Letter acknowledging interviews:* Always acknowledge an invitation for an interview, and in your letter, restate the dates, times, and places of the interview.
2. *Thank-you letters:* Thank-you letters are written to individuals with whom you have had interviews, acknowledging your gratitude for their time and interest in you. We also advise writing letters acknowledging important phone conversations. Such letters reinforce your name, credentials, and interest in the organization.
3. *Letter of acceptance:* When you receive a job offer and decide to accept it, a letter formally indicating your acceptance of the position is required (see the preceding section of this chapter).
4. *Letter of refusal:* If you decide to decline an offer, send a letter declining the opportunity but thanking the employer for the offer and for considering you. Be sure to send your letter of refusal as soon as possible.

All letters should be carefully written and edited. Have them professionally typed on bond paper, and be sure all names and addresses are spelled correctly. Be as thoughtful as you can, use common sense, and treat others with the same respect that you expect from them. Showing these common courtesies could be what makes you stand out from the other candidates.

Special Tactics for Job Seekers

The tactics for job seeking discussed throughout this chapter are the standard, traditional approaches, or "going in through the front door." There are other "back door" tactics that may be just as effective. Some of these are doing volunteer work, accepting part-time employment, or doing other odd jobs that get your foot in the door. These tactics may not at first lead to a career, but they build references and a reputation. An advantage of volunteer or part-time work is that you will learn of job openings before they are announced publicly. And as your accomplishments multiply, you may work yourself into a full-time job, or you may even create a new job. All these tactics are particularly valuable for the career seeker who has a definite career in mind but who cannot immediately get a starting position in that career.

Job sharing is a new tactic for job seekers that has grown in recent years. Job sharing refers to a job held by two people, each working part time. Job sharing may get you started in a career, and you may even find it a satisfactory career alternative.

Networking is also an important tactic for job seekers. All of us have a network of friends, relatives, and acquaintances. Some people rely on it to give them exposure to potential employers or to provide leads. Share your résumé with the people in your network. Let them know of your availability and your skills. When appropriate, volunteer for work or take part-time assignments. Ask if you might freelance or consult on a part-time basis with individuals in your network until an opportunity arises. Be creative in using your network, but above all be visible and let your availability be known to your contacts.

Tapping into the job market may often require such creative tactics and personal flexibility. In essence, you are doing whatever it takes to make your skills and availability known. By assertively marketing yourself using tactics like these, you will uncover a wider variety of opportunities than by merely taking the passive approach of letter writing or relying on your college placement service. We cannot overemphasize that jobs go not only to the most brilliant but also to those who want them the most and who do whatever is needed to get them.

Postscript

To close this chapter, we offer perspectives on three subjects: "rejection shock," mistakes job seekers make, and special procedures for government job seekers.

Postscript A: Rejection Shock

As Richard Bolles, author of *What Color Is Your Parachute?* pointed out, "rejection shock" is something that can happen to many of us when we seek jobs. We are confident that we are best for the job and will undoubtedly be recognized as such. Yet, after all the preparation and interviewing, we get a letter stating "we cannot offer you employment" or "no jobs are available at this time." This sometimes damages our self-esteem, self-confidence. The disappointment of being turned down can lead to lowered expectations and a willingness to accept a lower level of employment.

These reactions are wrong: Rejection occurs to all of us at some time or another during the job search. Just as you will not find every employer satisfactory for your interests and professional qualities, not all employers will see you as satisfactory for their needs. It is not that the system is wrong or bad, and it is definitely not the time to sulk or withdraw. Rather, it is the time to move on to the next opportunity. There always is another opportunity, as good as and often better than the one for which you were turned down. By far the best approach to rejection shock is to renew your efforts toward the next opportunities you are considering.

Postscript B: Mistakes Job Seekers Make

The following is a list of some of the more common mistakes that people make when seeking employment. Notice that many of these are mental mistakes, mistakes in attitudes, or a failure to think or take action.

- Lack of goals or well-defined objectives
- Lack of motivation or enthusiasm
- Misunderstanding, or lack of understanding, of the particular job for which you are applying
- Procrastination, or putting off until tomorrow what you should have done yesterday or today
- Not knowing facts or other information about the company or organization in which you are seeking employment
- Failing to highlight and emphasize your strongest selling points with respect to the job that you are seeking
- Having a poorly planned résumé or one that does not focus on your best qualities, experiences, and capabilities
- Putting too little commitment and effort into the job search and looking at too limited a selection of possible employers
- Looking at the wrong type of employer or employers that do not match your qualifications
- Lack of experience or an inability to demonstrate to the company that you have the necessary experience
- Unrealistic salary demands or unrealistic expectations of starting at a high-level position
- Failure to make personal contacts with employers through letters and telephone calls; failure to follow through on promises made in these and other contacts
- A feeling of desperation in the job search that is communicated to employers: sometimes saying "I'll do anything" if you'll just give me a chance and similarly taking any job out of desperation

- A know-it-all attitude conveying to the employer that surely no one else is as good as you are
- Negative attitude toward job search, such as saying there's no job for me or I have no positive qualifications for this job
- Overrelying on passive job seeking, such as sending résumés and hoping for good luck, rather than taking the initiative to make contacts
- The "Mom and Dad had it better" syndrome or "My friend Beth had it better" syndrome — the feeling that somehow others had an advantage over you
- Failure to use good etiquette and ethics at all stages of communications and job seeking

Postscript C: Special Procedures for Government Job Seekers

Seeking a career in the federal government is different from the job-seeking procedures discussed in this chapter. A useful book is David Waelde's *How to Get a Federal Job*, and newsletters such as the *Federal Jobs Newsletter* announce government job openings. One recommended way to start is by contacting the nearest Federal Job Information Center. These centers are located throughout the country (check your telephone directory under U.S. Government). Employment specialists with the center can explain procedures for seeking employment and tell you of current vacancies. They may also suggest agencies or individuals within agencies whom you may contact directly.

Applying for federal jobs usually works as follows: First you must find vacancies in agencies or governmental subunits in which you are seeking employment. The rules of government employment require that all vacancies be published in announcements, which you can obtain directly from agencies offering positions or from the Federal Job Information Center. The announcements describe the positions available, their rank and salary, responsibilities, qualifications, and the procedures for applying. Following the procedures for applying is extremely important. Usually they require submitting an "SF 171," Personal Qualifications Statement, which is like a résumé in that it describes in detail your education, work experience, and other qualifications. It is the most important application form for a government job and requires a careful, detailed, and accurate expression of your credentials. Type the form neatly, make sure there are no spelling errors, and describe your qualifications succinctly and positively.

Your completed SF 171, together with all other application forms or materials requested, should be submitted to the address listed in the job announcement. Your application is then evaluated and, if your credentials pass this inspection, is placed on a register of qualified candidates. It is necessary to get on this register of qualified applicants, for under civil service requirements this is the only pool from which candidates for the job may be selected. If yours is one of the better applications, your chances of selection from the register will be good because a number of qualified individuals are often hired at once. But if your application is passed over, it may be kept in the register for a future vacancy.

Some placement experts recommend that you personally contact actual supervisors or hiring officials of the federal agencies in which you are interested. Although this may not lead to a job, because you must still get on the register of qualified applicants, it may help supervisors form a favorable impression of you in advance of the hiring. Likewise, having contacts with the officials responsible for hiring may mean that you will hear about opportunities before they are announced.

Local government also offers many jobs for family and consumer professionals. To find job opportunities, start by checking the local government sections of telephone directories to find the programs and agencies in local governments in which you would like to work. You may then directly contact them to obtain information about employment opportunities. Many local governments also have employment offices or job information services. Look in the telephone directory in the local government section under "Personnel Department" or "Employment Department."

When seeking a career in local government, get acquainted with hiring officials and supervisory personnel. In this way you may gain entry to local careers, both because supervisors will know you and because you will have demonstrated your interests. Other ways to enter careers in local government are through internships, volunteer work experiences, summer employment, or work with local political parties or political action groups. Finally, look for local or regional newsletters on jobs. For instance, look in your library for *Western Cities, Job Finder*, and other newsletters that focus on city, county, and state government positions.

Questions and Exercises

1. Write a letter of inquiry to a company in which you are interested.
2. Write a practice letter of application.

3. Write a script for a telephone inquiry or interview. Practice it in a telephone call to a friend.
4. List some general questions you would like to ask in an interview.
5. Practice answering the typical questions asked by employers from this chapter. Tape-record your answers, and analyze them as if you were the employer.
6. Conduct mock employment interviews as a class project. Videotape and critique each interview.
7. Conduct an informational interview with a prospective employer. Find out what employers look for in an interview. Ask the questions you would ask in a job interview. Use this informational interview as a chance to practice presenting yourself professionally, including professional dress, neat grooming, a firm handshake, making eye contact with the interviewer, speaking clearly, and emphasizing the positive aspects of your personality.

Bibliography

Baron, Tony. "Using Your Connections," *National Business Employment Weekly* (August 13, 1989), 5–6.

Besson, Taunee. "A Stalled Job Search Can Be Pegged to Attitude," *National Business Employment Weekly* (July 30, 1989), 9–10.

Billingsley, Edmond. *Career Planning and Job Hunting for Today's Student: The Nonjob Interview Approach.* Santa Monica, CA: Goodyear, 1978.

"Breaking and Entering the Job Market with a Phone Call," *Career World* 12 (November 1983), 20–21.

Chase, Ellis. "Take the Stress Out of Interview Preparation," *National Business Employment Weekly* (February 18, 1990), 5–6.

Davidson, Jeffrey P. *Blow Your Own Horn: How to Market Yourself and Your Career.* New York: American Management Association, 1987

Engelbrecht, Joann D., and Joyce I. Nies. "Work/Family Interactions: Trends and Applications," *Journal of Home Economics* 80 (Spring 1988), 23–28.

Hadary, Sharon G. "Job Hunting Tips from the Front Line," *National Business Employment Weekly* (September 3, 1989), 5–6.

Helwig, Andrew A. "Information Required for Job Hunting: 1,121 Counselors Respond," *Journal of Employment Counseling* 24 (December 1987), 184–190.

Helwig, Andrew A., Randy Hiatt, and Joe Louis Vidales. "Job Hunting: Critical Knowledge and Skills," *Journal of Career Development* 15 (Spring 1989), 143–153.

Hoyt, Kenneth B. "The Career Status of Women and Minority Persons: A 20-Year Retrospective," *Career Development Quarterly* 37 (March 1989), 202–212.

Jackson, Tom. *Guerrilla Tactics in the Job Market*. New York: Bantam, 1983.

Jackson, Tom, and Davidyne Mayleas. *The Hidden Job Market for the Eighties*. New York: Times Books, 1981.

Krannich, Caryl Rae. *Interview for Success*. San Luis Obisbo, CA: Impact Publishers, 1990.

Medley, H. Anthony. *Sweaty Palms: The Neglected Art of Being Interviewed*. Belmont, CA: Lifetime Learning, 1984.

Olson, Richard F. *Managing the Interview: A Self-teaching Guide*. New York: Wiley, 1980.

Sincott, Michael Z., and Robert S. Goyer. *Interviewing*. New York: Macmillan, 1984.

Stoodley, Martha. "Choosing the Right Tool," *National Business Employment Weekly* (January 14, 1990), 9.

Waelde, David E. *How to Get a Federal Job*, 7th ed. Washington, DC: FEDHELP Publications, 1989.

Welch, Mary Scott. *Networking: The Great New Way for Women to Get Ahead*. New York: Harcourt Brace Jovanovich, 1981.

Yates, Martin John. *Hiring the Best: A Manager's Guide to Effective Interviewing*. Halbrook, MA: Bob Adams, 1988.

Career Development Following Graduation

Part IV looks at professional development after your career has started, focusing on topics such as successful career management and the future of your profession. The four chapters are the following:

- **Career Development and Career Transitions (Chapter 17)**
- **Managing a Successful Career (Chapter 18)**
- **Professional Associations, Organizations, and Memberships (Chapter 19)**
- **Future Directions for Family- and Consumer-Oriented Professions (Chapter 20)**

Career Development
and Career Transitions

Starting your new career is certainly one of the most exciting moments in your life. Not only does it mark what some people consider an official transition into adulthood; it also gives you an opportunity to take responsibility for your life and those around you.

In this and the following chapter, we discuss how to start your first job and how to succeed in your career. We also look at ways you can cope with some problems that arise in nearly everyone's early career. Of special interest to women are some of the problems that they may face.

TABLE 17.1   Basic Stages of Career Development

Stages	Specific activities
1. Preentry	Education, part-time experiences, internships
2. Entry into Career	Recruitment, interviewing, choosing among opportunities
3. Basic Training and Initiation	Adapting to first job and its "culture," completing traineeships, learning formal and informal routines, winning acceptance as part of the team
4. Settling in for the Long Term	Learning the job, assuming greater responsibility and authority, seeking higher status
5. Advancement and Mobility	Promotion, leveling off or becoming obsolete, updating or learning new skills, changing career directions
6. Reaching Continuing Status or Tenure in the Profession	Acceptance as a permanent member of the profession, reaching highest accomplishments, and eventual retirement (often as a senior consultant)

Source: Adapted from Schein, 1981, p. 29.

The Career Cycle

Let's begin by placing your lifelong career in perspective. It is useful at this time to reemphasize that you are beginning a long-term career, not just simply a first job. A career spans an entire lifetime and is a sequence of stages both in one's life-cycle and in one's professional growth. Over the years you will increase your skills and sophistication regarding your profession, advance your occupational position, and become a more complete professional person.

No two persons or professions have the same career cycles, but professionals in career planning believe that there are basic stages and transitions in the careers of most people. For example, Table 17.1 outlines the six typical stages of a career. These stages can apply to any type of organization, whether a small business, large business, government, or human service organization. Careers develop in a sequence of stages, including learning or socialization into the job, performance and advancement in the job, and an eventual culmination in which one either becomes obsolete or acquires new skills leading to further growth. A career is a series of passages and transitions, through which a person moves up an organization or perhaps laterally. Lateral moves are those at the same level, rank, and status in an organization and are considered important parts of career development in many businesses, government, and human service organizations.

During your career, you will probably go through some combination of these movements, both vertical and lateral. The important point is that a career is fluid and changing, involving continuous growth and transition through stages. You will learn how careers develop in your profession as you become more experienced. Every profession seems to be different, and every organization has its own pattern and rules determining stages of career development.

The career cycle may roughly parallel stages in the life cycle through which everyone passes. The idea of "stages in life," popularized in Daniel Levinson's *The Seasons of a Man's Life* and Gail Sheehy's *Passages*, is that the life cycle is a series of certain periods and major events. These events and periods have professional and personal overtones and show vividly how professional and personal lives become intertwined. Typical stages or transitions may be described as follows:

1. *The early adult transition (ages 18 to 22).* At this point in life the young adult begins to pull up roots, leaving the family environment and reducing dependence on family support or control. Going to college is one means for accomplishing this transition, but joining the military or taking some other job, or perhaps getting married, are transitional activities as well. Another transitional activity is career and job testing.

2. *Entering the adult world (ages 22 to 28).* This is a period in which the young adult tries on many uniforms (careers) in search of the correct fit. He or she explores the larger world and tries different responsibilities and perhaps different relationships, seeking a particular occupational niche though perhaps not finding a final lifelong occupation until later periods. The individual meets many significant people influencing his or her life and perhaps chooses one or more mentors. The result of this period is usually the formation of a "life structure" containing an occupational field and perhaps marriage and family. Most important, it is a time of exhilaration and excitement, a time when one has dreams that will guide entry and progression into later life.

3. *The age 30 transition (ages 28 to 32).* For some, this is one of the first major challenging periods in life. Here they might find some of the mistakes in early life or perhaps inadequacies in dreams and ideals. It is a time when such discontent or feelings of incompleteness can lead to shifts in careers and shifts in commitments. In short, the initial structure of one's life can be and may well be rebuilt at this time. This does not mean that careers are necessarily changed, but it does often mean that

career goals and career activities are redefined. This is also a time where personal relations in marriage and personal relations among friends may acquire a new structure and a new direction.

4. *The settling-down period (ages 33 to 40).* This is the period in life when occupation and personal life become more stable, organized, and orderly. It is a time of establishing roots and perhaps sending out new ones. Homes are bought, children are raised, and commitment to the most valued activities (whether work, family, or children) becomes deeper and more permanent. The goal now is to show that one has made it, and some people may even peak in their careers in their mid-to-late thirties. Promotion seeking and advancement are typical, and so this can be a period of considerable pressure. For some women this becomes a particularly difficult time of life because it is approaching the end of the childbearing years, and family life must be assessed or reassessed. For some women it is also the period when they reenter the working world following childbearing and rearing, and therefore, the period becomes especially engaging and exciting.

5. *The age 40 transition (ages 38 to 42).* A whole new perspective often emerges at this time. People realize that life is short and that their bodies and abilities are changing. It is also a time when they recognize their successes, limitations, and failures. They reassess where they have been and where they are going and often revise a major part of their life and career goals. They may become more self-accepting and more concerned with happiness, perhaps less concerned with achievement and more concerned with self-fulfillment. Whatever the case, this is an important time of transition and revision of life goals.

6. *Middle life and beyond (midforties and beyond).* At this time, people's career paths become more stable and clear, and people seem to accept where they are going. They are less dominated by other individuals or organizations and more concerned with enjoying work and life. Frequently this is the time of life when people achieve their greatest successes, happiness, and self-fulfillment.

The foregoing is an incomplete sketch of the stages in life, but it does illustrate the transitions, changing roles, and changing responsibilities or outlooks on life. The ages at which these transitions occur vary from individual to individual, depending on their maturity, circumstances, marriage, occupation, and the like. The point is to recognize life for what it is, a continuing set of transitions, ebbs, and flows. Perhaps there is no better time than now to learn the structures of careers, the stages in the career cycle, the stages in life, and the relationships among all of these. Professional and personal lives are closely intertwined.

Adjusting to Your New Job

Like everyone else, you will want to get a good start in that all-important first job (and all later jobs as well). Your first few days on the job are often crucial in getting off on the right foot. The following are some tips to help you get the right start, make the right impression, and begin work as smoothly as possible.

The starting place is with your supervisor. Very early in the game you will want to know your supervisor's needs and priorities and what he or she regards as most important or most fundamental. In other words, learn exactly what is expected of you, and if you don't understand, ask. Don't be afraid to ask questions, especially if you're confused or a bit overwhelmed. It is also reasonable to ask your supervisor to suggest other people with whom you should coordinate and cooperate. You won't want to bother your supervisor too much, and so it is important to find other helpful colleagues who can supply the answers.

Second, it is important to learn the office routines as soon as possible. By this we mean simple things such as starting time, lunch hours, breaks, quitting time, and other expectations regarding time management. Be sure to work within these time routines. If office routines indicate 8:00 A.M. sharp as starting time, be early and

---

SELF-ASSESSMENT EXERCISE 17–1

Your New Job—Part I

List unique situations or experiences that you encounter in your new job.

1. _____

2. _____

3. _____

4. _____

5. _____

never late; if office routine says the normal workday is eight hours, work at least eight and perhaps nine or ten. It is better to exceed expectations a little than to fail to meet them.

Avoid being pushy or overly aggressive until you learn the norms and expectations of the job setting. Naturally you will be eager to learn and to meet colleagues, but you simply cannot do all these things in the first few days or even the first few weeks of work. Move into your job assertively and with obvious enthusiasm, but don't push yourself on others. Let your fitting in with the organization, your new colleagues, and the new norms occur naturally over a period. Don't be the "hot shot" or know-it-all from the first day. Remember that not only are you adjusting to the organization and your new co-workers but also that they must adjust to you.

Read all you can about the company or organization you are entering. Many companies have procedures manuals or perhaps notebooks indicating their policies toward and expectations of employees. There also may be extensive files of memos, circulars, previously completed projects, client files, and many other things. Find out what you have access to and learn what is there.

Keep people informed about your whereabouts and what you are doing. Obviously you don't need to sign out every time you go to the restroom, but it's not a bad idea to let people know when you're

---

SELF-ASSESSMENT EXERCISE 17–2

Your New Job — Part II

What tasks will you perform during the learning period of your job (i.e., the first two to six months)?

1. _____

2. _____

3. _____

4. _____

5. _____

6. _____

7. _____

8. _____

going for lunch or to the organization's library. If you're visiting another office in the building, be sure people know where you're going. If you're working on particular activities or files, make sure that the appropriate people are aware of this. And be sure to keep all relevant co-workers and supervisors informed about the status of all your jobs and projects; otherwise, your supervisors will not know what you are doing and accomplishing.

Try to make a favorable first impression on everyone you meet. This means such little things as dressing appropriately, having a firm handshake, smiling, and making eye contact. It also means remembering people's names and their titles. This can be a big assignment, given the number of people you will meet the first few weeks on the job. Perhaps you can obtain a roster of the organization's employees and titles or an organizational chart to assist you. Take notes and take care to remember colleagues and co-workers. Remember too that the people you meet will make a first impression on you as well. First impressions are sometimes lasting, but keep an open mind and let your co-workers make their reputation by long-term actions rather than first impressions.

Your supervisor should take you around to meet the various co-workers in the organization. If not, ask to be introduced. The best entree into an organization is through introductions by others.

Finally, a certain amount of nervousness or apprehension on your first job is normal. It is probably most helpful to remember that you wouldn't have been hired if you hadn't been qualified. Why let unnecessary fear or apprehension interfere with your new job? In a short time, a few months in most cases, you will become a contributing member of the organization and feel that you belong.

Changes of Jobs and Careers

Changes and redirection are inevitable. You may advance in the organization, become more skilled, be given more responsibilities, or perhaps even change your career interests. Or you may change your values, goals, interests, and life-style. Such changes may lead you to a totally new career.

In the past, the prevailing assumption was that people should choose a single career and remain satisfied with it for life. In the occupational world of today, this attitude no longer prevails. As we pointed out in Chapter 10, many new careers and professions are emerging, and opportunities for entrepreneurship have never been better. Furthermore, it is now more acceptable to change careers.

There are also "comeback" professions, professions that once were thought to be dying but that are regaining importance (teaching is an excellent current example). People are discovering new skills and using them in new occupations. Being professionally flexible is thus becoming a desirable attribute for 1990s professionals.

Job shifts within the same profession or general career path are a part of career change. Most organizations and occupations have patterns of career development, whether they be upward in the hierarchical structure or lateral moves within different occupational areas. Such moves are job transitions in that they require adjustment to a new set of work routines, colleagues, occupational environments, and professional expectations. This is part of professional growth — learning to accept new responsibilities and proving that one's skills and experiences can be applied elsewhere. Updating or learning new skills will be necessary as well.

Example Career Path — Retail Merchandising

Paths vary from profession to profession, but the following is a typical series of jobs going up the organization.

Vice President of Merchandising
(and other senior management positions)
↑
General Merchandise Manager
↑
Divisional Merchandise Manager
↑
Buyer (specializing in a product)
↑
Department Manager
↑
Assistant or Associate Buyer
↑
Management Trainee
↑
Student Completing Degree

Job and career changes are also caused by terminations, layoffs, budgetary constraints, and firings. Nearly all of us will face the possibility of being terminated or fired. These events, whether inevitable or not, should not be taken as personal failures but, instead, as opportunities for renewal and growth (in fact, most terminations are not the fault of the individual but result instead from the organization's changing needs or priorities). This is the time to show courage and move forward to the next opportunity. Termination is part of occupational life and not a scarlet letter to be worn permanently.

How do you decide when it's time to change jobs or careers? Our first advice is to think before you switch and to ask yourself questions such as the following:

- Am I really unhappy with this career or just the job?
- What exactly about my current career do I dislike? The working conditions, colleagues, job responsibilities, working environment? Can I improve any of these and thereby increase my satisfaction with this career?
- Does this job conflict with my values and goals?
- What marketable skills do I have? How could I use them in a new job or career? What skills do I need to update?
- What new skills would I have to learn in order to obtain a new job or career?
- How would a change in jobs or careers change my life-style? Family relationships? Outlook on life in general? What would I have to give up?
- If I'm considering changing to a new career, am I really prepared to learn a new career or take an entry-level position elsewhere? Am I willing to give up my status, experience, and seniority for a new career? And what about those around me, my family and my friends?
- What are the psychological strains on my family and myself that would be involved with any changes? Could I and my family make the change successfully?
- If I have to relocate, can I handle problems such as financing the move, losing friends, and my spouse's losing his or her job?
- Will turning down an opportunity for career advancement or career change mean the loss of a future opportunity or a stalling of my career?

Career advancements and changes can be positive and exciting. They are a chance to advance in salary, status, and position. More important, they offer a fresh start in a new setting. They may add excitement to life when a career may be stalled or temporarily diverted. In a new work environment, changes also may relieve frustration and renew interest.

Once you have decided to move, there are many approaches you can take. First, many corporations and organizations have relocation specialists, people who smooth transition and movement from one job and location in the country to another. There are also outplacement specialists who assist employees who are facing termination. For those in executive occupations there are professional employment specialists, sometimes called "headhunters," who specialize in finding matches between professional executives and organizations needing new employees. To find such executive placement firms, check sources such as the *Directory of Executive Recruiters* or your telephone directory under placement services and executive search firms. Other proven techniques for career changes are looking for new opportunities through your network of professional colleagues, using the professional associations in which you are active, going to professional or local civic club meetings, and other techniques discussed in earlier chapters. Building a new professional résumé and portfolio is useful at this stage. A new technique, and one suitable for the seasoned professional, is to make a videotape presentation of one's portfolio in addition to the standard résumé and portfolio. These and many other techniques are useful for both job changes or major transitions. Much is being done to help those changing jobs or careers, and such moves are now regarded as beneficial and desirable.

Special Problems for Professional Women _____

A friend once said, "Life is more complicated for the professional woman, but it's more fun and exciting too!" Women now have more occupational options and roles open to them than ever before. The choices range from traditional home, family, and social roles to a wide variety of professional roles in the occupational world. Most women now expect to have successful lives not only as wives and mothers but also as professionals leading major corporations, governmental bodies, and human services organizations. Never have there been so many expectations and pressures on women as there are today.

Because we started by stating that being a professional woman is a challenge, we should also add that the professional woman has an advantage. First, people are becoming more aware of women's importance to the working world. Second, there are laws forbidding discrimination against women and minorities in the workplace. And third, perhaps the most controversial point, is that women's femininity is a positive characteristic for professional growth and development. On balance, then, women have both advantages and challenges in the working world.

Despite the laws, women still face discrimination, according to many feminists and experts in employment trends. Another problem is the lack of role models. At this time there is only a small minority of executive women in the highest echelons of business, government, and human services. Because women's representation in these managerial levels is lower, there is an inherent challenge in climbing the ladder. Sexual politics, office politics, and organizational gamesmanship are also obstacles. Furthermore, women mentors are scarce and rarely available. Fortunately, many of these problems do not apply to the professions that this book is emphasizing, professions serving consumers and families; in fact, women are well represented in them. Nevertheless, there is still a gap between women and professional development in many organizations, and it must be closed.

Another challenge for professional women is to be accepted as leaders and managers in organizations. Because few women have reached the higher levels of management, they are in unexplored territory. The lack of role models and accepted standards of executive female behavior are also problems. How do people expect women as leaders and managers to behave? Sometimes the executive woman placed in such a position simply does not know. Are they part of the old boy network, or should they form an old girl network? Should their relations with males and females differ, or should they be handled equally? In some instances men don't want to work with women or be led by women because they feel women lack political skills or clout. It is equally true that some women have difficulty leading other women, perhaps because many women are used to being led by men. They may also feel that women don't fit into what is still viewed as a man's game. Finally, some women lack the confidence and assertiveness to take charge of such situations. Professional women must meet these challenges, which are defined by their sex, not their capabilities.

One particularly thorny issue is women's salaries. That there are male-female differences in executive salaries for similar work is recognized, and many organizations are making significant progress toward removing these inequities. Yet differences do persist. The problem is that there is a long tradition of difference in salaries and that it will take time to overcome it. To remedy such inequities, the professional woman must gather all relevant facts and present her case for salary equity when it is in fact required.

Marriage and family relations are another challenge. Indeed, some people feel that marriage and having a family are not compatible with having a professional career, but this should not be the case. A dual-career family certainly faces more obstacles, particularly in apportioning time between family and work, but it still can be done — successfully. Some of the secrets to success are managing time well, sharing responsibilities with spouse, ensuring that children receive quality time, and using part-time help such as housekeepers if necessary. Avoiding such problems as becoming a workaholic and keeping romance and mutual respect at center stage are equally important to success. It requires such commitments for the dual-career family to achieve happiness and success, but many have and many will. In fact, recent research has shown that dual-career marriages, especially those in which work is shared, are the happiest and maybe the most successful.

What are the keys to overcoming obstacles and achieving success as a woman professional? There is much advice on this subject, ranging from courses or seminars on the entrepreneurial-professional woman and books with titles like *Management Careers for Women,* to professional women's magazines like *Working Woman* and *Executive Female.* All these are worth a look, if for no other reason than that they contain advice from others who have successfully faced similar problems. And probably most important, they also show that men and women face the same challenges and problems in reaching professional success.

The following are some tips that seem to be especially applicable to professional women:

- Have well-defined goals to achieve success, for both the short term and long term. And let people know you have such goals.
- Overcome sexual stereotypes. Especially important is to dispel the belief that you are temporary. It is still a widely held misconception that women are not in a job for the long term but that they will leave as soon as marriage and family life become more central to their lives.
- Don't avoid work situations, conferences, or meetings just because they seem to be mostly male. Instead, establish that you expect to be a part of all important business happenings.
- Develop a coping style. Learn to recognize special problems and take whatever steps are needed to control or eliminate them.
- Avoid being put in the position of being a token. Stay in the track leading to promotions and avoid watered-down jobs.
- Let the appropriate supervisors and organizational leaders know that you are mobile. If you can, show that marriage, family interests, and child care won't restrict your job performance, mobility, travel, or working late when necessary.

- Recognize that sex bias, even harassment, can exist. Do not give any cooperative signs, and don't let this interfere with your job performance.
- Establish a record for honest and open communication, and show that you work equally well with male and female colleagues.
- Find support in your personal life. Without support from family or friends, advancement, happiness, and success are virtually impossible.
- Find supportive co-workers and mentors, either male or female.
- Avoid getting involved socially and sexually with colleagues. Especially avoid romantic entanglements with co-workers and supervisors.
- Use your femininity. This means using the traits that have been associated with being a woman, such as empathy, concern for others, and positive human relations.
- Being feminine isn't the only personality trait for success. You should strive for a balance between those qualities traditionally associated with being male or female. Many people view this as the best combination for success.
- Develop assertiveness and competitiveness, and avoid submissiveness and a fear of challenge.
- Make special efforts to develop leadership skills. Demonstrate these skills, for they are perceived to be women's greatest limitation.

In conclusion, it is useful to remember that the ultimate determinant of success is performance, regardless of your sex. Success goes to those who are productive and efficient and who use the resources available to them in the most effective manner. This is true both for men and women: The advantage goes to those who achieve the organization's and their own goals.

Integrating Career with Life

In the rushed and pressured world of achieving success, it is easy to forget that life should be enjoyed. An enjoyable and successful life has many parts, including not only occupation but family and friends and fun as well. Some people take on a single central life interest such as occupational success and pursue it aggressively. This is not inherently wrong; in fact it may be right for some individuals. But for the majority, happiness is found by integrating work, leisure, and family life into a well-rounded whole. Strive for a balance of activities and interests in addition to your profession, and you'll then find the greatest success.

Questions and Exercises

1. Talk to a variety of people, such as parents or other friends, about how they dealt with the first few days of a new job.
2. Talk to people about how they have balanced their work and leisure time.
3. What problems do you anticipate in balancing your professional life with home and family life? Discuss this with your spouse or "significant other."
4. Interview a person who has recently changed jobs or careers. Ask questions on such topics as reasons for the change, difficulties experienced, anticipated benefits, and risks.
5. What are the special problems professional women face in our society? How are these problems similar to and different from the problems professional men face?
6. How will you keep updating your knowledge and skills as your career progresses?

Bibliography

Andrew, C., C. Coderre, and A. Denis. "Stop or Go: Reflections of Women Managers on Factors Influencing Their Career Development," *Journal of Business Ethics* 9 (April-May 1990), 361–367.

Azibo, Moni, and Therese Crylen Unumb. *The Mature Woman's Back-to-Work Book.* Chicago: Contemporary Books, 1980.

Bennett, Robert L. *Earning and Learning: A Guide to Individual Career Development.* San Mateo, CA: Action Link, 1980.

Bingham, Mindy, and Sandy Stryker. *More Choices: A Strategic Planning Guide for Mixing Career and Family.* St. Petersburg, FL: Ingram Publishing, 1987.

Birch, David L. "The Coming Demise of the Single-Career Career," *Journal of Career Planning and Employment* 50 (Winter 1990), 38–40.

Bird, Caroline. *The Two-Paycheck Marriage.* New York: Rawson, Wade, 1982.

Bird, Gerald A., Savannah Day, and Marilyn Cavell. "Housing and Household Characteristics of Single- and Dual-Earner Families," *Home Economics Research Journal* 19 (September 1990), 29–37.

Blotnick, Srully. *The Corporate Steeplechase: Predictable Crises in a Business Career.* New York: Facts on File, 1984.

Bolles, Richard N. *The Three Boxes of Life, and How to Get Out of Them.* Berkeley, CA: Ten Speed Press, 1981.

Brooks, Linda. "Encouraging Women's Motivation for Nontraditional Career and Lifestyle Options: A Model for Assessment and Intervention," *Journal of Career Development* 14 (Summer 1988), 223–239.

Burack, Elmer H., Maryann Albrecht, and Helene Seitler. *Growing: A Women's Guide to Career Satisfaction.* Belmont, CA: Lifetime Learning Publications, 1980.

Burke, R.J., and C.A. McKeen. "Mentoring in Organizations: Implications for Women," *Journal of Business Ethics* 9 (April-May 1990), 317–332.

Good, Linda K., James W. Gentry, and Grovalynn F. Sisler, "Work-Family Conflict and Retail Managers' Job Attitudes," *Home Economics Research Journal* 18 (June 1990), 323–335.

Hall, Francine S., and Douglas T. Hall. *The Two-Career Couple.* Reading, MA: Addison-Wesley, 1979.

Harren, Vincent A., M. Harry Daniels, and Jacqueline N. Buck. *Facilitating Students' Career Development.* San Francisco: Jossey-Bass, 1981.

Hill, Raymond E., Erwin L. Miller, and Malcom A. Lowther, eds. *Adult Career Transitions: Current Research Perspectives.* Ann Arbor: University of Michigan Graduate School of Business Administration, 1981. (See the chapters "The Individual, The Organization, and The Career"; "Career Transitions: Varieties and Commonalities"; and "Job Changes and the Middle Seasons of a Man's Life.")

Hoeflin, Ruth, Karen Pence, Mary G. Miller, and Joe Weber. *Careers for Professionals: New Perspectives in Home Economics.* Dubuque, IA: Kendall/Hunt, 1987.

Kanchier, Carole, and Wally R. Unruh. "The Career Cycle Meets the Life Cycle," *Career Development Quarterly* 37 (December 1988), 127–137.

Kelly, Marcia M. "The Work-At-Home Revolution," *The Futurist* 22 (November-December 1988), 28–32.

Ladewig, Becky Heath. "The Occupational Commitment of Men and Women: Personal and Family Variables," *Home Economics Research Journal* 18 (June 1990), 336–344.

Levinson, Daniel J. *The Seasons of a Man's Life.* New York: Ballantine, 1986.

Light, Harriett K. "Maintaining Momentum," *Illinois Teacher* 33 (January/February 1990), 96–99.

Loughead, Teri Anne. "The Use of Leisure in Career Development," *Journal of Career Development* 15 (Spring 1989), 154–163.

Mouat, Lucia. *Back to Business: A Woman's Guide to Reentering the Job Market.* New York: Sovereign Books, 1979.

Patterson, Barbara, Nancy Meadows, and Carol Dreger. *The Successful Woman,* Englewood Cliffs, NJ: Prentice-Hall, 1982.

Pinkstaff, Marlene Arthur, and Anna Bell Wilkinson. *Woman at Work: Overcoming the Obstacles.* Reading, MA: Addison-Wesley, 1979.

Reynolds, Caroline. *Dimensions in Professional Development,* 3rd ed. Cincinnati: South-Western, 1987.

Richardson, Douglas B. "How to Chart a Change in Careers," *National Business Employment Weekly* (December 31, 1989), 21–22.

Schein, Edgar H. "The Individual, The Organization, and The Career," in *Adult Career Transitions: Current Research Perspectives,* edited by Hill, Raymond E., Edwin L. Miller and Malcom A. Lowther. Ann Arbor: University of Michigan Graduate School of Business Administration, 1981.

Schnittger, Maureen H., and Gloria W. Bird. "Coping Among Dual-Career Men and Women Across the Family Life Cycle," *Family Relations* 39 (April 1990), 199–204.

Sheehy, Gail. *Passages: Predictable Crises of Adult Life.* New York: Dutton, 1976.

Shields, Laurie. *Displaced Homemakers.* New York: McGraw-Hill, 1981.

Steffy, Brian D., and Jack W. Jones. "The Impact of Family and Career Planning Variables on the Organizational, Career, and Community Commitment of Professional Women," *Journal of Vocational Behavior* 32 (1988), 196–212.

Westoff, Leslie Aldridge. "How to Capitalize on Hidden Talents," *Money* 11 (November 1982), 151–155.

Zey, Michael. *The Mentor Connection.* Homewood, IL: Dow Jones–Irwin, 1984.

CHAPTER 18

Managing a Successful Career

Achieving a successful career is a goal that most of us share. It means developing many personal characteristics and meeting many challenges. This chapter examines some of the principles for successfully managing your career.

Twenty-Seven Principles for a Successful Career _____

Successful people have many characteristics and strategies. Here are some that will enhance your career:

Understand the Culture of the Organization. This might also be called "understanding the rules of the game," or "how the organization conducts its activities." Every organization has its own rules, policies, procedures, protocols, and values. Some organizations have a very strict set of rules, and to violate them is to violate the fundamental principles according to which the organization operates. Although some of the rules may be written, most will not be. These rules are learned by observing, asking other people for advice, listening, perceiving, and synthesizing. Even if the rules seem foolish, don't violate them.

Learn the Power Structure. Most organizations have some kind of formal, written organization chart showing each position, titles, the chain of command (lines of authority), and so on. In addition to this formal structure, most organizations also have an informal structure. Understand these power structures, and learn how to operate within them. Learn who is really in charge and work with them. And do not, under any circumstances, challenge those in power.

A corollary to understanding the power structure is gaining some power yourself, that is, through leading and making decisions. To some people, seeking power is inherently distasteful because they may regard people with power as being manipulative. But without any power, it is difficult to perform and to achieve the organization's goals. Develop a style with which you are comfortable in leading and exercising your power.

Show Loyalty to the Organization. Demonstrate through your words and actions that you believe in the organization's goals, products, or services. Be an advocate of the organization in public. You can succeed in an organization only if you believe in it and express your loyalty openly.

For Success You Need

- Motivation
- Ambition
- Willingness to work
- Knowledge of job
- Responsibility
- Communications skills
- Enthusiasm
- Positive personality
- Appropriate appearance
- A good fit between you and your career

Know All the People Around You. You should know your co-workers, particularly those with whom you work most closely, on teams, on projects, or in other functions. And obviously you should know your supervisors as well as possible. In addition, know the secretaries, clerks, mailroom personnel, security guards, and the like. Attempt to be personal and personable with each. Not only is this an appropriate courtesy, but it creates a more pleasant and congenial environment and helps you perform more effectively.

To get to know the right people, invite them for lunch, coffee breaks, or whatever seems appropriate. Get to know people not only in the office but also away from the office where you can be more relaxed and informal. Perhaps more friendship, collegiality, and mutual respect develops over food and drink than any other human interactions.

Acquire the Special Skills Needed for Your Specific Job. No matter how good your education and training are, you may still need new managerial and technical skills. As you become more deeply involved in your job, you will need additional skills. It may be communicating orally or in writing, applying computer skills, or using basic technical skills needed to operate technological equipment such as a computer terminal. Whatever the case, acquire these skills on your own or by taking a college course.

Choose Mentors Carefully. Mentors are individuals who educate and guide you in the rules, regulations, and protocols of your job. They may be formal educators, such as your professors in college, or they may be co-workers you respect. Choosing mentors can be very important early in your career, for a good mentor will help you learn what is important, where to place your priorities, and how to achieve results. Mentors can also be important later in life when your career matures or as promotions become available. If at all possible, choose one or more mentors to be part of your personal support system.

Set Achievable Goals. Decide exactly what needs to be accomplished. Then, form a plan of action, step by step, to achieve these goals. Monitor your progress and reevaluate and revise your goals when necessary. Also establish timetables and deadlines for their achievement.

Decide What Needs to be Done. You will have many goals, and it's important to decide which are the most important. Then stick with them until you have achieved them. Finally, regularly evaluate and update your priorities.

Go That Extra Step in All Your Work. For each project, assignment, or responsibility, do more than meet the minimum requirements: Put in the extra effort to reach a truly outstanding result (often this takes only a little extra effort). Work longer hours if that achieves results. Look for extra responsibilities. Help a friend or colleague meet a deadline. Whatever the situation, put in that extra effort that changes good results to excellent.

Keep People Informed of Your Activities. It is especially important to keep your supervisor informed of what projects or activities you are currently working on and their scheduled completion dates. Also keep people informed of where you are and what you have accomplished. One of the biggest mistakes people make is to be identified as overly independent or as "the lone wolf" in doing projects. Don't be secretive; let the right people know what you are doing.

Make Your Supervisor's Job Easy. Take on responsibilities and extra tasks. Deliver your projects and assignments on time — early when possible. Do the extra little things, assisting your supervisor. Make your supervisors look good.

Be in the Right Place at the Right Time. Being in the right place means being able to select a job and a supervisor who will allow you to grow and develop. Taking concrete actions to be in the right place may also help: We know of one person who contacted an important supervisor simply by hanging around the elevator, "accidentally" getting on when he appeared and developing the accidental contact into an important conversation.

Work Effectively with Colleagues and Co-Workers. Build networks with your colleagues. Be a team player. Find ways to blend in with the group and help others. Cooperate and show common courtesies, and you should receive the same from many if not all of your professional associates. Part of all this is learning to play the game, learning how the organization actually operates, and fitting in with it. Another part of this is learning whom you can trust, who will carry out their responsibilities, and who are the most valuable players.

Be Independent. Although it is necessary to be a team player, it is also necessary to achieve some independence and self-reliance. Be ready to look after your own needs and interests. Realize that if you don't act, often no one else will.

Learn to Cope with Work-Place Conflicts. Conflicts between people are inevitable in any organization. Try to resolve them by negotiating with the individuals involved and compromising on a solution. If open discussion and resolution become impossible or if office politics becomes destructive, you must learn to live with the problem or leave the organization.

Be a Good Learner. Take every chance you have to learn. Have a positive attitude toward learning new approaches and better solutions to problems.

Be a Good Listener. Listen to everyone, especially to supervisors and upper management. This is how you learn what their goals are and what they want to accomplish. It is also wise to listen to the ideas of those with more experience or those who are slightly ahead of you in a similar career path.

Understand the Competitive System.   There is competition in all situations and systems: between organizations, between companies and business, and between individuals within an organization. Learn the dynamics of competition and cooperation that determine success. Many books have been written on competition in such areas as business, sports, and politics. Read those most relevant to you, for instance, *Henderson on Corporation Strategy* (by Bruce Henderson of the famous Boston Consulting Group), Tom Peters's, *Thriving on Chaos*, or Machiavelli's classic *The Prince* (a popular book in courses on the management of power).

Adapt to Change. Change is inevitable; learn to accept it. Being flexible and adaptable is the key to successful career development and transition.

Assume a Positive Attitude. Your attitude is perhaps one of the biggest determinants of your success or failure. Be idealistic and believe in yourself and your abilities. If adversity strikes, rebound with a positive attitude.

Give Praise Where Due. Give reinforcement, rewards, and praise where due. Look for what people are doing well, and praise them for it.

Always Be Well Prepared. Whether you are going to a meeting, leading a meeting, or presenting a paper at a conference, be prepared. Know with whom you will be dealing and organize for your role in advance. If you are to make a presentation or speech, put your ideas into a professional, organized, and visually attractive format. If you are leading a meeting, have a prepared, written agenda.

Present a Positive and Carefully Planned Image. It is first necessary to decide what image you want, to identify the qualities and personal characteristics you wish to project to others. Part of this is determining your appropriate visual image—professional dress, appearance, and mannerisms. Part of it also is personal characteristics such as your thoughtfulness, intellectual capability, drive, and willingness to work with others. Assess and improve your image in such areas as the quality and appropriateness of your professional dress, style of verbal presentation, relations with co-workers, relevance of what you say, body posture and gestures, and poise under pressure.

The way you keep your office and manage office communications is also a part of your image. Telephone manners and how you handle yourself in meetings are important. A sense of humor and a good disposition add to your image (bad moods, a bad temper, or inappropriate aggressiveness detract from it).

Practice Positive Self-Management. Know your strengths and limitations. Accept challenges and commitments, but avoid overcommitments. Know what you can and can't do. Learn to say no when a task or responsibility is not appropriately yours. Relax, don't overwork, eat right, exercise right, and get plenty of sleep. Doing all these will enable you to perform consistently and effectively and help you avoid stress and burnout.

Develop Consistent Work Habits. Desirable work habits can be as or more important than technical skills or great intelligence. Willingly taking on responsibilities, being on time, keeping people informed, and taking every step to accomplish your job efficiently are important. Most employers rate work habits as among the most significant factors in job success, even more so than technical or managerial skills.

Remember the Bottom Line. Remember the organization's goals and devote your efforts to satisfying those goals. In business, the bottom line is profitability. In government, it is service to the largest number of citizens. In human service organizations, it is the provision of programs for specific clienteles. Whatever your organization, there is always a bottom line by which its success is measured. Learn those measures and make sure that you make a visible contribution.

Emphasize Professionalism. Success is based on your total professionalism, the sum of your professional appearance, personal style, knowledge of your job, communication skills, willingness to lead, and willingness to take on responsibilities. Success is dealing fairly with others and working with a team toward the organization's goals. It is service to clients and customers. It is positive attitudes toward work, belief in self, commitment, and conscientiousness. In summary, a professional commitment to the principles we have discussed is the key to successful professional development.

The Problem of Stress Management _____

Work is filled with many pressures, mental strains, physical strains, and tension—in a word, *stress*. Some stress is normal, in fact desirable. However, the objective is to get enough stress but not too much. You must learn to cope with the stresses that are normal in your job and to reduce those that are unnecessary.

There are many *stressors* in the occupational environment. Examples are the deadlines you must meet, the long hours of work, daily dealings with clients, office politics, and the failures of others to carry out their responsibilities. Sometimes problems at home with children or spouse and financial matters can creep into the work setting. Professionals in consumer- and family-oriented professions have special stresses created by the interpersonal relations in their jobs. Teachers, government workers, those in the helping professions, and those in such business areas as marketing or the hospitality industry must interact daily with their clients, and this can be extremely stressful. In some cases the involvement is very close, as in the case of therapists working with clients who are facing serious personal or family problems. This involvement leads to a certain amount of empathy and stressful relationships. Every occupation has its own set of stressors that increase the difficulty of successful job management and the accomplishment of responsibilities.

How can you tell when you are stressed? Feelings of stress are sometimes difficult to identify because the causes differ so much from one person to another. Some people may feel little stress, but most do. Symptoms of stress are nervousness, tense muscles, headaches, stomach pains, insomnia, lethargy, short attention span, poor concentration, and boredom. Sometimes the stressed individual worries that the job cannot be accomplished and then feels depressed and guilty, which may lead to procrastination and even avoidance of work. Stress thus takes a toll in two ways: It interferes with the proper functioning of one's body, and it reduces one's efficiency or productivity.

Stressors in Life Come From

The Office:
Pressures of daily work routines
Relations with co-workers
Working long or irregular hours
Mismatch between you and job
Dealing with clients
Office politics
Deadlines

Home:
Family relations
Family economic and financial matters
Conflicts in personal values
Lack of communications
Differences in preferred life-styles (activities, roles)

How do you cope with stress? There is no simple answer to this question, but the following are some of the ways to cope. First, identify the stressors in your life. Look at specific things in your occupational environment: people, responsibilities, annoyances (such as telephones, computer terminals, other inanimate objects that invade life), or other things that interfere with activity. Some of these you can learn to cope with, and others can be eliminated. Control as much of your working environment and relationships as possible.

The National Institute of Mental Health recommends the following ten steps for handling stress:

1. Work off stress by exercising, playing tennis, running, gardening, or whatever physical activity you prefer.
2. Talk out your worries; share your thoughts with someone you trust who is sympathetic and constructive.
3. Learn to accept what you cannot change. Some things are beyond your control, and you must learn to accept them.
4. Avoid self-medication, whether it be pills, alcohol, or other habit-forming drugs and stimulants.
5. Get enough sleep and rest. Most people need seven to eight hours of sleep.
6. Balance work and recreation; you cannot work all the time, and some recreation should be a normal part of your life.
7. Do something for others, and get your mind off yourself and your problems.
8. Take one thing at a time, and decide on your priorities.
9. Give in once in a while—don't try to win every fight and every battle.
10. Make yourself available; if you're bored, do something.

There are many other techniques. Going to a movie, watching television, or reading will relax you. Slow down and try not to take on so many projects and responsibilities. Try to avoid getting angry or irritated. Learn to accept people and be more patient. And don't take everything too seriously; instead, look for the humor in all things. And finally, simply learn to relax and simplify things. A positive mental attitude can do more to relax stress than anything else.

Extreme stress can lead to "burnout." Burnout occurs when a job becomes unbearable, or the inability to achieve one's goals becomes overly frustrating. Often this leads to job failure or resignation. Avoid burnout at all costs.

Those most likely to burn out are the hard-working, dedicated, idealistic people who are among the most valued employees of any organization. Some family and consumer professionals are susceptible to burnout because they are typically more job involved and service oriented than many other professionals are. The desire to help others sometimes is not fulfilled, which can lead to frustration. The enthusiasm that such professionals find early in their career is later replaced by exhaustion, anger, or depression, and perhaps even self-doubt or physical illness. This situation is obviously serious, for it is career- and even life-threatening. It is important at this point that professional treatment be sought.

Many courses are offered today in stress management techniques. Some of these courses teach skills in socialization, relaxation, meditation, exercise, diet, and nutrition. Some organizations run seminars on adjustment to stress and burnout. Supervisors and managers are also being trained to help employees manage and reduce stress. Stress in the work place is now recognized as a problem that needs to be resolved.

The Challenge of Time Management _____

Managing time effectively is probably the most difficult of all challenges. Have you ever felt there was just not enough time to do everything? Every student has at some time experienced the pressures of deadlines, term papers, several projects due at one time, or several tests to study for at a time. These are really problems of effective time management. Similar problems of effective time management occur in the professional world as well.

Everyone can improve the management of time. The following are some of the techniques that the busiest and most successful professionals use to manage their time effectively:

1. *Keep a schedule of your time.* Most professionals keep an hour-by-hour schedule of work activities, appointments, and other events. On this schedule they also write target dates for completion of each project, or parts of projects.
2. *Plan activities in advance.* Spend some time planning your overall schedule of activities, events, and meetings, and include time for work, play, personal life, and social life.
3. *Establish goals and priorities.* At the beginning of the week, and perhaps even daily, make a list of what you want to get done. Rank these from most to least important. Check off each

item as it is completed. Keep these lists in a notebook as a log of your accomplishments, and review them periodically to see when you use time efficiently and where improvement is needed.

4. *Set completion dates.* Once deadlines are set, stick to them. Try to anticipate complications or new priorities that might interfere, and deal with them.

5. *Divide and conquer.* Break large or difficult jobs into smaller, more manageable parts.

6. *Take on one thing at a time.* It is easy to develop a routine of jumping from project to project. Instead, emphasize completing one task before turning to the next.

7. *Learn to make decisions in a timely manner.* Don't delay or put off decisions; make them and learn to live with them, or you may get nothing done.

8. *Learn to say no.* Many people will ask for your time. It's easy to say yes, especially for those in people-oriented and service-oriented professions. However, you must learn to say no once in a while to protect your time. Learn to say no as a way to avoid overcommitment.

9. *Establish "do not disturb" periods.* Set periods that no one can interrupt, or get away from your desk if possible. This includes getting away from the telephone.

10. *Schedule special periods for different activities.* For example, schedule an hour when you will return telephone calls. Set a weekly time for staff meetings and another time for memo writing. Protect those time periods for the activities intended.

11. *Use your peak time for priority work.* Each of us has a time of day when we work most efficiently. Some of us are morning people, others night. Do the most challenging or the highest-priority work at those times. Above all, don't waste that time on trivia.

Keys to Effectively Managing Time

- Keep a daily calendar of your activities and appointments.
- Set priorities with deadlines.
- Save time for yourself.
- Avoid procrastinating.
- Don't take on more than you can handle.

12. *Reduce paperwork.* Handle each piece of paper only once. Don't let paper stack up on you in your IN box. Move it out, and keep your desk clear.
13. *Delegate responsibility to others.* You can't do everything yourself, and there's no need to. Give appropriate responsibility and assignments to those around you.
14. *Fight against procrastination.* Putting off, or procrastinating, is the worst disease of the time waster. Jobs may look big and complex — conditions that encourage putting off. Determination and strength of character are needed to avoid this biggest enemy of achievement.
15. *Exercise self-discipline and self-management.* This is the summary statement for all the foregoing techniques. Time management means management of self, self-discipline. Exercise the discipline necessary to put all the preceding ideas into practice.

As you learn to be a more effective time manager, include positive rewards for yourself. Each time you complete a task by using time effectively or according to the plan scheduled, give yourself a reward for it. This may mean a short coffee break, going out for an ice cream cone, or perhaps a larger reward, if appropriate, such as going to a movie or buying a book. The point is simple: Give yourself strokes for doing a good job. This reinforces your feeling of accomplishment and your sense of self-worth.

Finally, find time for what is important to you. This means time to do the priority tasks at work and time to do things for yourself, for others, and with others. Some people find it desirable to identify separate periods for professional life, home life, social life, and time alone. And always remember, time is your most precious resource — put your time to the best use.

A Postscript on Success _____

It is often said that those who succeed in life are intelligent, practical, interested in people, confident, enthusiastic, energetic, personable, and on and on. It sounds like Superman or Superwoman, those who can do everything. In fact, success in life is simply finding one's own best qualities and emphasizing them to the fullest. Success is achieved by taking a long view of one's professional and personal life, establishing reachable goals, expecting transitions and changes, doing one's best, contributing, and enjoying life.

Questions and Exercises

1. From the twenty-seven principles for a successful career, list those that are the most important to you and explain why. Also list those that are the least important to you.
2. Discuss the following items related to stress:
   a. How do you feel (or know) stress?
   b. What causes stress for you?
   c. How do you deal with stress?
   d. What other strategies could you use to deal with stress?
3. In what ways are you now an effective manager of your time? How can you use your time more efficiently?
4. Identify the time management techniques listed in this chapter that would work most effectively for you.
5. What does success in a career mean to you?

Bibliography

Bingham, Mindy, and Sandy Stryker. *More Choices: A Strategic Planning Guide for Mixing Career and Family.* St. Petersburg, FL: Ingram Publishing, 1987.

Bird, Caroline. *The Two-Paycheck Marriage.* New York: Rawson, Wade, 1982.

Brooks, Linda. "Encouraging Women's Motivation for Nontraditional Career and Lifestyle Options: A Model for Assessment and Intervention," *Journal of Career Development* 14 (Summer 1988), 223–239.

Burack, Elmer H., Maryann Albrecht, and Helene Seitler. *Growing: A Women's Guide to Career Satisfaction.* Belmont, CA: Lifetime Learning Publications, 1980.

Hall, Francine S., and Douglas T. Hall. *The Two-Career Couple.* Reading, MA: Addison-Wesley, 1979.

Harragan, Betty Lehan. *Games Mother Never Taught You: Corporate Gamesmanship for Women.* New York: Warner Books, 1987.

Klassen, Marlene. "How to Get the Most Out of Your Time," *Supervision* 45 (April 1983), 9–10.

Krannich, Ronald L. *Network Your Way to Job and Career Success: The Complete Guide to Creating New Opportunities.* Manassas, VA: Impact Publications, 1989.

Lippert, Fred G. "Dealing with Stress," *Supervision* 45 (August 1983), 16–17.

London, Manuel, and Edward M. Mone. *Career Management and Survival in the Workplace: Helping Employees Make Tough Career Decisions, Stay Motivated, and Reduce Career Stress.* San Francisco: Jossey-Bass, 1987.

McConnel, Patricia. *Women's Work-At-Home Handbook: Income and Independence.* New York: Bantam, 1986.

Nave, James L. "Banishing Burnout," *Management World* 12 (June 1983), 30–31.

Niehouse, Oliver L. "The Road to Burnout in the Public Sector," *Supervisory Management* 28 (March 1983), 22–28.

Patterson, Barbara, Nancy Meadows, and Carol Dreger. *The Successful Woman,* Englewood Cliffs, NJ: Prentice-Hall, 1982.

Pinkstaff, Marlene Arthur, and Anna Beli Wilkinson. *Woman at Work: Overcoming the Obstacles.* Reading, MA: Addison-Wesley, 1979.

Reynolds, Caroline. *Dimensions in Professional Development,* 3rd ed. Cincinnati: South-Western, 1987.

Shaevitz, Marjorie Hansen. *The Superwoman Syndrome.* New York: Warner Books, 1985.

Steil, Kathy. "Success—What Does It Take?" In *More People Power for You,* proceedings of a retail personnel seminar on attracting, training, and retraining junior executives, March 18–20, 1981.

Stenberg, Laurie A., and Jack Elliot. "External Networking: The Untapped Resource," *Illinois Teacher* 33 (May/June 1990), 185–187, 190.

Zey, Michael. *The Mentor Connection.* Homewood, IL: Dow Jones–Irwin, 1984.

CHAPTER 19

Professional Associations, Organizations, and Memberships

Participating in associations and organizations is part of professional life. There are associations for every family and consumer professional — clothing specialists, fashion designers, interior designers, consumer affairs professionals, dietitians, family counselors, and many others.

Organizations and associations are important to your career. Their central function is contributing to your continuing education. They provide information, conferences, seminars, and publications in your area of interest. Associations also offer opportunities to meet with other professionals in your field and share ideas. Some sponsor research on topics of interest to the membership. Some help formulate public policy and represent the views of their membership to government. Nearly all have conventions or annual meetings at which the members get together as a group. Most, in some way or another, advance the interests of their profession.

Hundreds of organizations serve consumer- and family-oriented professionals. These include general, or "umbrella," professional associations, specialized professional associations, trade associations, civic clubs, service organizations, and social clubs. The Appendix lists the names, addresses, missions, and selected publications of many associations of interest to family and consumer professionals.

General Professional Associations _____

General professional associations are those whose members include professionals in a wide range of related and different specializations. General associations represent the viewpoints of many different people joined in one inclusive field of interest. Among the best-known general associations for family and consumer professionals are the American Home Economics Association (AHEA) and the American Vocational Association (AVA). There are other general professional associations for some consumer and family professionals, for example, the American Management Association, the National Association of Manufacturers, the American Psychological Association, the American Sociological Association, and the American Chemical Society. Although these sound somewhat specialized, they represent the interests of many different practicing professionals (for example, the American Psychological Association includes clinical psychologists, social psychologists, consumer psychologists, experimental psychologists, and cognitive psychologists).

The American Home Economics Association is one of the oldest, largest, and best-known general professional organizations in the family and consumer professions. Its membership includes high school teachers, college teachers, extension home economists, business professionals, and human service professionals. Like most professional organizations, it also has active student chapters at many colleges and universities.

There also are specialized sections of AHEA, including the Home Economists in Business, Cooperative Extension Service, Home Economists in Human Services, and Elementary, Secondary, and Adult Education. These and other professional sections offer programs and services for their members. The objective of the AHEA is to improve the quality of family life through education, research, and public information. Located near Washington, DC, it also attempts to influence public policy and legislation for the benefit of consumers and families. Its publications include the *Journal of Home Economics*, the *Home Economics Research Journal, AHEA Action* and books, pamphlets, and audiovisual materials. It holds an annual meeting in various cities around the country. That meeting, typical of other professional organizations, includes addresses by nationally known professionals speaking on the latest topics, displays of new publications, and professional presentations of new consumer products by companies exhibiting at the convention. Other activities are sponsoring smaller conferences, conducting special committees of interest to the membership, providing statistics on the changing demographics of the profession, offering awards for excellence, and sponsoring with other professional organizations the *Journal of Consumer Research.*

The AVA is another general association important to family and consumer professionals, particularly to vocational home economics educators, merchandising professionals, interior designers, and consumer affairs professionals. The AVA's objective is to develop and promote programs of vocational education leading to jobs that meet the needs of society. Located near Washington, DC, it also is involved in legislation, program development, conferences, and public information. Its publications include a journal (*Vocational Education Journal*), a newsletter (*Update*), books, pamphlets, and audiovisual materials. Its annual conference offers professional programs in all vocational fields of interest, professional speakers, exhibits of the newest publications, and the latest techniques in manufacturing and engineering.

Other general professional associations you may wish to join are listed in the Appendix. Because no list can include all organizations (there are over 15,000 associations listed in the *Encyclopedia of Associations*), you may wish to consult other lists as well, such as the *Encyclopedia of Associations*, your telephone book, your professors, or the American Society of Association Executives (Washington, DC).

Specialized Professional Associations _____

Specialized professional associations have a narrower focus. Examples are the American Council on Consumer Interests, the American Society of Interior Designers, the National Retail Federation, and the American Dietetic Association. Associations such as these have been growing rapidly and now are prominent parts of their professions.

The specialized professional associations vary in the content of their programs and the types of members they serve. For example, most of the members of the American Council on Consumer Interests are

SELF-ASSESSMENT EXERCISE 19-1

Key Activity

List the three organizations most important to your professional career:

1. _____

_____

_____

2. _____

_____

_____

3. _____

_____

_____

college professors, high school teachers, and government employees in consumer-oriented fields. The Society of Consumer Affairs Professionals in Business, on the other hand, has largely a business membership. The National Retail Federation has membership from large and small retail stores of all types. The services offered by specialized organizations vary just as much. Some have well-known publications and continuing education programs, and others focus on conferences or special meetings. Learn which special services are offered in your field and select those most relevant to you. You can write to them for further information or ask your professors about their programs and activities.

Local Chapters of National Organizations _____

Many national organizations sponsor local chapters in major cities throughout the United States. Sometimes these are statewide as well. Part of the dues or membership fees you pay to the national organizations are shared with the local chapters and support the local programs. The importance of the local chapters cannot be overestimated. They give you an opportunity to have face-to-face, frequent interactions with working professionals in your area. Local chapters often have monthly meetings to which they invite special luncheon or dinner speakers, and they may have social hours as well. Active local chapters also sponsor special programs and short conferences for members and guests. An active local chapter of a national organization may be of even greater value to the professions than the national organization is.

Some universities also have student chapters of national organizations. Check with your professors or watch the bulletin boards for announcements. If there is no student organization or professional club, get together with some students and one of your professors and organize one. National organizations are receptive to student membership and will give you all the privileges of membership (publications, newsletters, attendance at conferences) at a nominal cost. This is part of the total educational experience and introduction into professional life.

In many cities and communities, you will also find local organizations and professional groups that are not affiliated with a national organization. Examples are merchants' clubs or craft guilds in various specializations (fashion retailing, interior design, and others). Join these clubs or associations of professionals when possible.

Civic Clubs and Service Organizations _____

All cities and communities have civic clubs or service organizations with members from many professional communities. Consumer- and family-oriented professionals should join and participate in these community groups. Examples are the Kiwanis and the Rotary clubs. Other service clubs are listed in your local phone book and in publications of the chamber of commerce or other business groups. These organizations help you relate to many other professions outside the family and consumer specialties. Participating in them is a part of being a good citizen. Additional benefits are the professional interaction, a network of contacts, and opportunities for professional growth and self-improvement.

Social Clubs and Their Roles in the Professions _____

Many, if not all, of the professional organizations we have mentioned provide social outlets. But social clubs themselves are an important part of business and professional life as well. We mean golf clubs, tennis clubs, racquetball clubs, health clubs, swimming clubs, and other recreational sports clubs. Other special-interest clubs are investment clubs, bridge clubs, bird-watchers' clubs, hiking and camping clubs, and many others.

Clubs have obvious intended purposes, such as sports or some other social pursuit, but they are meeting places for professionals as well. Some clubs even become badges of membership in professions, for example, as racquetball and fitness clubs have become emblems of business executives. In fact, the social life of many professionals revolves around their clubs. It is also remarkable how many business and professional activities take place in clubs. The advice then is obvious: Seek out those clubs that are relevant to your profession, and enjoy their social as well as their professional benefits.

Benefits of Organizational Membership _____

Whatever organizations you join, you can expect certain benefits from a well-planned and well-run organization. The following are some of them, as suggested by the American Society of Association Executives:

- Up-to-date information about current trends and new events in your profession
- Reports on legislation and policy affecting your profession
- Data or research information on various topics in your field
- Effective representation of the profession in government, legislative bodies, and the public at large
- Public information and public relations programs
- Educational programs that assist you in professional development
- Information that helps you keep in touch with fellow members, such as directories and newsletters
- Professional conventions and meetings on subjects determined by the membership
- Things you can use in your own profession — operating procedures, training programs, public relations aids, and so forth
- Special benefits such as group insurance, travel opportunities, buying services, or other money-saving services
- An opportunity to elect officers and vote on policies affecting the organization
- Advice on your career development

- Careful financial management and financial responsibility by the officers of the organization ensuring your money is well spent

Your Role as a Member _____

As a professional member of an organization, you are expected to give as well as receive. In fact, no professional organization can survive for long without active participation by its members. This means such activities as the following:

- Paying your dues
- Attending conventions or meetings
- Reading publications by the organization
- Submitting ideas for programs
- Volunteering to be a participant or organizer of a program
- Presenting a paper at a meeting
- Becoming a member of a committee in the association
- Volunteering your time
- Running for office in the organization
- Offering constructive ideas and criticism when needed
- Actively promoting the profession of which you are a part, including its benefits to society and its clients

The Appendix lists associations in various areas of family- and consumer-oriented professions. A brief statement of the association's purpose and its publications follows each. We encourage you to look through the list to get an idea of just how many professional associations there are. Then choose several and write to them for information.

Questions and Exercises _____

1. Read the list of professional associations, and find the three that are the most interesting and applicable to you. Are there local chapters of these associations in your geographic region? Call or write your three choices for further information.
2. Talk to professionals working in your career area about the professional associations they belong to and the benefits they receive from them.
3. Attend a meeting of a local professional association.
4. Attend a regional or national meeting of a professional association.
5. Join the student chapter of some professional club or organization on

your campus (if you are not aware of any in your area of interest, ask your professors for information). If none is available, organize a group of students and start your own club or interest group. Be an active participant for at least one year in order to see the many benefits of your membership.

Bibliography _____

Associations: A Dynamic Force. Washington, DC: American Society of Association Executives, 1980.

Koek, Karin E. ed. *Encyclopedia of Associations.* Detroit: Gale Research, 1990.

Parker, Frances J. *Home Economics: An Introduction to a Dynamic Profession,* 3rd ed. New York: Macmillan, 1987.

Stenberg, Laurie A., and Jack Elliot. "External Networking: The Untapped Resource", *Illinois Teacher* 33 (May/June 1990), 185–187, 190.

CHAPTER 20

Future Directions for Family- and Consumer-Oriented Professions

It is said that forecasting the future is like "trying to drive a car blindfolded and following directions given by a person who is looking out of the back window."[1] The future holds surprises that are impossible to foresee. Yet, "futuring" has become a prominent topic today, owing in part to the great popularity of such books as Naisbett's *Megatrends* and *Megatrends 2000*, Toffler's *Future Shock* and *The Third Wave*, and publications such as *The Futurist*. Nearly everyone is interested in forecasting our future.

[1] Philip Kotler, *Marketing Management* (Englewood Cliffs, NJ: Prentice-Hall, 1972), p. 192.

And so it is in the spirit of futuring that we address our final topic. The following is a compilation of current and future trends that some experts feel will affect the professions serving consumers and families. We have grouped the trends into five categories: trends in family life, trends in work life, trends in education, economic trends, and consumer trends.

Trends in Family Life _____

1. There will be continued growth of new family forms, such as single-parent families, blended families, and cohabitating families. Family diversity is becoming the norm.
2. As women's horizons continue shifting from home to office, the number of dual-career families will continue to grow. This will have many side effects, such as increased affluence of the family unit and postponement of child rearing.
3. The high number of illegitimate births will continue. This is expected to be particularly persistent in such populations as teenagers and minorities.
4. There will be a continuing concern for day-care programs, as day care becomes more important to the rearing of children. Adult day care will also become available as a family service.
5. Family life for men and women will continue to become more equitable.
6. New technology such as computers in the home will create new life-styles and new "master entertainers" or centers of family life.
7. Tax policies influencing marriage, divorce, and family life — such as the current "marriage penalty," which puts married couples in a higher tax bracket than unmarried couples who live together — will come under greater scrutiny.
8. Life-styles of self-centeredness and hedonism will give way to a greater social concern for group interests and community. However, the hedonistic life-style will continue as an important goal for many, especially aging baby boomers.
9. There will be continuous change in the values held by the family pertaining to child rearing, mobility, roles of women, roles of men, status symbols, and consumption.
10. The trend toward increased leisure will continue through this century. The home will become a valued center for leisure

11. Concern for the quality of family life will continue, together with controversy over what constitutes that quality.

12. The communications revolution and the growing information society will affect all areas of family life.

13. The self-help movement will affect family life in such areas as consumer needs, medical care, health, and nutrition.

14. There will be an increased need for services for special groups, including the aged, those with health special needs, and the disadvantaged.

15. Delinquency among youth will continue as a major social problem.

16. Problems of family life such as divorce and child and spouse abuse will continue to be prevalent.

17. Many social programs aiding families will be discussed, but fewer will obtain the funding desired by their proponents. Major social programs such as Social Security and welfare will come under increasing scrutiny.

18. Society will be more open-minded, especially in regard to life-styles, morality, cultural diversity, and humanistic values affecting others.

19. Mobility from one part of the country to another will continue.

20. Single family housing will continue as the "American Dream." However, many families will choose multifamily housing, including townhouses and condominiums, rather than the traditional single-family house. This is likely to be most noticeable among younger families buying their first homes.

21. As people live longer and retire earlier, they will acquire new life-styles and new definitions of the good life.

22. Young adults will have conflicts between remaining single and marrying and/or having a family.

23. There will be greater conflict or controversy between women who prefer a career and those who prefer marriage and a family.

24. Overall there will be a greater emphasis on building cooperation, compassion, and positive human relations, both within family units and between family units.

25. The emphasis on conservative, middle-class values will continue to be the central force in the life-styles of the American family.

26. There will continue to be a growing fragmentation in values. Many new and sometimes individualistic values will exist, reflecting a culturally diverse society that explicitly allows many different family types, life-styles, and value orientations.

27. The working world will be more "family friendly"—offering day-care programs, maternity/paternity leaves, family-cen-

---

SELF-ASSESSMENT EXERCISE 20–1

Compare Today's and Tomorrow's Society— What Are the Implications for Changing Careers?

Factors to Compare	Describe Our Society Today	Describe Our Society in 20 Years
Family Composition	_____	_____
Clothing Worn	_____	_____
Foods Eaten	_____	_____
Typical Consumer Products	_____	_____
Life-Styles	_____	_____
Recreation	_____	_____
Travel	_____	_____
Work Life	_____	_____
Rapidity of Social and Technical Change	_____	_____
Education	_____	_____
Cost of Living	_____	_____
Roles of Men and Women	_____	_____
Status of Economy	_____	_____

---

tered activities, flextime work schedules, flexible benefits that can be tailored to unique family needs, and the like.

28. Health care will be a big family issue, particularly care for children and seniors (some of whom may move in with their children). How to finance health care, who is to provide it (doctors, nutritionists, therapists, paraprofessionals), and what levels of service to provide will all be central issues.

29. The American family will continue to be the basic structural unit of society, although the institution of the family will be reshaped by the trends described.

Trends in Work Life

1. The American economy will continue to be successful and generate many jobs for individuals. There may be a squeeze on midlevel professional opportunities because of competition among baby boomers. Centralization of businesses and increased efficiencies may also make some jobs more competitive, such as those in retailing or large service organizations.
2. Trends toward information-oriented and service-oriented careers will continue to grow.
3. There will be many jobs for family- and consumer-oriented professionals, as people realize the importance of these professions to a successful postindustrial society.
4. There will be continued trends toward automation, computers, and technological innovations in the work place. In some occupations the trend toward the "electronic cottage," or working at home, will increase.
5. New trends in the job market such as job sharing will receive increased attention by employers.
6. As the marketing of consumer products becomes more international, there will be more competition from imports in domestic markets. This will affect some careers, especially in those industries in which imports are the greatest competitor, but it will also create new careers in the international marketing of consumer products.
7. There will be greater equality in work for men and women. More men will enter traditionally female occupations, and more women will enter traditionally male occupations.
8. Unemployment problems among minorities will be a continuing problem. Government and business will build new partnerships to solve these problems, and education also will perform an important role in training minorities.
9. People with obsolete or outdated work skills will need to be retrained. Unemployment created by obsolete skills will become a persistent problem.
10. Employers will become more attuned to the home life and personal needs of employees. There will be more day-care centers in offices, more concern for maternity leaves for men as well as women, more benefits programs, and a general trend toward considering employees as part of a business's family.
11. Flexibility in careers, and particularly changes of careers, will become more prevalent. No longer will professionals stay on a single career path for their entire lives.

12. Work life will be restructured in some occupations, including more leisure time, more flexible work schedules, four-day workweeks, and ten- to twelve-hour workdays.
13. Continued professional development will be mandatory to meet the changing technology and structure of the job market. Lifelong learning will become the only means for maintaining capability as a professional.
14. Women will be taking an increasing number of senior, leadership positions in business, education, government, and human services.
15. There will be major growth in cultural diversity in the work place.
16. Early retirement will become possible and acceptable to more people. More people are now retiring by age sixty-two, but even earlier ages for retirement are the goals of some.

Trends in Education _____

1. Education will continue to be one of the most highly valued aspects of our culture. However, there will be continued concern for the quality of education at all levels.
2. The "computer invasion" will continue in education. Interest in computer literacy, computer-assisted instruction, computerized education at home, and Videotex systems will continue to be widely discussed and promoted.
3. Political action by teaching professionals will become more necessary as government at all levels takes an increasing role in educational systems.
4. The conflict between those advocating liberal education and those advocating vocational education will grow.
5. There will be a continuing and growing interest of students in education related to careers, including education aimed at entry into specialized family- and consumer-oriented careers. Educators will have to take into account this demand for professional, career-oriented education.
6. Educators will have to show the career relevance of their subject matter. It will be necessary for teachers of home economics, or related subjects, to show that consumer, family, and homemaking skills are directly applicable to the job market.
7. Consumer-oriented education in traditional subjects such as credit, insurance, consumer fraud, budgeting, and comparison

shopping will continue. However, it will be necessary to emphasize how the regulation of such major consumer industries as airlines, communications, banking, and consumer credit will require new consumer skills and coping strategies.

8. There will be continuing growth in the technological complexity of products and markets.

9. Family life education and home economics education will have to emphasize such "life management" subjects as stress management, time management, family nutrition, family self-help, personal health, well-being, and family resource management, including money management.

10. It will be desirable to expand home economics related occupations because there will be an increased need for service workers and managers.

11. Networking among teachers will become more active as the pressures on teachers increase.

12. Sex stereotyping in education will decrease. More males will be entering educational programs in home economics and family and consumer subjects; similarly, more women will find it feasible and acceptable to leave traditionally female educational programs.

13. The educational system will engage in more educational partnerships with local businesses, government, and human service organizations. Students will take more work experiences and internships as part of their education.

14. There will be increased attention to educating the handicapped, disadvantaged, and those with special needs.

15. Programs of adult education, particularly those leading to new careers, will receive greater attention. The emphasis on lifelong learning and retraining for changing careers will be prevalent.

16. Employers in business, government, and other settings will increasingly offer their own educational programs to their employees. In some cases the school systems and universities will come to the employer's facilities to offer courses, either through telecommunications or by actual instructors.

17. New educational technologies will continue to be developed, and a variety of teaching strategies will continue to be important in the classroom. However, the foundation of education will continue to be teachers, textbooks, and audiovisual aids.

18. There will be a growing need to adjust education to the evolving service and global economy, which will require new courses in many areas (e.g., consumer services, other languages, and other cultures).

Economic Trends _____

1. Concern with government spending and taxation will be the major economic issue for the remainder of this century.
2. Cycles of inflation and rising interest rates will continue.
3. The world will continue to be a single, complex, and interrelated economic system. All countries will be economically interdependent. Some countries will have economic problems that affect the entire world, such as the financial problems of the underdeveloped countries, which have affected the international financial system and credit of the weaker countries.
4. The United States economy will continue to generate new jobs and employment opportunities. However, there will be periodic unemployment problems created by changing business cycles and obsolete industries.
5. Families will become increasingly concerned with protecting the economic resources that they already have, including the better life-styles they have become able to afford. However, the belief that continuing growth of affluence is not the greatest goal is growing.
6. The possibility of slow growth and low inflation exists. But many people see our future as maintaining a high economic growth, high inflation, or even "stagflation," and so there is controversy.
7. There will be a continued change in appropriate financial investments for families—tax shelters, stocks, bonds, options, savings alternatives, real estate, collectibles, and the like. Management of investments and family financial resources will become more complex because of so many options.
8. Economic matters will be increasingly important determinants of such facets of family life as mate selection, marriage, family violence, and divorce.
9. Incomes will continue to increase. There will be greater general affluence and fewer individuals in the "very poor" categories. However, at present there appears to be a conflicting trend, with more families falling below the poverty line in income.
10. Inflation and unemployment will continue to be important economic and political issues.
11. Some people are predicting an economic decline and a reduced standard of living for Americans, pointing to trends in inflation, unemployment, deficit spending by government, and loss of our competitive position in world consumer markets as bases for those predictions.

12. Minorities and ethnic groups will attain greater economic equality with the rest of society.
13. As the world economy increases, there will be increased competition generated from increased world trade, and the United States's competitive position in some industries will be severely challenged (e.g., textiles, clothing, consumer electronics, automobiles). Some people see this as signifying a decline in our economy, and others see it as a natural transition toward a postindustrial, information society focused more on services.
14. The world economy will develop around three especially powerful and productive economic areas: the Pacific Rim, North America, and Europe.
15. There will be more saving and investing, particularly by the aging baby boomers as they secure higher incomes. The boom in consumer spending and borrowing of the 1980s will moderate in the 1990s.
16. New markets will emerge, particularly in Eastern Europe and the Soviet Union, as new policies of openness take effect.
17. As prices rise or as problems develop, there will be calls for increased federal, state, and local governmental regulation of markets and the economy in general.
18. Overall, the economic system of the United States will continue to be among the most prosperous in the world. This assumes that the work ethic and the desire to be productive and progressive continue to be valued in our society.

Consumer Trends

1. There will be continuing problems in the delivery of health care, caused largely by the rising costs of medical care. Some people will not receive the necessary health care as a result; many others will resort to self-help, self-medication, better nutrition, and exercise.
2. The availability of affordable energy resources will continue to be a question, although it appears that adequate resources will be available at increasing but relatively reasonable prices for the remainder of this century.
3. Consumers will continue to be more concerned with their diet, nutrition, and the role of exercise and relaxation in health.
4. New tax policies that discourage consumption will be considered and may be enacted (e.g., increasing sales taxes, taxes on "luxuries," value-added taxes).

5. The growing world economy will mean that there will be more imported consumer products, and consumers will have to recognize the various qualities of imported products.

6. There will be continued changes in consumers' eating patterns, with the growth of fast-food restaurants, ethnic food restaurants, gourmet specialty restaurants, takeout foods, supermarkets offering frozen or easy-fix meals, and so on.

7. In fashions there will be a continued growth of variety rather than uniformity of fashions. There will be many different fashion trends for different parts of people's life-styles and different subgroups (market segments) of the population.

8. Cluster housing, condominiums, and townhouses will continue to be major growth areas of residential housing.

9. Markets and consumer products will continue to become more complex, thus requiring consumers to make better-informed decisions based on information and education.

10. There will be controversy over the value of "high tech" versus simple products. Consumer movements toward simplification of products, voluntary simplicity, and preferences for natural foods will continue.

11. Many shopping alternatives will continue, such as shopping by computer, shopping by catalog, personal shoppers, and off-price merchandisers. Specialists in such areas as large-sized clothing and clothing for special needs will also find new markets.

12. Shopping malls will continue to grow, providing places for people to meet and find entertainment. Mass merchandising and hypermarkets will become more important as national department stores and mass merchandisers continue to grow.

13. Contrasting and contradictory trends toward affluence, hedonistic life-styles, voluntary simplicity, and "small is beautiful" will remain as themes of consumption of various segments of society.

14. The concern for the quality of consumer products and services will continue to grow.

15. Many consumers will become more aware of product safety and their environmental effects (pollution caused by products, trash problems).

16. Conservation of resources will continue to be an issue, especially conservation of energy resources but also other consumer resources (e.g., foods, textiles, and the preservation or renovation of older housing). Recycling and moderation in consumption will grow as forms of conservation, as will less materialistic life-styles. There will be more demand for high-quality, functional, long-lasting products.

17. Consumption of travel, sports entertainment, the arts, theater, cultural events, and literature will continue to grow in consumers' priorities. This goes hand in hand with increased education and upgraded tastes that have been a trend in our society for decades.

18. The service orientation of consumer-oriented businesses will continue to grow in centrality.

19. High technology will continue to grow in importance for consumer products and services (e.g., digital electronics, fiber optics, home electronics, home security, biotechnology/genetic engineering in foods and other consumer products, and high-tech hotels).

20. As international life-styles become more prevalent, there will be a continuing appreciation of cultural diversity and all that it implies for variety in consuming foods, arts, music, clothing, and so on.

21. The environment is moving to a top level of concern for many consumer-oriented businesses. This concern will shape the types of products offered (e.g., those that are biodegradable, those that do not exploit the environment, recyclable products, and non-polluting products and production technologies).

22. Overall, the United States will continue to be a consumer-oriented society. Mass consumption of standardized products and services will be replaced by a variety of alternatives tailored to the special needs and interests of various clienteles.

Some of these trends represent our hopes, others our fears, and still others what will surely be our reality. Some may never happen, but some are happening or will—for change is inevitable! And look for surprises, things that happen that are not on our list of expected changes.

In closing, we invite you to ask how these trends will affect you as a family or consumer professional. Develop alternative scenarios of the future—what you think it will be and what you want it to be, and then become an active participant in the most exciting of future professions, those serving families and consumers.

Questions and Exercises _____

1. What professional directions would you like the home economics profession to take in the next ten to twenty years?

2. Look at the trends listed in this chapter. Which do you think are likely, and which are less likely?

3. Think about how your career plans may be affected by changes in our society. How can your career take advantage of these changes? How may your career develop according to varying scenarios?

Bibliography

Armstrong, Barbara N. "A Cure for Future Shock," *Journal of Home Economics* 68 (September 1976), 23–25.

Boyd, Jillian R. "Families Coping in a Technological Society," *Illinois Teacher* 33 (January/February 1990), 110–114.

Burgess, Sharon L. "Home Economics and the Third Wave," *Journal of Home Economics* 75 (Fall 1983), 10–13.

Byrd, Flossie M. "Home Economics: Reflections on the Past, Visions for the Future," *Journal of Home Economics* 82 (Summer 1990), 43–46.

Carey, Max L. "Three Paths to the Future: Occupational Projections, 1980–1990," *Occupational Outlook Quarterly* 25 (Winter 1981), 3–11.

Cetron, Marvin J. "Career Direction During the '90s," *Journal of Career Planning and Employment* 50 (Winter 1990), 29–34.

———. "Getting Ready for the Jobs of the Future," *The Futurist* 17 (June 1983), 15–20.

Cetron, Marvin, and Thomas O'Toole. "Careers with a Future: Where the Jobs Will Be in the 1990's," *The Futurist* 16 (June 1982), 11–19.

"Consumer Agenda for the '90's," *Mobius* 8 (Fall 1989), entire issue.

Coulter, Kyle Jane, and Marge Stanton. *Graduates of Higher Education in the Food and Agricultural Sciences: An Analysis of Supply/Demand Relationships,* vol. II: *Home Economics.* U.S. Department of Agriculture, Science and Education Administration, Publication Number 1407, February 1981.

Coulter, Kyle Jane, Marge Stanton, and Norma Bobbitt. *Employment Opportunities for College Graduates in the Food and Agricultural Sciences— Home Economics.* Washington, DC: U.S. Department of Agriculture, November 1987.

Craig, Karen E. "Implications of Societal Transitions for Families: Today and Tomorrow," *Illinois Teacher* 32 (January/February 1989), 90–93.

Deacon, Ruth E. "Visions for the 21st Century (1987 AHEA Commemorative Lecture)," *Journal of Home Economics* 79 (Fall 1987), 62–70.

Dychtwald, Ken, and Joe Flower. *Age Wave.* Los Angeles: Jeremy Tarcher, 1989.

East, Marjorie. *Home Economics: Past, Present, and Future.* Boston: Allyn & Bacon, 1980.

Feingold, S. Norman. "Tracking New Career Categories Will Become a Preoccupation for Job Seekers and Managers," *Personnel Administrator* 28 (December 1983), 86–91.

Gallup, George, and William Proctor. *Forecast 2000: George Gallup, Jr. Predicts the Future of America.* New York: Morrow, 1984.

Godet, Michel, and Remi Barre. "Into the Next Decade: Major Trends and Uncertainties of the 1990s," *Futures* 20 (August 1988), 410–423.

Griffin, Sylvia F., "Futures Planning for Home Economists," *Journal of Home Economics* 81 (Fall 1989), 41–43.

Miller, Thomas A. W. "Forecasting Trends: The Roper Organization," *Mobius* 9 (Spring 1990), 5–7.

Henderson, Carter. "Exploring the Future of Home Economics," *Journal of Home Economics* 72 (Fall 1980), 23–26.

Hewes, Dorothy W. "From Home to Worksite: New Arenas for Home Economics," *Journal of Home Economics* 76 (Fall 1984), 33–37.

McFadden, Joan R. "Decades Ahead: Opportunities and Challenges for Home Economics," *Journal of Home Economics* 76 (Fall 1984), 14–16.

Miller, Lawrence. *American Spirit: Visions of a New Corporate Culture.* New York: Morrow, 1985.

Morf, Martin. "Eight Scenarios for Work in the Future," *The Futurist* 17 (June 1983), 24–29.

Nagy, Daniel R., and Lee Gurtin Wolf. "Workforce 2000: A Recruiting Challenge," *Journal of Career Planning and Employment* 50 (Winter 1990), 51–55.

Naisbitt, John. *Megatrends: Ten New Directions Transforming Our Lives.* Chicago: Nightingale Conant Corp., 1984.

Naisbitt, John, and Patricia Aburdene. *Megatrends 2000: Ten New Directions for the 1990's.* New York: Morrow, 1990.

Nickols, Sharon Y. "Families: Diverse but Enduring (1988 AHEA Commemorative Lecture)," *Journal of Home Economics* 80 (Fall 1988), 49–58.

Selmat, Navaleen Joy Schmitz. "Changing Role of Women," *Illinois Teacher* 25 (November/December 1981), 82–84.

Silvesti, George, and John Lukasiewicz. "Projections of Occupational Employment, 1988–2000," *Monthly Labor Review* 112 (November 1989), 42–65.

Sinetar, Marsha. "The New Careerists," *The Futurist* (March-April 1987), 24–25.

"Some Trends to Watch For," *Journal of Career Planning and Employment* 50 (Winter 1990), 34–36.

Spitze, Hazel Taylor. "Home Economics in the Future," *Illinois Teacher* 68 (September 1976), 19–22.

Toffler, Alvin. *The Third Wave.* New York: Bantam, 1984.

Vaughn, Gladys Gary. "Home Economics: An Agenda for the '90s," *Journal of Home Economics* 82 (Summer 1990), 50–54.

Wagner, Cynthia G., and Daniel M. Fields. "Futureview the 1990s & Beyond," *The Futurist* (November-December 1989), 29–38.

Wallace, Sharon A. "Science & Technology: Impact on Families (1989 AHEA Commemorative Lecture)," *Journal of Home Economics* 81 (Fall 1989), 46–52.

Williams, Sally K., Dorothy L. West, and Eloise C. Murray, eds. *Looking Toward the 21st Century: Home Economics and the Global Community.* Mission Hills, CA: Glencoe/McGraw-Hill, 1990.

Work, Clyde E., June H. Wheeler, and Jeanette V. Williams. "Guidance for Nontraditional Careers," *Personnel and Guidance Journal* 60 (May 1982), 553–556.

Appendix

Associations and National Organizations in Selected Family- and Consumer-Oriented Specialties

The following is a list of organizations relevant to the family and consumer professions. It is divided into groups of similar organizations, including general organizations, entrepreneurship organizations, education organizations, and organizations in specialized professional fields (e.g., child development, clothing and textiles, interior design, consumer affairs). Although the list is long, it is not complete. Interested professionals can find other organizations and associations through the *Encyclopedia of Associations*, national trade and professional associations, their own telephone directory, telephone directories in major cities, local chambers of commerce, local trade or professional groups, and their college or university.

General Professional Organizations

American Home Economics Association
1555 King St.
Alexandria, VA 22314

Works to improve the quality of family life through education, research, and information. Publishes *Journal of Home Economics*, *Home Economics Research Journal*, *AHEA Action*, and various booklets, pamphlets, reports, and audiovisual materials.

American Vocational Association
1410 King St.
Alexandria, VA 22314

Develops and promotes comprehensive programs of vocational education. Publishes *Vocational Education Journal, Update*, and various pamphlets, books, and teaching materials.

American Management Association
135 W. 50th St.
New York, NY 10020

Provides a wide range of services to managers in business, government, and human service organizations of all types. Publishes *Management Review* and many other materials of interest.

National Association of Manufacturers
1331 Pennsylvania Ave. NW, Suite 1500 N
Washington, DC 20014

Provides many services to manufacturers. Publishes bulletins, briefings, legal studies, and other items of interest.

National Federation of Business and Professional Womens Clubs
2012 Massachusetts Ave. NW
Washington, DC 20036

Promotes interests and opportunities for business and professional women through education. Publishes an association newsletter.

American Business Women's Association
P.O. Box 8728
9100 Ward Parkway
Kansas City, MO 64114

An educational association promoting interests of women in business, government, education, and service companies. Publishes *Connect* (newsletter) and *Women in Business*.

Entrepreneurship and Small Business Management ___

Center for Entrepreneurial Management
180 Varick St., Penthouse Suite
New York, NY 10014

Provides materials and education on developing business plans and organizing a business. Publishes *Entrepreneurial Manager* and a newsletter.

American Federation of Small Businesses
407 S. Dearborne Street
Chicago, IL 60605

Provides information and support to small businesses in services, retail, and other fields. Publishes *Bi-Monthly Letters* and reports.

National Association of Women Business Owners
600 S. Federal St., Suite 400
Chicago, IL 60605

Serves women who own and operate their own businesses. Publishes *Statement* and directories of women-owned businesses.

National Family Business Council
60 Revere Dr., Suite 500
Northbrook, IL 60062

An organization of owners or directors of family-oriented businesses. Publishes *Family Business Letter* and *Resource Guide to Family Business*.

Center for Family Business
P.O. Box 24268
Cleveland, OH 44124

An organization of owners of family-owned businesses that develops educational programs in business and management. Publishes *The Family in Business* and books on family business.

National Association for the Cottage Industry
P.O. Box 14850
Chicago, IL 60614

Provides information and organization ideas for people who operate businesses out of their homes. Publishes *Cottage Connection*.

Education and Extension

The American Home Economics Association and the American Vocational Association (listed earlier) are the two most important organizations for teachers, educators, and extension specialists. These two organizations, together with the Home Economics Education Association (listed below), form the Coalition of Home Economics.

Home Economics Education Association   3/94
~~1201 16th Street~~ NW   *P. O. Box   603*
~~Washington, DC 20036~~   *Gainsville, Va 22065*

An organization of teachers and supervisors of home economics education promoting effective teaching of home economics. Publishes newsletter and booklets of interest to educators.

National Association of Teacher Educators for Vocational Home
Economics
c/o Dr. Virginia Clark
College of Home Economics
South Dakota State University
Brookings, SD 57007

An organization of individuals involved in preservice and in-service education of home economics teachers. Publishes *Journal of Vocational Home Economics Education, Directory,* and *Insider.*

National Association of Vocational Home Economics Teachers
c/o M. Josephine Hampton
1514 Sugargrove Ct.
Creve Coeur, MT 63146

A professional organization of home economics teachers who are also members of the American Vocational Association. Publishes newsletters and association news in *Vocational Education Journal.*

National Association of State Supervisors of Vocational Home
Economics
c/o Judith Heatherly

Texas Education Agency
1701 N. Congress Ave.
Austin, TX 78701

An organization of supervisors of state home economics programs
and other state staff members who oversee the administration of
home economics education programs. Publishes a newsletter.

National Association of Extension Home Economists
1801 Robert Fulton Dr., Suite 400
Reston, VA 22091

An organization of extension home economics educators and extension specialists. Publishes *The Reporter.*

National Extension Homemakers Council
4089 Snake Island Rd.
Sturgeon Bay, WI 54235

An organization of homemakers who are members of state extension
homemakers councils in various states. Publishes *The Homemaker
Magazine* and *The Homemaker Update.*

Child Development

Society for Research in Child Development
University of Chicago Press
5720 Woodlawn Ave.
Chicago, IL 60637

A professional interdisciplinary society including educators, psychologists, sociologists, nutritionists, pediatricians, and others doing research on child development. Publishes *Child Development, Child
Development Abstracts and Bibliography*, a newsletter, and reviews.

Association for Childhood Education International
11141 Georgia Ave., Suite 200
Wheaton, MD 20902

Provides education and information on childhood education. Publishes *Journal of Childhood Education*, books, and bulletins.

National Association for the Education of Young Children
1834 Connecticut Ave. NW
Washington, DC 20009

An organization focused on the education of children. Publishes *Young Children* and other books and materials.

National Black Child Development Institute
1463 Rhode Island Ave. NW
Washington, DC 20005

An association focused on support and guidance for black children. Publishes *Black Child Advocate* and other materials.

Child Find
P.O. Box 277
New Paltz, NY 12561

An organization of parents of missing children and service organizations supporting the finding of missing children. Publishes *Child Find*, a directory (with photographs or descriptions of missing children), and other items.

Child Welfare League of America
440 First St. NW, Suite 310
Washington, DC 20001

An organization focused on improving care and services for deprived or neglected children and youth. Publishes *Child Welfare*, a directory, books, and newsletters.

Parents United
P.O. Box 952
San Jose, CA 95108

An organization of individuals and families who have experienced child molestation. Publishes a newsletter.

International Society for Prevention of Child Abuse and Neglect
1205 Oneida Street
Denver, CO 80220

An organization concerned with alleviating child abuse. Publishes *International Journal of Child Abuse and Neglect*.

Family Relations _____

National Council on Family Relations
3989 Central Ave. NE, Suite 550
Minneapolis, MN 55421

An interdisciplinary group of professionals in family relations, including clergy, counselors, educators, home economists, psychologists, social workers, and others. Publishes *Journal of Marriage and the Family, Family Relations, Journal of Family History*, and a newsletter.

American Association of Marriage and Family Therapists
1717 K St. NW, #407
Washington, DC 20006

An organization of marriage and family counselors, including a referral service. Publishes *Family Therapy News* and a directory.

Family Service America
11700 West Lake Park Dr.
Milwaukee, WI 53224

A federation of individuals and counseling services providing all types of family counseling and education. Publishes *Families in Society*, a directory, and various informational materials.

National Academy of Counselors and Family Therapists
55 Morris Ave.
Springfield, NJ 07081

An interdisciplinary organization of psychologists, counselors, and social workers. Publishes *Family Letter*, a newsletter, and other materials.

United Families of America
P.O. Box 6098
Arlington, VA 22206

An organization of individuals promoting family and related public policies. Publishes *National Family Reporter*.

Parents Without Partners
8807 Colesville Rd.
Silver Spring, MD 20910

An organization promoting the solutions of single-parent family problems. Publishes *The Single Parent* and a directory.

Step Family Association of America
602 Joppa Rd.
Baltimore, MD 21204

An organization promoting interests of stepparents, remarried parents, and their children. Publishes *Bulletin, Learning to Step Together*, and other materials.

Family Planning International Assistance
810 Seventh Avenue
New York, NY 10019

An organization promoting responsible parenthood.

Big Brothers/Big Sisters
230 N. 13th St.
Philadelphia, PA 19107

Provides guidance to young boys and girls in parent-absent homes. Publishes an agency directory and other informational publications.

National Association of Area Agencies on Aging
West Wing, Suite 208
600 Maryland Ave. SW
Washington, DC 20024

An organization of agencies focused on the aged. Publishes a directory of agencies and other materials.

National Alliance of Senior Citizens
2525 Wilson Blvd.
Washington, DC 22201

An organization advocating advancement of the interests of senior Americans. Publishes *Senior Guardian* and *Our Age*.

International Center for Social Gerontology
117 N. First St., Suite 204
Ann Arbor, MI 48104

An organization to advance the well-being of older citizens through research and education. Publishes bulletins and manuals.

Clothing and Textiles _____

Association of College Professors of Textiles and Clothing
P.O. Box 1360
Monument, CO 80132

An organization of college professors in two-year and four-year colleges and universities. Publishes *Clothing and Textiles Research Journal* and *ACPTC Newsletter*.

American Association of Textile Chemists and Colorists
P.O. Box 12215
Research Triangle Park, NC 27709

An association of business, government, and educational representatives working in all phases of textile processing and testing. Publishes *Textile Chemist and Colorist*.

Textile Research Institute
P.O. Box 625
Princeton, NJ 08540

A research institute on all aspects of textile processing and manufacturing. Publishes *Textile Research Journal*.

Costume Society of America
55 Edgewater Dr.
P.O. Box 73
Earleville, MD 21919

An organization focusing on the historical analysis of dress and fashion. Publishes *Dress* and a newsletter.

American Textile Manufacturers Institute
1801 K St. NW, Suite 900
Washington, DC 20006

An organization of textile mills manufacturing all types of textile products. Publishes *Textile Trends, Textile Hi-lights,* and other materials.

American Apparel Manufacturers Association
2500 Wilson Blvd., Suite 301
Arlington, VA 22201

An organization of manufacturers of all types of men's, women's, and children's apparel. Publishes *Apparel Management Letter, Import Digest*, a newsletter, and other informational materials.

National Association of Fashion and Accessory Designers
2180 E. 93rd St.
Cleveland, OH 44106

An organization of people in fashion design and related fields. Publishes a newsletter.

National Association of Uniform Manufacturers and Distributors
1156 Avenue of the Americas
New York, NY 10036

Members are manufacturers and distributors of all types of uniforms. Publishes a newsletter and other materials.

National Association of Decorative Fabrics Distributors
3008 Milwood Ave.
Columbia, SC 29205

An organization of wholesalers and distributors of drapery and upholstery fabric. Publishes a newsletter and other materials.

Knitted Textile Association
386 Park Ave. South
New York, NY 10016

An association of manufacturers of knitted fabrics of all types. Publishes *Knitted Fabrics Resource List*.

Textile Designers Guild
c/o Graphic Artists Guild
11 W. 20th St., 11th Floor
New York, NY 10011

An organization of textile artists and designers. Publishes *The Update*, a newsletter, and other materials.

Costume Designers Guild
14724 Ventura Blvd.
Sherman Oaks, CA 91403

An organization of costume designers and artists in the motion picture and television industry.

Council of Fashion Designers of America
1412 Broadway, Suite 1006
New York, NY 10018

An organization of people in creative fashion design.

Custom Tailors and Designers Association of America
17 E. 45th St.
New York, NY 10017

An organization of designers of men's apparel. Publishes *Custom Tailor*.

Bureau of Salesmen's National Associations
P.O. Box 49086
Atlanta, GA 30359

An organization of wholesale sales representatives of women's, men's, and children's apparel and accessories.

Textile Quality Control Association
P.O. Box 76501
Atlanta, GA 30328

An organization of executives and quality control supervisors in the textiles industry.

The Fashion Group International
Nine Rockefeller Plaza
New York, NY 10020

An organization of women executives in fashion and related fields. Publishes *Your Future in Fashion*, a newsletter, and other materials.

Foods and Nutrition

American Dietetic Association
216 W. Jackson Blvd., Suite 800
Chicago, IL 60606

A professional association of dietitians in all types of institutions, schools, day-care centers, businesses, and industry. Publishes *Journal of the American Dietetic Association.*

American College of Nutrition
722 Robert E. Lee Dr.
Wilmington, NC 28412

Association of research scientists, dietitians, and nutritionists providing education on experimental developments in the field of nutrition. Publishes *Journal of the American College of Nutrition* and a newsletter.

American Institute of Nutrition
9650 Rockville Pike
Bethesda, MD 20814

A professional society of nutritional scientists from government, universities, and industry. Publishes *American Journal of Clinical Nutrition, Nutrition Notes*, and other materials.

Food and Nutrition Board
2101 Constitution Ave. NW
Washington, DC 20418

A group that evaluates nutrition and science as they relate to human nutrition and public health. Publishes a directory and monographs on nutrition and human health.

Community Nutrition Institute
2001 S St. NW, Suite 530
Washington, DC 20009

An organization advocating improved nutrition and health. Publishes *Weekly Report* and various booklets and training materials.

Nutrition Education Association
3647 Glen Haven, P.O. Box 20301
Houston, TX 77225

An organization of health professionals and other individuals promoting good nutrition. Publishes various books and brochures on nutrition and health.

Natural Food Associates
P.O. Box 210
Atlanta, TX 75551

An association of professionals and consumers interested in natural foods and organic farming. Publishes *Natural Food and Farming, Natural Food News*, and other materials.

Food Distribution Research Society
c/o Dr. John Brooker
Department of Agricultural Economics
Box 1071
University of Tennessee
Knoxville, TN 37901

An association of individuals from business and education interested in food distribution. Publishes *Journal of Food Distribution Research* and a newsletter.

Food Marketing Institute
1750 K St. NW, Suite 700
Washington, DC 20006

An organization of grocers and wholesalers. Publishes various reports and informational brochures.

Institute of Food Technologists
221 N. LaSalle St.
Chicago, IL 60601

A professional society of technical personnel in the food industries and product development. Publishes *Food Technology, Journal of Food Science*, and other materials.

American Dairy Association
6300 N. River Road
Rosemount, IL 60018

A federation of regional and state dairy farmers' associations.

National Nutritional Foods Association
150 E. Paularino Ave., #285
Costa Mesa, CA 92626

An organization of retailers, wholesalers, and manufacturers of special natural, nutritional, and dietary foods. Publishes a newsletter and other materials.

Potato Chip–Snack Food Association
1711 King St., Suite 1
Alexandria, VA 22314

An organization of manufacturers of various snack foods. Publishes *Chipper/Snacker* and other materials.

The Hospitality Industry (Hotels, Restaurants, Institutional Food Services)

American Hotel and Motel Association
1201 New York Ave. NW, Suite 600
Washington, DC 20005

A federation of hotel associations that represents over a million hotel and motel rooms. Publishes *Construction and Modernization Report, Lodging*, and other materials.

International Hotel Association
89 Rue Faubourg-Saint Honoré
Paris, France

Represents national hotel associations in seventy-six countries around the world. Publishes *International Hotel Review* and other materials related to international hotels.

Hotel Sales and Marketing Association International
1300 L St. NW, Suite 800
Washington, DC 20005

An organization of executives and managers in the hotel business devoted to the education of executives. Publishes *Update, Marketing Review*, and other materials.

Hospitality Lodging and Travel Research Foundation
c/o Raymond C. Ellis, Jr.
American Hotel and Motel Association
1201 New York Ave. NW, Suite 600
Washington, DC 20005

Conducts management research, management programs, and information programs on operating hotels and motels. Publishes various manuals on the operation of lodging facilities.

National Restaurant Association
1200 17th St. NW
Washington, DC 20036

An organization of restaurants, cafeterias, clubs, and other food services. Publishes *Washington Report, News,* and other materials.

Council on Hotel, Restaurant, and Institutional Education
1200 17th St. NW
Washington, DC 20036

An organization of schools offering education in various fields of the hospitality industry. Publishes *Hospitality Educator, Journal of Hospitality Education,* and other materials.

Food Service and Lodging Institute
1919 Pennsylvania Ave. NW
Washington, DC 20006

An organization of major multiunit food service and lodging organizations. Publishes *Washington Report* and other materials.

Society for Food Service Management
304 West Liberty Street, Suite 301
Louisville, KY 40202

An organization serving the needs and interests of food service executives and managers. Publishes a newsletter and other materials.

Society for the Advancement of Food Service Research
304 W. Liberty St., Suite 301
Louisville, KY 40202

An association of restaurant operators, dietitians, professors, food service directors, and other people doing research in food services.

Food Service Consultant Society International
12345 30th Ave. NE, Suite A
Seattle, WA 98125

A professional organization of people who design food service facilities and provide management consulting on food service. Publishes *The Consultant, Spec Sheet,* and other materials.

United Soft-Serve and Fast-Food Association
516 S. Front St.
Chesaning, MI 48616

An organization of owners of fast-food stores and soft-ice-cream stores. Publishes a newsletter.

Food Service Equipment Distributors Association
3332 South Michigan Ave.
Chicago, IL. 60604

An organization of distributors of all types of food service equipment. Publishes *News and Views* and other materials.

American Culinary Federation
P.O Box 3466, Ten San Bartola Rd.
St. Augustine, FL 32084

An organization of professional chefs. Publishes a monthly periodical and various materials and guides for culinarians.

Commercial Food Equipment Service Association
9240 N. Meridian St., Suite 355
Indianapolis, IN 46260

An organization of firms that manufacture food preparation equipment. Publishes *On Target* and other materials.

National Food Service Association
P.O Box 1932
Columbus, OH 43216

An organization of food service firms, schools, hospitals, clubs, institutions, retirement centers, and nursing homes with food services.

National Association of Food Equipment Manufacturers
c/o Smith, Buckland & Associates, Inc.
111 E. Wacker Dr.
Chicago, IL 60611

An organization of manufacturers of commercial food service equipment and supplies for restaurants, hotels, and institutions. Publishes a newsletter.

National Institutional Food Distributor Associates
280 Interstate Parkway
Atlanta, GA 30339

An organization of wholesale food distributors that distribute food products to all types of food services.

National Institute for the Food Service Industry
20 N. Wacker Dr., #1400
Chicago, Il 60606

An educational foundation supported by restaurants, food service companies, equipment manufacturers, and trade associations. Publishes *News* and other materials.

American School Food Service Association
1600 Duke St., 7th Floor
Alexandria, VA 22314

An organization of professionals in school food services. Publishes *School Food Service Journal, School Food Service Research Review,* and other materials.

Housing and Household Equipment

American Association of Housing Educators
College of Architecture
Texas A&M University
College Station, TX 77843

An organization of professors, researchers, and government employees in various aspects of housing. Publishes *Housing and Society,* a newsletter, and other materials.

National Association of Homebuilders of the U.S.
15th and M St. NW
Washington, DC 20005

An organization of single and multifamily home builders and others associated with building (remodelers, developers, utilities, architects, financial institutions, retail dealers, etc.). Publishes *Builder Newsletter, Builder Magazine, Economic Newsnotes, Library Bulletin*, and other materials.

National Association of Realtors
430 N. Michigan Ave.
Chicago, IL 60611

An organization of state and local real estate boards whose members are titled realtors and realtor-associates. Publishes *Realtor News, Real Estate Today*, and other materials.

National Association of Real Estate Brokers
1629 K St., NW #2, Suite 605
Washington, DC 20006

An organization of various members of the real estate industry. Publishes *Realtist Flyer, Realtist Magazine*, and other materials.

American Society of Real Estate Counselors
430 N. Michigan Ave.
Chicago, IL 60611

A professional society of realtors who provide counseling and advice. Publishes *The Counselor, Real Estate Issues*, and other materials.

Apartment Owners and Managers Association of America
65 Cherry Plaza
Watertown, CT 06795

An organization of builders and managers of multifamily housing units. Publishes *Apartment Management Report*, a newsletter, and various bulletins.

National Apartment Association
1111 14th St. NW, Suite 900
Washington, DC 20005

A federation of associations of investors, developers, owners, builders, and managers of rental properties. Publishes *Multi-Housing Advocate, Multi-Housing Mainstream*, and other materials.

Institute of Real Estate Management
430 N. Michigan Ave.
Chicago, IL 60611

A professional organization of property managers. Publishes *CPM Aspects, Journal of Property Management, Operating Techniques, Bulletin*, and other materials and books.

American Institute of Real Estate Appraisers
430 N. Michigan Ave.
Chicago, IL 60611

An organization of appraisers of all types of property. Publishes *The Appraiser, Appraiser Journal*, and other publications.

National Council of the Housing Industry
15th & M St. NW
Washington, DC 20005

An organization of manufacturers of goods and services for the housing industry. Publishes *News*.

National Association of the Remodeling Industry
1901 N. Moore St., Suite 808
Arlington, VA 22209

An organization of manufacturers of building products, lending institutions, distributors, and remodeling contractors. Publishes a newsletter.

National Association of Plumbing-Heating-Cooling Contractors
P.O. Box 6808
180 S. Washington St.
Falls Church, VA 22046

A federation of organizations for all aspects of plumbing, heating, and cooling. Publishes a newsletter.

National Association of Women in Construction
327 S. Adams St.
Ft. Worth, TX 76104

An organization of women in the construction industry. Publishes *Image* and other materials.

Vacation Ownership Council
1220 L St. NW, Suite 510
Washingtin, DC 20005

A council of developers of time-sharing resorts. Publishes *Consumers Guide* and *The Resort Time Sharing Industry.*

National Society of Professional Resident Managers
1518 K St. NW
Washington, DC 20005

An organization of property managers. Publishes a newsletter and other materials.

National Association of Housing Cooperatives
200 Park Ave. S
New York, NY 10003

An organization of housing cooperatives controlled by member-owners. Publishes *Cooperative Housing Bulletin* and other materials.

National Homeowners Association
1906 Sunderland Place NW
Washington, DC 20036

A national organization of homeowners. Publishes *Homefront* and other materials.

Association of Home Appliance Manufacturers
20 N. Wacker Dr.
Chicago, IL 60606

An organization of companies manufacturing major appliances and portable appliances. Publishes *Appliance Letter* and other materials.

Gas Appliance Manufacturers Association
1901 Moore St., Suite 1100
Arlington, VA 22209

An organization of manufacturers of gas appliances. Publishes *Patent Digest.*

Cookware Manufacturers Association
P.O. Box 1177
Lake Geneva, WI 53147

An organization of manufacturers of cooking utensils and accessories.

International Sleep Products Association
333 Commerce St.
Alexandria, VA 22314

An organization of manufacturers of mattresses and sleeping equipment. Publishes *Bedding/Bed Times*.

National Bath, Bed and Linen Association
15 E. 26th St., Suite 1602
New York, NY 10110

An organization of manufacturers of domestic textiles and related products. Publishes *National Show Directory*.

National Housewares Manufacturers Association
1324 Merchandise Mart
Chicago, IL 60654

An organization of manufacturers of housewares and small appliances. Publishes *Housewares Exposition Directory*.

Interior Design

American Society of Interior Designers
1430 Broadway
New York, NY 10018

An organization of professional interior designers and associates in design fields. Publishes *ASID Report* and other materials.

American Society of Furniture Designers
P.O. Box 2688
High Point, NC 27261

An organization of furniture designers and people in activities related to design. Publishes *Bulletin* and other materials.

Institute of Business Designers
341 Merchandise Mart
Chicago, IL 60654

An organization of professional interior designers in contract (nonresidential) design, such as designers of offices, hotels, and other commercial businesses. Publishes *In-Depth, Digest*, and other materials.

Interior Design Society
P.O. Box 2396
High Point, NC 27261

An organization of retail designers and design-oriented firms. Publishes *Portfolio* and a newsletter.

Interior Design Educators Council
14252 Culver Dr., Suite A–311
Irvine, CA 92714

An organization of educators in interior design. Publishes *Journal of Interior Design Education and Research*.

Industrial Designers Society of America
1142 E. Walker Rd.
Great Falls, VA 22066

A professional society of industrial designers. Publishes a newsletter and other materials.

Carpet and Rug Institute
P.O. Box 2048
Dalton, GA 30722

An organization of manufacturers of carpets, rugs, bedspreads, and suppliers of raw materials. Publishes *Report, News, Carpet Specifiers Handbook*, and other materials.

International Drapery Association
7052 Orangewood Ave., Suite 5
Garden Grove, CA 92641

An organization of custom drapery merchants. Publishes a newsletter and other materials.

National Kitchen and Bath Association
124 Main St.
Hackettstown, NJ 07840

An organization of firms in retail kitchen sales and manufacturers of kitchen equipment. Publishes *Drawing Board* and other materials.

National Decorating Products Association
1050 N. Lindberg Blvd.
St. Louis, MO 63132

An organization of distributors and retailers of paint and wallpaper products. Publishes *Decorating Retailer, Decorating Retailers Wallcovering Directory*, and other materials.

International Association of Lighting Designers
18 E. 16th St., Suite 208
New York, NY 10003

An organization of professionals in lighting design. Publishes two newsletters.

Interior Plantscape Division
405 N. Washington St., Suite 104
Falls Church, VA 22046

An organization of owners, suppliers, growers, and providers of materials related to the plant business.

Painting and Decorating Contractors of America
3913 Old Lee Hwy., Suite 33B
Fairfax, VA 22030

An organization of painting and wallpapering contractors. Publishes *Professional Decorating and Coating Action* and other materials.

Society of Certified Kitchen Designers
124 Main St.
Hackettstown, NJ 07840

An organization of kitchen designers. Publishes *The Professional to Consult* and *Kitchen Industry Technical Manual*.

National Home Fashions League
P.O. Box 58045
107 World Trade Center
Dallas, TX 75258

An organization of professional women in all aspects of interior design. Publishes *Newsbriefs, Journal*, and other materials.

Leisure and Recreational Services for Families _____

American Society of Travel Agents
1101 King St.
Alexandria, VA 22314

An association of travel agents and representatives of carriers, hotels, resorts, and other tourist organizations. Publishes *Astanotes, ASTA Travel News*, and other materials.

American Sightseeing International
309 Fifth Ave.
New York, NY 10016

An organization of independent sight-seeing companies. Publishes travel information.

Association of Retail Travel Agents
1745 Jefferson Davis Pkwy., Suite 300
Arlington, VA 22202

An organization of retail travel agents. Publishes *ARTAFACTS*.

Association of Travel Marketing Executives
P.O. Box 43563
Washington, DC 20010

An organization of travel marketing executives. Publishes *Travel and Tourism Executive Newsletter* and other materials.

National Ski Areas Association
P.O. Box 2883
20 Maple St.
Springfield, MA 01101

An organization of ski areas. Publishes *News* and other materials.

Cross Country Ski Areas Association
259 Bolton Rd.
Winchester, NH 03470

An organization of owners and operators of ski-touring facilities. Publishes *Nordic Network* and other materials.

Bowling Proprietors Association of America
P.O. Box 5802
Arlington, TX 76011

An organization of bowling establishments. Publishes *The Bowling Proprietor*.

Golf Course Association
8030 Cedar, Suite 228
Minneapolis, MN 55425

An organization of owners of public and private golf courses. Publishes a newsletter and other materials.

Ice Skating Institute of America
1000 Skokie Boulevard
Wilmette, IL 60091

An organization of ice rink operators and managers. Publishes *Recreational Ice Skating Magazine*, a newsletter, and other materials.

National Employee Services and Recreation Association
2400 S. Downing Ave.
Westchester, IL 60154

An organization of corporations and governmental agencies that sponsor recreational and related service programs for their employees. Publishes *Keynotes Newsletter, Employee Services Management*, and other materials.

Sauna Society of America
1001 Connecticut Ave.
Washington, DC 20036

An organization of owners, importers, and manufacturers of saunas. Publishes a newsletter and other materials.

International Racquet Sports Association
132 Brookline Ave.
Boston, MA 02215

An organization of racquet sports manufacturers, racquet ball clubs, and tennis clubs. Publishes a journal and other materials.

International Physical Fitness Association
415 West Court St.
Flint, MI 48503

An organization of physical fitness centers of all types. Publishes *Membership Roster.*

National Golf Foundation
1150 S. U.S. Hwy. One
Jupiter, FL 33477

An organization of golf-oriented businesses, including clubs, associations, and equipment. Publishes *Golf Market Report, Architects Directory*, and other materials.

Sporting Goods Manufacturers Association
200 Castlewood Dr.
N. Palm Beach, FL 33408

An organization of manufacturers of athletic equipment and sporting goods. Publishes *Action Update, International Trade Review*, and other materials.

National Sporting Goods Association
1699 Wall St.
Mt. Prospect, IL 60056

An organization of manufacturers, wholesalers, and retailers of athletic equipment and sporting goods. Publishes a monthly magazine and various other materials and statistical studies.

Recreation Vehicle Industry Association
1896 Preston White Dr.
P.O. Box 2999
Reston, VA 22090

An organization of recreation vehicle manufacturers and associated businesses. Publishes *Marketing Report* and other materials.

Consumer Affairs and Family Resource Management __

American Council on Consumer Interests
240 Stanley Hall
University of Missouri
Columbia, MO 65211

An organization of educators, government officials, and business
executives in consumer affairs and consumer education. Publishes
Journal of Consumer Affairs, ACCI Newsletter, and other materials.

Association for Consumer Research
c/o Keith Hunt
Graduate School of Business
Brigham Young University
Provo, UT 84602

An organization of educators, business persons, and government officials interested in conducting consumer research. Publishes *Advances
in Consumer Research* and a newsletter.

Society of Consumer Affairs Professionals in Business
4900 Leesburg Pike, Suite 400
Alexandria, VA 22302

An organization of business persons specializing in programs of consumer education, consumer information, consumer protection, complaint handling, and other consumer concerns. Publishes *Mobius* and
other materials.

Consumer Federation of America
1424 16th St. NW, Suite 604
Washington, DC 20036

An organization of a wide range of consumer groups. Publishes *CFA
News* and other materials.

Public Citizen
P.O. Box 19404
Washington, DC 20036

An organization formed by Ralph Nader to support citizen advocates
of various consumer issues. Publishes various reports and materials.

Major Appliance Consumer Action Panel
20 N. Wacker Dr.
Chicago, IL 60606

An organization of independent consumer experts that represents
consumer views and resolves consumer complaints in the appliance
industry.

International Organization of Consumers Unions
Emmastraat 9, NL–2595 EG
The Hague, Netherlands

An association of consumer organizations around the world. Publishes *Consumer Currents, Consumers Directory*, and other materials.

International Anti-Counterfeiting Coalition
818 Connecticut Ave. NW, 12th Floor
Washington, DC 20006

An organization of American, European, and Asian companies desir-
ing to stop the counterfeiting of brand-name merchandise. Publishes
Bulletin and other materials.

American Association of Credit Counselors
P.O. Box 372
Grayslake, IL 60030

An organization of persons engaged in family financial counseling.

American Financial Services Association
1101 14th St. NW
Washington, DC 20035

An organization of companies lending to consumers or purchasing
finance paper regarding consumer products. Publishes *Credit Week,
Consumer Finance Law Bulletin, Finance Facts, Credit, Thrift Reporter*, and other materials.

International Association for Financial Planning
2 Concours Parkway, Suite 800
Atlanta, GA 30328

An association of financial planners assisting members in obtaining
education and information related to financial planning and financial

services. Publishes *Financial Planning News, Financial Planning*, a directory, and other informational items.

National Association of Personal Financial Advisors
1130 Lake Cook Rd., Suite 105
Buffalo Grove, IL 60089

An association of fee-only financial planners. Publishes *NAPFA News* and a membership directory.

Associated Credit Bureaus
P.O. Box 218300
16211 Park Ten Place
Houston, TX 77218

An international association of credit reporting and selection services. Publishes *Communicator, Management*, and other materials.

Credit Research Foundation
8815 Center Park Dr.
Columbia, MD 21045

An organization of credit and financial executives that supervises research and educational programs at the National Association of Credit Management. Publishes *National Summary of International Trade Receivables* and other credit management papers.

Credit Union National Association
P.O. Box 431
Madison, WI 53701

An association of local credit unions. Publishes *Credit Union Newswatch, Credit Union Magazine, Credit Union President, Everybody's Money*, and other materials.

International Consumer Credit Association
243 North Lindbergh Blvd.
St. Louis, MO 63141

An organization of credit executives in all fields of consumer credit. Publishes *Consumer Trends, Credit World*, and other materials.

National Association of Credit Management
8815 Center Park Dr.
Columbia, MD 21045

An organization of credit and financial executives representing all types of businesses involved in credit. Publishes *Credit Manual of Commercial Laws* and other materials.

National Association of Federal Credit Unions
P.O. Box 3769
Washington, DC 20007

An organization of federally chartered credit unions. Publishes *Update, The Federal Credit Union*, and other materials.

CWI Credit Professionals
6500 Chippewa, Suite 225
St. Louis, MO 63109

An organization of women employed in credit or collection departments. Publishes *International*, a newsletter, and other materials.

National Foundation for Consumer Credit
8701 Georgia Avenue, Suite 507
Silver Spring, MD 20910

An organization of businesses and finance companies interested in public education and counseling for consumers in the area of credit and credit management. Publishes a newsletter and other materials regarding counseling.

National Institute for Credit
8815 Center Park Dr.
Columbia, MD 21045

An organization offering classes in credit and financial management to people employed in the credit field. Publishes *Business Credit Magazine* and other books and items of interest.

Mortgage Bankers Association of America
1125 Fifteenth St. NW
Washington, DC 20005

An organization of all types of financial institutions — including banks, insurance companies, title companies, and savings and loans — interested in lending and investor interests. Publishes *Washington Report, Mortgage Banking*, and other materials.

Independent Bankers Association of America
One Thomas Cir. NW, Suite 950
Washington, DC 20005

An organization of medium-sized and smaller banks. Publishes
Washington Weekly Report and other materials.

National Association of Bank Women
500 N. Michigan Ave.
Suite 1400
Chicago, IL 60611

An organization of women officers and members in the banking
business. Publishes a journal, newsletter, and other materials.

Life Insurance Marketing and Research Association
P.O. Box 208
Hartford, CT 06141

An organization of life insurance companies conducting research and
educational programs on insurance. Publishes *Managers Magazine,
Market Facts*, and other materials.

Insurance Institute of America
720 Providence Rd.
Malvern, PA 19355

An organization sponsoring educational programs for property and
liability insurance professionals. Publishes *Catalogue* and other
materials.

Independent Insurance Agents of America
127 Peyton
Alexandria, VA 22314

An organization of agencies handling various types of insurance. Publishes *IIAA Action News, Management Service*, and other materials.

Insurance Information Institute
110 William St.
New York, NY 10038

An organization representing insurance companies. Publishes *Journal
of Insurance, Insurance Facts*, and other materials.

Investment Counsel Association of America
20 Exchange Pl.
New York, NY 10005

An organization of investment counseling firms providing advice on securities to clients. Publishes various materials on investment counseling.

Independent Investment Protector League
P.O. Box 5031
Ft. Lauderdale, FL 33310

An organization seeking to protect investors.

Investment Company Institute
1600 M St. NW, Suite 600
Washington, DC 20036

An organization of open-end investment companies (mutual funds). Publishes *Mutual Fund News, Trends in Mutual Fund Activity*, and other materials.

National Association of Securities Dealers
1735 K St. NW
Washington, DC 20006

An organization of investment brokers and dealers. Publishes *NASDAQ Notes, Executive Digest*, and other materials.

Society of Professional Journalists
53 W. Jackson Blvd., Suite 731
Chicago, IL 60604

An organization of broadcasters specializing in financial and economic news. Publishes *The Quill* and various reports.

Council of Better Business Bureaus
4200 Wilson Blvd., Suite 800
Arlington, VA 22203

An organization of local better business bureaus supported by business and professional firms in all consumer and retail fields. Publishes *Annual Report*, consumer education leaflets, and other materials.

Retail Merchandising _____

School of Business Administration
New York University
Washington Square
New York, NY 10003

Conducts educational programs and research of interest to the retail industry and educators. Publishes *Journal of Retailing* and other materials.

American Marketing Association
250 South Wacker Dr., Suite 200
Chicago, IL 60606

A professional organization of marketing executives, professors, and practitioners in all areas of retailing, consumer behavior, and marketing. Publishes *Journal of Marketing, Journal of Marketing Research, Marketing News*, and other materials. Co-sponsors *Journal of Consumer Research.*

National Retail Federation
100 West 31st St.
New York, NY 10001

An organization of department, chain, mass merchandise, and specialty stores retailing all types of apparel and home furnishings. Publishes *Stores, Retail Control*, and other materials.

National Mass Retail Association
570 Seventh Avenue, Suite 900
New York, NY 10018

An organization of mass retailing chain stores. Publishes various reports, surveys, and a membership guide.

International Center for Companies of the Food Trade and
Industry
3800 Moor Pl.
Alexandria, VA 22305

Members are food-industry chain stores and suppliers. Publishes *Quarterly Review*, a newsletter, and other materials.

International Council of Shopping Centers
665 Fifth Ave.
New York, NY 10022

An organization of owners, developers, retailers, and managers of shopping centers. Publishes *Shopping Centers Today, Leasing Opportunities*, and other materials.

American Mail Order Association
444 Lincoln Blvd., #107
Venice, CA 90291

An organization of retailers selling by mail. Publishes various books, booklets and manuals.

National Association of Catalog Showroom Merchandisers
P.O. Box 725
Hauppauge, NY 11788

An organization of catalog showroom operators. Publishes *News* and other materials.

National Association of Retail Dealers of America
Ten E. 22nd St.
Lombard, IL 60148

An organization of retailers and distributors of consumer electronics, refrigerators, washers, furniture, television sets, and other appliances. Publishes *NARDA* News.

Menswear Retailers of America
2011 I St. NW
Washington, DC 20006

An organization of retailers of men's and boys' clothing. Publishes *Better Retail Salesmanship* and a newsletter.

National Grocers Association
1825 Samuel Morse Dr.
Reston, VA 22090

An organization of independent retailers and wholesale distributors. Publishes various materials and reports.

International Development and Trade

International Federation of Home Economics
5 Avenue de la Port-Brancion
Paris, France

An international organization of home economics groups. Publishes *L'Economie Familiale* and other items of interest.

American Association of Exporters and Importers
11 West 42nd St.
New York, NY 10036

An organization of importers and exporters of products and raw materials. Publishes *International Trade Alert, Newsletter*, and other materials.

International Traders Association
c/o The Mellinger Company
6100 Variel Ave.
Woodland Hills, CA 91367

Association of individuals and firms in export and import businesses. Publishes *Trade Opportunities Magazine* and books on trade.

World Trade Center of New Orleans
Two Canal St., Suite 2900
P.O. Box 52020
New Orleans, LA 70130

An organization of U.S. and foreign business leaders promoting international trade, friendship, and understanding. Publishes *Tradewinds, Trading Post*, and other materials.

Trade Relations Council of the United States
c/o Stewart Trade Data
808 17th St. NW, Suite 580
Washington, DC 20036

An organization of trade associations, manufacturers, and agricultural interests that conducts research and sponsors education on trade. Publishes materials related to trade.

Other organizations with interest in international development include the United Nations (New York), the Peace Corps (Washington, DC), and the United States government (Agency for International Development, U.S. Department of State, and U.S. Department of Commerce).

Index

415